STUDIES IN THE HISTORY
OF CHRISTIAN MISSIONS

R. E. Frykenberg
Brian Stanley
General Editors

Christian Identity and *Dalit* Religion in Hindu India, 1868-1947

Chad M. Bauman

WILLIAM B. EERDMANS PUBLISHING COMPANY
GRAND RAPIDS, MICHIGAN / CAMBRIDGE, U.K.

Published 2008 by

Wm. B. Eerdmans Publishing Co.

2140 Oak Industrial Drive N.E., Grand Rapids, Michigan 49505 /
P.O. Box 163, Cambridge CB3 9PU U.K.

Printed and bound in Great Britain by
Marston Book Services Limited, Didcot

13 12 11 10 09 08   7 6 5 4 3 2 1

Library of Congress Cataloging-in-Publication Data

Bauman, Chad M.

Christian identity and Dalit religion in Hindu India, 1868-1947 /
Chad M. Bauman.

p.   cm. — (Studies in the history of Christian missions)

Includes bibliographical references.

ISBN 978-0-8028-6276-1 (cloth: alk. paper)

1. Missions — India — Chhattisgarh. 2. Christianity —
India. 3. India — Religion. 4. Satnamis — India —
Chhattisgarh.   I. Title.

BV3265.3.B38   2008

266.00954′3 — dc22

2008016712

www.eerdmans.com

Contents

Contents

Acknowledgments

On 7 February 2004, after a three-hour ride during which I lurched my way over some of Chhattisgarh's dustiest, most pockmarked roads, and worried incessantly about puncturing the tires of my trusty Hero Honda Street, which all of my Indian friends assured me was an *aurat-vālī* (girl's) motorcycle, I arrived at Girodpuri for the annual *Satnami melā* (religious fair). After another half-hour of slithering my way through unyielding *melā*-related traffic, I finally arrived at the parking lot, a rock-strewn open field.

From there, my *Satnami* guide and I set out on foot, joining other pilgrims on a circuitous route toward the central shrine (the direct route would have led us through a field that had been used as a latrine by those camping at the festival, and was therefore prohibitively "mined"). We were accompanied by thousands of pilgrims, a few of whom had traveled to the *melā* by fully prostrating themselves in the direction of the shrine, reaching forward, standing up where their fingers had come to rest, and repeating the procedure over, and over, and over again. The sides of the narrow path were lined with makeshift shops from which aggressive shopkeepers emerged to hawk sweets, music, toys, and religious objects. *Satnami* devotional tunes, some of which I recognized from the Christianized versions sung by *Satnami* converts, blared at us from both sides. An old *Satnami* whom I had previously interviewed, and whom I had jokingly instructed to look for the only *gorā* (white person) at the *melā*, spotted me among the pilgrims and appeared, laughing and smiling, to give his greetings. Heat rose up from the asphalt and mingled in the air with dust, music, and the spirited voices of pilgrims.

We entered the dimly lit and incensed shrine to receive a blessing from the old *bābā* in attendance, and with his permission I took a photo that I developed some time later. Inexplicably, the photo and the digital file from which it had been printed contained a streak of light, suspended downward on the right side of the image, like a fluorescent snake. One particularly pious Hindu friend of mine would not accept the occurrence as a coincidence, and, to be honest, nothing remotely like this had ever happened with my camera (nor has it ever since). My friend hypothesized that it had something to do with the revered serpents that live in a tree just outside the shrine, which pilgrims jostle and crane to see. Whatever the source, my friend assured me, it was a sign that the gods had smiled on my research.

The gods did seem to smile on my research in Chhattisgarh, though perhaps this is just another way of saying that I was fortunate to have the friendship and assistance of a number of extraordinary people. Dr. Abha Pal, Professor of History at Pt. Ravishankar Shukla University in Raipur, advised me ably, beginning more than a year before my arrival in Chhattisgarh. Her student, Mr. Manish Tiwari, was indispensable, and capably provided logistical and linguistic support. Mr. Tiwari and Mr. Ranjit Nandi, my C.E.O. (Chief Entertainment Officer), also provided much-needed companionship and amusement, as did the pious and refreshingly juvenile Gifty (Brijpal Sandhu) and Shakti (Pal Singh Rathor). The owners, workers, and patrons of Manju Mamta, Raipur's hippest restaurant, especially Raja and Priti, my adopted siblings, provided a home away from home. So did the entire staff of the Mungeli Christian Hospital. The Bais brothers, owners of Sun City Cyber Café, kept me "wired" and in good company, and — by getting married on the same day — provided the venue for my enjoyable (if embarrassing) *bhangrā* dancing debut. Christopher Tavares, the director of Gass Memorial Centre in Raipur, appeared to delight in solving all of my problems, as did Mr. J. S. Lal. *Dada* and *Dadi* Francis (Daniel and Clementina), Uncle Keshav Rao, Auntie Geeta Pardiwalla, and *bhaiya* Samson Samuel accepted me as a member of their respective families. While I was in Bishrampur, Khrist and Kamal Dayal compensated for some of the necessary austerities of village life with the best meals in India. Dr. Satish Gyan, mentor and friend, helped me in innumerable ways. To all of these friends and guides, I am eternally grateful.

Though it would be impossible to thank all of those who assisted me in the collection of oral histories, several must be recognized for their special service. Padri Samsher Samuel, Church of North India pastor and Amway salesman *extraordinaire,* is personally responsible for the success of my interviews in the Bishrampur area, as are C. P. Samuel, Matthew Jahani, and P. C. Julius for those conducted around Takhatpur, and Kesar Das for those in Champa. Banjari, who uses only one name, accompanied me to a variety of *melās* (including the one described above). For the extraordinary competence, companionship, and guidance of each of these, I give my deepest gratitude.

My research also benefited greatly from the skillful aid of archivists at the Disciples of Christ Historical Society in Nashville, Tennessee, the Archives of the Evangelical Synod at Eden Theological Seminary (especially Lowell Zuck), the Heritage Room at Christian Theological Seminary Library, and the Mennonite Church USA Archives in Goshen, Indiana. Dr. Saurabh Dube, of El Colegio de México, and Dr. Ramdas Lamb, of the University of Hawaii, graciously and enthusiastically helped me in various ways throughout the project, even though it was clear from the start that I would be revisiting, as it were, some of their academic ground. I would like also to thank Drs. Joyce Burkhalter Flueckiger, Corinne Dempsey, Darrell Guder, Arun Jones, Eliza Kent, Vijay Gambhir, Selva Raj, Luis Rivera-Pagan, Laurie Patton, Stephen Teiser, and all of the editors and blind reviewers who have worked with me for their contribution to the success of this project. I also owe a debt of gratitude to Kate Bullis, my research assistant, for her work on the index.

Dr. Charles Ryerson kindly tolerated my many intrusions into the first six years of his retirement, and offered perceptive observations and suggestions at all stages of my research for this project. Dr. Andrew Walls took time away from his international perambulations to comment on earlier drafts of the manuscript. Drs. Ryerson and Walls are responsible for the earliest, formative years of my scholarly training, and their influence lies just beneath the surface of the following text. Dr. Richard Fox Young, trusted advisor, read several versions of this text with patience and acuity, sacrificing, for my benefit, far too much of a well-earned sabbatical from Princeton Theological Seminary in the fall of 2004. To each of these scholars, mentors, and friends I give my heartfelt thanks.

Sections of this book have been previously published elsewhere. Material similar to that in Chapter 4, "Allopathic Medicine and the Allure of Efficacy," appeared in *Miracle as Modern Conundrum in South Asian Religious Traditions*, a volume edited by Corinne G. Dempsey and Selva J. Raj (SUNY Press, 2008). And portions of the Simon Patros section of Chapter 6 appeared separately in 2006 as "Singing of Satnam: Blind Simon Patros, *Dalit* Religious Identity, and *Satnami*-Christian Music in Chhattisgarh, India," in the *Journal of Hindu-Christian Studies*, vol. 19. Finally, some material from chapter 5 appeared first as "Redeeming Indian 'Christian' Womanhood? Missionaries, *Dalits*, and Agency in Colonial India," in the *Journal of Feminist Studies in Religion*, vol. 24.2 (Fall 2008). My thanks to SUNY, JHCS, and JFSR for granting permission to reprint the overlapping material.

Finally, I must also thank colleagues and friends for sustaining me through the writing and revising process with friendship and good humor. I must especially thank two of these friends, Mr. Joerg Albrecht and Mr. Enrico Bocker, for their assistance in the translation of German texts. Special thanks also to my parents-in-law, Carol and Wade Mullet, and to my parents, Glenn and Christine Bauman, who have never wavered in their support for my personal and scholarly endeavors. To other members of the Bauman family, Chloe and the Sisters "B," who provided companionship through what could otherwise have been very lonely periods of research and writing, I am grateful. Finally, to my wife, Jodi, whose love, patience, hard work, and selflessness have made this all possible, I offer my inadequate but humble and sincerest gratitude.

A Note on Language

All words of Indian origin are italicized, except in the case of those (like "guru") that are commonly found in English. Words used in English less frequently, but included in the *Merriam-Webster Unabridged Dictionary* (such as "sari," "samaj," and "dhoti") are given with italics but without diacritics. Words that are better known to English speakers in their Sanskritic (rather than Hindi) forms are thus given (e.g., "karma," not "karm"). *Jāti* names appear capitalized and italicized, but without diacritics (thus "*Chamar*," and "*Gond*"); *varṇa* names appear with italics, but are not capitalized (thus "*brahman*," and "*sudra*"). In the case of proper names and nouns for which more than one English rendering is common, I have generally chosen the spelling that most resembles the original Hindi (e.g., "Jagjivandas" rather than "Jagjiwandas," and "Ravat" rather than "Rawat," or "Raut").

For all other words, including the names of Indian scriptures, I have followed the transliteration pattern of R. S. McGregor's *Oxford Hindi-English Dictionary,* with three exceptions: First, I have chosen to render vowel nasalizations with an "n" rather than an "m" as McGregor does, because, in most cases, "n" better approximates the actual pronunciation than "m" (thus, "*angrezī*" and "*sanskār*"). I have, however, rendered true *anusvāras,* when they occur at the end of a word, with "*ṃ*" (thus "*ājñāyeṃ*"). Second, I have not followed McGregor's inclusion of a subscript dot under syllables (such as "kha") to indicate when their source, and thus their pronunciation, is of Persian rather than Sanskrit origin. I have made this decision primarily because most Indian presses have stopped making the distinction in *devanagari* and Romanized Hindi. Third, I have not employed McGregor's superscript "ˇ" to indicate elided vowel sounds (thus "*satya,*" not "*satyă*").

With the diacritic renderings, most English speakers should be able to venture a guess as to a word's correct pronunciation, but should keep in mind that all "c's" are pronounced as "ch," "e's" are pronounced as the "ay" in "hay," and "v's" are pronounced somewhere between the English "v" and "w." Since there are no capital letters in the *devanagari* script, I have capitalized only the first word of Hindi titles. For plurals I have simply added an "s" to the singular Hindi words, rather than complicate things with the Hindi plural form. All unfamiliar words from Indian languages that appear more than once are also defined in the glossary at the end of the text.

In the early years of the period under study, British and missionary records generally made a distinction between *"Satnamis"* (i.e., the followers of Ghasidas) and members of the *Chamar* caste from which most of them came. In fact, followers of Ghasidas successfully petitioned census officials, in 1926, to have *Satnamis* distinguished from *Chamars* in all official documents. One side effect of this change was that *"Satnami"* came to be used as a caste name. Slowly, even *Chamars* who had no connection to Ghasidas began to embrace the term, happy to abandon *"Chamar,"* a name associated with low status and ritual impurity. Today, almost nobody in Chhattisgarh uses the term *"Chamar,"* and one can be called into court if one applies it to a *Satnami*.

To bring some organization to this confusion, I have therefore used *"Chamar"* as the caste name before the founding of the Satnampanth, and *"Satnami"* as the caste name afterwards. Doing so unfortunately blurs the distinction between members of the caste who accepted Ghasidas's religious reforms and members of the caste who did not. In the beginning of the period under study, there were still a good number of *Chamars* who did not follow Ghasidas, and therefore did not embrace the name *Satnami*. But over time, as indicated above, many *Chamars* who had nothing to do with Ghasidas began calling themselves *Satnamis*. Attempting to differentiate clearly between the *Satnamis* who followed Ghasidas and those who merely took *Satnami* as their caste name is therefore nearly impossible. Any attempt to do so would create as much confusion as it would prevent. Moreover, it would unnecessarily reify a distinction which was clear neither in reality nor in the documentary evidence upon which my research drew. I have for this reason chosen to embrace an accurate ambiguity rather than a misleading clarity. That said, in most cases, the context should make the intended meaning plain.

Abbreviations

BJP	Bharatiya Janata Party
CG	Chhattisgarh, India
COCC	Chhattisgarh and Orissa Church Council of the United Church of North India
CWBM	Christian Woman's Board of Missions (Disciples)
DCHS	Disciples of Christ Historical Society archives, Nashville, TN
DOM	Division of Overseas Mission (Disciples)
AES	Archives of the Evangelical Synod at Eden Theological Seminary, St. Louis, Missouri
FCMS	Foreign Christian Mission Society (Disciples)
HCS	H. C. Saum files, Disciples of Christ Historical Society archives
IMD	India Mission District (Evangelical)
INC	Indian National Congress
RSS	Rashtriya Swayamsevak Sangh
SUNY	State University of New York
UCMS	United Christian Missionary Society (Disciples)
UCNI	United Church of North India
VHP	Vishva Hindu Parishad

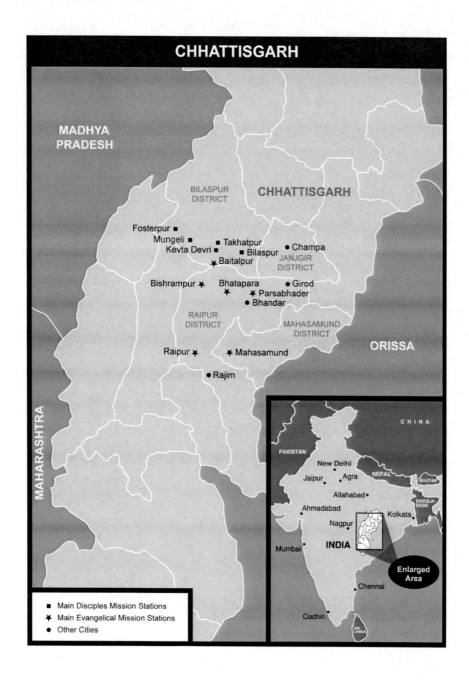

Introduction

This book, which deals in various ways with whether and to what extent conversion to Christianity in Chhattisgarh, a new state in Central India, entailed a process of "deculturation," or "denationalization," could not have come at a more historically apposite — some might say controversial — time. Indians continue to debate the nature of their national identity, and many consider Hinduism, or Hindu-ness *(Hindutva)* to be a central and intrinsic aspect of it. For those who hold this view, Christianity represents a culturally indigestible leftover of the nation's colonial past. Political parties such as the Bharatiya Janata Party (BJP), and organizations such as the Rashtriya Swayamsevak Sangh (RSS) and the Vishva Hindu Parishad (VHP) exploit popular fears regarding the growth of Christianity for political gain, equating conversion with denationalization. The accusation is nothing new. Gandhi himself called the evangelical efforts of Bishop Vedanayagam Azariah "anti-national" as early as 1937. And more recently, Arundhati Roy, the activist and novelist whose literary abilities I admire a great deal, drew upon the strength of popular sentiments against "missionary" activities when she called the forces of globalization "the new missionaries" in a published speech at the World Social Forum in Mumbai.[1]

In late 2003, during state legislative assembly elections in the state of Chhattisgarh, a local nationalist organization calling itself the Hindu Raksha Manch (the Hindu Protection Platform) ran a political cartoon in local papers depicting the region's Catholic Bishop, Rev. Joseph Augustine, next to a fierce-looking *goonda,* who is menacingly holding a *lathi* over a man presum-

1. Arundhati Roy, "Do Turkeys Enjoy Thanksgiving?" *Hindu,* 18 January 2004.

1

ably being forced to become Christian. Behind these three is a prison full of others awaiting the same fate. The cartoon's already obvious implication was explained by its caption, which referred to the Bishop: "Agent of the Pope — A Servant of Madam [Sonia Gandhi]. . . . Changing religion means changing nationality [*dharmāntaraṇ yāṇi rāṣṭrāntaraṇ*]. Change the government in Chhattisgarh and we can stop conversion."

The Italian birth of Sonia Gandhi, daughter-in-law of one former Indian prime minister, wife of another, and leader, at the time, of the more secular Congress Party, had led to rumors suggesting a papal conspiracy to Christianize the nation, and the cartoon implied that Augustine was part of the plot. The real target of the cartoon, however, was Ajit Jogi, the standing Chief Minister, who was a member of the Congress Party and also, significantly, a Christian (and whose political fate the elections would indirectly decide). Under his tenure, it was alleged, Christian conversions had increased exponentially, though there is little evidence that this was the case.

During the race, Dilip Singh Judev, a local BJP leader and Union Minister of State for Forests and Environment at the time, launched "Operation Homecoming" *(ghar vāpasī)*, aimed at reconverting "Christians" to Hinduism. (Some of the "reconverted" later admitted that they had never been Christian in the first place.)[2] Vishva Hindu Parishad state president Ramesh Modi vowed that his organization would not tolerate the "continuous suppression of Hindus" in the state by "churches guided and controlled by those who have roots in foreign countries."[3] Jogi's party was defeated in the election.

Arriving just after these elections, I feared that the tense political climate would adversely affect my research, partly because a variety of (usually urban and educated) Indians had warned me that this would be the case. In some ways, my fears were well founded. Christians occasionally hesitated to speak openly with me until they were certain that it was safe to do so, and some Hindus also initially treated me with suspicion. Nevertheless, in the rural areas in which I conducted the majority of my research, the highly publicized political tensions between Christians and Hindus simply did not exist. The political situation *did* shade the information I gathered from informants, but in a fashion contrary to my expectations — members of all communities went out of their way to indicate how well they got along with each other, almost as if they were attempting to correct what they believed to be mis-

2. For an interesting and scholarly, but clearly defensive Christian account of these events, see Rajendra K. Sail, *Conversion in Chhattisgarh: Facts and Myths* (Raipur: Indian Social Action Forum, 2003).

3. Council for World Mission, "VHP Rails against Christians in Chhattisgarh," 17 December 2003, accessed 17 December 2003; available from http://www.cwmission.org.

perceptions nurtured by the (again, urban and educated) press and exploited by certain prominent figures for political gain.

As these stories suggest, conversion is one of the most politically charged acts in contemporary India. While Hindu nationalist groups like Judev's conduct highly publicized and theatrical ceremonies in order to reconvert Christians and Muslims to Hinduism, Hindus continue, sometimes in great numbers but generally a few at a time, to convert to other faiths. On the recent fiftieth anniversary of B. R. Ambedkar's[4] conversion to Buddhism, for example, hundreds of *dalits,* members of India's lowest castes, gathered to convert, some to Buddhism and others to Christianity, explicitly rejecting Hinduism, a religion they claim oppresses and demeans them.

In the logic of Hindu nationalism, conversion to "foreign" faiths, especially Christianity and Islam, entails a denationalization that diminishes the convert's loyalty to *Bharat Mata,* or "Mother India" (increasingly conceived of today as a Hindu goddess). Conversion to Christianity is particularly distasteful, given its association with Britain, the former colonizer, and America, the global superpower with what many Indians perceive to be neo-colonial ambitions. In fact, many Indians perceive in Christian evangelism the seditious designs of a "foreign hand" — either that of the Pope or, as suggested in a recent issue of *Tehelka,* an Indian periodical, of that putative über-Christian, George W. Bush.[5] According to these Indians, conversions to Christianity represent yet another threat to India's unity, autonomy, and right of self-determination.

Because of this, Indians have at various times and by various methods attempted to curtail evangelism and conversion. The British East India Company itself did for some time prohibit certain kinds of evangelism, but lifted the prohibition in 1813. On the other hand, many of India's princely states, quasi-autonomous vassals of the Raj until India's Independence (1947), had enacted anti-conversion laws to keep foreign missionaries and Indian Christians out of their territory. For example, Raigarh promulgated a "Conversion

4. Dr. Ambedkar, the Columbia University–educated lawyer and sometimes opponent of Gandhi, was the most prominent of Indian *dalit* leaders in the first half of the twentieth century, and converted from Hinduism to Buddhism in 1956 to protest the former's treatment of the lowest castes. On this, see Christopher S. Queen, "Dr. Ambedkar and the Hermeneutics of Buddhist Liberation," in *Engaged Buddhism: Buddhist Liberation Movements in Asia,* ed. Christopher S. Queen and Sallie B. King (Albany: State University of New York Press, 1996). See also Christopher Jaffrelot, *Dr. Ambedkar and Untouchability: Fighting the Indian Caste System* (New York: Columbia University Press, 2004).

5. V. K. Shashikumar, "Preparing for the Harvest," *Tehelka (Online Edition),* 7 February 2004.

Act" in 1936, Patna in 1942, Sarguja in 1945, and Udaipur in 1946. Other princely states followed suit.

At Independence, however, these states were integrated — some more quickly than others — into the Indian Union, and the laws of the former gave way to those of the latter, which did not regulate conversion. Consequently, the various states of newly constituted India began to pass individual laws regarding conversion from one community to another. In 1967, Orissa passed the "Freedom of Religion Act," and in 1968 Madhya Pradesh enacted a similar law, entitled "Dharma Swatantraya Adhiniyam." Arunachal Pradesh joined them in 1978.[6] More recently, the states of Tamil Nadu (2002), Gujarat (2003), and Himachal Pradesh (2007) have passed laws regulating conversion, and similar regulations are being considered by state governments in Chhattisgarh, Uttarakhand, and Rajasthan.

All of these laws prohibit conversion due to force, fraud, inducement, or allurement. A few of them require that those wishing to convert (and those wishing to convert them) notify local authorities well in advance of the actual ceremony. Those who support such laws argue that they prohibit only underhanded evangelical strategies, and that they therefore exist for the sole purpose of ensuring that "foreign" faiths cannot lure adherents with the vast sums (by Indian standards) of money and influence to which they have access. They cite as support for their argument the fact that until recently, very few people had been convicted under the laws.

Christians, on the other hand, claim that the mere existence of such laws gives courage to more extreme Hindu nationalists, leading to increased harassment and maltreatment of Christians. Moreover, Christians allege, opponents of Christian conversion use such laws, through false accusations, in order to intimidate Christian leaders and potential converts. They therefore perceive these laws to be a blunt instrument with which Hindu nationalists bludgeon and browbeat India's religious minorities and the primarily lower-caste Hindus who would join them. Adding support to their argument is the fact that the laws in question do not generally regulate reconversion *to Hinduism*, despite evidence that allurement is sometimes involved therein.

The *dalits* are caught in the crossfire. Though many of the earliest Christian missionaries in India focused on members of the higher castes, believing that faith in Christ would trickle downward from them to the uneducated lower classes, the vast majority of converts to Christianity in the last three centuries have come from India's *dalit* and tribal communities. Despite generous reserva-

6. For more on the history of these laws, see Arpita Anant, "Anti-Conversion Laws," *The Hindu (Online Edition),* 17 December 2002.

tions for such communities in India's government and educational institutions that have raised their economic prospects (and caused some members of the upper castes to talk of reverse discrimination), independent India has failed to eradicate the social stigma of lower-caste status, particularly in its rural areas. Some *dalits* have therefore converted to Christianity in order, among other reasons, to live in a world (theoretically) free of caste discrimination. Yet doing so means relinquishing their eligibility for governmental and educational reservations, and facing minor or major forms of social censure. Beaten down and neglected by the religion to which they adhere, yet risking marginalization, harassment, or even violence should they convert, India's *dalits* are caught in the middle — damned, as it were, if they do, damned if they don't.

The complexity of these issues cannot be fully understood without reference to the past, and to the lives of specific Indians and Indian communities. Leaving current events to the sociologists, therefore, as historians are wont to do, this book takes a step back in time just beyond the glare of contemporary controversies in order to explore the experiences of one community of *dalits,* the Satnampanth of Chhattisgarh. The Satnampanth is a Hindu sectarian community founded in the early nineteenth century by an illiterate *dalit,*[7] Guru Ghasidas, a member of the *Chamar* caste. Ghasidas's message was similar to that of many Hindu reformers who had come before him. He told his followers, among other things, to abandon the worship of images, to devote themselves entirely to the one and only deity (whom he called "Satnam," i.e., the True Name), to avoid eating meat, and to reject the use of *brahmans* as religious functionaries. The Guru's following grew, slowly at first, but by his death in 1850 he claimed a quarter of a million disciples, and by the century's end nearly all members of the *Chamar* caste in Chhattisgarh had joined his *panth* (a community of followers), calling themselves *Satnamis.*

In 1868, eighteen years after Ghasidas's death, the first western missionaries, sent by German Evangelicals living in the United States, arrived in Raipur and later set up camp nearby, in Bishrampur. In 1885, Disciples of Christ mis-

---

7. Though the term *"dalit"* (broken, or oppressed) has existed since at least the 1970s, it has only recently come to be used widely with reference to the "untouchables," or what the British called the "depressed classes." These lower castes, which are now officially called "scheduled castes," have become increasingly conscious of their oppression and solidarity in a process that has been called "dalitization." Nevertheless, Chhattisgarh's lower castes still do not generally use the term self-referentially, preferring Gandhi's *"harijan."* To use the term with reference to Chhattisgarhis in the late colonial period would therefore be historically inaccurate. For this reason I used the term *"dalit"* when writing generally about lower-caste communities, but have avoided it when describing specific historical and contextual matters.

sionaries would join them, working outwards from the town of Bilaspur.[8] Hearing from an unknown source that a *Satnami* guru had prophesied their coming, these missionaries came to expect that all *Satnamis* would soon become Christian. Only a small percentage of *Satnamis* ever did convert, but the great majority of today's Christians in this area can trace their ancestry to the Satnampanth.

This book analyzes the interaction of *Satnamis* and Christians, an interaction involving roughly eighty years of intense cultural and religious conversation in the midst of which a *Satnami*-Christian identity emerged, distinct both from that of the *Satnamis* and of the missionaries. The interaction was most intense between 1868, when missionaries arrived, and 1947, when India received her independence and missionary influence began to wane, and it occurred primarily within the cartographic quadrangle formed by connecting the cities of Raipur, Mahasamund, Bilaspur, and Mungeli (see map, p. xv). I have therefore located my investigation within these temporal and spatial boundaries. And rather than focus on missionary history, as so many studies of "Indian Christianity" have done, this work attempts to highlight the experiences and beliefs of Chhattisgarhis themselves.

The most central of the book's claims is that while the transformations wrought in the developing *Satnami*-Christian community during this period were overwhelmingly the result of contact with a heterogenetic[9] religion (Christianity), a religion made attractive by, among other things, its putative association with colonial structures of power and wealth, and with the aura of novel and potent sources of authority (e.g., "logic," science, and literacy), the trajectory of these transformations was at the same time orthogenetically altered. That is, the trajectory was conditioned in appreciable and significant ways by pre-existing *Satnami* structures of thought, belief, and behavior, by the community's unique set of hopes and dreams, its methods of determining "truth" and "falsity," its "history" and "tradition." Therefore, the Christianization of Chhattisgarh — limited as it was — also entailed the *Chhattisgarhization* of Christianity.

---

8. Other Christian denominations, such as the Catholics, American Methodists, and Mennonites (both General Conference and Mennonite Conference), also worked in the region, but they arrived later and their interaction with the *Satnamis* was, generally speaking, much less intense. I have therefore chosen to focus on the Evangelical and the Disciples of Christ mission fields.

9. Midway through the twentieth century, anthropologists such as Milton Singer began to distinguish changes that originated from within a culture ("orthogenetic" innovations) from those that had their provenance on "foreign" soil ("heterogenetic" innovations). I find the terminology useful for discussing religious change as well.

A community's identity is, in many ways, like a dream. Like a dream, it is a pastiche, constructed (whether consciously or unconsciously) of excerpts and fragments, pieces and bits, disparate and sometimes unrelated elements, some borrowed, some close at hand, some creatively imagined. Yet, as in dreams, these elements are woven into an apparently seamless fabric, reworked into a convincing and "natural" communal self-image. To argue, therefore, that the communal identity of *Satnami*-Christians involved both heterogenetic and orthogenetic elements is not, therefore, to suggest that it is in this way different from any other communal identity.

From the inception of Christianity, Christian missionaries working in lands other than their own have frequently been confronted with the difficulty of disentangling culture and religion, and in the last two centuries western scholars like Marx, Weber, and Durkheim have dealt with this difficulty in a more systematic way. Religion is, as Clifford Geertz has put it, a "cultural system,"[10] and a particularly important one in societies like India where the distinction between what westerners call "religion" and "culture" is blurrier and more difficult to discern than the proverbial line in the sand.

Religion, as I understand it, is a symbolic system that brings order and coherence to the world and shields believers from the disruptive potential of realities such as suffering, injustice, and death. It is a lens through which the world is viewed, a gloss on its inherent contradictions, a denial of meaninglessness, chaos, and disorder. Such an understanding brings me close to the view of the late cultural anthropologist, Clifford Geertz. However, Geertz and others like him have rightly been criticized by scholars like Talad Asad and Peter van der Veer for not adequately taking into consideration the fact that the interpretation of experience and articulation of beliefs do not take place in a social vacuum, but are rather enmeshed in social patterns of power and weakness, wealth and poverty, status and inferiority.[11] Nevertheless, while such criticisms offer a much-needed corrective, it appears to me that the differences between Geertz and many of those who criticize him on this account are relatively small, and Geertz's general framework need not, therefore, be entirely abandoned. A scholar like Talal Asad stands in relationship to Geertz as a corrective, not a refutation.

I therefore understand religion to be: (1) A dynamic, diverse, and contested system of symbols which acts to (2) condition a person's experience of

10. "Religion as a Cultural System," Chapter Four in Clifford Geertz, *The Interpretation of Cultures* (New York: Basic Books, 1973).

11. For a well-reasoned critique of Geertz, see Peter van der Veer, *Gods on Earth: The Management of Religious Experience in a North Indian Pilgrimage Center* (Delhi: Oxford University Press, 1988), pp. 46-47.

the world by (3) placing that experience within a larger, more consequential, and ostensibly unalterable framework of meaning (a worldview), while at the same time (4) rendering the framework of meaning believable and persuasive by (5) invoking the very same conditioned experience of the world as evidence of its appropriateness.[12] Furthermore, while religion as it is here described involves the symbiosis of experience (the world as lived) and worldview (the world as imagined), it must be kept in mind that it is neither impervious to change nor entirely insulated from the possibility of manipulation by those in possession of social power and authority.

The Context: Chhattisgarh, the *Satnamis,* and *Satnami*-Christians

In November of 2000, the eastern sliver of Madhya Pradesh, a state in what has been termed the "Hindi Heartland" of India, was carved off to form the new state of Chhattisgarh, which encompasses an area of 83,847 square miles (roughly the size of Kansas). According to the 2001 Census of India, Chhattisgarh's twenty-one million residents live in around twenty thousand villages and towns, and 80 percent of the population lives in rural areas.[13] The centrally located and quickly growing capital, Raipur, is the largest of the state's cities, and is home to three million people. In 1901, 95 percent of the region's inhabitants reported that Chhattisgarhi, a dialect of Eastern Hindi (along with Awadhi and Begheli), was their mother tongue. By the 1961 census that number had decreased to 65 percent, Hindi having become more popular in the urban areas.[14] Though Hindi is on the rise, English has yet to become a popular language in the state. As recently as 2003, fewer than one-fifth of the Chief Minister's cabinet members were fluent in English.[15] Chhattisgarhi is a language raised in the dust and soil of a farmer's life, a language of earthy idioms, lurid abuses, and evocative imagery. To those who speak it fluently, it is a language of pride and belonging.

Though it has only recently been granted statehood, Chhattisgarh has long been recognized as a distinct region with a certain geographic, linguistic,

---

12. Geertz's definition, which informs my own, appears in Geertz, *Interpretation of Cultures,* p. 90.

13. Office of the Registrar General, "Census of India, 2001," accessed 23 June 2004; available from http://www.censusindia.net/results/.

14. Joyce Burkhalter Flueckiger, *Gender and Genre in the Folklore of Middle India* (Ithaca, NY: Cornell University Press, 1996), p. 7.

15. Times News Network, "Chhattisgarh: Past Imperfect," 2003, accessed 29 September 2003; available from http://www.timesofindia.com.

ethnic, and historical integrity. The large and fertile crop-producing plain of Chhattisgarh, watered by the Mahanadi, Son, and Seonath river basins, is surrounded by several forest-covered hilly tracts: the Satpura Hills and the Maikala Range in the west, the Sonpar Hills and Chotanagpur Plateau in the north, and the Bastar and Albaka hills in the south. These mountainous areas forbid easy transportation and have sheltered the region from commerce with the outside world. A large part of the state is still accessible only by oxcart, foot, or hardy motorcycle.

Such physical isolation has resulted in the development of distinct Chhattisgarhi folkways. Chhattisgarh is not, however, an ethnographic monolith. Until more recent urbanization, the peoples of Chhattisgarh could be roughly divided into the "Hindus" of the plains and the "jungly" *ādivāsī*[16] communities of the hills, which were less fully integrated into the Hindu caste system.[17] Chhattisgarh is known for its Scheduled Tribe and Caste population. Nearly two-thirds of the Scheduled Castes and a large majority of undivided Madhya Pradesh's *ādivāsī* communities were found in the region. Due to these demographics and its geographic inaccessibility, Chhattisgarh has often been perceived by outsiders as a refuge for miscreants and Corybants. In 1867, Gazetteer Charles Grant described the region in this way: "Land-locked on every side by deep forests of hill-passes, and remote from all centres, whether of eastern or more modern western civilization, this little principality was till of comparably late years the least known portion of the obscurest division of India."[18] In 1869, the Raipur Settlement Report spoke of Chhattisgarhi religiosity in a similar vein: "Chhuteesgurh to orthodox Hindoos is not only hateful as the land of the *Dasyus* [thieves, barbarians] and witches, but as the headquarters of religious dissent, as it is to its secluded wilds that all those who opposed the prevailing tenets fled to escape from their persecutors, and consequently Hindooism sits lightly on most of the people, while large numbers are avowed dissenters belonging to the Kubeerpuntee and Sutnamee sects." Today, references to the state in conversations with modernized Indians often provoke comment on its "backwardness" and unflattering comparisons to underdeveloped Bihar. However, because of their sheer numerical strength, and the absence of a large high-caste

16. Though the Indian government still officially uses the term "tribal" when speaking of "Scheduled Tribes," "*ādivāsī*," meaning "original inhabitant," is currently used by most scholars and writers in India and is considered a less pejorative term.

17. Lawrence A. Babb, *The Divine Hierarchy: Popular Hinduism in Central India* (New York: Columbia University Press, 1975), p. 11.

18. Charles Grant, ed., *The Gazetteer of the Central Provinces of India* (New Delhi: Usha, 1984), p. 56.

population — among caste Hindus, *sudras* predominate — Chhattisgarh's low castes have been able to contest their domination by high castes in a variety of ways, and in many villages they are in fact the dominant caste, statistically and otherwise.[19]

Much of the population is rural and the economy is largely agricultural. The land is bone-dry and dusty from November to June, and green with rice paddies in the rainy months between July and October. Chhattisgarhis consider their state India's *dhān kā kaṭorā* (rice bowl), and indeed the region's ample average yearly rainfall of forty-nine inches allows for fruitful production of the crop, which is usually planted midway through June. In between rice-growing seasons, Chhattisgarhis cultivate a variety of cereals, oilseeds, and pulses. Sal and teak trees dominate the region's forests.

Until the end of the first millennium CE, the region was known as Dakshin (south) Kosala, and governed by a series of monarchic dynasties, among them the Gupta.[20] Around 1000 CE the Kalachuris of the Haihaya dynasty mastered the territory. Their capital was at Ratanpur, where several ancient temples from the period still stand.[21] In the fourteenth century the Kalachuri dynasty split, and each of the two realms was divided into eighteen districts, protected by forts. The most likely provenance of the name Chhattisgarh derives from these thirty-six forts *(chattīs gaṛh)*. In 1742, Maratha armies passing through the region on their way to lay siege to Orissa pacified the Haihayavanshis, bringing a measure of political stability to the region.[22]

Maratha rule, executed through local governors, or *sūbāhdārs*, continued until 1817, when the British defeated the Bhonsles[23] of Nagpur at the battle of Sitabaldi. A British official, Major Vans Agnew, administered the territory temporarily until the Bhonsle ruler, Raghoji III, came of age in 1830. In 1854, Raghoji III died without offspring, and under the doctrine of lapse the British annexed the region as part of the territories of Nagpur, which were in 1861 in-

19. Ramdas Lamb, *Rapt in the Name: The Ramnamis, Ramnam, and Untouchable Religion in Central India* (Albany: State University of New York Press, 2002), p. 12.

20. Stanley Wolpert, *A New History of India*, 5th ed. (New York: Oxford University Press, 1997), p. 88.

21. The oldest is the Kanthi Deval Shiva temple, built in 1039 CE. See Makhan Jha, "Ratanpur: Some Aspects of a Sacred City in Chhattisgarh," in *Chhattisgarh: An Area Study*, ed. Ajit Kumar Danda (Calcutta: Anthropological Survey of India, Govt. of India, 1977).

22. Saurabh Dube, *Untouchable Pasts: Religion, Identity, and Power among a Central Indian Community, 1780-1950* (Albany: State University of New York Press, 1998), pp. 27-28.

23. A Maratha clan.

cluded in the newly organized Central Provinces.[24] In 1857, during the Indian Mutiny (or "First War of Independence," as it is called by some), a small section of the Raipur Indian military force broke ranks, but the insurrection was promptly and fiercely put down. Chhattisgarhis participated in the development and growth of the Indian National Congress (INC, formed in 1885), though they were by no means central players. Upon India's Independence, Chhattisgarh was included with other regions of the Central Provinces and Berar in the new state of Madhya Pradesh (a Hindi rendering of "Central Province").

Both Maratha and British rulers extracted revenue from Chhattisgarh through a hierarchy of local and regional tax officials who received a percentage of what they collected in exchange for their services. Under the Marathas, village heads, called *gaunṭiyās*, extracted taxes from those working the land in their village, took a portion of the yield, and sent the rest to regional *paṭels*, who did the same and passed the remainder up the hierarchy until the revenue reached the provincial *sūbāhdārs* and through them the Bhonsle Maratha treasury.[25]

Though the system encouraged officials at all levels to maximize the revenue extracted from those in their jurisdiction, and abuses were certainly common, the fact that labor (rather than arable land) was scarce in the region shielded the Chhattisgarhi peasantry from the worst injustices. *Gaunṭiyās* and *paṭels* who attempted to extract exorbitant amounts from their subordinates were in danger of provoking migration to other areas.[26] Nevertheless, low-caste farmers were at particular risk of falling prey to graft because they were generally disconnected from centers of power and had no recourse when exploited.[27]

Hoping to increase production after taking control of the region in 1854, the British introduced the *khalsā* and *zamindari* land tenure systems. The *khalsā* system granted *gaunṭiyās*, or *malguzars* as they were known under the new system, ownership of the villages from which they had extracted revenue for the Bhonsles. The lands controlled by *malguzars* were divided into a *sīr* (a home farm, over which the *malguzars* claimed ownership and complete control) and a *khudkāśt* (the outlying lands on which tenants retained certain

---

24. Grant, ed., *Gazetteer*, p. 56. At the founding of the Central Provinces, Chhattisgarh was divided into two districts, Raipur and Bilaspur. Under the doctrine of lapse, implemented midway through the nineteenth century, any vassal state of the British East Company would be annexed if its ruler died without a male heir.

25. Dube, *Untouchable Pasts*, pp. 28-30.

26. Dube, *Untouchable Pasts*, p. 30.

27. Dube, *Untouchable Pasts*, p. 31.

rights). The reforms served to strengthen the hand of former *gauṇṭiyās* and *paṭels* (who were generally members of the high castes and the former Maratha elite), and to weaken that of the belabored, often lower-caste farmers. In addition, by granting land ownership rights, the British made land *transferable*, raising the possibility that impoverished peasants might be driven from good land by those laying claim to it.

Along with the *khalsā* land revenue arrangement, British officials implemented a system of land tenure called the *zamindari* system. The *zamindars* were essentially landlords who controlled large estates, sometimes encompassing several hundred square miles. As much as 50 percent of Chhattisgarhi land under the British was controlled by *zamindars*.[28] *Zamindars* received all the leviable revenue in their domains, paid a fixed tribute to the British, and were in return responsible for ensuring law and order at their own expense.[29]

Tenants in Chhattisgarh, as elsewhere in India, were bound to the dominant landholding communities in their villages through the *jajmānī* system — a reciprocal exchange of privileges and services. Each caste community received certain hereditary perquisites in exchange for carrying out a variety of services for other villagers, and especially for members of the dominant community. The rights and services rendered by a particular community were usually related to that community's traditional occupation. For Guru Ghasidas's *Chamars*, this meant, among other things, the right to dead cattle, to a certain share of the harvest, to fuel (dung) and cuttings from the village lands, and to gifts on special occasions in exchange for their services as leather-workers, as agriculturalists, and — for the women — as midwives.[30] The system ensured the interdependence of all communities in a village, but the exchange of goods, privileges, and services was of course in control of the dominant landholding group, and thus weighted in its favor.

Because of their numerical strength, the *Chamars* of Chhattisgarh enjoyed, throughout the eighteenth century, a higher social position in Chhattisgarh than many of their caste-mates elsewhere. If unscrupulous landowners taxed them unfairly or attempted to extort an unusually high amount of *begar* (corvée labor)[31] from them, they could migrate *en masse*

28. William Wilson Hunter, Sir, and others, eds., *Imperial Gazetteer of India*, vol. 8 (Oxford: Clarendon Press, 1908), pp. 226-27.

29. Grant, ed., *Gazetteer*, p. 153.

30. John C. B. Webster, *A History of the Dalit Christians in India* (San Francisco: Mellen Research University Press, 1992), p. 17.

31. It was a common and accepted practice for landlords to extract free labor from their tenants, especially for village projects such as digging reservoirs, etc. But the exact amount was not predetermined and was frequently a cause of conflict.

and deal their landlords a significant financial blow. There is also evidence that during this period *Chamars* owned a fair number of villages, some of them occupied by no other caste. But if these villages allowed *Chamars* a haven from the oppression of the higher castes, they also aroused the jealousies of the same, provoking high-caste landlords to deal more harshly with *Chamars* under their control.[32]

While not all religious (and cultural) change should be assumed to be the result of external forces, it is indeed very often the case that external disruptions provide the catalyst for momentous religious change. Frequently, the source of religious disillusionment — figurative and literal — is a radical shift in the social order that renders it impossible to experience and interpret the world as before. Whether the source of disruption is political, demographic, or natural, or whether it results from the appearance of new sources of power or authority, individuals and communities generally respond by attempting to reestablish the perception of order, of *eunomie*. This reconstruction requires either that the social order be somehow returned to its previous state of perceived equilibrium or that the world be imagined in new ways.

This book focuses on one such rupture, or rather a set of ruptures that shook the foundations of the social order in nineteenth-century Chhattisgarh, and led to a significant degree of religious unrest among the region's lowest castes. It is difficult to confidently determine which of them was most catalytic — was it the cumulative effect of colonization, a reality that made itself felt, in this region, midway through the nineteenth century? Was it the emergence of another alternate religious system (Christianity), which appeared at roughly the same time?[33] Was it the series of mid-nineteenth-century British land tenure reforms that played, for the most part, into the hands of elite landholding communities? Was it the disintegration of traditional village patterns of intercaste patronage and the exchange of goods and services known as the *jajmānī* system? Was it withering poverty, devastating famines, or epidemic disease? Or was it a general state of oppression that could be borne no longer?

32. Dube, *Untouchable Pasts,* pp. 7, 25, 32.

33. Berger suggests that the appearance of alternate religious systems "deobjectivates" religion by robbing it of its "taken-for-granted status." "The premodern individual," he says, "was linked to his gods in the same inexorable destiny that dominated most of the rest of his existence; modern man is faced with the necessity of choosing between the gods." Certainly Christianity represented another and powerful alternative to various forms of Hinduism in Chhattisgarh, but Islam had preceded it by several centuries. Peter Berger, *The Heretical Imperative: Contemporary Possibilities of Religious Affirmation* (Garden City, NY: Anchor Press/Doubleday, 1980), pp. 24-25.

Whatever the most salient cause of social disruption, the *Chamars*, a caste of leather-workers and agriculturalists at the lower reaches of the socio-religious hierarchy, appear to have experienced it more profoundly than others. For many, the symbiotic and circular relationship between the world as lived and the world as imagined had ruptured — or at least it had begun to distend. However, the upper-caste (and, later, British) domination prevented them from attempting to alter their social situation in public, direct, and confrontational ways, despite being the largest community in the region. Drawn into the political realities of the colonial Raj, buffeted by the vagaries of the natural world, and slipping down the rungs of socio-economic status, the *Chamars* were in need of a cultural revolution, of a new and imaginative *collective effervescence*.

It was in circumstances such as these that Ghasidas went into the forest, in the 1820s, and returned with a message for his people. The Guru's message helped many *Chamars* to reimagine themselves and the world in which they lived. His insistence on the relative equality of all castes, and his refusal to rely on *brahman* religious functionaries, provided a source of pride and dignity to the downtrodden community, altered its self-perception, and therefore its *experience* of reality (though not, to the same extent, the "reality" itself).

There was, therefore, already a considerable degree of religious restlessness in Chhattisgarh when the first missionaries arrived in 1868, which may lend credence to Robin Horton's thesis, articulated in the context of Africa, that modern pressures provoked the rationalization of traditional religions (involving, among other things, the increased importance of a "single" high God), and that the growth of more "macrocosmic" religions such as Islam and Christianity was more opportunistic than catalytic; that is, they were *manifestations*, rather than causes, of change.[34] Evangelical missionaries, and the Disciples of Christ mission workers that followed them three decades later, quickly concluded that they might be able to turn this religious ferment to their advantage, and focused their efforts on the *Chamars* who became *Satnamis*. Despite evangelical expectations, most *Satnamis* remained members of the *panth*. But for some, Ghasidas's reinvention of the community had

---

34. See Robin Horton, "On the Rationality of Conversion," *Africa* 45, no. 3 (1975); and Robin Horton, *Patterns of Thought in Africa and the West: Essays on Magic, Religion, and Science* (New York: Cambridge University Press, 1993). Robert Frykenberg disputes the relevance of Horton's thesis to India, arguing that even *bhakti* movements were aimed at "intermediate" deities. The *Satnamis*, however, appear to represent a rather clear, if, as we will see, abortive and incomplete move towards a single "high" God. See Robert Eric Frykenberg, "On the Study of Conversion Movements: A Review Article and a Theoretical Note," *Indian Economic and Social History Review* 17, no. 1 (1980): 136.

not gone far enough, had not achieved significant and tangible enough results, or worse, by articulating a vision of a better world, had succeeded only in drawing attention to the deplorable existing state of affairs. Missionaries, of course, are always and in every situation agents of change, rabble-rousers, intruders, disturbers of the status quo; not surprisingly, they exacerbated this dissatisfaction by providing it with an outlet.[35] For some disillusioned *Satnamis,* Christianity became an appealing alternative.

Plan of the Book

Chapter 1 provides more detail on Chhattisgarhi history, social structure, and religious practices. In it I argue, with reference to Louis Dumont, that the caste system, prevalent in Chhattisgarh as elsewhere in India, is a socio-religious hierarchy based on commonly held perceptions of purity and pollution. Yet I also show, by drawing upon the work of M. N. Srinivas, that this hierarchy was never entirely stable, and that there was in fact an element of flexibility in the system which allowed caste communities that gained a certain degree of economic, numerical, or political power to move up, if rather slowly, the rungs of the hierarchical ladder. As Srinivas's work indicates, and as post-colonial scholars have pointed out, Dumont's theory neglected the political and economic side of the caste hierarchy, and in particular the fact that those with power could wield some influence over it. Even the British, as Nicholas Dirks and others have shown, may have contributed to an ossification of the system by enumerating and ranking castes in their decennial censuses.

Chapter 1 also more fully discusses the origins of the Satnampanth. Though most *Satnamis* believe Ghasidas to have been divinely inspired during his forest retreat, many alternative views exist. One view, perpetuated most frequently by Christians in the region, is that while on a pilgrimage, Ghasidas encountered and was inspired by a Christian missionary, and there are indeed certain superficial similarities between Ghasidas's message and that of Christian missionaries. (The tension between Christian and *Satnami*

---

35. See Robert Eric Frykenberg, "Introduction: Dealing with Contested Definitions and Controversial Perspectives," in *Christians and Missionaries in India: Cross-Cultural Communication since 1500,* ed. Robert Eric Frykenberg (Grand Rapids: Eerdmans, 2003), p. 11. Duncan Forrester claims that Christianity was, in many parts of India, the first to respond "religiously" to *dalit* restlessness; see Duncan B. Forrester, "The Depressed Classes and Conversion to Christianity, 1860-1960," in *Religion in South Asia: Religious Conversion and Revival Movements in South Asia in Medieval and Modern Times,* ed. G. A. Oddie (New Delhi: Manohar Publications, 1977).

beliefs about the origin of Ghasidas's message animates Chapter 3.) Others, however, both *Satnami* and non-*Satnami*, have asserted that Ghasidas drew his message from that of two earlier movements which went by the name "*Satnami*" (both originating in the seventeenth century, one in the Punjab, and the other in what is today Uttar Pradesh). Still others, however, like the scholar Lawrence Babb, have linked Ghasidas's message to the Kabirpanth, a religious community which reveres the north Indian *sant* (poet-saint), Kabir, and which was prevalent in Chhattisgarh during Ghasidas's life.

In Chapter 1, however, I argue that Ghasidas probably drew less from these specific sources than from the more general *bhakti* (devotional Hindu) tradition and the north Indian *sants* who were inspired by it. The *sants* circumvented brahmanical hegemony by rejecting orthodox deities and temple ritual. They focused their devotion on abstract *nirgun* deities (deities "without qualities"). And they tended to downplay caste distinctions. Ghasidas's most significant innovations, therefore, follow rather closely the *bhakti-sant* blueprint.

This context, then, is the focus of my study, but though it lies in the past, it is not at all unrelated to the contemporary controversies discussed at the beginning of the chapter. For example, all of the post-Independence laws regulating conversion prohibit conversion by means, in a commonly used phrase, "of force, fraud, or inducement." But what in actual fact constitutes "inducement," or, to use another common term, "allurement"? There are some acts that nearly everyone would consider unacceptable — the explicit offering of money or employment in exchange for conversion, for example. But beyond these things, the issue gets more complicated. Has the *dalit* who converts to Christianity because Christians will educate his children and Hindus will not (because of their low ritual status) been improperly induced? And what of the *dalit* who joins the Christian community because she is inspired by its relatively more egalitarian social views? Is the promise of an escape from caste discrimination (whether fully delivered or not) an unfair allurement? What about the diseased person who converts to Christianity after receiving competent and much-needed care at a Christian medical facility — would this conversion constitute "force, fraud, or inducement"? Is the ability of Christian medical facilities to provide healing in areas where the government cannot itself an allurement? Or, stating the question more broadly, does the mere association of Christianity with western power, money, and status mean that any convert can be accused of having motives other than the purely religious?

The variety of motives driving conversion to Christianity is the focus of Chapter 2, which discusses the extent to which those who became Christian can be considered "agents" of their own history, and asks why it was that some *Satnamis* found Christianity attractive, while most did not. The chapter begins with a discussion of "agency" itself, and suggests, following Talal Asad, that the current obsession of western scholars with agency, with those who *acted* (rather than those who were *acted upon*) reflects western prejudices regarding what is worthwhile, respectable behavior and, moreover, obscures the undeniable fact that structures of colonial power always and in various ways conditioned and circumscribed the actions of colonial subjects. I therefore draw upon the work of Anthony Giddens to argue that religion, and religious behavior, is "dually constructed," a function both of intentional individual actions and of the institutional and social realities that delimit and influence them. Chhattisgarhis were therefore not by any means "free" agents. But they did act in their own interests to the extent that circumstances allowed.

Chapter 2 also investigates the act of conversion itself, and in particular the two predominant sociological theories used to explain it. The first of these, the "interest" theory, which has been developed extensively by Marxist theorists, suggests that people convert for reasons of material interest. The other predominant view is called the "strain" theory, and would interpret conversion as an attempt to resolve some kind of social dysfunction. As I see it, however, both theories are problematic because they imply that human behavior is determined at all times by rational calculation regarding the perception of problems and their solution (strain theory), or the identification of material goals and their attainment (interest theory). My own position, which I call "primordialist," is that though conversion does represent the pursuit of interests and a response to social strain, these interests and strains are *felt* more than rationally grasped, based on intuited (but not fully articulated) desires more than intentional, rational calculation. I call these desires primordial because they have to do with basic and universal human needs such as security, health, and meaning.

The chapter makes the argument, therefore, that while the social circumstances of *Satnamis* who converted to Christianity were largely determined by forces beyond their control, they nevertheless did not simply accept these circumstances, but searched for ways to alter, domesticate, and control them. For some, the search ended in Christianity and in this context conversion to Christianity cannot therefore be reduced to the result of economic and political concerns alone, though these undoubtedly played important roles. Rather, some Chhattisgarhis embraced Christianity because of what Max Weber would have called "ideal" interests, because it embodied a compelling vision of the "good life," a vision that involved both indigenous values and values imported by the missionaries.

Along with the allegation that Christians use improper means to lure Hindus to their fold, another of the central claims of those who oppose con-

version to Christianity, as indicated above, is that conversion entails denationalization, that one cannot adhere to a foreign faith without assimilating
disruptive foreign values and loyalties. Chapters 4 and 5 of this book address
that very issue, exploring whether and to what extent those *Satnamis* who became Christian also became, by that act, somehow less Indian.

Satnami-Christians, as I discovered in missionary archives and in my field
research, frequently mobilized their use of western, or allopathic, medicine
(the topic of Chapter 4) and their "better" treatment of women (the topic of
Chapter 5) as markers of group difference and pride. Scholars have tended to
interpret such social changes under the rubric of modernization. In this view,
when a "traditional" community (e.g., the *Satnami*-Christians) comes into
contact with a more "modernized" community (e.g., the missionaries), the
former is thereby modernized. Such modernization, it is moreover assumed,
is the ultimate end of all traditional peoples in the modern world. Chapters 4
and 5, however, call such evolutionary and deterministic thinking into question in three ways: 1) by demonstrating that it is difficult to define tradition
and modernity, let alone disentangle the two, 2) by arguing that what might
appear on the surface to be "modern" behavior is very often just "traditional"
behavior applied to changed circumstances, and 3) by suggesting that judged
by contemporary standards missionary behavior was no more consistently
"modern" than Indian behavior was "traditional." Because of this, I prefer to
speak of "tradition" and "innovation," for though what the missionaries
brought to Chhattisgarh was clearly new, it was not in every case "modern."

For example, as I investigated the *Satnami*-Christian use of allopathic
medicine further, it became clear that they had not simply assimilated the values and behaviors of evangelical missionaries, but had, rather, understood
these values and behaviors according to indigenous criteria. Chapter 4 therefore argues that *Satnami*-Christians assessed and appropriated (or rejected)
allopathic medical innovations introduced by missionaries according to traditional criteria of efficacy, leading to a process of medical "itineration"
among the medico-spiritual treatments of *baigās*, the ayurvedic solutions of
baids, and the allopathic services of mission-founded institutions. At the
same time, missionaries, by asserting that the Christian God (rather than
good science) was behind their medical ability, actually exhibited a rather
un-modern understanding of medical cause and effect that was similar, in
significant ways, to that of the "traditional" Indians with whom they worked.

In Chapter 5, I argue that traditional Hindu norms regarding respectable
upper-caste womanhood played a significant role in the *Satnami*-Christian
community's evaluation and *selective* assimilation of missionary notions of
"Christian" womanhood. Drawing on the work of Eliza Kent, I suggest that in

this "discourse of respectability," *Satnami*-Christians did assimilate certain Victorian-era values regarding the proper treatment and behavior of women. But they tended to assimilate much more quickly and vigorously those values that were also shared by local upper-caste communities, thereby allowing them to assert a higher social status. Interestingly, Victorian values were not always more "modern" than those of the *Satnamis*, particularly with regard to women. In fact, it appears to be the case that by adopting missionary values regarding women (which, not insignificantly, corresponded with upper-caste Hindu views on the same), *Satnami*-Christians actually *restricted* female mobility and the range of roles considered appropriate for women. Both Chapters 4 and 5 therefore suggest that becoming Christian did not entail a break with Chhattisgarhi culture, but rather involved a process during which elements of the community's "old" and "new" worldviews intermingled and mutually informed one another. *Satnami*-Christians assessed their new religion according to traditional criteria, and appraised their cultural traditions according to new criteria.

The question of communal identity looms large in contemporary Indian politics. What does it mean to be an Indian? What does it mean to be a Hindu? And, perhaps more importantly, does the former identity require the latter? Such questions are not foreign to the context of this study, as the *Satnami*-Christians of Chhattisgarh constantly struggled with what it meant to be both Christian *and* Indian. Chapter 3, for example, discusses the *Satnami*-Christian community's fluid identity, and in particular its changing attitudes towards the *Satnami* past. From the beginning of Christianity in Chhattisgarh, Christian leaders — both American and Indian — highlighted the continuities between Christianity and the Satnampanth. In collaboration with *Satnami*-Christian converts, Christian leaders reconfigured the *Satnami* past in order to portray conversion to Christianity as a fulfillment — rather than a rejection — of Guru Ghasidas's message. The earliest Christians appear to have appreciated these purported continuities with their *Satnami* past. But having achieved a modicum of social respect and status, the Christian community later sought to alter its tradition once again in order to obscure its mostly *Satnami* origins. In this case, the *Satnami*-Christians altered their "tradition" — which had in any case been largely "imagined" for them by non-*Satnami* leaders — in order to better suit their cultural goals and emergent self-understanding.

Many contemporary Indian opponents of conversion to Christianity postulate the essential and timeless *Hindu-ness* of Indian identity. Nevertheless, based on the history just articulated, and drawing on the work of theorists Stuart Hall and Paul du Gay, I argue in Chapter 3 that communal identities are social facts, part, as Paul Veyne has argued, of the "constitutive imagina-tion," which is a social (not individual) product. They are "imagined" — con-structed, whether consciously or unconsciously, by members of the groups that embrace them. This is true of *all* identities, whether *Satnami*-Christian, Indian, or any other. Symbols of cultural identity are culled from a commu-nity's "tradition" with meticulous (though not necessarily conscious) dis-crimination, from "histories" selectively remembered. Identities thus forged, however, do not appear imagined to those who embrace them. If they did, they would have no meaning.

Not only is a community's cultural identity imagined, it is also constantly evolving; it is contested, protean, emerging, and fluid.[36] Cultural identity, and thus religious identity, as I understand it, involves a *process* whereby the sym-bolic markers of group uniqueness, solidarity, and difference, as well as the parameters of inclusion and exclusion, are socially constructed, "invented," to use the terminology of Eric Hobsbawm, Terence Ranger, and Roy Wagner, in such a way as to be self-perpetuating, though not impervious to modification and change.

The notion that identity is fluid and negotiable is reinforced by Chapter 6, which narrates the stories of five Chhattisgarhi men of *Satnami* origin. Though I repeatedly asked my informants and searched in the archives for in-formation regarding prominent *Satnami*-Christian women, I was simply not able to suitably reconstruct the story of a single one. This may say something about my abilities as a researcher, but it also surely reflects the cultural biases of both Chhattisgarhis and the missionaries who encountered them. In any case, the five men whose stories are told in Chapter 6 constantly and in a vari-ety of ways struggled to find their place in the world, some by conversion to Christianity, others by aggressively resisting Christian influence in their com-munities. They embody many of the issues discussed in the book as a whole, and are therefore fitting metaphors, exemplary cases, symbolic personages.

Methodological Notes

The book that follows is a historical ethnography of a religious community, an interdisciplinary work informed by methodologies in the study of religion,

---

36. This language, and the discussion that follows, draws liberally from Stuart Hall's introduction to Peter Berger, *The Social Construction of Reality: A Treatise in the Sociology of Knowledge* (Garden City, NY: Doubleday, 1966); and Stuart Hall and Paul du Gay, eds., *Questions of Cultural Identity* (London: Sage, 1996), pp. 1-3.

history, and anthropology. I have attempted to inform my reading of historical "texts," archival and otherwise, with an ethnographic sensibility, and to
bring my fieldwork into conversation with the historical record. Susan
Wadley has asserted that the difference between anthropologists and historians of religion is that the former examine their texts in context, while the latter do not.[37] Though the distinction is perhaps overly simplistic, given that
few "historians of religion" these days immure themselves in dimly lit archives and read only from the dusty pages of hoary antiquity, it is Wadley's vision of the anthropologist who brings texts into conversation with context
that I wish to emulate. (In her defense, Wadley was writing in 1978 and arrived at her conclusions in conversation with a Sanskritist.)

To the extent, therefore, that what is contained in this book is history, it is
episodic history, a series of snapshots rather than an unbroken catalog of
events and occurrences. But as anyone who has suffered through the interminable video recordings of another's family vacation can tell you, snapshots often offer a more meaningful and evocative (not to mention sufferable) record
of events than the strict and monotonous play-by-play of video recordings.

Scholars working under the rubric of post-colonial studies and — in the
context of South Asia — subaltern studies have also affected my approach to
this project. Publications of the Subaltern Studies Collective constitute a resource of mixed utility for scholars of religion. On the one hand, their imaginative critique of South Asian historiographies, particularly those historiographies that uncritically accept colonial and western forms of constructing
historical truth, has been an indispensable corrective. Moreover, particularly
since the 1990s, Subaltern Studies research has tended to conceive of religion as
a significant part of the "subaltern consciousness" and therefore not only as a
potential site of domination, but also of *resistance* to it.[38] On the other hand,
however, few religionists have been part of the Subaltern Studies project and
religion therefore remains for it a kind of theoretical "blind spot."[39] This is

37. Susan S. Wadley, "Texts in Context: Oral Tradition and the Study of Religion in
Karimpur," in *American Studies in the Anthropology of India,* ed. Sylvia Vatuk (New Delhi:
Manohar Publications, 1978), p. 310.

38. See, for example, Partha Chatterjee, "Agrarian Relations and Communalism in
Bengal, 1926-1935," in *Subaltern Studies I: Writings on South Asian History and Society,* ed.
Ranajit Guha (Delhi: Oxford University Press, 1982); Partha Chatterjee, "Caste and Subal-
tern Consciousness," in *Subaltern Studies VI,* ed. Ranajit Guha (Delhi: Oxford University
Press, 1989); and Ranajit Guha, "The Prose of Counter-Insurgency," in *Selected Subaltern
Studies,* ed. Ranajit Guha and Gayatri Spivak (Delhi: Oxford University Press, 1988).

39. Christian Novetzke, "The Subaltern Numen: Making History in the Name of God,"
History of Religions 46, no. 2 (2006): 125.

particularly so with regard to Christianity in India, which inhabits a rather ambiguous place in South Asian historiography. For while conversion to Christianity provided one avenue of revolt against upper-caste domination, it was also construed (then, by critics, and today, by many historians and anthropologists) as a kind of regrettable "capitulation" to the dominant colonial religion. For this reason, conversion to Christianity continues to constitute something of an elephant in the room of subaltern studies.

Despite this, I have been particularly influenced by the attempt by subaltern studies scholars to highlight the voices of subaltern peoples — however difficult and problematic such an endeavor might be, especially for a western scholar — and to reject facile bifurcations such as east and west, indigenous and foreign, tradition and modernity, agency and passivity, sovereignty and subjugation. I therefore consider this book a work of subaltern history, and if I do not consistently employ the academic language associated with the field of subaltern studies, it is only because, very often, that idiom is unintelligible to the uninitiated.

I have drawn my information primarily from three sources. The first, scholarly treatises such as those by Lawrence Babb, Saurabh Dube, Joyce Burkhalter Flueckiger, and Ramdas Lamb, supplied contextual details on the history, cultures, and religions of Chhattisgarh.[40] Of these, Dube's *Untouchable Pasts* was the most serviceable. This exceptional text not only provides an overview of *Satnami* history, but also places that history within a theoretical framework thoroughly informed by recent studies on gender, power, and colonial history. I read *Untouchable Pasts* early in my research and then set it aside, fearing that its cogent and persuasive voice might overwhelm my own. Returning to it again after having established my own conclusions, I found those contained in it all the more convincing. Nevertheless, whereas Dube concentrates on the Satnampanth itself, and deals only in a more impressionistic and tangential way with its interactions with Christianity, my research focuses more intensely on those interactions, and on the *Satnami*-Christian community that emerged as a result of them.

British colonial texts and missionary writings, both published and archival, provided a second important source of material for the project. With notable exceptions, few *Satnamis* or *Satnami*-Christians produced written works containing firsthand ethnographic observations of any kind. For these I have had to rely on British ethnographers, and on missionaries with an eye for the culturally significant. However, embedded in colonial texts and hid-

---

40. Babb, *Divine Hierarchy;* Dube, *Untouchable Pasts;* Flueckiger, *Gender and Genre;* and Lamb, *Rapt in the Name.*

den away in the drawers and files of missionary archives there are letters, "testimonies," and research papers attributed to *Satnamis* and *Satnami*-Christians, and these have provided much of my primary source material. British officials and western missionaries each had their own agenda, their own constituencies, and their own audiences, and this primary source material is, therefore, very often framed in such a way that the extent to which it reflects the actual experience of Chhattisgarhis is difficult to determine. Nevertheless, the subaltern *do* speak in these sources, and if one listens carefully it is sometimes possible to hear their whispers beneath the din of western voices that framed, filtered, and interpreted them.[41]

Oral histories provided a third important source of material for the study. During the first half of 2004 I traveled to Chhattisgarh and conducted interviews with nearly a hundred Chhattisgarhis (most were over seventy years old). Through the memories of older Chhattisgarhis and the oral histories passed down from generation to generation, I found that I could, with some patience and prodding, obtain information pertaining to the period back as far as 1900 (and sometimes farther). These interviews of *Satnamis*, Christians, and members of other communities were therefore especially useful in developing a sense of the Chhattisgarhi experience during the latter half of the period under investigation (1868-1947).

There are, of course, problems attendant to the collection of oral history, none more intractable or disturbing than discovering contradictory versions of "what really happened." In particular, convert testimonials tend to become refined, embellished, and stylized over time.[42] One of the ways that I have at-

41. On the potential hazards of using British and missionary texts and archives as sources of information on Indians, see Frykenberg, "Contested Definitions and Controversial Perspectives," p. 8; Arun W. Jones, *Christian Missions in the American Empire: Episcopalians in Northern Luzon, the Philippines, 1902-1946* (New York: Peter Lang, 2003), pp. 21-22; Dick Kooiman, "Untouchability in India through the Missionary's Eye," *Itinerario* 7, no. 1 (1983); Dick Kooiman, *Conversion and Social Equality in India* (New Delhi: South Asia Publications, 1989), p. 5n; Dick Kooiman, Otto van den Muijzenberg, and Peter van der Veer, eds., *Conversion, Competition and Conflict* (Amsterdam: Free University Press, 1984), pp. 15, 19; William L. Merrill, "Conversion and Colonialism in Northern Mexico: The Tarahumara Response to the Jesuit Mission Program, 1601-1767," in *Conversion to Christianity: Historical and Anthropological Perspectives on a Great Transformation*, ed. Robert W. Hefner (Berkeley: University of California Press, 1993), p. 153; and John C. B. Webster, "Dalits and Christianity in Colonial Punjab: Cultural Interactions," in *Christians, Cultural Interactions, and India's Religious Traditions*, ed. Judith M. Brown and Robert Eric Frykenberg (Grand Rapids: Eerdmans, 2002), p. 93.

42. David A. Snow and Richard Machalek, "The Sociology of Conversion," *Annual Review of Sociology* 10 (1983); and B. Taylor, "Recollection and Membership: Converts' Talk and the Ratiocination of Commonality," *Sociology* 12 (1978).

tempted to circumvent this problem is by concentrating not so much on history, as on the *perception* of history. Dealing with sources in such a way, what "really" happened thus becomes less important than what the various versions of history say about those who tell them. Nevertheless, like any source, the "firsthand" accounts of "native" informants must be treated with caution and care.

Following this logic, my own version of events, the image that I create of the object of my study, says something about me as well. Though I have attempted to read *through* the prejudices of my sources in order to understand and interpret the logic of Chhattisgarhi manners, behaviors, and beliefs in such a way that they would be intelligible to readers, my own version of events will, no doubt, expose different biases.

Furthermore, ethnographic interpretations, even historical ones, are, as Clifford Geertz has said, "constructions of other people's constructions of what they and their compatriots are up to," and are therefore removed from actuality by at least two degrees of separation.[43] They are works of creativity; they are fictions (though some are "truer" fictions than others).[44] Moreover, no story is "just a story." Rather, all stories, or at least those that interest us as humans, are allegorical. Accepting the notion that ethnographic writing is allegorical prompts us, James Clifford suggests, "to say of any cultural description not 'this represents, or symbolizes, that,' but rather, 'this is a (morally charged) *story* about that.'"[45]

There is a bias, in the academic world, against studies of this kind, against investigating Christianity, particularly Christianity in the nonwestern world, as a *religion* like any other. In the secular academy, anthropologists conducting research in Africa, Asia, and Latin America have tended to focus on "autochthonous" religions, rather than "imported" ones, such as Christianity, which are seen as intrusions upon the "unspoiled" cultures under investigation. This is not surprising, given the historical roots of anthropology in the movement to preserve endangered cultures from extinction. Thankfully, however, more recently anthropologists have begun to lose some of their predecessors' naïve romanticism, and if postmodern scholarship has taught us anything, it is that *no* culture or religion is purely "autochthonous." Rather,

43. Geertz, *Interpretation of Cultures*, p. 9.

44. James Clifford, "Introduction: Partial Truths," in *Writing Culture: The Poetics and Politics of Ethnography*, ed. James Clifford and George E. Marcus (Berkeley: University of California Press, 1986), pp. 6-7.

45. James Clifford, "On Ethnographic Allegory," in *Writing Culture: The Poetics and Politics of Ethnography*, ed. James Clifford and George E. Marcus (Berkeley: University of California Press, 1986), p. 100.

this world is one of interaction, hybridity, and blurred distinctions. All cultures are constantly undergoing change as a result of both internal and external forces, and there is no justifiable *a priori* reason to avoid investigating those cultures that are undergoing more radical change than others (even if that change results from contact with the "outside world").

Because of prejudices such as these, the various manifestations of Christianity around the globe have — more, perhaps, than those of other religions — escaped the gaze of scholars equipped with the methodological tools of modern academia. But times are changing. Anthropologists such as Jean and John Comaroff have brought a measure of respectability to the anthropological study of Christianity in colonial contexts, provoking scholars to reconsider their initial reticence to carry out similar studies.[46] In *Contested Belonging,* an extraordinary anthropological analysis of Rabha culture, Bengt Karlsson speaks of his own transformation from an anthropologist who saw conversion to Christianity as a disruption of ancient ways to one who realized that he could not ignore asking what the fact that some Rabhas converted to Christianity said about their culture.[47]

The 2002 publication of *Popular Christianity in India: Riting between the Lines,* a collection of essays edited by Selva Raj and Corinne Dempsey, heralded the maturation of scholarship on Christianity in India, and reflected the growth of scholarly research on Christianities in the nonwestern world more generally (a development that makes sense given the fact that more than half of the world's Christians are now or will soon be located in the nonwestern world). The volume included contributions from several of the most prominent and theoretically sophisticated scholars in the field, such as Eliza Kent and Corinne Dempsey, who have themselves produced influential monographs in the field (*Converting Women,* 2004, and *Kerala Christian Sainthood,* 2000, respectively).

I have been particularly influenced by three aspects of this emerging work. The first is that unlike previous research on Christianity in India, much of which either bemoaned its existence as a vestige of colonialism or promoted its propagation as the cure for India's social and soteriological woes, this more recent scholarship has treated the existence of Christianity in India as an ethnographic and historical fact, which, as such, is worthy of scholarly study.

---

46. See Jean Comaroff and John Comaroff, *Of Revelation and Revolution: Christianity, Colonialism, and Consciousness in South Africa* (Chicago: University of Chicago Press, 1991).

47. The Rabhas are a tribe in northeastern India. See Bengt G. Karlsson, *Contested Belonging: An Indigenous People's Struggle for Forest and Identity in Sub-Himalayan Bengal* (Richmond, VA: Curzon, 2000), p. 152.

While scholars such as Dempsey, Kent, and Karlsson are certainly aware of the ways that religion conditions and is conditioned by social structures and relations of power, they allow neither Christianity's proponents nor its critics to derail their honest analysis of various (Christian) religious phenomena.

A second significant aspect of this new scholarship is the methodological shift from belief to practice. In the popular western imagination, religions are conceived of as receptacles of propositional truth recorded in canonized texts. The modern Christian who encounters a person of another faith generally asks, "What do you *believe?*" not "What do you *do?*" This is no doubt related to the rationalizing effect of the Enlightenment, but also reflects the self-understanding and peculiar nature of western Christianity. Such a conception of religion has far-ranging implications, from the way we in the western academy teach (and mis-teach) about non-Christian religions to the way that non-Christians living in the west have had to reformulate and rearticulate their own religions to conform to rationalized and doctrinal western templates of what constitutes a religion (or at least a respectable one).

The problem with conceiving of religion as a matter of belief and scripture is not merely, however, that such a conception is (or at least was) largely alien to the Indian context, even, for the most part, the Indian *Christian* context. Rather, the larger problem is that such a conception reifies a complex set of phenomena and suggests that religions are hermetically sealed one from another, that adherents of one are easily distinguished from adherents of another, and that religions remain somehow unaffected by their cultural context. When Indian Christianity has been described in terms of its beliefs only, it comes off very frequently looking quite alien. The fact that much of the early scholarship on Christianity in India was conducted by missionaries, most of whom were rather theologically inclined, simply exaggerated the impression.

While not ignoring belief, however, more recent scholarship on Christianity in India has turned its gaze upon ritual and everyday practices. By doing so, as the subtitle of Raj and Dempsey's volume *(Riting between the Lines)* suggests, one not only attends to a significant aspect of religious life previously undervalued in religious scholarship, but also begins to usefully complicate the notion that religions are discrete, independent, and self-contained.

Such a move is related to the third aspect of emerging research on Indian Christianity that I find methodologically useful: its attention to syncretism, hybrid religious identities, and to the moments, which appear more commonly in the realm of practice than in the realm of belief, when the lines between religions simply cease to exist. As I suggested above, conceiving of religion in terms of belief alone suggests against the facts that religions are unaffected by the cultural contexts in which they find themselves. But there is no such thing as a cultureless religion, and therefore no such thing as a cultureless Christianity. Blissfully unaware of the fact that western Christianity was merely the latest in a series of cross-cultural dispersions beginning with the early Christian articulation of Jesus' rather Jewish ideas in the idiom of Greco-Roman thought, and thereby certain of the superiority and purity of their form of Christianity, western Christian missionaries in India, especially Protestant ones, generally felt confident in distinguishing true Christianity from that which showed too clearly the influence of Indian culture, which they labeled and censured as "syncretism." Given the fact that for many years scholars of religion left the study of nonwestern Christianities to missionaries, there was therefore in earlier research on Indian Christianity a tendency, a few notable exceptions aside, towards condemnation of syncretism and hybrid religious identities.

Contemporary research on Indian Christianity, however, conceives of syncretism like it conceives of the existence of Indian Christianity itself — as an ethnographic and historical fact, and an instructive one at that. For attending to the ways in which religious people do not always fit easily into western religious categories contributes to the development of a more sophisticated scholarly understanding of religious identities. It is for this reason that I have tried, in this book, to attend both to the ways that *Satnami*-Christians were affected by their interaction with missionaries and to the ways in which they were affected, in their articulation and practice of Christianity, by their own cultural context.

It is clear that my own method, influenced as it has been by scholars such as Kent, Dempsey, Karlsson, and others, represents a move away from ethnographies and histories of Indian Christianity executed from an explicitly Christian or missionary perspective. Lest it be alleged, however, that I have uncritically dismissed the possibility that such scholarship might have something to offer, let me admit that much of what we know about the history of Christianities in the nonwestern world has come from the work of Christian historians, many of them missionaries. Similarly, the field of anthropology was largely built on the backs of missionaries, without whose descriptions of non-Christian peoples the earliest anthropologists, some of whom never left home, would have had little about which to write.[48] Admittedly, much of what Christians and missionaries reported about the areas in

---

48. For a discussion of the ambiguous relationship between anthropologists and missionaries, especially with reference to Bronislaw Malinowksi (1884-1942), see Kenelm Burridge, "Introduction: Missionary Occasions," in *Mission, Church, and Sect in Oceania*, ed. James A. Boutilier, Daniel T. Hughes, and Sharon W. Tiffany (Ann Arbor: University of Michigan Press, 1978), p. 5.

which they worked was influenced by a decidedly triumphalist perspective, and modern scholars justifiably view it with suspicion. Nevertheless, there were always noteworthy exceptions. Moreover, though interested in and attuned to the theological implications of their work, contemporary Christian scholars such as Andrew Walls and Lamin Sanneh have raised the study of Christianity's interaction with local cultures in Africa, Asia, and Latin America to a new standard of erudition. I have therefore not avoided consulting texts written by missionaries or from an explicitly Christian perspective. But I have attempted to account, at all times, for their perspective and potential bias just as one should when reading the work of those virulently opposed to Christian conversion (and everyone in between).

Broader Issues

As is perhaps already clear to the perceptive reader, the issues raised by this study, though rooted in the late nineteenth and early twentieth centuries, are not unrelated to contemporary debates regarding religion in contemporary India. For example, one of the recurrent questions raised implicitly by this study has to do with the nature of freedom of religion. Independent India's constitution ensures it. But what exactly does religious freedom entail? Does religious freedom entail the right merely to practice one's own religion, or must it by definition include the right to propagate? To evangelize? To convert? And how far does religious freedom extend? At what point must a nation's obligation to maintain order, harmony, and a smoothly functioning society trump its commitment to religious freedom?

Closely related to these issues is that of the proper place of religion in a secular state. India, like America, is an extremely religious society directed by an officially secular government. The definition of secularism differs, to some extent, between India and America — Americans generally understand secularism to mean keeping religion out of government (and government out of religion), whereas Indians conceive of it in the more limited sense of not privileging one religion over another. One question haunting India today is how Hindus, who constitute 80 percent of the population, should relate to the nation's religious minorities. To what extent do Hindus have the right to consider their values universally (or at least nationally) valid? In a secular democracy, should the values of the religious majority be legislated, or would the imposition of Hindu values on the minority constitute a "tyranny of the majority"?

At the heart of all these questions is this one: Do minority religious viewpoints (and practices) represent, by their very existence, a threat to the cohesiveness and integrity of the democratic nation-state? And, if so, is accepting that threat part and parcel of the democratic experiment, or should a democracy seek to limit the growth and expression of such viewpoints? These are issues that are of interest not only in the world's largest democracy, India, but also in the most powerful and oldest democracies of the west, and which I therefore hope will be of interest to the reader. I will return to them again in the Conclusion.

CHAPTER 1

Contextualizing the Study

The present chapter provides a brief introduction to Chhattisgarhi social structure and religious patterns before moving on to a discussion of the Satnampanth and the origin of Christianity in the region. It is a congeries of cold facts, histories (mythic and otherwise), and contextual details. I have intended it as a bare minimum introduction so that the remainder of the discussion might be grounded in the proper soil. The chapter provides proportionately less coverage of the region's Christians, as subsequent chapters will focus on their story.

Chhattisgarhi Social Structure

As in other parts of India, the caste system was an influential factor in the structure of Chhattisgarhi social life in the late nineteenth and early twentieth centuries. The originally Portuguese but now anglicized word "caste" is a misleadingly simple designation for the complex *varṇa-jāti* system. The fourfold social division indicated by the term *"varṇa"* — *brahmans* (priests), *kshatriyas* (rulers and warriors), *vaisyas* (merchants and traders), and *sudras* (peasants) — is given a metaphysical justification in the ancient Vedic scriptures. What the British called "outcastes," "untouchables," or the "depressed classes," were considered outside the four *varṇas* by the Vedas; they constituted a marginal "fifth category" *(pañcama)* because of their association with ritually impure occupations.

The reality, however, has been much messier — particularly in the area between the extremes of high and low caste — and is characterized by the labyrinthine hierarchical relationships of thousands of local, regional, and pan-Indian endogamous groups, or *jātis*. Whereas the hierarchical position of each *varṇa* is easily ascertained, no such certainty exists with regard to the relative rank of various *jātis*. Unfortunately, bifurcating the term "caste" into *varṇa* and *jāti* does not do away with all confusion.[1] For instance, a nineteenth-century *Satnami* asked his or her *jāti* might have responded with a *varṇa* designation *(pañchama)*, a caste *(Chamar)*, a sub-caste *(Satnami)*, or even an exogamous *gotra* (clan) name.

Louis Dumont has suggested that the ideational justification for a particular *jāti's* position in the caste hierarchy is the extent to which that *jāti* has contact with objects or is involved in activities considered ritually impure.[2] Contact with animal skins, hair, fingernails, sweat, saliva, feces, or menstrual fluids is polluting, as is drinking alcohol and eating meat. Tanner, barber, and sweeper *jātis* are therefore among the lowest castes, whereas *jātis* that avoid polluting objects and activities have a generally higher position.

In the ritual hierarchy, *brahmans* usually rank highest, due to their perceived conscientiousness about maintaining purity and the association of *brahman* priests with proper conduct and ritual propriety. Following them are the other two twice-born *(dvīj)* castes, the *kshatriyas* and *vaisyas*.[3] Below these three are the *sudras,* a group of liminal communities that are of ambiguous ritual status. Finally, below all these are the "untouchables," or *dalits*. However, to say that *dalits* are considered ritually impure is not to suggest that they have no role in Hindu religious practices. Though Indian villages were and are often ghettoized, with *dalit* communities inhabiting a separate *pārā* (quarter), lower-caste communities still perform vital functions at village religious ceremonies and festivals. The old British term "outcaste" is therefore somewhat misleading.

The depth of feeling regarding purity and impurity varies from region to region, as does the relative rank of particular *jātis*. M. N. Srinivas has sug-

1. Louis Dumont, *Homo Hierarchicus* (Chicago: University of Chicago Press, 1980), p. 62.

2. Dumont, *Homo Hierarchicus*. See also Louis Dumont and David Pocock, "Pure and Impure," *Contributions to Indian Sociology* 3 (1959). For a more theoretical and phenomenological discussion of notions of purity and pollution in world religions, see Mary Douglas, *Purity and Danger: An Analysis of Concepts of Pollution and Taboo* (London: Routledge & Kegan Paul, 1966).

3. "Twice-born" refers to the rite of initiation that these three castes perform during their youth. Biological birth is considered the first, and the initiation rite a second. See G. M. Carstairs, *The Twice-Born: A Study of a Community of High-Caste Hindus* (London: Hogarth Press, 1957).

gested, "To the average peasant . . . the names of castes in other linguistic areas are pure abracadabra. They make sense only when they are fitted into the Procrustean frame of *varṇa*."[4] Barber *jātis*, for instance, are found all over India, but their hierarchical status differs from place to place.[5] Eating, drinking, or close physical contact with other *jātis* is generally considered polluting, especially if the other *jāti* is of a lower ritual status. For this reason, members of a *jāti* tended to conduct most of their social affairs within their own *jāti*, or sometimes even within a subdivision of it, though in urban settings this social insularity is of course less easily maintained.

While ritual purity is unquestionably the symbolic and ideological basis for structuring the *varṇa-jāti* system, it is not the only factor. Dumont has been criticized by Marxist social theorists and more recently by post-colonial scholars for failing to take into account the element of economic and political power in the determination of social rank. To his credit, though he chose to focus on "ideological" factors, Dumont recognized that "politico-economic" actualities were an important aspect of the caste system. This element of power is largely responsible for the dynamic nature of the *varṇa-jāti* system. For example, a *jāti* that attains a certain degree of numeric, economic, or political power may be able to move up in the hierarchy over time, especially if the *jāti* is within the ranks of caste Hinduism (i.e., one of the four *varṇas*).

This process of social mobility, referred to as sanskritization and discussed at greater length below, involves ascent of the ritual hierarchy by means of taking on the symbols of high-caste purity, such as teetotalism and vegetarianism. The appropriation of the insignia of high-caste status requires legitimation — a community's claims to higher status must be recognized and accepted by the locality's dominant castes. Power is therefore reticulated with notions of purity and pollution in the determination of ritual hierarchy. Accordingly, I understand the *varṇa-jāti* system to be a hierarchical socio-religious system based on common if not uncontested understandings of purity and pollution as symbolic markers of a social and hierarchical order, never entirely settled (but more stable at the extremes), which is established and maintained through a complex matrix of power and status relations involving the overlapping interests of local, regional, all-India, and even foreign communities.

I have included the last phrase of this definition, "even foreign communities," because scholars have recently suggested that the British significantly

---

4. M. N. Srinivas, *Social Change in Modern India* (Berkeley: University of California Press, 1966), p. 3.

5. Dumont, *Homo Hierarchicus*, p. 34.

altered the *varṇa-jāti* system by conducting ethnographic surveys and decennial censuses.[6] Ethnographic surveys established caste as the organizing principle of Indian sociological analysis, and the censuses, which began in the late nineteenth century, inventoried the Indian population and described it according to a variety of factors, including caste (other factors were age, sex, religion, literacy, etc.). By putting these caste names on the record, defining them, and even occasionally attempting to rank them, the British contributed to a calcification of the system. Even today, Indian scholars writing about the country's castes refer frequently to works by official English ethnographers like R. V. Russell and census takers such as H. H. Risley.[7] At the same time, the decennial censuses became the focus of identity politics as castes attempted to affect their social status by petitioning for new names and a higher rank.

The British did not by any stretch of the imagination *create* caste. But the censuses helped ossify a system that previously included a strong element of flexibility, leading scholars of India to mistakenly posit an immalleable and intractable *varṇa-jāti* structure as part of the definitive essence of Indian culture.[8] Dumont himself has been accused of reading colonial Indian social structures into the pre-colonial past. "Hierarchy," argues Nicholas Dirks, "in the sense of rank or ordered difference might have been a pervasive feature of Indian history, but hierarchy in the sense used by Dumont and others became a systematic value only under the sign of the colonial modern."[9]

Chhattisgarhi Religiosity

Hinduism is by far the predominant religion[10] on the plains of Chhattisgarh, but such a statement must be accompanied immediately by two caveats. The

6. See, for example, Nicholas B. Dirks, "The Original Caste: Power, History and Hierarchy in South Asia," *Contributions to Indian Sociology* (n.s.) 23 (1989); and Nicholas B. Dirks, *Castes of Mind: Colonialism and the Making of Modern India* (Princeton: Princeton University Press, 2001). See also Peter van der Veer, *Gods on Earth: The Management of Religious Experience in a North Indian Pilgrimage Centre* (Delhi: Oxford University Press, 1988), p. 53.

7. See, for example, K. S. Singh, *The Scheduled Castes*, rev. ed. (Calcutta: Oxford University Press, 1999).

8. On this, see Ronald Inden, *Imagining India* (Oxford: Blackwell, 1990).

9. Dirks, *Castes of Mind*, p. 14.

10. Despite my free use of the term "religion" in this context, it must be remembered that no cognate term exists in any Indian language. On this, see Wilhelm Halbfass, *India and Europe: An Essay in Understanding* (Albany: State University of New York Press, 1988),

first regards "Hinduism" itself, which is a rather ambiguous and disputed term. Its etymological forerunners were first used by foreigners such as the Greeks and Persians to refer to the people on the far side of the river Indus. It wasn't until the sixteenth century that the term began to appear in texts written by Indians themselves. Even then, it was a self-reflexive, oppositional term, used to distinguish "Hindus" from the *"mlecchas"* (barbarians) or *"yavanas"* (foreigners, Greeks, Muslims, Europeans). It was only after the eighteenth century that the term began, slowly, to refer not to Indians themselves, but to their religion.[11] Some have suggested that scholars abandon the term "Hinduism" altogether as an invention of colonial scholarship. While the ways that colonial knowledge-making influenced the developing self-understanding of Hindus is itself an interesting topic explored ably by Brian Pennington,[12] it is beyond the purview of this book.

Part of the problem with the term "Hinduism" stems from the fact that there is no word in any Indian language that denotes the exact meaning of the English term "religion" or its romance language cognates.[13] The closest terms to "religion" in North Indian languages would be *dharm, sanātana* (eternal) *dharm,* or *ārya* (noble) *dharm.*[14] A Chhattisgarhi asked his or her *"dharm"* would be likely to respond with the name of a *jāti* or a *panth,* but not with

---

pp. 310ff. Jonathan Z. Smith has gone so far as to suggest that religion is "solely the creation of the scholar's study," and Wilfred Cantwell Smith and others have suggested that the term be dropped entirely. See Jonathan Z. Smith, *Imagining Religion: From Babylon to Jonestown* (Chicago: University of Chicago Press, 1982), p. xi; Jonathan Z. Smith, "Religion, Religions, Religious," in *Critical Terms for Religious Studies,* ed. Mark C. Taylor (Chicago: University of Chicago Press, 1998); and Wilfred Cantwell Smith, *The Meaning and End of Religion: A New Approach to the Religious Traditions of Mankind* (New York: Macmillan, 1963), pp. 18, 50-51. To my mind, such invasive surgery is not necessary, as the term continues to have heuristic value as an "ideal type." As Wittgenstein suggested, "Isn't the indistinct [picture] often exactly what we need?" Quoted in Kathleen M. Sands, "Tracking Religion: Religion through the Lens of Critical and Cultural Studies," *CSSR Bulletin* 31, no. 3 (2002): 71-72. One must, however, keep in mind the ultimate *untranslatability* of the term into non-Romance languages.

11. Robert Eric Frykenberg, "Emergence of Modern 'Hinduism' as a Concept and as an Institution," in *Hinduism Reconsidered,* ed. Günther-Dietz Sontheimer and Hermann Kulke (New Delhi: Manohar Publications, 1991).

12. See Brian Pennington, *Was Hinduism Invented? Britons, Indians, and the Colonial Construction of Religion* (New York: Oxford University Press, 2005).

13. See Halbfass, *India and Europe,* pp. 310ff. This is not merely reflective of linguistic differences, but also of the historical fact that India has not as yet undergone anything resembling the privatization of religion experienced by western countries in the post-Enlightenment period.

14. Frykenberg, "Emergence of Modern Hinduism," p. 31.

"Hindu."[15] The connotation of *"dharm"* is much wider than the English term "religion." In addition to the significations of the English term "religion," *"dharm"* connotes "custom," "law," "essence," and "duty." To use the term "Hinduism" in reference to a particular religion (in the English sense) thus poses some immediate difficulties; to speak of the "Hindu *religion*" is a double reification.

The second problem with the terms "Hindu" and "Hinduism" is that they represent the generalization of an extremely variegated set of phenomena. As one scholar put it, Indians have from ancient times "acquired the most lucid habit of seeing with many eyes and speaking with many tongues."[16] There is no homogeneous single community of Hindus, nor is there one set of easily defined Hindu beliefs or practices. Robert Frykenberg asserts that too often scholars mistake one style of Hinduism — whether it be called *"bhakti"* (devotional), "temple," "popular," "village," "tribal," or some other term — for the whole.[17] In fact, the variety of forms contained under the term is indeed so vast that some scholars have suggested that no such thing as a Hindu really exists (unless by the term one means no more than "Indian").[18]

Though I agree that one must recognize the diversity of configurations encompassed by the term "Hindu," I would argue that Hinduism is no less useful a term than "Christianity," which, though also a reification of a multiplicity of *Christianities*, nevertheless sits comfortably on the shoulders of western scholars as a heuristic term. One could argue that there is among these various forms of Hinduism what Wittgenstein referred to as a "family resemblance."[19] It is in this sense that I will use the term, while recognizing that it is in fact an abstraction, detached from any single reality.

One way that scholars in the past have attempted to organize the multiformity of Hinduism is by speaking of "little" and "great" tradition Hinduism. Robert Redfield developed the terminology from insights gained in his studies, *The Folk Culture of the Yucatan* (1941) and *The Primitive World and Its Transformations* (1953). The terminology came to be popular among anthro-

---

15. For a similar claim regarding Hindus in the Punjab, see Mark Juergensmeyer, *Religion as Social Vision: The Movement against Untouchability in Twentieth-Century Punjab* (Berkeley: University of California Press, 1982), p. 2.

16. Chaturvedi Badrinath, "Max Weber's Wrong Understanding of Indian Civilization," in *Recent Research on Max Weber's Studies of Hinduism*, ed. Detlef Kantowsky (London: Weltforum, 1986), p. 46. See also Smith, *The Meaning and End of Religion*, p. 66.

17. See, for example, Frykenberg, "Emergence of Modern Hinduism," p. 32.

18. Frykenberg, "Emergence of Modern Hinduism," p. 29.

19. Quoted in Julius Lipner, *Hindus: Their Religious Beliefs and Practices* (New York: Routledge, 1998), p. 6.

pologists based at the University of Chicago and was developed more fully in the context of India by Redfield and Milton Singer in a 1954 article, "The Cultural Role of Cities."[20] In any particular civilization, they argued, there are "the 'high' cultural traditions of the reflective few (the 'great tradition'), and the 'low' folk traditions of the unreflective many (the 'little tradition')."[21] The great tradition is a systematization, or "specialization," of the various local traditions and is embodied in "sacred books" or "classics," sanctified by a cult, expressed in monuments, sculpture, painting, and architecture, and served by the other arts and sciences.[22]

India's great tradition has often been called "Sanskritic," or "textual," because it centers on the cult of certain all-India gods (e.g., Vishnu, Shiva, and Brahma) and goddesses (e.g., Durga and Kali), and information about these deities and their proper worship is found in Sanskrit scriptures such as the Vedas, Puranas, and Epics (e.g., the *Mahābhārata* and the *Rāmāyaṇa*). Others have called "great" tradition Hinduism "brahmanical" because of the central priestly role of some (but not all) *brahmans* in the worship of pan-Indian deities. Sanskrit scriptures have no doubt played an important formative role in the development of India's religions, and in most parts of India *brahmans* have a significant, if contested role in the functioning of cultic activities. However, one could only with great difficulty find someone among the 75 percent of India's population that is rural whose religious life never strays beyond the rather stereotyped beliefs and practices of the "Sanskritic" or "brahmanical" tradition. Most of India's Hindus, especially those in rural areas, are primarily concerned with the multitude of small-time gods and local goddesses.

There is, however, a complex and symbiotic relationship between India's great and little traditions — pilgrimage practices, traveling specialists and artists, extra-village marriage norms, and other social realities link each village with others around it. Through this interaction, local religious rituals, festivals, and gods and goddesses become connected with all-India cognates through a process of "accretion." Once associated, the little tradition is "universalized," taking on the characteristics of its great tradition equivalents, while the great tradition is "localized," and begins to resemble the little traditions with which it is connected.[23]

---

20. Robert Redfield and Milton Singer, "The Cultural Role of Cities," *Economic Development and Cultural Change* 3, no. 1 (1954).

21. Milton Singer, "The Social Organization of Indian Civilization," *Diogenes* 45 (1964): 92.

22. Redfield and Singer, "Cities," pp. 63, 70; and Singer, "Social Organization," p. 93.

23. McKim Marriott, "Little Communities in an Indigenous Civilization," in *Village India: Studies in the Little Community,* ed. McKim Marriott (Chicago: University of Chicago

Chhattisgarhi religion is entangled in this symbiotic relationship of great and little traditions. Certain practices and beliefs in the region clearly connect to great tradition Hinduism. For instance, as in other parts of India, *pūjā* (worship or homage) is the fundamental religious ritual in Chhattisgarh, and involves the symbolic offering of food or other items to the gods.[24] Having been offered to the gods, food becomes *"prasād,"* a most valued possession, and worshipers eat and share it with delight. Most *pūjās* take place in the home, and involve the worship of one or more family deities on a quasi-regular schedule. Women are more frequently than men responsible for carrying out the family's ritual obligations. Other deities may be honored during crises, or before undertaking a large project or embarking on a long journey. There are in Chhattisgarh's villages few sizeable temples, though roadside shrines are ubiquitous. These generally include little more than one or two red-painted rocks symbolizing deities, and a small construction that offers them modest protection from the elements. They are frequently found under trees, and are rarely attended by a full-time priest.

In addition, like other Hindus, Chhattisgarhis participate in a variety of life-cycle rituals, called *sanskārs*. Many *sanskārs* are designed to combat impurity incurred in the normal transitions of life. Giving birth, for instance, is considered highly polluting and requires a purificatory period, during which new mothers are often not bathed or fed solid food. Death is also polluting for the family of the deceased, and overcoming this pollution generally requires offering a meal to one's *jāt*-fellows. Death rituals must be properly performed, or the deceased is liable to become a troublesome ghost. Marriage is the one exception to the general rule that life's transitions are polluting and involves a grand reversal in which the bride and groom are treated as gods for the duration of the festivities.

As in other parts of India, Chhattisgarhi religious passions surge in the celebration of festivals, or *melās*. Religious festivals, such as *navrātra, dīwālī,* and *holī,* are generally set according to a lunar calendar, most falling on *pūrṇimā* (full moon) or *amāvasyā* (new moon). Festivals are celebrated to commemorate the birth and exploits of the gods (e.g., *akshay tṛtīya, daśahrā*), to propitiate malevolent forces (such as the smallpox goddess, Shitala), or to

---

Press, 1955). Very often these connections with Sanskritic gods and goddesses are invoked as a way of communicating with outsiders unfamiliar with the local deities.

24. See Lawrence A. Babb, *The Divine Hierarchy: Popular Hinduism in Central India* (New York: Columbia University Press, 1975). This study is perhaps the most frequently quoted text on northern Indian village religious practices in general, and Babb conducted his research in Raipur District, Chhattisgarh, making it of special use in the context of this study.

ensure future safety, happiness, and success in worldly affairs (e.g., *sāvitrī, govardhan*). In Chhattisgarh, the most important of all *melās* is that held each year at Rajim. Like fairs, *melās* are attended not only by the devout, but also by the entertainment-seeking and entrepreneurial, and *melā* grounds are usually lined with the shops of souvenir hawkers. (At the 2004 *melā* in Rajim, jeeps towed parasailers across the sands of a dry riverbed for seventy-five rupees, roughly two dollars.) The religious aspect of *melās* generally involves a ritual bath in a river, or confluence of rivers, and a subsequent visit to the *melā's* primary deity or deities.[25]

At times, rural Chhattisgarhis worship all-India gods and goddesses, and ever since the Haihaya dynasty, the region has been particularly enamored of Ram (an *avatār*, or incarnation, of Vishnu).[26] Ram is a Sanskritic deity mythologized in Valmiki's *Rāmāyaṇa*, but most Chhattisgarhis receive their information about Ram from local or regional versions of these scriptures. The most important of these is Tulsidas's *Rāmcaritmānas*, an Awadhi vernacularization of Valmiki's *Rāmāyaṇa* which has for some time been available in Hindi. Through this same text Chhattisgarhis have come to know and love the monkey-god Hanuman, Ram's friend and an intermediary between humans and the hero. Also important in Chhattisgarh is Devi, the Goddess, who makes herself known in a variety of forms, as Durga, Kali, Mahamaya, and others.[27]

Alongside these Sanskritic beliefs and rituals, which are generally directed and attended by *brahman* priests, there are in Chhattisgarh a host of more autochthonous traditions, not entirely distinct from great tradition Hinduism but at the same time tinctured with local flavor. During *dīwālī*, for instance, Chhattisgarh's *Gonds*, an *ādivāsī* community, the second largest in Chhattisgarh after the *Chamars*, celebrate *gaura*. Despite its association with the all-India festival, *gaura* involves rituals specific to Chhattisgarh, such as the dancing of *Suā Nāc* (the Parrot Dance).

Alongside India's Sanskritic Epics, Chhattisgarh has its own hero *(vīr)* stories, such as the *Candainī* and the *Paṇḍvānī*.[28] And though on certain occasions and for certain reasons they will worship and celebrate the deities of great tradition Hinduism, rural Chhattisgarhis are particularly fond of their regional gods and goddesses. Most important among these are Mata, a ge-

25. Babb, *Divine Hierarchy*, pp. 123-76.

26. Ramdas Lamb, *Rapt in the Name: The Ramnamis, Ramnam, and Untouchable Religion in Central India* (Albany: State University of New York Press, 2002), p. 35.

27. Babb, *Divine Hierarchy*, p. 191.

28. Joyce Burkhalter Flueckiger, *Gender and Genre in the Folklore of Middle India* (Ithaca: Cornell University Press, 1996), p. 12.

neric catch-all for a variety of local goddesses (such as the Seven Sisters, or Twenty-One Sisters), and Thakur Dev, a godling who is a servant of the goddess and the protector of villages.

These local deities have not resisted association with Sanskritic gods and goddesses. Chhattisgarhi manifestations of the goddess are easily connected to the all-India Devi. Thakur Dev has been associated with Bhairav, and through him to Shiva.[29] But whereas the cult of Sanskritic gods and goddesses requires the services of *brahman* priests, these local deities are generally attended by a class of non-*brahman* priests and local healers called *baigās*. And whereas the gods of great tradition Hinduism primarily grant boons of *general* well-being, local deities are consulted for specific and immediate exigencies.[30]

If there are in Chhattisgarh these local and regional traditions that are capable of being related with great tradition Hinduism, there are also a host of other beliefs and practices that, although properly called religious, have little relation to what is generally understood by the term "Hinduism." These practices verge on the magical, and have led foreign commentators, from scholars to missionaries, to suggest that they are indeed a different form of religion — "animism," "superstition," "spirit worship," or (depending on the commentator's perspective) "devil worship." "Magical" practices are by no means unique to Chhattisgarh — indeed H. H. Risley, Census Commissioner from 1901 to 1910, remarked that India's Hinduism was "animism more or less transformed by philosophy, magic tempered by metaphysics."[31]

The religion of rural Chhattisgarh in the nineteenth and early twentieth centuries was (and in many ways still is) about power and control, about survival, protection, and order. It was about the concerns of the everyday, about diagnosing illnesses, interpreting omens and signs, and about performing rituals intended to smooth one's pathways in this life and the next. It was about propitiating the powers that could be easily swayed, and foiling the plans of those that couldn't. It was a religion of place, embodied in local anecdotes, quasi-mythological stories, and songs written in Chhattisgarhi. It tackled the problems of everyday life with the obsessive performance of daily rituals, the *ad hoc* utilization of amulets and charms, and the protective repetition of *mantras*.

---

29. These associations are most often invoked for the purposes of communicating with outsiders. For example, when I would ask to which god or goddess a particular temple was dedicated, Chhattisgarhis would frequently use the name of a local deity, and then, sensing my confusion, would state the name of the all-India deity with which the local deity has come to be associated.

30. Babb, *Divine Hierarchy*, pp. 215-46.

31. Quoted in Louis Dumont, *Religion/Politics and History in India: Collected Papers in Indian Sociology* (Paris: Mouton, 1971), p. 34.

Rural Chhattisgarhis understood their environment to be one in which malicious or at least mischievous spirits milled about the air and gathered around trees, brooks, dark places, and crossroads, and in which malevolent forces — witches and sorcerers — cast jealous glances at beloved children under the cover of darkness. To protect their clients from such dangers, local healers mixed concoctions of roots, leaves, exorcisms, and magic. It is this layer of religion that was the most pervasive in Chhattisgarh's villages, and also the most ecumenical, permeating even the thought-worlds of Muslims, Christians, and other non-Hindus.

David Mandelbaum has posited the existence of two distinct aspects of religion in India, the "pragmatic" and the "transcendental." The "transcendental complex," he argues:

> is used to ensure the long-term welfare of society, to explain and help maintain village institutions, to guarantee the proper transition of individuals from stage to stage within the institutions. It is concerned with the ultimate purposes of man. The pragmatic complex, by contrast, is used for local exigencies, for personal benefit, for individual welfare.[32]

While the transcendental complex is regulated by hereditary priests, generally *brahman,* the pragmatic complex is controlled by "ritualist-exorcists" whose status is achieved, not ascribed. The two complexes do not compete, but are complementary.[33] The question of whether the "pragmatic complex" of Chhattisgarhi religiosity can be properly called Hindu is a valid one. But it is my contention that it is an integral aspect of village Hinduism, and that to exclude it would be to deny a large portion of the religious concerns and practices of rural Indians (and thereby to suggest that the majority of Indians are not in fact Hindus).

The Satnampanth

The *Chamars* are the largest *dalit* caste in India, and in Chhattisgarh, where most have changed their name to *Satnami,* they are the largest of all communities. In the first census conducted in the Central Provinces (1866), which did not yet distinguish *Satnamis* from *Chamars,* the caste constituted roughly

---

32. David G. Mandelbaum, "Transcendental and Pragmatic Aspects of Religion," *American Anthropologist* 68 (1966): 1168. Quoted in Babb, *Divine Hierarchy,* pp. 178-79.
33. Babb, *Divine Hierarchy,* p. 179.

one-fifth of the region's population.[34] The *Chamars* were traditionally associated with tanning and leather goods. They were also expected to remove cow, bullock, and buffalo carcasses from the village (other castes and tribes were responsible for the hides of other animals). In return they were granted the carrion as nouriture. *"Chamar"* is, in fact, a derivative of *camṛā,* i.e., hide or skin. *Chamar* women, or *Chamarin,* are frequently called upon as midwives *(daīs),* increasing the caste's ritual pollution through their contact with birthing fluids.

The *Chamars* are associated in the popular imagination with filth and foul odors, and anyone who has been within smelling distance of a village tannery will admit that it is a fetid and feculent business indeed.[35] *Chamars* were considered latent or actual criminals, and in Chhattisgarh they were perceived to be fervid cattle poisoners (which would have had obvious economic advantages). Other communities considered them dunces and scoundrels to be treated with circumspection and firm discipline. One proverb suggests: "Hemp, rice, and a *Chamar;* the more they are pounded the better they are."[36] Another says, "The shoemaker *(Chamar)* gets a smack in the face with a shoe of his own making" (being struck with the sole of a shoe is considered a gross insult).[37] The very name *"Chamar"* has overtones of obscenity, and a related word, *camṛā,* when used in the proper context, is among the worst of all possible abuses.[38] Not surprisingly, *Chamars* in various parts of northern India have attempted to change their name.[39]

Because of this association with the skins and bodies of dead animals, and in particular the sacred cow,[40] *Chamars* were excluded from entry into Hindu temples and considered among the most ritually polluting of all castes, de-

34. Saurabh Dube, *Untouchable Pasts: Religion, Identity, and Power among a Central Indian Community, 1780-1950* (Albany: State University of New York Press, 1998), p. 50.

35. For more on the process of tanning and leatherwork among *Chamars,* see George Weston Briggs, *The Chamārs* (Calcutta: Association Press, 1920), Appendix B.

36. Robert Vane Russell, *The Tribes and Castes of the Central Provinces of India,* vol. 1 (London: Macmillan, 1916), p. 422.

37. H. H. Risley, *The People of India* (Delhi: Oriental Books Reprint Corporation, 1969), p. 321.

38. I was once shushed (by a *brahman*) in an Indian library after pronouncing the name *Chamar,* and was told in no uncertain terms that the word was "perverted."

39. On *Chamars* in Uttar Pradesh who call themselves "Raidasi," see Bernard Cohn, "The Changing Status of a Depressed Caste," in *An Anthropologist among the Historians and Other Essays,* ed. Bernard Cohn (Delhi: Oxford University Press, 1987), p. 264.

40. Not all animal skins are considered impure, and even religious mendicants can be found wearing deer and tiger skins. See Russell, *Tribes and Castes of the Central Provinces (1),* p. 418.

spite the fact that a large portion of *Chamars* in Chhattisgarh had abandoned their traditional occupation for agriculture.[41]

It was into this community that Guru Ghasidas, founder of the Satnampanth, was born, in the 1770s.[42] His birthplace was Girod, near the Sonakhan forest, in what is now Raipur District (but was at the time in Bilaspur District). Tradition[43] has it that he showed signs of precocity and began performing miracles while still young. Later he became the farm servant of a *Marar* (vegetable-growing *jāti*) in order to support himself, his wife, Safura, and their children. One day the *Marar* noticed that Ghasidas's plough was moving on its own, and declared himself his servant's servant.[44]

News of the miracle spread and Ghasidas gained a following, mostly among the *Chamars*. But then a series of tragedies struck the blossoming guru. According to one tradition, Ghasidas's favorite son was suddenly struck down. (Other accounts indicate that all of the couple's children died suddenly of various causes.) In grief, Ghasidas retired to the forest near his home,[45] around 1820, hoping that a wild animal might put an end to his life. None did, and instead a tiger sat benignly beside him for several hours.[46] Word spread among his followers that he had entered the forest and would emerge in half a year with a message for them. Six months later, Ghasidas emerged from the forest and told the gathered crowd that he had been miraculously sustained

41. For a discussion of references to the *Chamar* in Vedic literature and in the writings of Manu, see Briggs, *The Chamārs*, pp. 11-17.

42. The tradition places his date of birth much earlier, in 1756. This seems unlikely given his death in 1850. Evangelical missionary Theodore C. Seybold claims that the date was actually 1785. See Theodore C. Seybold, *God's Guiding Hand: A History of the Central Indian Mission 1868-1967* (Philadelphia: United Church Board for World Ministries of the United Church of Christ, 1971), p. 16.

43. Here, and in similar contexts, "tradition" or "*the* tradition" refers to the collection of stories that a community tells *about itself* (as opposed to the stories others, including historians, tell about them). In the historical context under investigation, there were few textual accounts of Ghasidas's life and the history of the Satnampanth, and none considered by all to be "authoritative." The "tradition" was therefore largely an oral one. To indicate a disputed or idiosyncratic interpretation of history, I will generally speak of "*a* tradition."

44. Dube, *Untouchable Pasts*, p. 39.

45. Retiring to the forest as a hermit *(vānaprasth)* is the third of four stages *(āsramas)* in the idealized traditional life progression of Hindu men.

46. From "Notes on the Sutnamee Chumars of the Raepore District from Information Gathered Orally from the Gooroo, Agur Dass, and His Disciples, and from Chumars Generally in 1868." This unsigned typescript, which appears to have been published as a supplement to Temple's 1867 Gazetteer of Central India, can be found in HCS, box 3 of 4 (no folder).

and had communed with a higher power, whom he called *Satnam* or *Satpuruṣ* (the true supreme person, or source of the universe), and who had given him a message to deliver to the *Chamars*.[47]

Ghasidas instructed his followers to abandon their idol worship and to believe only in Satnam. His followers were to be called *Satnamis,* rather than *Chamar,* because of the latter's disparaging connotations, and they were to avoid eating meat and certain red vegetables and pulses (which resembled meat or blood). They were to abjure the use of alcohol and tobacco, they were to refrain from using cows for cultivation (buffalos were allowed) and from plowing after midday, and they were to abandon occupations that brought them into contact with leather and carrion. These prohibitions were clearly aimed at disentangling *Satnamis* from the ritual pollution associated with things such as meat eating and alcohol consumption, misuse of the sacred cow, and contact with the skin of dead animals. Ghasidas also enjoined his community to use only brass utensils (which, because more easily cleaned than clay, were considered less polluting). Ghasidas clearly accepted prevailing Hindu notions of purity and pollution, and sought to manipulate them for the improvement of his community.

There were other symbols of the Hindu ritual hierarchy, however, which Ghasidas reworked or rejected. For example, he forbade the worship of anthropomorphized deities, whether of local or all-India provenance. The tradition holds that he once gathered together all the gods and goddesses of a certain village and threw them on a rubbish heap. He also urged his followers to reject caste distinctions. He denied the priestly importance of *brahmans* and replaced *purohits* (family and village priests) with *bhandārīs,* members of the *Chamar* caste who were responsible for the execution of *Satnami* life-cycle rituals and for mediating *Satnami* disputes in the villages where they lived. He dissociated popular festivals from the Hindu gods and goddesses with whom they were connected, and provided an alternate meaning for the celebrations from the history and beliefs of the *panth*.[48]

As a positive symbolic marker of *Satnami* identity, Ghasidas encouraged his followers to wear the *kanṭhī,* a necklace of small *tulsi* (wood of the basil plant) beads associated with the Kabirpanthis and other Vaishnavas. Instead of the usual village greeting, "Ram, Ram," Ghasidas encouraged his followers to greet each other with "Satnam." Later in the nineteenth century, the *jait khambhā* (victory pillar), a bamboo or cement pole with a white flag at the top, came to symbolize the presence of *Satnami* communities and the authority of the guru.

47. Dube, *Untouchable Pasts,* p. 40.
48. Dube, *Untouchable Pasts,* p. 45.

Towards the end of his life, Ghasidas became the *malguzar* of village Bhandar, where he had established his *gaddī* (guru seat). As a result, the location grew in importance and became the destination of *Satnami* pilgrimages, complementing (if not entirely replacing) pilgrimages to places like Rajim.[49] Ghasidas also initiated *ramat,* the practice of touring in order to allow his followers *darśan,* a vision of the Guru, and to deal with problems of discipline and social harmony within the community. On these tours and in Bhandar, where Ghasidas had taken residence, *Satnamis* offered the Guru coconuts and money in exchange for *caraṇāmṛit* (literally, "nectar of the feet") — water in which the Guru's foot had been dipped or washed. Stories soon multiplied of the miraculous powers of this substance. It was believed to counteract infertility, warm the body, heal injuries and sicknesses, and cure snakebites.[50] Other stories of the Guru's miraculous powers emerged over time. Informants indicated, for example, that upon returning from his forest seclusion Ghasidas raised his wife from the dead, and that he was able to perform an impossible agricultural feat given to him by residents of his village as a test of his spiritual awakening. He was said to have been of an unusually fair complexion and to have had a "rather imposing appearance," which belied his "sensitive, silent" nature and proclivity towards seeing visions.[51]

By the time of his death in 1850, Ghasidas claimed a quarter of a million followers.[52] Forty years later, the 1891 Census of India reported that roughly 88.5 percent of the *Chamars* in Raipur District had become *Satnami* (54.7 percent in Bilaspur District).[53] In the 1901 census 471,566 Chhattisgarhis, or 14.36 percent of the region's inhabitants, returned their caste as *Chamar* (245,126 in Raipur and 209,517 in Bilaspur);[54] in the same year, 343,468 Chhattisgarhis identified themselves as *Satnami,* indicating that roughly 75 percent of *Chamars* considered themselves members of the *samaj* (society or association).[55] A large portion of the 25 percent who did not join were Kanaujia *Chamars,* a major sub-section of the caste in Chhattisgarh which refused to

49. Charles Grant, ed., *The Gazetteer of the Central Provinces of India* (New Delhi: Usha, 1984), p. 56.

50. Dube, *Untouchable Pasts,* p. 44.

51. *Report on the Land Revenue Settlement of the Belaspore District, 1868,* by J. W. Chisholm. Quoted in Russell, *Tribes and Castes of the Central Provinces (1),* p. 309.

52. Dube, *Untouchable Pasts,* p. 40.

53. Dube, *Untouchable Pasts,* p. 50.

54. The next largest communities were the *Gonds,* who returned 421,942 members (13 percent of the population), the *Telis,* who returned 343,212 (10.5 percent), and the *Ahirs* (a *Ravat,* or grazier caste), who returned 328,728 (10 percent).

55. India Census Commissioner, *Census of India, 1901,* vol. 8 (Part 2, Statistics) (Bombay: Government Central Press, 1902-3).

give up its traditional occupations. Not surprisingly, the *Satnamis* avoided contact with them.

Not all of Ghasidas's followers were *Chamars*. The Guru accepted disciples from all castes except those he considered below the *Chamars*, such as the *Dhobis* (launderers), *Ghasias* (grass-cutters), and *Mehtars* (sweepers).[56] But although there were during Ghasidas's lifetime a significant number of *Telis* (oil pressers, the largest *sudra* caste in Chhattisgarh) who became *Satnamis,* they constituted a rather small percentage of the community, and because there were no distinctions within the community (i.e., all *Satnamis* ate and drank with one another) outsiders perceived all members of the *panth* to be *Chamars*.[57]

The *panth* did not, of course, die with Ghasidas, but continued on under the leadership of his offspring in the *Satnami* guru *pārampara* (lineage). Soon after the Guru's death, Balakdas, his son, took control of the *samaj*. If Ghasidas provided the initial charisma for the *Satnami* movement, Balakdas can be credited with fervently establishing its institutional foundations, and it was under him that the *Satnami* religious bureaucracy expanded. Whereas the sect was at one time ruled by Guru Ghasidas alone, in the latter half of the nineteenth century a hierarchy developed, involving the Guru, his various assistants, regional leaders called *mahants,* and local village heads called *bhandārīs*.[58]

Having forbidden the worship of Hindu gods and goddesses, Ghasidas effectively reinforced his own and his descendants' status (whether this was his intention is another matter). The Satnam, having no anthropomorphic form or symbolic image, could not readily be shown affection, and with no other permitted outlet for religious devotion, *Satnamis* focused their worship on the Guru himself. If Ghasidas the ascetic householder was at all uncomfortable with this role, his sons and grandsons were not.

By seizing the insignia of upper-caste Hindu purity (e.g., vegetarianism, teetotalism, etc.) Ghasidas succeeded in raising the self-esteem of the *Chamars* who became *Satnami*. However, he had done little to directly resist the structure of brahmanical Hindu society. *Brahmans* and other high castes welcomed Ghasidas's reforms, in part because they fit within an accepted and familiar pattern of lower-caste religious change. Balakdas, however, was somewhat more confrontational. Whereas Ghasidas had instructed his fol-

---

56. Russell, *Tribes and Castes of the Central Provinces (1),* pp. 312-14.

57. Lamb, *Rapt in the Name,* p. 56.

58. The institutionalization of *Satnami* leadership has its parallels in other Hindu reforming sects such as the Swaminarayan movement in Gujarat in the early nineteenth century. See Raymond Brady Williams, *An Introduction to Swaminarayan Hinduism* (Cambridge: Cambridge University Press, 2001), pp. 33ff.

lowers to wear *kaṇṭhīs*, Balakdas began distributing the *janeū* (sacred thread and symbol of the twice-born castes). At the same time, he personally appropriated the use of two symbols of temporal and religious status, the elephant and horse.[59] Balakdas's reforms had the effect of arousing the passions of high-caste religious leaders and local economic and political strongmen, and thereby foreshortening his own life. In 1860, he was killed by a group of *Rajputs* (to whom many *Satnamis* would have been indentured). He was succeeded by his younger half-brother, Agardas. But as soon as he became old enough to make a believable claim to the *gaddī*, Sahebdas, son of Balakdas and his kept wife Radha (or Rahi Mata), disputed Agardas's claim to the Guru's authority. In order to settle the dispute, leadership of the *panth* was officially divided by the British government, but conflicts regarding leadership of the community have continued into contemporary times.

Though the tradition holds that Ghasidas received his message from *Satpurus*, the question still remains whether in addition to this the Guru was in any way inspired by the ideas of other religious leaders or movements. Much of the debate concerns what exactly happened during those six months that Ghasidas remained away from his community. At different times in the late nineteenth and early twentieth centuries, groups of *Satnamis*, Hindus, and Christians attempted to give the *Satnamis* a pedigree and a narrative that favored their own understanding both of the *Satnamis* and of themselves.

For example, in the local Christian version of the story Ghasidas makes a pilgrimage to the Jagannath temple at Puri (Orissa), but stops off in Cuttack where he encounters some white-faced *ṭopī-vālās* (literally "people with hats," i.e., the pith helmet-wearing missionaries) who speak of Jesus as Truth (*Sat* or *Satya*). By the time Ghasidas arrived home, so the story goes, he had forgotten much of the message, and the Satnampanth, a kind of degenerated Christianity, was the result. Later, high-caste Hindus attempting to draw the *Satnamis* into the political process gave them a more respectable and orthodox ancestry by linking them directly to the *sants* (a group of poet-saints living around the fifteenth and sixteenth centuries).[60]

Satnami tradition asserts that Ghasidas received a vision from *Satpuruṣ* while on a pilgrimage to the Jagannath temple. Along the way, in the town of Sarangarh, a divine figure appeared to the traveler and told him that the worship of images (for which the Jagannath temple was famous) was ineffectual. Convinced, he abandoned his pilgrimage and returned home, punctuating

---

59. Dube, *Untouchable Pasts*, p. 61.

60. These outsider appropriations of the *Satnami* narrative will be discussed at more length in Chapter 5.

his journey with praises of the one God, whom he called Satnam. The villagers, who had gathered upon his return to receive Jagannath *prasād,* were at first unconvinced of the veracity of his message, and Ghasidas began retreating to the forests, from which, as discussed above, he later emerged transformed and brimming with charismatic power.

There are other competing accounts, however. Many people, from *panth* members to nineteenth-century British officials to current historians, assert that Ghasidas found some inspiration in two previous movements that went by the name of *Satnami.* The earliest of these appeared in seventeenth-century Punjab. The community followed the patterns of *nirgun bhakti* (devotion to a deity without anthropomorphic qualities), and was, according to Mughal chronicles, a mixture of "gold smiths, carpenters, sweepers, tanners and other ignoble beings."[61] The sect seems to have been fairly sizeable, but found itself on the wrong side of history when it opposed a taxation scheme of the religiously inclined but authoritarian Mughal emperor, Aurangzeb, whose armies utterly annihilated it in 1672.

A second group of *Satnamis* in Uttar Pradesh emerged not long after this one. This group was led by Jagjivandas (1669-1760), who may or may not have been inspired by the earlier movement. He also was a *nirgun bhakt* (a devotee of the divine without qualities), and instructed his followers to chant *"satya nām"* (true name). Jagjivandas promulgated a list of seven tenets of his sect that are virtually indistinguishable from those of Ghasidas; it therefore seems unlikely that Ghasidas was not in some way influenced by him.[62] Unlike the earlier movement of the same name, this group of *Satnamis* survived.[63] Most *Satnamis* deny or are unaware of any historical connection between their guru and these earlier movements, and there are indeed some discontinuities, such as the fact that neither of the earlier movements included a large number of *Chamars,* and the fact that both allowed for the worship of Hindu deities, despite their *nirgun bhakti* proclivities.

Another likely source of inspiration for Ghasidas was the Kabirpanth. Though much of the scholarship relating to the Kabirpanth has focused on its founder, Kabir (ca. fifteenth century), and on the *panth's* Varanasi *śākhā*

---

61. Quoted in Stephen Fuchs, *Rebellious Prophets: A Study of Messianic Movements in Indian Religions* (New York: Asia Publishing House, 1965), p. 98.

62. Some present-day *Satnamis* combine the pilgrimage to Jagannath with inspiration by Jagjivandas, asserting that Ghasidas met the religious leader on the way to Puri (a historical impossibility if traditional dates given for the two leaders are correct).

63. A Disciples missionary working in Chhattisgarh and obsessed with the history of all three *Satnami* communities, H. C. Saum, carried on correspondence with early twentieth-century gurus of this *Satnami* group.

(branch), the Chhattisgarhi *śākhā*, founded by a disciple of Kabir named Dharamdas, has in fact at least since the beginning of the twentieth century been the larger of the two branches.

Kabir, one of the best known of the *sants*, was born into a family of Muslim weavers.[64] Though it is historically unlikely, the tradition holds that Kabir took a famous Vaishnava, Ramananda, as his guru. Kabir rejected *sagun bhakti* (devotion to deities with attributes, usually in the form of images), and believed that the chanting of *Rāmnām* (the name of Ram) was the most efficacious path towards union with the *nirgun brahman*, the impersonal animating principle of the cosmos who was beyond the distinctions of Hindu and Muslim.[65] Worshiping the divine in *nirgun* form allowed Kabir to bypass the authority of *brahmans*, who controlled the mythology and worship of *sagun* gods and goddesses. This circumnavigation would have appealed to Kabir's followers, many of whom came from the lower castes.[66] Both his iconoclasm and his absolute rejection of *sagun bhakti* have become attenuated in the *panth* that bears his name.

Dharamdas was born near Jabalpur, in Madhya Pradesh, into a *vaisya* family. Despite his high-caste background, the *śākhā's* membership derives largely from *dalit* and *ādivāsī* peoples. And whereas the Varanasi *śākhā*, highly influenced by the hyper-orthodox surroundings of its holy city, has in the past made moves to restrict its membership to the high castes, the Chhattisgarhi *śākhā* has done nothing to check the influx of *dalits* and *sudras*. Today *Pankas* (weavers and agricultural workers) and *Telis* (oil-pressers) constitute the majority of the *śākhā*. Though the *panth* recognizes caste distinctions regarding commensality and endogamy, Kabirpanthis observe various rituals that symbolically undermine the importance of caste alterity, such as a common meal held annually on the date of Kabir's birth (August 13th). And if in reality Dharamdas's Kabirpanth does in fact perpetuate certain of the forms of Hindu hierarchy, the ideals it espouses are generally inimical to it.[67] The Chhattis-

---

64. The traditional dates of Kabir's life are 1398-1518, but he probably lived in the first half of the fifteenth century.

65. Lamb, *Rapt in the Name*, p. 49.

66. David N. Lorenzen, "The Kabir-Panth and Social Protest," in *The Sants: Studies in a Devotional Tradition of India*, ed. Karine Schomer and W. H. McLeod (Berkeley: Berkeley Religious Studies Series, 1987), p. 287.

67. See David N. Lorenzen, *Kabir Legends and Ananta-Das's Kabir Parachai* (Albany: State University of New York Press, 1991), p. 276. On the Kabirpanth more generally, see Lorenzen, "The Kabir-Panth and Social Protest." The "classic" texts on the *panth* are F. E. Keay, *Kabir and His Followers* (Calcutta: Association Press, 1931); and G. H. Westcott, *Kabir and the Kabir Panth* (Calcutta: Susil Gupta, 1953).

garhi *śākhā* of the Kabirpanth was founded before the birth of Ghasidas, but by 1901 the Satnampanth had eclipsed it in terms of size, returning 342,468 Chhattisgarhi members in the census to the Kabirpanth's 277,111.[68]

Lawrence Babb, who argues that "very little of what Ghasi Das said or did was without precedent," suggests that Guru Ghasidas probably borrowed his model for hereditary guru-ship and many of his doctrines and practices from the Kabirpanthis.[69] The *kaṇṭhī*, a sign of strict vegetarianism borrowed from the Kabirpanth, allowed Ghasidas to assert his community's purity as well as forge a link to the great *sant*. The *Satnamis* also appropriated the Kabirpanthi *caukā*, a simple chalk-lined worship space, and reconfigured it for use in their own religious services. Finally, the *Satnami* emphasis on *nirguṇ bhakti*, its distaste for caste-based social distinctions, and its *mantra*, "satyanām," are all elements found within the Kabirpanth.

However, many of these symbols, themes, and practices are common to India's *sant* tradition more generally, and the *bhakti* movement that helped inspire it. Before the writing of the *Bhagavad Gītā* (fifth century BCE–second century CE), the term *"bhakti"* simply meant "affection" or "attachment."[70] But in the *Gītā*, Krishna, *avatār* of Vishnu and divine charioteer, described *bhakti* as a religious *mārg*, or path to *mukti* (liberation), adding it to the well-established paths of *karma* (doing one's *dharma* without regard for the results), and *jñāna* (knowledge and the pursuit of spiritual awakening). On the verge of battle, Krishna tells the warrior Arjuna, third oldest of the five Pandava brothers, "Be it a leaf or flower or fruit or water that a zealous soul may offer Me with love's devotion, that do I [willingly] accept, for it was love that made the offering. . . . For whosoever makes Me his haven, base-born though he may be, yes, women too and artisans [*vaisyas*], even serfs [*sudras*], theirs it is to tread the highest way" (9:26, 32).[71] Though the text itself is rather restrained, it paved the way for a number of movements characterized by effusive devotion to a god or goddess.[72]

68. India Census Commissioner, *Census, 1901.*

69. Lawrence A. Babb, "The Satnamis — Political Involvement of a Religious Movement," in *The Untouchables in Contemporary India*, ed. Michael J. Mahar (Tucson: University of Arizona Press, 1972), p. 144. K. S. Singh also sees a connection between Ghasidas and Kabir, but through the mediation of Jagjivandas. It is curious, if Singh was aware of the Kabirpanthi presence in Chhattisgarh, why he felt this explanation more likely. See Singh, *The Scheduled Castes*, p. 353.

70. Karen Pechilis Prentiss, *The Embodiment of Bhakti* (New York: Oxford University Press, 1999), p. 5.

71. Quotation from *The Bhagavad-Gītā*, trans. R. C. Zaehner (New York: Oxford University Press, 1973).

72. Dumont, *Religion/Politics*, p. 56.

The *Āgamas* and *Purāṇas* of the fifth to seventh centuries CE recorded and multiplied the mythologies of anthropomorphized deities like Vishnu and Shiva, and asserted that in the *Kalī Yuga* (the cosmic period of moral darkness), humans were incapable of practicing austerities or studying the Vedas, and should therefore seek refuge in the mercy of the deity. Combining the *Gītā's* devotionalism with this Puranic focus on *saguṇa* gods and goddesses, a number of *bhakti* movements appeared in the Tamil-speaking South between the seventh and tenth centuries CE. These early movements, says A. K. Ramanujan:

> . . . used whatever they found at hand, and changed whatever they used. Vedic and Upaniṣadic notions, Buddhist and Jaina concepts, conventions of Tamil and Sanskrit poetry, early Tamil conceptions of love, service, women, and kings, mythology or folk religion and folksong, the play of contrasts between Sanskrit and the mother tongue: all these elements were reworked and transformed in *bhakti*.[73]

The euphoria of *bhakti* movements soon intoxicated the North, and contributed to an awakening among groups like the Vaishnava Gaudiyas in Bengal, the cult of Vithoba in Maharashtra, and the Ramanandi order based in Ayodhya, as well as among the Shaiva Nath sect, which mediated earthy tantric practices to the masses between the twelfth and fifteenth centuries.

The *sants* drew inspiration from these northern Vaishnava *bhakti* movements and the Nath cult, and were also significantly influenced by the presence of mystical Sufi orders. Kabir, perhaps the most important of the *sants,* wove these three forms of devotionalism into a coherent (if eclectic) whole that was fueled by passion for the formless Absolute. Guru Nanak (1469-1539), considered the founder of Sikhism, and Ravidas (ca. fifteenth century), a *Chamar* shoemaker from Varanasi, drew from similar sources and advanced analogous themes. But the *sant* tradition diverges from *bhakti* devotionalism in several ways. Most importantly, whereas *bhakti* sects tended to focus on a highly anthropomorphized external deity imagined as a friend, lover, or master, the *sants* directed their devotion to a *nirguṇ* conception of the divine understood to be *within* the devotee. Their devotion, however, was no less impassioned.

The *bhakti* and *sant* poets and leaders were not prophets of social uplift, but their emphasis on devotional expression over the performance of prescribed social and religious duties encouraged the growth of movements that disregarded, downplayed, and sometimes even contested the ritual hierarchy

---

73. A. K. Ramanujan, *Hymns for the Drowning* (Princeton: Princeton University Press, 1981), p. 104.

and its caste-based social distinctions.[74] Their lack of concern about *varṇa-jāti* restrictions gave them the appearance of concern about social equality.[75] It is therefore not surprising that many of the leaders and participants of these movements came from the lower castes. Ravidas (or Raidas), one of the most popular of the *sants,* was a *Chamar.* And Kabir, of a lowly weaver community, has come to be a potent symbol of hope for India's *dalits.*

However, the movements have generally failed to materialize the ideals they espoused. Lloyd and Susanne Hoeber Rudolph argue that the *bhakti* and *sant* movements "have usually been ambivalent, at once rebellious and compliant, with respect to the dominant high culture definitions, damning ritual and social barriers but failing to convert critique into reform and remaining within the framework of Hinduism."[76] Most devotional sects, after gaining some measure of respect, have again begun to accept high-caste ideology, especially brahmanical markers of purity and impurity, some of which we see in the *Satnami* community, particularly after the death of Ghasidas. Their rebellion against the hegemonic religious order improves their self-image, but their compliance ensures their assimilation back into the very society they despise. Their cultural identity is transformed, but their social reality is not.

The *sant* tradition represents a circumvention of brahmanical hegemony by means of a rejection of orthodox deities and ritual forms (especially the temple cult). Ghasidas took many things from the *sants* — devotion to a *nirguṇ* deity, the diminished importance of hierarchical obligations and privileges, and a disregard for *varṇa-jāti* distinctions. Hinduism, Julius Lipner asserts, "is *par excellence* the religion of the back door."[77] But Hindu communities have a peculiar way of reining in the centrifugal forces of religious reform movements, and most *sant* movements, believing themselves to be exiting by the back door, found themselves entering again by the front (or perhaps, more appositely, by the side). In the late nineteenth and early twentieth centuries, the Satnampanth underwent a similar process. Ghasidas's charisma was tamed, the *panth's* effervescence routinized, and its beliefs and rituals sanskritized.

---

74. Most movements for social change in India are, in fact, expressed in a religious idiom. On this topic, see Fuchs, *Rebellious Prophets;* David G. Mandelbaum, *Society in India* (Berkeley: University of California Press, 1970); and Suman Lata Pathak, "Religious Conversion and Social Change," in *Reform, Protest and Social Transformation,* ed. Satish K. Sharma (New Delhi: Ashish Publishing House, 1987).

75. Juergensmeyer, *Social Vision,* p. 211.

76. Lloyd I. Rudolph and Susanne Hoeber Rudolph, *The Modernity of Tradition: Political Development in India* (Chicago: University of Chicago Press, 1967), p. 139.

77. Lipner, *Hindus,* p. 57.

Satnamis and Sanskritization in the Twentieth Century

Though roots of this transformation can be found in the late nineteenth century, its effects are more appreciable in the opening decades of the twentieth. The Government of India Act of 1909 defined India as a nation of diverse "interests" that needed to be consulted for the purposes of fair and just government.[78] This notion was given more support when, in 1917, Edwin Montagu rose in front of British parliamentarians and announced that His Majesty's policy was to work towards "the increasing association of Indians in every branch of the administration and the gradual development of self-governing institutions with a view to the progressive realisation of responsible government in India as an integral part of the British Empire."[79] This meant more positions of power for Indians under the British Raj. In 1919, constitutional reforms directed that these positions be distributed according to a principle of "separate electorates," whereby Muslims and Sikhs were granted certain numbers of reserved seats. In 1932, Ramsay MacDonald announced the Communal Award, which expanded the privilege of separate electorates to Indian Christians, Anglo-Indians, Europeans, and the "depressed classes." Fearing their wholesale political defection, Gandhi began a fast-unto-death against the differentiation of what he called *"harijans"* from the greater Hindu community. He and Dr. B. R. Ambedkar, leader of the lower-caste Indians, worked out a compromise whereby the depressed caste communities would be included in the Hindu electoral bloc, but would be given a number of reserved seats.

These events served instantly to increase the political cachet of lower-caste communities, especially larger ones. *Dalit* communities realized their numbers were a valuable commodity and formed political caste associations, such as the Adi Dravida movement in South India, and the Ad Dharm and Adi Hindu movements in Uttar Pradesh.[80] Finding themselves wooed by the high castes, many *harijan* communities attempted to translate their newfound political power into higher status in the traditional ritual hierarchy by taking advantage of an age-old process that M. N. Srinivas has called sanskritization.[81]

Sanskritization is: "The process by which a 'low' Hindu caste, or tribal or

78. For more on India's "politics of numbers," see John C. B. Webster, *A History of the Dalit Christians in India* (San Francisco: Mellen Research University Press, 1992).

79. Stanley Wolpert, *A New History of India,* 5th ed. (New York: Oxford University Press, 1997), p. 294.

80. Juergensmeyer, *Social Vision,* p. 22.

81. For a detailed chronological treatment of the formation of Srinivas's theory of sanskritization, see Simon Charsley, "Sanskritization: The Career of an Anthropological Theory," *Contributions to Indian Sociology* (n.s.) 32, no. 2 (1998).

other group, changes its customs, ritual, ideology, and way of life in the direction of a high, and frequently, 'twice-born' caste. Generally such changes are followed by a claim to a higher position in the caste hierarchy than that traditionally conceded to the claimant caste by the local community. The claim is usually made over a period of time, in fact, a generation or two, before the 'arrival' is conceded."[82]

The *varṇa-jāti* system, Srinivas argued, was never immutable, and contains three "axes of power" — the ritual, the economic, and the numerical. Possession of power on any of the three axes enables the acquisition of power on the other two, though numerical strength seems to be the most important of the three.[83] If a caste managed to increase its political or economic condition, sanskritization generally followed as a means of reconciling secular and ritual rank.[84]

Though in his early writings Srinivas emphasized the importance of *brahmans* in the process of sanskritization, he later disclaimed that emphasis, and in subsequent treatises he spoke more of the "dominant caste."[85] For example, *brahmans,* by dint of their traditional priestly function, possess ritual power, but they do not always — and in fact quite frequently do not — possess political or economic power, and so it is common that non-brahmanical castes will exert dominance over a particular locale.

Orthodox Hindu society forbade the *dalits* to appropriate the signs and symbols of the high castes, such as the *janeū*. But the prohibition seems to

82. Srinivas, *Social Change,* p. 6. For an alternate definition, see M. N. Srinivas, "The Cohesive Role of Sanskritization," in *India and Ceylon: Unity and Diversity,* ed. Philip Mason (London: Oxford University Press, 1967), pp. 67-68.

83. M. N. Srinivas, "A Note on Sanskritization and Westernization," *Far Eastern Quarterly* 15, no. 4 (1956): 483, 492. In modern India, with its more developed networks of communication and its "secular" democratic political structure, the importance of numerical strength has grown exponentially. See Srinivas, *Social Change,* p. 11. See also "Introduction," in M. N. Srinivas, *The Dominant Caste and Other Essays* (Delhi: Oxford University Press, 1987), p. 8. Srinivas occasionally also spoke of a "Western" form of dominance, which could be wielded by communities with a large number of highly educated members. See "The Dominant Caste in Rampura," in M. N. Srinivas, *Collected Essays* (New York: Oxford University Press, 2002), p. 75.

84. Srinivas, *Social Change,* pp. 28, 32-42; and M. N. Srinivas, "Mobility in the Caste System," in *Structure and Change in Indian Society,* ed. Milton Singer and Bernard Cohn (Chicago: University of Chicago Press, 1968), pp. 189-92. Under the British, both political instability and the availability of land decreased, but other avenues of political and economic advance were opened up such that by the early twentieth century a far greater and more diverse number of castes were undergoing the process of sanskritization.

85. M. N. Srinivas, "The Social System of a Mysore Village," in *Village India,* ed. McKim Marriott (Chicago: University of Chicago Press, 1955), p. 18.

have made those symbols all the more desirable, such that they became a natural inducement for the *dalits* to adopt the customs and behavior of the highest castes. Sanskritization has thus been a centripetal force in the history of India, pulling lower and marginal communities towards central high-caste symbols, myths, philosophical concepts, and social institutions.[86]

Because of the changes in British India discussed above, high-caste Chhattisgarhi Hindus attempted to court the favor of the same low-caste communities they had until the 1920s portrayed as *outside* the Hindu fold (e.g., with respect to temple entry). In 1925, two *Satnamis,* Naindas and Anjordas, founded the Satnami Mahasabha, a political organization through which the *Satnamis* were to become both more politically involved and more fully sanskritized. Naindas and Anjordas had first worked together to oppose the government slaughterhouses in Raipur and Bilaspur Districts, indicating their earlier interest in appropriating the symbols of high-caste status, such as cow protection. Joined later by Ratiram, a powerful *malguzar* of Kevta (pronounced kay-OWN-ta) Devri, and Agamdas, one of several great-grandsons of Ghasidas claiming the guru *gaddī,* they went to the Kanpur meeting of the INC, where leaders "purified" them by granting them the sacred thread. As its first initiative, the Mahasabha petitioned the Governor of the Central Provinces, Sir Montagu Butler, to have official government documents distinguish between *Chamars* who followed Guru Ghasidas and those who did not. He agreed, and after 1926 the *Chamars* who had joined the *panth* were officially called *Satnamis.*[87]

At Kanpur, the *Satnamis* met Baba Ramchandra, a Maharashtrian *brahman* who had been the leader of an aggressive farmers' movement in the region of Awadh. Ramchandra became enamored with the *Satnamis* and authored two texts on the movement, *Ghāsīdāsjī kī vanśāvalī* (Genealogy of Ghasidas) and *Satnām sagar* (Ocean of Satnam). The latter of these texts purported to be a history of the *Satnamis,* but invented for the *panth* a respectable genealogy and an orthodox set of beliefs. In the text, Ghasidas is given only a supporting role in a drama where the very gods and goddesses he ignored are the stars and the real agents of history.[88] Though Ramchandra's

---

86. M. N. Srinivas, "Note on Sanskritization and Westernization," pp. 482-85; and M. N. Srinivas, *Religion and Society among the Coorgs of South India* (New York: Asia Publishing House, 1965), pp. 31, 209, 213, 227.

87. Dube, *Untouchable Pasts,* pp. 150-51. During this period census offices were swamped with similar petitions, leading many census-takers to abandon the practice of recording the population according to caste. For similar name-changing efforts among south Indian communities, see Rudolph and Rudolph, *Modernity of Tradition,* pp. 39-62.

88. Dube, *Untouchable Pasts,* pp. 14-15, 116-17.

emphasis on the deities of the Sanskritic pantheon contravened one of Ghasidas's main teachings, it was not entirely out of step with the practice of common *Satnamis,* who had again begun (or perhaps never stopped) worshiping Hindu deities, particularly Thakur Dev.[89] By the beginning of the twentieth century, little separated the religious practices of most *Satnamis* from the villagers around whom they lived.[90]

The Satnami Mahasabha continued its reforms throughout the 1920s and '30s, publicly forbidding members of the *panth* to employ themselves in occupations involving leather and carrion, and passing resolutions threatening punishment to those who disobeyed. They also persisted in their appropriation of high-caste Hindu symbols. At one 1925 meeting in Mungeli, the Mahasabha adopted a flag with a picture of a cow on it.[91] Their moves, however, had little impact on the way that high-caste Hindus perceived them, except that high-caste politicians now saw them as political allies. William Baur, an Evangelical missionary, reported the following encounter at a *Satnami melā* in 1938:

> Finally I discovered one well-fed Brahmin walking about with a Satnami Mahant. This Mahant was boasting about the fact that the Satnamis were really Hindus. And the Hindu brother was smirking and smiling and seemed to be happy that the Satnamis were so well Hinduized again. The Mahant did not realize how true his words were. For Satnamiism has again reverted to popular Hinduism and Hinduism has once more demonstrated its power to neutralize and absorb anything like a reform which starts from within.[92]

Here, the Christian trope of *Satnami* decline does not obscure the fact that sanskritization was in the interest of both *Satnamis* and their high-caste political allies and advisors.

89. *Satnamis* had even begun to build temples. Around 1933, near Champa (on the General Conference Mennonite mission field), Mahadev (Shiva) appeared to one Budhwaroo *Satnami,* "bull [Shiva's mount, Nandi] and all." Budhwaroo built a temple on the site to commemorate his vision. See H. C. Saum to J. W. Pickett, 3 July 1934, in HCS, box 1 of 4 (no folder).

90. Babb, "Satnamis," p. 146. Though the social reality may not have changed significantly, the cultural reality did; that is to say that though their practices may have differed little from those of other villagers, their identity remained distinct.

91. Untitled, undated, unsigned, Hindi text found in HCS, box 3 of 4 (folder: Unrest Ramnamis).

92. "Second Quarterly Report — 1938," AES 82-14 Qu2, Baur, Wm., Quarterly Reports, Articles, Newsletters, 1927-58.

At the time of Independence, the *Satnami* faction represented by Agamdas and the Mahasabha succeeded in establishing itself at the center of the community's power, despite the fact that rival claimants to the position of guru controlled the symbolic guru *gaddī* in the village of Bhandar. The difference was that while Agamdas and the Mahasabha had aligned themselves with the INC and indirectly with high-caste Hindus, the rival claimants, led by brothers Muktavandas, Jagtarandas, and Atibaldas, had sided with lower-caste Chhattisgarhis, Ambedkar's All India Scheduled Caste Foundation (formed in 1942), and the region's pro-British forces.[93] Clearly the two factions represented different visions of the *Satnami* community. Muktavandas and his brothers emphasized the lower-caste identity of the *Satnami* community and played on fears that the interests of the INC leadership were not in line with those of the *Satnami* community. Agamdas, on the other hand, hitched his wagon to the INC, which became the dominant political force in independent India. For the moment, at least, his vision had emerged victorious.[94]

There is a curious paradox here, that while the Mahasabha and the *Satnami* leadership more generally was attempting to manipulate the symbols of high-caste Hinduism and claim higher status, it was at the same time loudly reminding British officials of its disabilities as a depressed caste, in hopes of gaining political and educational concessions. It simultaneously pursued the symbols of traditional status (like cow protection, the sacred thread, and teetotalism) and of the colonial regime (such as literacy, education, and political representation). The two processes may, in fact, have complemented each other, as literacy increases access to the written mythologies of the Sanskritic gods.[95] And though the illiterate Ghasidas left behind no scriptures, his twentieth-century disciples increasingly claimed Tulsidas's *Rāmcaritmānas* as their own. As will be shown later with regard to *Satnami*-Christians, whose religious identity combined both traditional and modern status symbols, the history of the Satnampanth in the early twentieth century resists interpretations that position sanskritization and Christianization as discrete and competing processes.[96]

Ghasidas's legacy is still a matter of much discussion in Chhattisgarh. Was he an original saint? A wily imposter? A social reformer? A political agitator?

93. In 1946, Muktavandas became the president of the Chhattisgarh Scheduled Caste Federation. Dube, *Untouchable Pasts*, p. 180.

94. Agamdas successfully ran as a Congress Party parliamentary candidate in Chhattisgarh in 1950. Dube, *Untouchable Pasts*, p. 181.

95. Cohn, "The Changing Status of a Depressed Caste," p. 297.

96. For more on this topic, see "Mobility in the Caste System," in Srinivas, *Collected Essays*, p. 194.

An advocate of the downtrodden? Not surprisingly, many current interpretations of the *Satnami* heritage throw history by the wayside and say more about those who advance them than about Ghasidas or the Satnampanth. H. L. Shukla, writing in a climate of anti-conversion politics in the region, argues that, "Guru Ghāsīdāsa was against the process of Christianization which was very much rampant in those days. . . ."[97] (The fact that Christian missionaries did not enter the region until eighteen years after Ghasidas's death seems to be of little import to the author.) With similar historical anachronism, the Government of Chhattisgarh's website portrays Ghasidas as an anti-British nationalist leader.[98] Alternatively, *Satnami* leaders wishing to improve the *panth's* Sanskrit Hindu credentials deny that the Satnampanth was ever a reformist religious sect, preferring to interpret it as just another *jāti*. My own view is that the *panth* was primarily a religious movement which by improving the self-esteem of members of the *panth*, created the basis for claims of higher social status, sometimes in the arena of traditional status symbols, sometimes in the realm of colonial politics.

No matter how one interprets the *Satnami* movement, it is clear that it represents a movement of social and religious ferment — of orthogenetic change long before the arrival of missionaries. By midway through the nineteenth century there were several religious options available to Chhattisgarh *Chamars*. They could remain as they were, despised and religiously marginalized, or they could join a Hindu reform movement such as the Satnampanth, or the important but smaller Ramnami movement.[99] In 1868, a third option arrived from across the seas — a source of heterogenetic innovation that would prove appealing to many of Chhattisgarh's *Satnamis*.

97. Hira Lal Shukla, *Chattisgarh Rediscovered: Vedāntic Approaches to Folklore* (New Delhi: Aryan Books International, 1995), p. 37n.

98. Government of Chhattisgarh, "Official Website, Govt. of Chhattisgarh," 2004, accessed 28 June 2004; available from http://www.chhattisgarh.nic.in/profile/corigin.htm #seed.

99. Parasuram, the *Chamar* founder of the Ramnami Samaj, was born in Chhattisgarh midway through the nineteenth century. In a moment of crisis, he had an encounter with a mysterious *sadhu* (a wandering ascetic) who told him that Ram was pleased with his devotion, and that the name of Ram would appear written on his chest during the night. It did, and Parasuram's family and villagers celebrated the miracle. In addition to tattooing Ram on their bodies, the Ramnamis have developed several other distinctive practices. They are encouraged to wear *ordhni*, cloth covered entirely with the name of Ram, when chanting the name of Ram. In addition, Ramnami men — and occasionally women — wear *mukut* (literally, "crown"), a hat made with peacock feathers, which are traditionally associated with incarnations of Vishnu, such as Ram. See Lamb, *Rapt in the Name.*

The Origins of Christianity[100] in Chhattisgarh

On 9 March 1865, pastors from six denominations in the New Jersey area gathered together to form *"Die Deutsche Evangelische Missionsgesellschaft in den Vereinigten Staaten."*[101] A year later, the German Evangelical Mission Society, as it came to be known, decided to commission Rev. Oscar Lohr, a German immigrant to America who had had to abandon his first assignment as a Gossner missionary in Chota Nagpur on account of the Indian Mutiny. Arriving in India with his family in 1868, Lohr attended a Bombay missionary conference where Rev. J. G. Cooper, of the Free Church of Scotland in Nagpur, described the need for work among the *Satnamis* of Chhattisgarh, and assured his audience that the work would have the support of the Division's British Commissioner, Colonel Balmain.[102]

Lohr went first to Nagpur, and then on to Raipur, where he remained for some time laying the foundation for his work. Encouraged by his reception

---

100. Catholicism figures prominently in post-Independence debates on conversion in Chhattisgarh, largely because of its growth in the northeastern regions of what is now Chhattisgarh. Nevertheless, in the late nineteenth and early twentieth centuries Catholicism did not have a significant presence in Chhattisgarh, especially rural Chhattisgarh. In 1901, for example, of the 6,463 Christians in the Chhattisgarh Division of the Central Provinces, only 556 (8.6 percent) were Roman Catholic, and of this number 201 were either Europeans or Eurasians. The percentage of Catholics in Chhattisgarh decreased in the 1911 and 1921 censuses (to 8 and 6.8 percent, respectively). See India Census Commissioner, *Census, 1901;* India Census Commissioner, *Census of India, 1911,* vol. 10 (Part 2, Statistics) (Calcutta: Superintendent of Government Printing, 1911); and India Census Commissioner, *Census of India, 1921,* vol. 11 (Part 2, Statistics) (Nagpur: Government Press, 1923). Moreover, during the period under study, Catholic missionary activity was largely confined to the larger cities where priests were assigned to minister to already established Catholic communities. When they did begin to work more intentionally among un-Christianized peoples, they avoided the already established mission stations and worked to the northeast of the geographical focus of my study. Because of this they had little contact with the *Satnamis,* and this book therefore focuses more on the two most prominent Protestant denominations in the region, the Evangelicals and Disciples of Christ. Recently, however, Chhattisgarhi Catholics have come to focus their work on the *Satnamis,* as the Disciples and Evangelicals did before them. See Jose Madappattu, *Evangelization in a Marginalizing World: With Special Reference to the Marginalised Satnamis in the Diocese of Raipur* (Nettetal: Steyler, 1997).

101. The six denominations involved were the German Reformed, Evangelical, Dutch Reformed, Lutheran, German Presbyterian, and Moravian Brethren. The Society was later taken over by the Evangelical Synod of North America, which merged with the Reformed Church in 1934. Later the merged denominations joined the Congregational Christian Churches of the U.S. to become the United Church of Christ. Seybold, *God's Guiding Hand,* p. 6.

102. Seybold, *God's Guiding Hand,* pp. 13-17.

and advised by some English friends, Lohr started a school for *Satnamis* in an effort to nurture leadership for the church he hoped would develop. On the occasion of the annual *Satnami guru pūjā* and pilgrimage, held during the Hindu festival of *daśahrā*, Lohr traveled to Bhandar, headquarters of the Satnampanth. He reported:

> As I approached the village, I saw a great mass of people milling about and making their way toward me. Soon they had completely surrounded me. I tried to address them, but found this to be impossible. Then in the midst of this crowd of from three to four thousand people, I saw the Chief Priest coming toward me. Like all the rest of the men he wore only a loin cloth and his body was dripping with sour milk, which had been poured over him by his followers.[103] When we reached his residence he had me sit next to him, and after some semblance of order had been achieved with the help of considerable clubbing and beating, I was able to speak to this great mass. I explained to them that they really had no right to call themselves Satnamis, as they did not know the 'True Name' given to men that they might be saved, the name of Jesus Christ. For four long hours I continued speaking, then sat down, weary and exhausted. The Chief Priest himself now served me some refreshments of which I was in dire need. The next morning the crowd assembled once more and I was able to speak to them again.[104]

Afterwards, the *Satnamis* stroked Lohr's beard, a gesture the missionary interpreted to be a sign of their pleasure and interest in his message.

There are a variety of ways to interpret Lohr's reception in Raipur and Bhandar. Lohr appears to have perceived the *Satnamis'* reception as a sign that they believed his message and were ready for conversion. Missionaries writing later and viewing the encounter in the less roseate light of experience interpreted the friendly Bhandar reception as a calculated response by *Satnamis* who desperately desired social uplift (and believed Lohr might be a sympathetic white patron). In any case, the story took on mythic proportions among Evangelical missionaries, who retold, reworked, and embellished it for many subsequent generations.[105]

---

103. Sour milk is often poured over images of Indian gods to "cool" their potentially destructive powers and make them approachable.

104. From Lohr's unpublished autobiography, quoted in Seybold, *God's Guiding Hand*, p. 19.

105. H. A. Feierabend, for instance, inflated the number of *Satnamis* in the crowd to 10,000. See Herman Hans Feierabend, *Life of a Jungle Missionary: Herman August*

It is uncertain how the *Satnamis* themselves understood Lohr's visit. Was their stroking of Lohr's beard a sign of pleasure, or simple curiosity about the texture of foreign hair? Was the offer of refreshments from the guru an anointing, a sign of friendship to a foreign guest, or an attempt to manage the disruption caused by Lohr's arrival? Did the guru *himself* serve Lohr refreshments — the text is ambiguous — or did he have someone else do it (a significantly different gesture)?

It is likely that there were those in the crowd who were genuinely interested in Lohr's religion, which, after all, bore similarities to their own. But it is equally likely that much of the enthusiasm for Lohr's visit was a simple function of its rarity. If the guru ever considered Lohr's message to have been "true," a few moments of sober reflection would have convinced him that if he wished to retain his perquisites as guru, he could not endorse the foreigner's message. Indeed, after this reception the *panth's* attitude towards Lohr cooled significantly.

Colonel Balmain, who was "burdened with the spiritual destitution of the Chamars, that of the Satnami sect in particular,"[106] soon facilitated and helped finance Lohr's purchase of a tract of land north of Raipur, just off the Raipur-Bilaspur road. The land, which locals referred to as "The Tiger Hole," was in a forested area infested by wild animals. One of the tigers for which the area was known would eventually kill Lohr's son. On receiving official ownership papers for the land in 1870, Lohr named it Bishrampur (City of Rest). In the meantime, Lohr had also purchased the village of Ganeshpur, which adjoined the property. Lohr himself became *malguzar* of the two villages, which means that within them he had proprietary rights over the distribution and use of land, and a responsibility to determine and collect taxes.

At Christmas in 1868, Lohr held a service in Bishrampur which British officials and as many as one thousand *Satnamis* attended. But the period of goodwill ended abruptly the next week when Lohr conducted his first three baptisms. During the ceremony, Lohr asked the *Satnami* converts to remove their *kanthīs*.[107] As a result, all thirty-five of Lohr's *Satnami* students, who presumably were considering becoming Christian, threatened to abandon the school, which was now being held in Bishrampur, if they too would be asked

---

Feierabend (U.S.A.: n.p., 1999), p. 45. For another discussion of this encounter, see Saurabh Dube, *Stitches on Time: Colonial Textures and Postcolonial Tangles* (Durham, NC: Duke University Press, 2004), pp. 36-37.

106. Edith Moulton Melick, *The Evangelical Synod in India* (St. Louis: Eden Publishing House, 1930), p. 49.

107. Dube argues, mistakenly I believe, that the converts were asked to remove their sacred *threads (janeū)*. See Dube, *Untouchable Pasts*, p. 72.

to give up their sacred necklace. Lohr refused to budge, and they made good on their promise, though twenty-two returned later in the day.[108] Lohr reported six months later, however, that the matter was still unsettled and prevented him from baptizing any others.[109]

The incident underscores the fact that there were between Lohr and the *Satnamis* disparate understandings of the nature of Christianity.[110] There is no question that Lohr and others — for the same confusion would later plague the Disciples of Christ missionaries — understood Christianity to be a religious tradition entirely distinct from Hinduism. Yet they tried strenuously to forge connections with *Satnami* and Hindu modes of thought. They understood these adaptations as superficial adjustments, mere marketing strategies. But the adaptations were effective to the extent that, at least at first, *Satnamis* understood Christianity to be a *panth*, a school of thought or way of spiritual praxis that could be investigated and explored without compromising their connection to the *Satnami* community.[111]

As such they welcomed its presence, particularly since association with it appeared to have certain social and economic advantages in the colonial context. Missionary reports, letters, and books are saturated with stories about *Satnamis* who liked to listen to missionaries, attended church, read the Bible, and spoke lovingly of Christ but yet who displayed no interest in baptism.[112] Missionaries generally interpreted this reticence as a sign that *Satnamis* were unwilling to give up their "profligate ways" such as polygamy and adultery.[113]

---

108. Oscar Lohr, "Von Bisrampoor (1)," *Der deutsche Missionsfreund* 4, no. 5 (1869): 1.

109. Oscar Lohr, "Von Bisrampoor (2)," *Der deutsche Missionsfreund* 4, no. 6 (1869): 1.

110. As discussed above, the English word "religion" resists translation into Indian languages. In different contexts one might use the Hindi words *qaum* (a word of Arabic origin which, in some areas, signifies a large religious community like Christianity or Islam), *dharm* (which comprises the customs, mores, and social responsibilities of a community), and *panth* (a spiritual lineage, or an informal community of like-minded sojourners). See Juergensmeyer, *Social Vision*, pp. 2, 87. There are a variety of other words that are roughly synonymous with *panth* and connote different aspects of the English word "sect": *mat* (akin to "school of thought"), *marg* (path or way), and *sampradāy* (an established system of teaching such as Vaishnava or Shaiva). For more on these terms, see M. S. A. Rao, "Religion, Sect and Social Transformation: Some Reflections on Max Weber's Contributions to Hinduism and Buddhism," in *Recent Researches on Max Weber's Studies of Hinduism*, ed. Detlef Kantowsky (London: Weltforum, 1986), p. 194.

111. Interestingly, there is still some disagreement among *Satnamis* over whether Ghasidas's movement itself is a *dharm* or a *panth*.

112. For one typical account, see H. A. Feierabend's "Annual Report, 1935-36," AES 82-13a Pr91, Annual Reports, no. 20, 1935.

113. Donald A. McGavran, *The Satnami Story: A Thrilling Drama of Religious Change* (Pasadena: William Carey Library, 1990), p. 21.

There is some evidence that Christian moral standards were an obstacle to *Satnamis* otherwise interested in joining the community, but the more important factor appears to have been that baptism entailed a dislocating social and economic ostracism, a loss of belonging, security, and identity tantamount to social death.

It is for this reason that when Lohr deprived his first converts of their *kanṭhīs*, a symbol of *Satnami* identity, he inadvertently provoked such an intense backlash. Until that moment, or so it appears, the *Satnamis* had considered Christianity a *panth*, that is, as a way of thinking and acting that complemented, rather than required the rejection of, their *Satnami* beliefs and practices. Moreover, joining this Christian *panth* would have granted *Satnamis* access to certain social and economic advantages while not disrupting their social lives.[114] Little is known of the content of Lohr's early evangelistic messages, but it is clear from his own accounts that he portrayed Jesus as the Satnam of which Ghasidas had spoken.[115] It is therefore not surprising that *Satnamis* may have initially understood Christianity in this way.

The Evangelical mission continued to grow slowly through the rest of the nineteenth century; Lohr and other missionaries founded schools, orphanages, hospitals, and a printing press, and brought most converts into the spatial and economic orbit of the mission compound. In 1871 a mission was opened in Raipur, and then others in Bethelpur (1886, a Christian town that is now called Baitalpur), Parsabhader (1893), Mahasamund (1907), and Tilda (1929). Devastating famines at the end of the century greatly increased the frequency of conversion (and also reversion). The Christian community grew beyond these mission centers, and soon Indians were moving into leadership positions. Simon Ramnath Bajpai became the first Indian to be ordained in the region (in 1920), and others followed. Few of the early Indian leaders, however, were Chhattisgarhis, and fewer still *Satnamis*.

In 1874, Disciples of Christ women formed the Christian Woman's Board of Missions (CWBM). A year later the denomination also began mission work under the Foreign Christian Missionary Society (FCMS). In 1882, the two boards agreed to begin a mission in Asia, and by the end of the year two families from the FCMS and four single women from the CWBM set up camp at Harda, 416 miles northeast of Mumbai (Bombay) in what is now

114. For a discussion of a similar set of divergent opinions regarding the nature of Christianity among *Chamars* in Delhi, see John C. B. Webster, "Missionary Strategy and the Development of the Christian Community: Delhi, 1859-1884," in *Popular Christianity in India: Riting between the Lines*, ed. Selva Raj and Corinne Dempsey (Albany: State University of New York Press, 2002), p. 224.

115. Oscar Lohr, "Beginning of Work: Bisrampur," undated, AES 83-3 Bis54.

Madhya Pradesh.[116] In 1885, the mission expanded into the Chhattisgarh region with a station at Bilaspur. The Bilaspur mission did not explicitly target the *Satnamis*, yet many of the mission's first converts came from the community. In 1886, hoping to have more contact with the caste, the Disciples established a mission in Mungeli, a town thirty-one miles west of Bilaspur around which a high proportion of the population was *Satnami*.

Already in 1885, a resident of Bilaspur named Bhagwani Satnami had become the first convert, and a year later, Hira Lal, a *Satnami* who would eventually become a famous Christian doctor, joined the Christian community in Mungeli. As on the Evangelical mission field, the amicable relationship between Disciples missionaries and *Satnamis* was disrupted when it became clear that the missionaries expected converts to renounce certain of their *Satnami* beliefs, practices, and folkways.

The Disciples mission in Chhattisgarh continued to produce converts to Christianity, especially in the period after the famines of the 1890s. Accordingly, the Disciples extended their schools, orphanages, leper asylums, and hospitals into more and more villages. In 1926, the Disciples opened a mission at Takhatpur, midway between Bilaspur and Mungeli, in another region of *Satnami* predominance. Though there was never anything resembling a mass movement among *Satnamis*, Disciples missionaries considered the *Satnami* field so promising that in 1916 they closed down missions in other areas in order to focus more of their resources on the regions of *Satnami* concentration.

One can trace the ebb and flow of the *Satnami*-Christian community only with great difficulty. The primary problem is that the mission agencies generally reported statistics for the entire mission and both the Disciples and Evangelicals had mission stations outside of these areas where *Satnamis* predominated. Even when the statistics given do speak of specific stations or villages, they usually do not distinguish between *Satnami* and non-*Satnami* members or converts. To understand the patterns of conversion, non-conversion, and reversion we must therefore first analyze general trends pertaining to the entire region, a particular region or a single village, and then attempt to determine to what extent those general trends held true for the *Satnami* community.

The Christian community in Chhattisgarh grew slowly at first. For the first twenty years (1868-1888), Indians joined the Evangelical Church in small groups, never more than forty-five in a year. The same can be said for the Disciples, after their arrival in 1885. The number of converts around the Evangelical Bishrampur station remained unremarkable until the 1890s (see Figure 1

116. Homer P. Gamboe, "The Missionary Work of the Disciples of Christ in India and Its Development" (B.Div. thesis, the College of the Bible, 1918), pp. 1-2.

in the Appendix), the single most significant decade in the history of Christianity in Chhattisgarh.

In the 1890s, Chhattisgarh suffered a series of ravaging famines, impoverishing tens of thousands of people. The first severe famine came in 1896-97 and hit Uttar Pradesh, large parts of the Punjab, and the Central Provinces. Streams and wells dried up and brackish waters became contaminated, fueling an opportunistic cholera epidemic. The Bubonic Plague, which had begun in Bombay, also made an appearance. Mothers wandered the countryside desperately offering their children for sale; orphaned children straggled about in search of food. The dead lay about on the roads, and the living were too weak or fearful to bury them. A second famine, more severe than the first, struck the region between 1898 and 1899. But the government was more prepared for this second disaster, and though still deadly, it claimed relatively fewer victims.

The famines significantly and permanently altered the nature of mission work in Chhattisgarh. The British government funneled large amounts of money and grain to mission workers with which they were to feed and employ famine victims in useful work. During the first famine, Evangelical missionaries were feeding more than two thousand people daily in the Bishrampur area, over one thousand in Parsabhader, and around six thousand in Raipur.[117] Out of desperation and gratitude, Chhattisgarhis became Christian in droves. The missions established orphanages that were immediately filled to capacity (by 1900, there were well over six hundred parentless children under the care of Evangelical and Disciples missionaries).

Despite the fact that the missionaries had been wary of baptizing "rice Christians," many of those who became Christian during the famines reverted to their previous faiths afterwards. In 1901 alone, the Evangelicals lost 429 members, and from 1903 to 1908 the community declined from nearly five thousand to 3,160 communicants.[118] Census figures show that the entire Christian community in Chhattisgarh declined in that decade, though in the next three decades Christian growth outpaced that of every other major community (see Figures 2 and 3 in the Appendix). The post-1911 increase was partly due to the large number of famine orphans who came of age in that period and asked for baptism. The decennial censuses show the following figures for the Christian community in all of Chhattisgarh: 6,392 (1901), 8,077 (1911), 11,544 (1921), 15,336 (1931), 20,693 (1941), and 44,695 (1951).

Estimates regarding the proportion of these Christians who could trace

---

117. Seybold, *God's Guiding Hand,* pp. 41, 43.
118. Seybold, *God's Guiding Hand,* p. 46.

their ancestry to *Satnami* ancestors range from 75 to 95 percent. The figures vary, of course, from region to region. A 1943 study indicates that the highest proportion of *Satnami*-Christians on the Evangelical mission field was in the vicinity of Baitalpur (88 percent), followed by Bishrampur (85 percent), Parsabhader (82 percent), and Bhatapara (80 percent).[119] In 1939, a Disciples of Christ missionary working in Mungeli declared that around 95 percent of the area's Christians were *Satnami*-Christians.[120] H. C. Saum, who worked in Takhatpur, Mungeli, and Bilaspur from 1905 to 1940, claimed that during his tenure 90 percent of converts in the region had been *Satnamis*.[121] Figures from the late 1930s suggest that approximately three to four thousand *Satnamis* had converted to Christianity in all of Chhattisgarh since 1868, and that with their children and grandchildren, they numbered fifteen thousand.[122]

There is a modicum of uncertainty in these figures because it is unknown whether the missionaries included *Chamars* who had not become followers of Ghasidas when speaking of "*Satnamis*." And whereas in the 1870s and '80s a good number of *Chamars* had not yet become followers of Ghasidas, by 1901 roughly 73 percent of Chhattisgarhi *Chamars* returned their "religion" in the Census as "*Satnami*."[123] By the 1930s and '40s nearly all *Chamars* were calling themselves *Satnamis* (which had become accepted as a *caste* name), whether or not they possessed any substantial knowledge about the *panth*. In any case, I am inclined to believe that in the rectangular region that is the focus of my study, the percentage of Christians of *Satnami* ancestry was around 85 to 90 percent, with most of those having been associated as well with the Satnam-panth.

The percentage had not always been that high. Though Lohr's first three converts were *Satnamis,* the next group of four included a *brahman* and a *Kurmi.* Throughout the first few years roughly 60 percent of the converts had been *Satnamis.*[124] But as the number of *Satnamis* who became Christian in-

119. M. P. Davis, "A Study of Christians [*sic*] Descendants from Chamars and Satnamis," 1943, AES 80-1 Sat8.

120. Donald A. McGavran, "So He Went and Told His Brethren," *World Call,* March 1939, p. 27.

121. H. C. Saum to "Dear Friends," undated, in HCS, box 4 of 4 (folder: Satnami Mss.).

122. McGavran, *Satnami Story,* p. 160. See also "Minutes of the Satnami Evangelization Council, October 15, 1938, at Bishrampur," AES 80-1 Sat8.

123. This statistic assumes that only a negligible number of *Satnamis* were from castes other than *Chamar.* In the Census, 471,566 people returned their caste as *Chamar* in the Chhattisgarh division of the Central Provinces; 343,468 people returned their "religion" as *Satnami.* India Census Commissioner, *Census, 1901.*

124. Bishrampur Baptismal Registry, AES 83-1a Bap22, and "Second Annual Report of the Chutteesgurh Mission, 1870-71," AES 82-13a Pr91, 1870-83 (Annual Reports).

creased, the perception grew among Hindus more generally that to become Christian was to affiliate with *Satnamis* (and thus, in essence, to become a *Satnami*). Because of the *Satnami* association with ritual pollution, as the proportion of *Satnami*-Christians grew, the percentage of non-*Satnami* converts declined. In 1954, for example, an Indian Christian leader working near Takhatpur said that 98 percent of the sixty people who had converted in that area in the four previous years had been *Satnami*.[125]

Both mission societies experienced an appreciable lull in conversions in the first decades of the twentieth century, and from 1901 to 1911 the *Satnami* community actually grew at a faster rate than Christianity (see Figures 2-4 in the Appendix). If the Christian community at Bishrampur is any indication, there was little growth in *Satnami* areas until the mid-1930s (see Figure 5 in the Appendix), perhaps due to the promise of political options for social advancement discussed above.[126]

In the mid-1930s, *Satnami* conversions to Christianity began again to rise, due in part to a new, focused attempt by both missions to evangelize the *Satnamis* according to the findings of Methodist mission theorist J. Waskom Pickett's mass movement research, and the perfervid conviction of Disciples' missionary Donald McGavran that the best way to induce a mass movement into Christianity was to encourage the conversion of an entire community (or in this case a caste) *en masse*, rather than focusing on individuals or single families.[127] No mass movement came, but there were signs that certain *Satnami* groups did consider it an option. Already in 1917, the leaders of as many as fifty thousand Chungia[128] *Satnamis* met near Mungeli to discuss becoming Christian as a group, but they were prevailed upon by the local police authorities to remain within the fold of Hinduism. Throughout the 1930s and '40s there was

125. Sita Ram Goel, ed., *Vindicated by Time: The Niyogi Committee Report on Christian Missionary Activities (1956)* (New Delhi: Voice of India, 1998), p. II.A.76.

126. Bishrampur, however, may not be representative, as the community there was well established much earlier, and much of its growth was the result of Christian children joining the church when they came of age.

127. See J. W. Pickett, *Christian Mass Movements in India* (New York: Abingdon Press, 1933); and J. W. Pickett, *Church Growth and Group Conversion* (Lucknow: Lucknow Publishing House, 1956). After returning to America, McGavran would develop this conviction into a controversial theory of missions and the "Church Growth Movement." See Donald A. McGavran, *The Bridges of God* (New York: Friendship Press, 1955); and Donald A. McGavran, *How Churches Grow* (New York: Friendship Press, 1959).

128. The Chungias had broken away from the main *Satnami* faction in the 1860s because of their desire to smoke *chūngīs* (village leaf-pipes), and their argument that Ghasidas received a subsequent revelation rescinding his prohibition against the use of tobacco.

significant interest in Christianity among the *Satnamis* of Mungeli and Takhatpur. Conversions did increase slightly in that period, though many of the missionaries at the time seemed convinced that the new political opportunities available to *Satnamis* would prevent them from ever risking social ostracism and entering the Christian community in large numbers.[129] It seems to be the case that until the 1920s a not insignificant number of Chhattisgarhis saw Christianity as an attractive option. But in light of the successes of the national-ist movement and its progressively more explicit criticism of Christianity and Christian missions, Chhattisgarhis came to perceive Christianity as part of the problem, the faith of "foreigners" and British loyalists.

By 1945, there were 3,669 baptized Christians associated with the Disciples' mission, a thousand of them in the area just around Takhatpur.[130] At the same time there were 4,822 communicants within the Evangelical mission. But only 1,435 of these were in the four areas of highest *Satnami* concentration (listed above).[131] It is evident from these figures that there was never anything resem-bling a "mass movement" to Christianity from among the *Satnami* commu-nity. By 1931, for example, only around 2.5 percent of *Satnamis* had become Christian (in Bilaspur the figure was around 1.3 percent).[132]

As indicated earlier, the historical focus of this study is the period between 1868 and 1947, though the conclusion ranges beyond 1947 to the present day. The justification for beginning in 1868 is obvious enough, as this date marks the arrival of the first missionaries in the region. On 15 August 1947, India achieved its independence from Britain. Independence brought with it a range of social, cultural, and political changes, and transformed the nature of the Indian Christian community's search for a meaningful and contextually appropriate communal identity.

In the period before Independence, the Indian Christian community devel-oped under the watchful gaze of foreign missionaries. These missionaries con-

---

129. One piece of legislation in particular, the Government of India (Scheduled Castes) Order of 1936, defined Christians out of the Scheduled Castes and paved the way for them to be denied reservations and other privileges enjoyed by the Scheduled Castes.

130. Nelle Grant Alexander, *Disciples of Christ in India* (Indianapolis: United Christian Missionary Society, 1946), p. 38.

131. "Statistical Report, 1944-45," AES 82-15 St2.

132. These figures assume that 85 percent of Christians in Raipur and Bilaspur districts were of *Satnami* origin or ancestry. As discussed above, the exact percentage is unknown, so the figures should be taken as an estimate. In Raipur district there were, in 1931, 174,528 people who returned their religion as *Satnami*. In Bilaspur the number was 143,928. The number of Christians in Raipur and Bilaspur, respectively, was 5,216 and 2,174. W. H. Shoobert, *Census of India, 1931*, vol. 12: *Central Provinces and Berar (Part 2-Tables)* (Nagpur: Government Printing, C.P., 1933).

trolled, for the most part, mission institutions, appointments, and budgets. Moreover, in places like Chhattisgarh, where there had been no major "mass" movements into Christianity, the lives of Indian Christians revolved around the central mission stations and institutions. Because of this, missionaries were very much a part of the development of the local Christian consciousness.

Already before Independence, however, and especially in the 1930s and '40s, this situation had begun to shift. Prompted by the intuition that they might not be welcome in an independent India and spurred on, at times, by Indian Christians whose desire for independence extended also to ecclesiastical affairs, mission societies began to devolve responsibilities on Indian leaders.[133] By all accounts, this process of devolution — the "decolonization" of missions — proceeded rather slowly until 1947, when India itself became an independent nation. Within several years, the Government of India began delaying and, in some cases, denying visas for foreign missionaries. The transfer of power from foreign to Indian Christians thus became more urgent, and missionary numbers began to dwindle along with their influence. As the Indian Christian community developed in the post-Independence era, therefore, the relative importance of foreign and national conversation partners shifted in favor of the latter.

As the desire for political independence grew in India, so too did Indian Christians' desire for ecclesiastical independence in Chhattisgarh. The Evangelical and Disciples missionaries responded to this pressure — and also acted upon their own desire to "indigenize" the church — by progressively transferring authority to Indian leaders. In 1925, Evangelicals organized the India Mission District (IMD) of the Evangelical Synod of North America, which merged the leadership of the mission and the church. Not everyone was pleased with this arrangement, and in the 1930s, there was a brief schism among Evangelical Christian Indians in Bishrampur.[134] But plans to transfer powers from the mission society to Indian church leaders continued. In 1936, leaders of the IMD decided to join the United Church of North India (UCNI), which had been formed in 1924.[135] In 1938, they were accepted into

133. George Thomas, *Christian Indians and Indian Nationalism 1885-1959* (Frankfurt: Peter Lang, 1979), p. 185.

134. The immediate provocation appears to have been the India Mission District's defense of Boas Purti, whom members of the schismatic community considered an adulterer. See "Minutes of the Special Meeting of Immanuel Mandli, Held at Ganeshpur Church on the 10th of August, 1933," AES 83-3 Bis54. See also my discussion of the schism in Chapter 3.

135. By joining the UCNI, the Evangelicals joined the United Church of Canada, the Presbyterian Churches of Canada, England, Ireland, New Zealand, and Wales, the Church

the union, and the IMD became the Chhattisgarh and Orissa Church Council (COCC) of the Synod of Gujarat, Rajasthan, and Mid-India of the UCNI. In 1947, Indians were given responsibilities for evangelism, and in 1954, all authority was transferred to Indian leaders. At the same time, the mission's properties were transferred to the COCC.[136] The trajectory of Disciples of Christ devolution followed a similar pattern, though the Disciples churches in Chhattisgarh never joined the UCNI. In 1970 they did, however, join with member denominations of the UCNI and several other denominations in North India to form the Church of North India.

By 1868, all the pieces were in place for an intense and sustained intercultural and interreligious encounter in Chhattisgarh. Slowly, a small but significant community emerged that embodied that encounter: the *Satnami*-Christians. In the next chapter I analyze the reasons — to the extent that they can be known — that Chhattisgarh's *Satnamis* became (or did not become) Christian.

---

of Scotland, the London Missionary Society, the Congregational Churches of America, and the Moravian Church. For more, see Seybold, *God's Guiding Hand,* p. 102.

136. Seybold, *God's Guiding Hand,* pp. 102-9.

CHAPTER 2

Factors in Becoming
(or Not Becoming) Christian

As a social phenomenon religion is, to use Anthony Giddens's phrase, "dually constructed" — emerging both from the ideas and intentions of individuals and from the institutions and circumstances that constrain and routinize the world in which people act, often outside their full awareness.

Robert Hefner, "World Building
and the Rationality of Conversion"

. . . when [Marshall] Sahlins protests that local peoples are not "passive objects of their own history," it should be evident that this is not the equivalent to claiming that they are its "authors."

Talal Asad, *Genealogies of Religion*

Post-colonial scholars bear a certain antipathy towards conversion that sometimes borders on outright hostility. Many of them share with anthropologists of an earlier era a romantic nostalgia for the *status quo ante* and view Christianity as a disruption (never mind that the *status quo* for which these scholars pine had been established by a series of previous disruptions). In addition, many citizens of post-colonial countries, India foremost among them, consider conversion from majority to minority faiths tantamount to sedition.[1]

---

1. I do not wish to downplay the degree to which the arrival of missionaries, and their explicit attempts to draw people from one religion to another, represents a cultural pertur-

The sentiment is particularly strong with regard to converts to Christianity, who come to be seen as collaborators with the forces either of colonization or — after Independence — globalization. Conversion to Christianity is therefore a rather controversial matter, both in academic discussion and in the world at large.

One aspect of the controversy within academic circles involves the extent to which colonial subjects were *agents* of their own history. Post-colonial historians have demonstrated a decided preference for the rebels, the revolutionaries, for those who took their fate into their own hands and resisted the hegemony of indigenous and foreign powers. Conversion to Christianity, on the other hand, is seen as a concession, a passive admission of defeat. Talal Asad maintains that this predilection to speak of colonial subjects as "agents" is a reflection of modern, western notions about what is worthwhile behavior (e.g., active, self-guided, autonomous, individual, etc.), and thus usually says more about western scholars than the subjects of their enquiry. In addition to projecting modern concerns into earlier histories, describing colonial subjects as "agents" runs the risk of obscuring the ways in which structures of colonial power conditioned and circumscribed action.[2]

All action takes place in the context of social and cultural arrangements that make certain behaviors possible or likely and others impossible or unlikely. No one is fully and without qualification a "free" agent. Neither, however, is a person's or a community's behavior fully determined by their sociocultural circumstances. *Powergame,* a painting by the Icelandic artist, Eyjólfur Einarsson, portrays a male figure on a verdant landscape, attached by strings like a marionette to a puppeteer's handle hovering in a purple-gray sky with ominous dark clouds approaching. The painting might be an expression of the sentiment that fate and human behavior are determined by an unseen hand, by circumstances out of one's control, but for the fact that the figure is fiercely pulling on the strings, as if flying the handle like a kite.[3] The social

---

bation. Quoting from the Book of Wisdom (2:14), and drawing on Kenelm Burridge's *In the Way: A Study of Christian Missionary Endeavors,* Richard F. Young writes that in merely existing, missionaries can disturb a culture's equilibrium: "Before us he stands, a reproof to 'our way of thinking.'" Richard Fox Young, "Some Hindu Perspectives on Christian Missionaries in the Indic World of the Mid Nineteenth Century," in *Christians, Cultural Interactions, and India's Religious Traditions,* ed. Judith M. Brown and Robert Eric Frykenberg (Grand Rapids: Eerdmans, 2002), p. 40.

2. Talal Asad, "Comments on Conversion," in *Conversion to Modernities: The Globalization of Christianity,* ed. Peter van der Veer (New York: Routledge, 1996), p. 271.

3. Eyjólfur Einarsson, *Valdabarátta (Powergame),* Oil on canvas, 150 x 150 cm., 2002 (whereabouts unknown). There is an interesting parallel here to one of the poems of the

and economic ground of the *Satnamis* in the late nineteenth and early twentieth centuries was shifting according to seismic forces largely out of their control. These forces delimited the range of possible and likely *Satnami* behavior. They did not, however, determine that behavior. *Satnamis* attempted in a variety of ways to address their circumstances effectively and meaningfully. They were, as it were, pulling on their marionette strings. Those who became Christian embodied one option, but there were others. Were they "free" agents? Certainly not in any absolute sense. But they did act in their own interests according to the exigencies of the time. In Chhattisgarh as in other places, religion is therefore, as Giddens put it, "dually constructed."[4]

I have spoken here of conversion as a "choice," but it must immediately be added that conversion often does not entail the conscious weighing of and eventual decision between alternatives. There are two primary sociological interpretations of the social determinants of "ideology" (and accordingly of religious dogma): the "interest" theory and the "strain" theory.[5] According to the interest theory, developed extensively by Marxist theorists, ideology is a cover for the material interests of those creating or embracing it. Seen in this light, conversion — the shift from one "ideology" to another — would satisfy certain material or political desires. Strain theorists, on the other hand, maintain that ideology is a response to a situation of social dysfunctionality. According to this view, conversion would represent an attempt to establish, or reestablish, equilibrium in a situation of disequilibrium. To use Geertzian terminology, according to the strain theory conversion is an attempt to reestablish harmony between the world as lived and the world as imagined.[6] The interest theory involves the satisfaction of desires, the strain theory the solving of problems. The two interpretations are of course not mutually exclusive, because a perceived "strain" may be nothing more than an impediment in the pursuit of interests.

Though I prefer the strain theory, it shares with the interest theory a basic

---

great Maharashtrian Christian poet, Narayan Vaman Tilak, who expresses frustration against missionary paternalism in his poem, *Abhang* (no. 160): "We dance as puppets while you hold the strings; / How long shall this buffoonery endure?" Quoted in Gauri Viswanathan, *Outside the Fold: Conversion, Modernity, and Belief* (Princeton: Princeton University Press, 1998), p. 40.

4. On this topic, see also Peter Berger, *The Sacred Canopy: Elements of a Sociological Theory of Religion* (Garden City, NY: Doubleday, 1967), pp. 3-4.

5. Clifford Geertz, *The Interpretation of Cultures* (New York: Basic Books, 1973), p. 201. See also Sherry Ortner, "Theory in Anthropology since the Sixties," *Comparative Studies in Society and History* 26, no. 1 (1984): 151-52.

6. Geertz, *Interpretation of Cultures*, p. 112.

weakness: Both imply that human action is driven at every moment by rational calculation regarding the perception of problems and their solution (strain theory) or the identification of material goals and their attainment (interest theory). At least since the time of Weber, the pitfalls of such a purely "intellectualist" interpretation of human behavior have been obvious.[7] The "interiorist" position popularized by William James, which sees religion and religious change as something interior, psychological, and private, is similarly inadequate, because it fails to take into account the social context of religious expression.[8]

My own position, which one might call "primordialist," is that conversion does indeed represent the pursuit of interests and a response to strain, but interests and strains *felt* more often than intellectually recognized, intuited more frequently than rationally grasped. Accordingly, the choice to shift allegiance from one religion to another is informed not by the conscious and cynical weighing of pros and cons, but rather by a certain pre-cognitive insight. If in fact a person does intellectually "choose" to change from one religion to another, the choice renders the new religion ultimately less believable, less persuasive. For a religion that is *chosen* lacks the taken-for-granted, unquestionable authority of a religion by which one has *been chosen*, to which one *submits*.[9]

Decisions to move from one religion to another, if they are more than a ruse, most frequently arise not from ratiocination but from certain not-fully-articulated desires. Though religious conversion may be, for some, a logical step in the pursuit of interests — material or ideal — the transforma-

---

7. Weber hypothesized four types of action: instrumental (the logical pursuit of ends and means), value-rational (in which either the end or means — or both — were determined by values), traditional (in which behavior followed stereotyped patterns), and affectual (determined by passionate emotional states). Max Weber, *Economy and Society,* ed. Guenther Roth and Claus Wittich (Berkeley: University of California Press, 1978), pp. 24-25. See also Robert W. Hefner, "Of Faith and Commitment: Christian Conversion in Muslim Java," in *Conversion to Christianity: Historical and Anthropological Perspectives on a Great Transformation,* ed. Robert W. Hefner (Berkeley: University of California Press, 1993), p. 119.

8. William James, *The Varieties of Religious Experience* (New York: Mentor Books, 1958). Another form of the interiorist argument posits a radical "change of heart" under "divine" inspiration (e.g., by the Holy Spirit). This understanding of conversion finds its roots in the Christian tradition, and even the New Testament, which influenced James's work. Whether such transempirical inspiration is possible must, unfortunately, be a question bracketed in this study (as it was in James's), for it is not historically or scientifically investigable.

9. Cf. Peter Berger, *The Heretical Imperative: Contemporary Possibilities of Religious Affirmation* (Garden City, NY: Anchor Press/Doubleday, 1980), p. 26.

tion will not become believable to the convert unless the "decision" arises from the pre-rational depths of his or her spirit with all the force and believability of an external revelation. It is these desires I call primordial, because they are fundamental, basic. They include such things as a desire for security (though not necessarily great wealth), health, dignity, a meaningful interpretation of life's experiences (good and bad), and a program for appropriate action in the world.

In the context of this study, I take conversion to be a transition from one worldview to another, from one way of life to another, and, almost of necessity, from one community to another.[10] It is a transition symbolized by an event or events, but entailing a longer process of acculturation to new ways of thinking and acting, as well as some degree of "syncretism" or "hybridity." It is a transformation that takes place in the context of social and cultural realities that condition and constrain the range of possible human behaviors.

Though this transformation may in fact diminish or even resolve certain concrete problems or satisfy immediate needs and interests, the convert does not generally consider his or her transition from one religion to another as a cynical gesture but rather as the expression of some deeply felt but only inchoately intuited desire, a desire that finds its roots in sentiments as diverse as desperation and inspiration. At the risk of being accused of not taking converts at their word, I would argue, for instance, that a *Satnami* who admits to converting in order to gain for his or her children an education and yet remains in the community after they have completed that education is not only acting according to self-interest, but expressing a desire to be part of a community where education, even for those who were historically denied access to it, is a *possibility*.[11]

I share Max Weber's great suspicion of uni-causal explanations of history, and particularly of the materialist reduction of religious history. Ideals and

10. This definition relies heavily on that found in Robert Eric Frykenberg, "On the Study of Conversion Movements: A Review Article and a Theoretical Note," *Indian Economic and Social History Review* 17, no. 1 (1980): 129. See also G. A. Oddie, "Old Wine in New Bottles? Kartabhaja (Vaishnava) Converts to Evangelical Christianity in Bengal, 1835-1845," in *Religious Change, Conversion and Culture,* ed. Lynette Olson (Sydney: Sydney Association for Studies in Society and Culture, 1996), p. 3.

11. Their continued involvement in the community, despite, perhaps, initially less-than-exemplary motives, may also reflect the transformative effect of participation in the life of the community. On this, see Hefner, "Of Faith and Commitment." In another context, Buswell argues that involvement in Zen monastic life often remolded the initial motivations of those who joined the community (many of whom did so for purely "materialistic reasons") into more "exemplary" ones. Robert E. Buswell, *The Zen Monastic Experience* (Princeton: Princeton University Press, 1992), p. 76.

values are often hidden away in the crevices of what appears to be purely material activity. This, however, is often overlooked, and just as a seemingly flat surface can seem pockmarked and rugged under a microscope, history, when duly investigated, defies simple explanation. Explanations that attempt to account for the full spectrum of historical causes, factors, and consequences tend to sound unconvincing and contradictory. Despite this, I have sought in this chapter to illuminate a wide range of factors — including material *and* ideal interests — that might have contributed to the growth of Christianity in Chhattisgarh.

Famine, Misfortune, and the Economics of Conversion

The famines of the 1890s were devastating events. The first (1896-97) followed three years of scarcity and inflation.[12] By February 1897, after the rains of 1896 had failed, 7 percent of the population in Raipur District was employed in public relief work as part of an ameliorative work-for-food program. By December, jackals and wild dogs were dragging parts of corpses into villages, and large groups of people abandoned their homes for work in the tea plantations far to the north. Acts of thievery and dacoity increased exponentially, and at least some of the crimes were perpetrated with the expressed purpose of getting into jail, where basic nourishment was assured. Forty-two percent of the region's inhabitants required food from famine kitchens.[13] With mission and government funds, missionaries put thousands to work in exchange for food or a small wage.[14] Though the government was better prepared to counter the effects of the 1899-1900 famine, Chhattisgarhis fared little better struggling through it and the cholera epidemic that accompanied it. There were also other famines throughout the early part of the twentieth century, though none of them were as devastating as those of the 1890s.

Whole families and villages came to the missionaries offering to convert if they would be fed, an offer most missionaries were wise enough to refuse.[15]

---

12. Leta May Brown, *Hira Lal of India: Diamond Precious* (St. Louis: Bethany Press, 1954), p. 148.

13. Martin P. Davis, *Sadhu Hagenstein: A White Man among the Brown* (St. Louis: The Board for Foreign Missions, Evangelical Synod of North America, 1930), pp. 83, 86.

14. Interestingly, some missionaries paid upper-caste workers double wages. See Davis, *Sadhu Hagenstein*, p. 86.

15. Since there were no mass conversion movements among the *Satnamis*, people joined the community in small groups, and conversions generally involved the decision of a (usually male) head of a household. But if the initial decision was made by an individual,

The missionaries generally disbursed what food and employment they had at their disposal to all who came, regardless of their religious affiliation, and emphasized that no one should become Christian thinking they would receive special treatment. Many, however, seemed to believe that their chances for survival would increase if they became Christian. And missionaries, despite their rhetoric of fairness, could not always resist lending special assistance to members of their community. In 1942, for instance, after three successive crop failures, Disciples missionary Donald McGavran wrote, "We have set it as a goal to be reached that 'no Christian who will work shall starve,' and believe that God will provide the resources for giving work to *at least the Christian people.*"[16]

Consequently, many were baptized during the famines. At the time, missionaries interpreted their conversions as acts of gratitude,[17] but it seems just as likely, if not more, that the destruction of wealth and body had brought many to a state of desperation, in which neither pride nor *jāti* loyalty was of any consequence. A Chhattisgarhi proverb says, *"vakt pare bākā to gadhe lā kahe kakā"* (In times of necessity a man will call an ass his uncle).[18] Of the two thousand people baptized by the Evangelical mission during the famines (who were almost all *Satnamis*), roughly six hundred later abandoned the Christian community.[19]

As Chhattisgarhis struggled to make sense of the famines, a variety of divergent and competing interpretations emerged. Some Christians, who despite everything did have an easier time of the famines than others, interpreted the natural disasters as a judgment on those who refused to convert. One unidentified Indian catechist recorded the following exchange at the home of Kali Ram Satnami in Bimcha during another year of minor famine, 1909: "They complained of the scarcity of rain. I explained that God sometimes threatens people for repentance, when there is plenty people do not care for him and when the harvest is disappointing they cry for the rains . . .

---

his family and the families of his younger brothers often followed suit. It must therefore be kept in mind during the following discussion that while there was a range of motivating factors in the conversion of *Satnamis* to Christianity, the great majority of those who became Christian would have been following the decision of a spouse, parent, or elder sibling.

16. Donald A. McGavran, "Evangelism in Central India," *World Call,* February 1942. (Italics added.)

17. For one example, see Brown, *Hira Lal,* p. 155.

18. E. M. Gordon, *Indian Folk Tales: Being Side-Lights on Village Life in Bilaspore, Central Provinces* (London: Elliot Stock, 1909), p. 74.

19. J. W. Pickett, *Church Growth and Group Conversion* (Lucknow: Lucknow Publishing House, 1956), p. 87.

You lavish money at . . . Bhandar [the *Satnami* gaddī] and depend upon them for help, but the Bhandaris are also men, they cannot help you . . ."[20] At the same time, other Christians interpreted them in the opposite direction. A sizeable number of those who had become Christian before the famines left the Christian community, some of them perhaps because they considered the disaster a divine judgment.[21]

The famines flooded existing mission orphanages with malnourished, weak, and diseased children, and missions had to create such institutions where none had existed. The Evangelicals opened up homes for orphans in each of their four main stations in 1897. Hundreds of despairing and despondent children were sheltered by the mission. Not surprisingly, nearly all those who came to the orphanages at a young age eventually became Christian and were, when old enough, married to other Christians.

It cannot be said that these famine orphans *chose* Christianity for material reasons. Powerless and without possession, they had few options other than entering or being entered into an orphanage. Most were not baptized until they were older, but regardless of the reason they eventually entered the Christian community in this more formal way, famine-induced loss — a material reality — was the precipitating factor of their relationship with the mission. The same must be said of the adults who converted during famines. Even when told, as they were by most missionaries, that Christians received no special treatment, some Chhattisgarhis were willing to join the community, hoping that by doing so they might secure for themselves and their families the few extra crumbs per day that could mean the difference between life and death.

In addition to food in a time of famine, there were other material factors that contributed to the appeal of Christianity. For instance, non-Christians perceived Christianity as a guarantor of employment. But whereas non-Christians saw the mission as a provider of jobs — *any* jobs — those who had been Christian for some time seemed to see Christianity as a shelter from difficult and degrading work. For example, *Satnami*-Christians often refused to do work considered polluting, such as the removal of carcasses, work with

20. Entry in diary, unnamed catechist, 11 September 1909, found in the journal of S. J. Scott, Mahasamund catechist, AES 83-5 Di54 #1. For a discussion of how historians should read this and other similar texts, see Saurabh Dube, "Conversion to Translation: Colonial Registers of a Vernacular Christianity," *South Atlantic Quarterly* 101, no. 4 (2002).

21. On a similar situation among South Indian Christians in time of famine, see Jose Kananaikil, *Christians of Scheduled Caste Origin* (New Delhi: Indian Social Institute, 1986), p. 10; and Dick Kooiman, *Conversion and Social Equality in India* (New Delhi: South Asia Publications, 1989), p. 189.

leather and bones, or the cleaning of latrines and village reservoirs. *Satnami-*Christians recalled that as *Satnamis* these tasks had been a symbol of their degradation and, once Christian, they avoided them. As *Satnamis* they had been responsible, for instance, for a disproportionate amount of *begar,* but as Christians they at times refused to work on vital village projects as directed by the missionary-*malguzar,* even when offered payment (under the *begar* system they would have received no compensation).[22] Avoidance of degrading or strenuous work was a mark of wealth and traditional status, and it appears that Christians, especially educated Christians, were appropriating this traditional status symbol as a way of asserting their own social worth.[23] Not only Christians but non-Christians as well perceived Christianity as an escape from menial labor, much to the chagrin of missionaries who, operating under a dissimilar but still religiously informed "work ethic," wished to instill a sense of the nobility of "honest work" among Chhattisgarhi Christians.[24]

Missionaries occasionally helped Chhattisgarhis with debt relief, particularly just before or after they became Christian. The missionaries perceived this aid as a way of helping Christians make a clean break from their past, especially since the immediate effects of conversion were likely to be economically disruptive. As elsewhere, the debt system in village Chhattisgarh was positively crushing. Lenders charged exorbitant interest rates, keeping small-time farmers constantly in debt and on the verge of financial bankruptcy, which, if and when it occurred, would be alleviated with yet another extortionate loan, resulting in virtual bondage.[25]

Missionary aid, however, contributed to the perception that Christians had been enticed from their communities for the sake of help. Indeed, some

22. For example, in the mid-1930s, Christians in Bishrampur refused to help clean the *tālāb* (village reservoir), even though the missionary promised to pay them. *Malguzars* generally expected villagers to periodically clean the *tālāb* in exchange for its sludge (which they used as fertilizer). See William Baur's "Annual Report, 1935-36," AES 82-13a Pr91, Annual Reports, no. 21, 1936.

23. Mary Kingsbury, a Disciples missionary, reported in 1896 that: "Manual labor is considered degrading, particularly by those who have received a little education, even a *very little* education." Mary Kingsbury, "Orphanage Work in India," *Missionary Tidings,* December 1896, p. 191. The problem was particularly acute in the orphanages, which suggests that they did not entirely shelter their wards from outside influences.

24. For instance, "Sadhu" Hagenstein, an Evangelical missionary working in Parsabhader, told villagers, "God never blesses laziness. The mission is no cow to be milked by lazy Indian Christians. He who does not work shall not eat, hence Americans don't want me to feed lazy people." Davis, *Sadhu Hagenstein,* p. 108.

25. For a provocative depiction of rural debt and village resistance, see Mehboob Khan, "Mother India," ed. Wajahat Mirza and S. Ali Raza (Bombay: 1957).

missionaries did seem willing to use the funds at their disposal in this way. Before the important 1917 meeting of Chungia *Satnami* leaders mentioned earlier, for example, Disciples missionary H. C. Saum arranged for a sum of five thousand rupees (quite a large amount at the time) for alleviation of the leaders' debts.[26]

These advantages continued beyond the time of conversion. The Christian community appears to have been able to nurture the ability of its members to cooperate financially. Christians formed common lending institutions and other cooperatives, particularly after the 1930s. Around 1942, Maqbul Masih, an Indian Christian working in the Fosterpur area, asked pastors under his supervision what evidence they saw of "growing love" among Christians in their villages. Most of the answers he received had to do with economic cooperation — banding together to help a poor member replace an ox that had strayed or to purchase utensils for a recently converted family whose possessions had been pillaged during a post-conversion period of persecution.[27] And when times became truly rough, *Satnami*-Christians turned to the missionaries as a safety net. With funds at their disposal from churches at home or the colonial authorities, missionaries were able, for instance, to order the timely construction of a needed building or well as an excuse to employ impecunious and distressed Christians.[28]

There were other factors in the conversion of Chhattisgarhis to Christianity that mixed material and religious interests. For instance, one rather unexpected theme that emerges from an analysis of *Satnami* conversions to Christianity is that a great number of *Satnamis* perceived Christianity as an escape from expensive and inconvenient religious rituals. In fact the trope of Christianity as "freedom" from burdensome rituals is quite strong in written and oral accounts of conversion.[29] As part of what may be called the Protestantiz-

26. The information comes from the prominent *Satnami*-Christian, Hira Lal, who attended the meeting. See Leta May Brown to H. C. Saum, 14 January 1953, HCS, box 1 of 4 (no folder).

27. Donald A. McGavran, "Training Leaders for a New Christian Movement," *World Call*, February 1942.

28. See Homer P. Gamboe, "The Story of a Well," *World Call*, December 1942.

29. For the theme of conversion as escape from expensive rituals among converts to Christianity elsewhere in South and Southeast Asia, see Barbara Boal, *The Konds: Human Sacrifice and Religious Change* (Warminster, Wilts, England: Aris & Phillips, 1982); and C. A. Kammerer, "Custom and Christian Conversion among Akha Highlanders of Burma and Thailand," *American Ethnologist* 17, no. 2 (1990). For a discussion of these authors with reference to the Rabhas in India's Northeast, see Bengt G. Karlsson, *Contested Belonging: An Indigenous People's Struggle for Forest and Identity in Sub-Himalayan Bengal* (Richmond, VA: Curzon, 2000); and Bengt G. Karlsson, "Entering into the Christian Dharma:

ation process, *Satnamis* who converted to Christianity assimilated values of thrift, frugality, and longer-term economic planning.

Satnamis, many of whom admitted that their religious rituals were a financial burden, envied this aspect of Christian practice. After encountering a *Satnami* guru conducting *ramat,* an Evangelical missionary asked a disillusioned *Satnami* what the guru did when he passed through villages. "Nothing," responded the *Satnami,* "but whispers something in our ears and takes our money."[30] Occasionally, the prosperity of the Christian community vis-à-vis its *Satnami* neighbors led to tensions between the two communities. Around 1932 in Parsabhader, village *Satnamis,* who the missionary believed had been "squandering their money on useless caste customs and [had] little cash on hand," boycotted the Christians after a period of two years in which they (the Christians) had bought fifty acres of land from indebted *Satnamis.*[31]

Of *Satnami* religious rituals, the most expensive involved weddings and funerals, both of which required providing meals for a large number of people, sometimes (in the case of weddings) over the course of several or even many days.[32] In addition to expensive funeral meals, *Satnamis* could also expect a post-funereal visit from a *mangan,* a non-*Satnami* medium who visited the aggrieved and asked for a donation or something owned by the deceased in exchange for acting as an intermediary between the living and the dead.[33] Most *Satnamis* were glad to curtail these practices when they became Christian; nevertheless, elaborate weddings remained a sign of status, and the death feast given to caste fellows of the aggrieved — which was considered necessary for aiding the deceased spirit's transition into the next world — did occasionally find its way back into the Christian community, even during the missionary era. M. P. Albrecht reported, in 1938, that "One of the new problems now arising is whether or not to permit death feasts. Among non-

---

Contemporary 'Tribal' Conversions in India," in *Christians, Cultural Interactions, and India's Religious Traditions,* ed. Judith M. Brown and Robert Eric Frykenberg (Grand Rapids: Eerdmans, 2002).

30. Elise Kettler, "The Hindus' Life Giving Water," undated, AES 82-14 Qu2, Kettler, Elise, Quarterly Reports, Articles, Newsletters, 1910-1933.

31. M. P. Davis, "Annual Report, Parsabhader, 1932/33," AES 82-13a Pr91, Annual Reports, no. 18, 1933.

32. In the 1930s, the average *Satnami* wedding cost around one hundred rupees, much of which had to be borrowed at interest upwards of 37 percent; see H. A. Feierabend, "New Opportunities and Difficulties in Evangelistic Work," ca. 1936, AES 82-14 Qu2, Feierabend, H. A., Quarterly Reports, Articles, Newsletters, 1933-1941.

33. See "Mangan System among the Satnamis," undated, probably written by H. C. Saum, HCS, box 4 of 4 (folder: India — History).

Christians this is of course the custom. At the present there is at least one of the larger congregations where it is practised by an influential section of the people."[34]

There were also a variety of smaller religious expenses for the average *Satnami* — gifts to the guru and his *mahants*, fines paid to the same for violations of caste customs, and the fees of *bhandārīs* and their assistants, *santidars*, who were necessary officiants at every village ceremony.[35] In the process of becoming Christian, *Satnamis* rationalized their rituals and celebrations and simplified their ceremonies. Even their *melās* — Christians throughout Chhattisgarh established an annual *melā* at Madku Ghat in 1909 — were simpler and cheaper.[36] They came to see non-Christian ritual obligations as wasteful and vacuous. Christian rituals were cheap, simple, and convenient.[37]

There were certain material factors, no doubt, which encouraged conversions to Christianity, but for many of those who became Christian, the immediate economic effects were disastrous. Most convert families were socially ostracized, cut off from their family and friends, financially boycotted by *jāti*-fellows and other people of their villages, disinherited, and treated harshly by moneylenders who often chose the occasion to call in debts. They were declared traitors and spoilers of their caste. Others suffered an even worse fate, being beaten or abducted by family members, or harassed by extra-*Satnami* organizations such as the Arya Samaj engaged in reconversion (*śuddhi*) campaigns.[38] Still others lost their homes to arson, their crops to vandalism, their few possessions to thievery, and their lives to poison or suspicious illnesses.[39] Though there were plenty of indirect inducements to

34. M. P. Albrecht, "Annual Report, 1938," AES 82-13a Pr91, Annual Reports, no. 23, 1938. M. M. Paul, a pastor working in Mahasamund with the Evangelicals, said that new Christians who discovered they were not allowed to perform death feasts were prone to abandoning the community; see his "Report of the Work at Pithora, Mahasamund for the Year 1938-39," AES 82-13a Pr91, Annual Reports, no. 24, 1939.

35. See the findings of a study researched by Simon Patros, son of *Satnami* converts on the Evangelical mission field, and written by an unnamed missionary: "How Much Do Satnamis Give for Religious Purposes?" ca. 1930, AES 80-1 Sat8.

36. Christians were discouraged from attending Hindu *melās*.

37. This is perhaps not surprising given their association with Protestant missionaries, who generally equated the "excessive" ritualism of Hinduism with that of "Popery."

38. The Arya Samaj was particularly active in the region in the late 1930s. See M. M. Paul, "Yearly Report of Pithora Sub-Station for the Year 1940-41," AES 82-13a Pr91, Annual Reports, no. 26, 1941.

39. See letter from Evangelical missionary Rev. J. Gass to H. C. Saum, 8 July 1935, included with letter from Saum to J. Waskom Pickett, 29 December 1935 (or 1936), HCS, box 1 of 4 (no folder).

Christianity, there is no evidence of any physically forced conversion to Christianity; there is, however, evidence that some were physically coerced to reconvert. However, these forms of direct persecution were generally ephemeral, and so despite the fact that the short-term effects of conversion were unpleasant and difficult, for those who survived, the long-term effects were often quite beneficial.[40]

One of the reasons that becoming Christian generally entailed long-term economic improvement was that converts and their children received education and vocational training from the mission.[41] This training was particularly significant for Christian women, who as trained teachers and nurses were able to secure better-paying jobs than their *Satnami* counterparts. There is evidence that at least some converts became Christian as a way of investing in their future by educating their children. Some, for example, became Christian until their children had received a (mission-subsidized) education and then promptly recanted. And one *Satnami* considering baptism told a Disciples missionary, "WE cannot be uplifted but there is hope for our children."[42]

At least by the beginning of the twentieth century (and probably even earlier), education became a highly valued commodity, and *Satnamis* banked on their relations with Christian leaders in order to secure their share of the resource. The diary of one unidentified Indian (and Evangelical) catechist records the following encounter at the home of Menghu Satnami in Bimcha:

> Having read from the Gospel of Luke about the birth of Christ I explained the need of an incarnation to fulfill the law of God which could not be fully obeyed by man because being born in sin he is naturally weak to satisfy God [sic]. Therefore Christ took the human form not only to satisfy the demands of the law but also to make a propitiation for the sins of the world by offering himself. *Menghu suggested that a school*

---

40. This is especially true in areas without mass movements, as the slow pace of conversion allowed for more intensive treatment of each new Christian. On a mass conversion movement that had little economic effect on those who became Christian, see Dick Kooiman, "Mission, Education and Employment in Travancore (19th Century)," in *Conversion, Competition and Conflict,* ed. Dick Kooiman, Otto van den Muijzenberg, and Peter van der Veer (Amsterdam: Free University Press, 1984), p. 185.

41. Susan Harper, in fact, has argued that the long-term benefits of Christianization in the Dornakal Diocese were more educational than economic, as the educated often moved to urban areas and away from their rural family members. See Susan Billington Harper, "The Dornakal Church on the Cultural Frontier," in *Christians, Cultural Interactions, and India's Religious Traditions,* ed. Judith M. Brown and Robert Eric Frykenberg (Grand Rapids: Eerdmans, 2002).

42. Ann Mullin, "Among the Depressed Classes," *World Call,* February 1937.

should be opened there for the low castes because they are prohibited to be taught along with high castes in Mahasamund School . . .[43]

Whether this report describes a continuous flow of conversation or two separate conversations is difficult to determine, but either way the juxtaposition of evangelical and *Satnami* aims could not be more jarring.

Christian missionaries also helped converts and potential converts by shielding them from extortionist moneylenders, overbearing *malguzars* (especially those of the upper castes), and sometimes the justice system itself. It is a baneful myth that missionaries and the British government worked together towards some sinister common colonial goal. But the missionaries did enjoy a significant degree of power because of their relationship, as mutual foreigners, with British officials, many of whom were also evangelically inclined. That power allowed them to interfere in village politics on behalf of those they favored — to find "justice" (as they interpreted it) for those they desired to help.

This official leverage allowed missionaries to encourage acts of resistance among lower-caste communities that would not have been possible otherwise, at least not without the risk of a dangerous backlash. For example, in the 1930s, around twelve *Satnami* families abandoned the village of Kevta Devri, near Takhatpur, because of a quarrel with its *Satnami malguzar*, the notoriously ill-behaved and difficult Ratiram, who was one of the leaders of the Satnami Mahasabha (for more on Ratiram, see Chapter 6). Ratiram had required what they perceived to be an exorbitant amount of *begar* and their previous attempts to resist had resulted only in vicious beatings, so they left the village in protest. In their absence, Ratiram claimed their fields, destroyed their houses, and began constructing his own buildings. Around 1938, two of the families sought out the Disciples missionary, Donald McGavran, and became Christian. One of the families was that of Awadh Masih (formerly Awadh Ram), whose house Ratiram had destroyed. McGavran organized a group of forty people who marched towards the village from Takhatpur, camped on the bank of a nearby river, and then under cover of darkness crossed it and surreptitiously infiltrated the village and began rebuilding Masih's house. Ratiram was out of the village at the time, but when he returned he took the matter to the sub-inspector of police, who took Ratiram's view of the matter. McGavran intervened again, and used his influence to have the sub-inspector transferred elsewhere, and then threatened Ratiram

43. Entry for 1 April 1908, found in the journal of S. J. Scott, Mahasamund catechist, AES 83-5 Di54 #1 (italics added).

with legal harassment if he should ever again beat a Christian.[44] Missionaries soon came to be seen as advocates for the oppressed (or those they perceived to be oppressed).

It is clear that some *Satnamis* perceived conversion to Christianity as a method of blunting or blocking the workings of the justice system. Rupdhar, a *Satnami malguzar* of Parsabhader who harassed the missionaries for some time after their arrival there in 1893, was implicated with his wives in the murder of a Pathan moneylender. Evangelical missionary "Sadhu" Hagenstein interceded for him and the courts lightened the sentence. In jail Rupdhar became a Christian, but in the words of the missionary, after being released he "became a dealer in skins and hides, rejoined the Satnami caste and died a backslider."[45] In several towns around Takhatpur, a fair number of Christians can trace their ancestry to notorious robber families, who after ostensibly having given up their "trade" in the 1930s and '40s, became Christian in hopes of gaining missionary help in ending police harassment (they were successful).[46]

More than any of the missionaries in the region, Disciples mission-worker Donald McGavran, who worked in the Takhatpur area, seems especially to have sought out *Satnamis* in economic, legal, or social tight spots in hopes of wooing them to Christianity. His methods produced a large number of converts, but also a significant number of reversions when those who had become Christian for his advocacy no longer found it necessary. Some Christian informants therefore expressed ambivalence about McGavran's legacy. One story, shared by informants involved in it, illustrates his methods. During

---

44. I have followed the account of these events given by Awadh Masih, who was still living when I conducted my fieldwork. Other sources have verified the details. When asked why he became a Christian, Masih answered plainly, "Because Ratiram would not allow us to go to our fields." Interview by author, Kevta Devri, CG, 18 February 2004. Though mission advocacy attracted some Chhattisgarhis to Christianity, Saxena and Mitra overgeneralize: "As a matter of fact [Chhattisgarhi Christian converts] did not change their religion for the sake of conviction but because Christianity brought them a defense against the oppression of their landlords." Abha Saxena and Mitashree Mitra, "Christian Missionaries in Chhattisgarh," in *Reform, Protest and Social Transformation,* ed. Satish K. Sharma (New Delhi: Ashish Publishing House, 1987), p. 234.

45. Davis, *Sadhu Hagenstein,* p. 68.

46. The police had for many years made a practice of visiting the homes of these families in the middle of the night to make certain that the suspected thieves were in bed and not involved in spreaghery. Christian descendants of these families in Chhattisgarh find their past mildly embarrassing, and are prone to hide it or create new histories for their ancestors. For a similar story in the Bishrampur area, see William Baur's "First Quarterly Report, January 15, 1938," AES 82-14 Qu2, Baur, Wm., Quarterly Reports, Articles, Newsletters, 1927-58. See also Homer P. Gamboe, "The Missionary Work of the Disciples of Christ in India and Its Development" (B.Div. thesis, College of the Bible, 1918), p. 76.

World War II, the British, expecting a Japanese invasion of India, set up an artillery range in the Takhatpur area, displacing a good number of Chhattisgarhis, including 150 Christians. Some *Satnamis* from the village of Sonbandha found unexploded ordnance on the range and brought it back to their village. One of the men involved, Baula, decided the ordnance would make a good lamp, and — fire not mixing well with combustibles — the bomb exploded, injuring several people and generally causing a great deal of *garbar* (disturbance, uproar, agitation). Baula was also seriously injured, but was nursed back to health by doctors at the mission hospital in Mungeli. The residents of Sonbandha, however, were justifiably unhappy with Baula, who was still living when I conducted my fieldwork, and pressured him to leave town with his relatives. At this point McGavran offered to settle the families on land owned by the mission in what came to be called Shantipur. The families moved in and were soon baptized. (Some of them, however, soon recanted and returned to Sonbandha.)

Until the 1930s, the prevailing *modus operandi* of mission workers in Chhattisgarh was to construct a mission station or outpost, and then develop schools, dispensaries, hospitals, and other institutions around it. These centers possessed a certain magnetism, drawing new Christians out of their social contexts and into the economic, social, and cultural ambit of the mission. The approach made sense — the region was in need of these basic institutions, and Christians, whose decision to leave their former religion generally meant social and economic marginalization, required an alternative support system. The mission, so its workers believed, was simply providing basic help to compensate new Christians for the sacrifices their conversion had entailed.

Though it was not the intention of missionaries, the result of this mission compound approach was that many Chhattisgarhi Christians came to depend on help from the mission in finding homes, jobs, and land. This paternalism, or *ma-bap-ism*, as Indians and missionaries referred to it (employing a Hindi term for mother-father, or parents) led to a situation in which both Christians and non-Christians viewed the relationship of converts towards the mission as one of total dependence. Even missionaries who avoided building up institutions and helping Christians and potential converts in any material way could not escape this perception. J. W. Pickett, who conducted a number of his mass movement studies in the Chhattisgarh area, was severely critical of such an approach.[47] Influenced by his conclusions, some missionaries in the area attempted to disentangle themselves from the perception of

---

47. J. W. Pickett, *Mass Movement Survey Report for Mid-India* (Jubbulpore, Central Provinces, India: Mission Press, 1937), p. 38.

the missionary as patron, beginning around the end of the 1930s.[48] The choice to change their methods was not so much an ethical decision as it was a pragmatic one. Mission paternalism had served to spatially and economically distance converts from their families, villages, and *jāti*-fellows, and the missionaries knew that in such a situation the mass movements they so desired would never materialize. But missionaries soon found that when they stressed only the spiritual benefits of conversion, interest in Christianity rapidly subsided.

Despite these shifts, Christians continued to believe that the mission was responsible for supporting them materially. One older *Satnami* who became Christian in the Champa area said that in the 1940s and '50s, Christians often greeted missionaries with the phrase, *"ham ko thorā sahāyatā cāhiye"* (We need a little help). Non-Christians, even those who harbored no ill-feelings for the missionaries, continued to perceive the Christian community as a place for the desperate, an economic "last chance" saloon. One Muslim informant, who had been a *malguzar* near Takhatpur and a personal friend of Disciples missionary Donald McGavran, reported flatly that the *Satnamis* who became Christian in his village in the 1940s did so because of poverty and drought, and not for any other reason. Even those who needed nothing perceived Christianity to be a religion of economic boon. The perception was as old as the mission itself. In 1872, Lohr reported: "The leading man of a large village and underpriest of the sect [either a *bhandārī* or a *mahant*], has repeatedly made proposals to me to give him a living on the estate and he would then embrace Christianity with a thousand of his followers, but he was informed . . . that Christianity was not to be purchased and that we could not accept any proposal from himself or others without an unconditional surrender of themselves both Soul and body to Christ."[49] Given that the Christian community had largely taken shape during the famines of the 1890s, it is not surprising that the missions developed as they did, and that Chhattisgarhis, both Christian and others, would view Christianity as a refuge in time of crisis.

Missionaries were uncomfortable with this perception, and generally tried to be certain that those becoming Christian did so for "spiritual" reasons. In 1940, an Evangelical missionary said of a new *Satnami*-Christian: "He hopes to

48. Some missionaries, in particular the Disciples missionary Donald McGavran, resisted this shift well into the 1950s. For a discussion of missionaries as patrons in the Punjab, see John C. B. Webster, "Dalits and Christianity in Colonial Punjab: Cultural Interactions," in *Christians, Cultural Interactions, and India's Religious Traditions*, ed. Judith M. Brown and Robert Eric Frykenberg (Grand Rapids: Eerdmans, 2002), p. 104.

49. "Third Annual Report of the Chutteesgurh Mission, 1871-72," AES 82-13a Pr91, 1870-83 (Annual Reports).

get his children . . . educated and find a better opportunity for their future than he could have for them as a Satnami. He professed that his chief reason for becoming Christian was to find salvation from sin, peace for his soul and eternal life."[50] Here it seems certain that the missionary's presence prompted the unnamed *Satnami* to profess the paramountcy of his "spiritual" motivations even when it is clear there were additional motives. One wonders to what extent the missionary's description of the profession reflects the *Satnami's* words — "salvation from sin," for instance, is unlikely to have been the idiom chosen by the convert, unless it had been previously learned.[51]

Health, Healing, and Leaving One's Religion

If material and social factors were prominent in the growth of the Christian community in Chhattisgarh, they were not alone. Many *Satnamis* first encountered Christians at the mission hospitals, leprosaria, and dispensaries. The implications of this fact will be discussed at greater length in Chapter 4, but suffice it to say here that in the popular imagination Christianity became linked with health and healing, and many *Satnamis* who found health in Christians institutions, particularly if traditional forms of medicine had failed them, became Christian. David Jordan has suggested that, "The success or failure of a therapeutic method, particularly a medical therapy, is an important logic both for conversion and for sustained loyalty to a particular cult, sect, or system or practice." He also argues that many Taiwanese in the 1960s became Christian in order to secure for themselves access to Christian hospitals.[52] The same was true in Chhattisgarh, especially among lepers. After being socially ostracized for their disease and then given care at Christian institutions, lepers were especially prone to join the community that symbolized the reversal of their social fortunes.[53]

50. H. A. Feierabend, "An Inquirer Comes to the Missionary," 1940, AES 82-14 Qu2 Feierabend, H. A., Quarterly Reports, Articles, Newsletters, 1933-1941.

51. For another passage reflecting missionary ambivalence regarding material factors in conversion, see Donald A. McGavran, *The Satnami Story: A Thrilling Drama of Religious Change* (Pasadena: William Carey Library, 1990), p. 53.

52. David K. Jordan, "The Glyphomancy Factor: Observations on Chinese Conversion," in *Conversion to Christianity: Historical and Anthropological Perspectives on a Great Transformation*, ed. Robert W. Hefner (Berkeley: University of California Press, 1993), p. 293.

53. Ironically, Christian missionaries sometimes quoted from Leviticus 13:45 (KJV), "And the leper in whom the plague is, his clothes shall be rent, and his head bare, and he shall put a covering upon his upper lip, and shall cry, Unclean, unclean," to describe the social ostracism of lepers in Hindu communities.

In addition, it was the perception among Christians and some *Satnamis* that Christian mothers and children survived the trauma of pregnancy and birth at a greater rate than the *Satnamis*. This perception seems to have been based in fact, which is not surprising, given the missionary emphasis on hygiene and proper and timely medical intervention. The importance of this factor in a context where large families are a matter of pride cannot be discounted.[54] The death of a child could also be an occasion for conversion. Despairing parents sometimes found help in their grief by turning away from the gods they considered responsible for having inflicted death on their offspring.

Christianization and Social Status

Social factors also made becoming Christian attractive to some *Satnamis*.[55] Even after Ghasidas's reforms, the *Satnamis* were a despised community with no real short-term hope of improving their ritual status. Some *Satnamis* saw in Christianity a potential source of social improvement and adopted it as part of their quest for respect and dignity. There is some evidence, for instance, that after becoming Christian, certain *Satnamis* were no longer considered untouchable by members of the higher castes. The day after he converted, for instance, Chungia *Satnami* Hira Lal was warmly welcomed into the office of a post-office clerk who told him he could no longer be considered a member of the low castes.[56] (For more on Hira Lal, see Chapter 6.) However, this improvement in status appears to have been limited to prominent and respected members of the community, whereas for the great majority conversion brought little appreciable short-term difference.

Becoming Christian did, however, increase the chances that one would gain ground according to modern indicators of status, such as education, respectable employment, and wealth. Christian teachers, for example, taught

54. Birgit Meyer suggests that healing was a prominent motivation for conversion among the West Africa Ewe (comparatively cheap death rites was another). Birgit Meyer, "Modernity and Enchantment: The Image of the Devil in Popular African Christianity," in *Conversion to Modernities: The Globalization of Christianity*, ed. Peter van der Veer (New York: Routledge, 1996).

55. Whereas in the context of mass conversion movements within a single caste, the bid for social mobility seems to be a more prominent factor than material considerations, in this context material factors seem to overshadow concern about social status. For comparison, see Walter Fernandes, *Caste and Conversion Movements in India: Religion and Human Rights* (New Delhi: Indian Social Institute, 1981).

56. Brown, *Hira Lal*, p. 173.

members of all castes, and this position of power and influence was a source of great pride as Indians became increasingly aware of the economic value of literacy in the colonial milieu. Moreover, the Christian community as a whole came to be far more literate than other communities in the region.

Convinced Protestants that they were, missionaries and evangelists among the *Satnamis* feared that illiteracy would prevent their converts from being exposed to "the Word" in the Bible, tracts, and hymnbooks.[57] Missionaries expended a large portion of their resources, both human and financial, on teaching people to read. They produced magazines for mass consumption, and published books, tracts, and pamphlets, mostly in Hindi and Chhattisgarhi, at a feverish pace. Sales of mission publications on the Evangelical mission rose from four thousand in 1932 to nearly twenty-eight thousand in 1936.[58] Even those Christians who could not read were required to memorize texts such as the Ten Commandments, the Lord's Prayer, the Twenty-Third Psalm, and the Apostles' Creed.[59]

The Christian effort to eradicate illiteracy produced tangible results. By 1943, 28 percent of Christian women on the Evangelical mission field could read and write.[60] At roughly the same time, Evangelical M. P. Davis figured that 40 percent of *Satnami*-Christians were literate (as opposed to 8 percent of Chhattisgarhis and 13 percent of Indians).[61] In 1952, an unnamed Disciples missionary reported that 93 percent of adults in the Mungeli congregation, most of them with *Satnami* ancestry, were literate.[62] These percentages were even higher than the average among all Christians in Chhattisgarh (on this, and on literacy in Raipur, Bilaspur, and Chhattisgarh more generally, see Figures 6-8 in the Appendix).[63]

---

57. Emil W. Menzel, *I Will Build My Church: The Story of Our India Mission and How It Became a Church* (Philadelphia: Board of Missions, Evangelical and Reformed Church, 1943), p. 32.

58. See P. D. Gottlieb, "Annual Report for 1931-32," AES 82-13a Pr91, Annual Reports, no. 17, 1932; and "Report of the President, 1935-36," ibid., no. 21, 1936.

59. McGavran, *Satnami Story*, p. 41.

60. Menzel, *I Will Build My Church*, p. 69.

61. Martin P. Davis, *India Today and the Church Tomorrow* (Philadelphia: The Board of International Missions, Evangelical and Reformed Church, 1947), pp. 59-60.

62. "Brief Report on the Christian Church, Mungeli," ca. 1952, DCHS, UCMS Records, DOM, India, box 14 (folder: India-Orientation). These and earlier figures do not distinguish between those who were literate in Hindi and those who were literate in Chhattisgarhi.

63. Christianization did not always entail great increases in literacy, and due to mass movements in other parts of India in the 1920s, which brought large numbers of illiterate Christians into the fold and overwhelmed missionary institutions, Christians, who had

Particularly among those who had been Christian for some time, the "value" of education and literacy seemed obvious, and *Satnami*-Christians were known to go to great lengths to get their children educated. The change, as will be discussed in Chapter 5, was most pronounced among women and girls. While literacy rates remained deplorably low, literacy itself came to be universally valued.

Historically, *Satnamis* and other *dalit* communities had been denied access to traditional forms of education, and were even generally barred from learning, reading, or writing Sanskrit, the language of Hindu scriptures and learning. Upper-caste Hindus such as the famous theologian-philosopher Shankara (ca. 788-820) and like-minded nineteenth- and twentieth-century scholars were loath to educate members of communities whose low birth, they believed, was a mark of karmic retribution. Egalitarian access to the sacred text was therefore, in this context, the most radical element of Christian teaching, and it is therefore not surprising that *Satnamis* who became Christian should so earnestly embrace the possibility of education.

Many non-Christian *Satnamis*, however, either did not consider education useful or recognized (and wished to avoid) the possibility that a missionary education might significantly alter one's thought patterns and beliefs. It was rumored, in fact, that Ghasidas had at one time forbidden education to his followers (but that he eventually withdrew the objection). An Evangelical, formerly *brahman* evangelist Ramnath Bajpai, reported that Agardas and Sahebdas, dual claimants to the guru *gaddī* after Balakdas, had told a government official who wished to encourage their education, "We do not require these black letters, as [God] has ordained us to mind our work with the stick called Tutari [a stick with which one drives bullocks]."[64] Even into the 1930s, *Satnami* gurus discouraged members of the *Satnami* community from attending mission-run schools.[65] Non-Christian *Satnamis* did eventually come to desire literacy and education, but only later, and in smaller numbers than Christians. To the extent, therefore, that more modern criteria of social status such as education and literacy became important in Chhattisgarhi society, the Christian community's social position improved. Eventually they came, in general, to be treated much better than *Satnamis* by members of the higher castes.

Conversion, or rather the threat of conversion, could also be used by

---

previously ranked first in literacy, fell to fourth after the Parsis, Jains, and Buddhists. See "Official Census of India (Reprinted from the Missionary Herald)," *World Call*, July 1924, p. 37.

64. *Some Facts about the Satnamis*, 1921(?), HCS, box 2 of 4 (no folder).
65. Martin P. Davis, "The Satnami Tragedy," *Evangelical Herald*, 1 June 1933, p. 429.

Satnamis to improve their social condition within the *panth*. Milau, a recognized leader of the *Satnamis* in his area by dint of his education at the mission school, had a dream in which, he said, "I saw myself with a Gospel-bag on which was the sign of the cross, just like evangelists use; I was walking from village to village selling Christian books." Milau claimed that if he converted, many members of his village would convert with him. The missionaries and evangelists therefore paid him much respect and attention. But so too did the *Satnami* community leaders who feared his defection. In the end, it seemed clear that Milau had simply been threatening his conversion and making it seem a possibility in order to procure for himself special favors from the *Satnami* hierarchy.[66]

Satnamis in Chhattisgarh lived under the dominion of certain behavioral restrictions. *Satnami* men were not allowed to wear full-length *dhotis*, turbans, or shoes in front of members of the upper castes. *Satnami* women were prevented from wearing *saris* with brightly colored borders or ornaments of silver or gold, and were made to leave their torsos exposed before the higher castes. *Satnamis* also had to use a different area of the village *tālāb* for bathing and washing clothes. In addition, *Satnamis* were not allowed to make use of umbrellas, ride horses or elephants, or use palanquins at their weddings.[67] By joining the Christian community, *Satnamis* could avoid many of these and other similar *varṇa-jāti* restrictions.[68]

In one case, becoming Christian may have allowed a prominent *Satnami* to circumnavigate his caste restrictions and fulfill his father's deathbed request. According to one version of his story, Tularam of Lata village became Christian because his father had requested that the *Gītā pāṭh* (recitation of passages from the *Gītā*) be read after his death (a ritual usually reserved for members of the upper castes, but which the father believed would ensure his success in the afterlife). As no *brahman* would agree to perform the ritual for a *Satnami*,

66. M. P. Davis, "That Downward Pull," ca. 1937, AES 82-14 Qu2, Davis, M. P., Quarterly Reports, Articles, Newsletters, 1936-1940.

67. These latter were all signs of temporal and ritual status. See Saurabh Dube, *Untouchable Pasts: Religion, Identity, and Power among a Central Indian Community, 1780-1950* (Albany: State University of New York Press, 1998), p. 55.

68. Christian missionaries across India were seen as opponents of caste prejudice at least since the Revolt of 1857, after which missionaries argued for government interference in caste relations. See Duncan B. Forrester, "The Depressed Classes and Conversion to Christianity, 1860-1960," in *Religion in South Asia: Religious Conversion and Revival Movements in South Asia in Medieval and Modern Times*, ed. G. A. Oddie (New Delhi: Manohar Publications, 1977), p. 39. This was especially true of Protestants because of their greater reluctance to allow caste distinctions in the church. See Fernandes, *Caste and Conversion Movements in India*, p. 28.

Tularam became Christian and, on the advice of missionaries, traveled to South India to find *brahman*-Christians who would perform the ceremony.[69] Here, paradoxically, Christianity allowed the proper fulfillment, via *brahman*-Christians, of a dying lower-caste man's upper-caste Hindu aspirations.

Abandoned, divorced, and widowed women also frequently embraced Christianity as an escape from the difficulties and dangers of single female life. Suffering at various times from economic problems, neglect, abuse, and sexual exploitation, these women found shelter in Christian hostels and boarding schools. Women involved in polygynous unions or threatened by abusive husbands also sometimes saw in Christian boarding schools the possibility of escaping what they perceived to be an unsatisfactory life. This was especially true in the area of Takhatpur, where missionaries and Indian workers made a special effort to shelter women in need.[70] Many of those who did enter the mission's boarding schools and hostels received an education. According to an informant who worked at a women's hostel, almost all converted and were eventually married or remarried to Christian men.

The Christian message of social equality brought a measure of self-respect and dignity to *Satnamis* who became Christian, regardless of whether their conversion brought any appreciable or immediate change in social status.[71] But the Christians in Chhattisgarh were not the only community to deny the validity of caste differences and caste restrictions. Ghasidas's message included a strong egalitarian strain, though he too excluded members of the even lower castes from his *panth*. Kabirpanthi beliefs and practices also symbolically undermined the importance of caste distinctions. Yet both of these movements eventually attempted, with little success, to sanskritize their rituals and symbols and move up within the *varṇa-jāti* hierarchy. Though essentially rejecting distinctions based on caste as did the *Satnamis* and Kabirpanthis, Ramnamis resisted the urge to follow the path of sanskritization and instead drew inward, repudiating the use of *brahmans* in their rituals and cer-

69. For another version of the story, and more about Tularam, see Chapter 5. This version is from I. D. Paul (son of Tularam), interview by author, Takhatpur, CG, 19 February 2004.

70. During the Christian Missionary Activities Enquiry of 1954, some Hindus expressed alarm, claiming that "Women who have quarrels with their husbands are converted." Sita Ram Goel, ed., *Vindicated by Time: The Niyogi Committee Report on Christian Missionary Activities (1956)* (New Delhi: Voice of India, 1998), p. II.A.75.

71. For a similar argument regarding Christians in South India, see Sundararaj Manickam, *The Social Setting of Christian Conversion in South India: The Impact of the Wesleyan Methodist Missionaries on the Trichy-Tanjore Diocese with Special Reference to the Harijan Communities of the Mass Movement Area, 1820-1947* (Wiesbaden: Steiner, 1977).

emonies. Building on this autonomy and their unique symbolic markers, they developed a strong sense of communal solidarity.[72]

Nevertheless, these movements resulted only in *positional* change within the socio-religious hierarchy and did not effect fundamental, *structural* change.[73] Neither did the Christian community, largely because of its paucity. But its rhetorical rejection of caste distinctions was perhaps more consistent and would have appealed to those who joined these other communities, particularly those who had not experienced any appreciable improvement in social status as a result. Christian missionaries, evangelists, and catechists emphasized the socially egalitarian message of Christianity, as well as the fact that worth and status were theoretically to be based on achieved merit rather than ascription. *Satnamis,* even those who did not become Christian, recognized and respected this aspect of Christianity. When asked why some *Satnamis* had become Christian in his childhood (1940s and '50s), one *Satnami* said that the community was treated poorly by upper-caste Hindus, and so when *Satnamis* saw that Christians respected them, that they were willing to associate with them, and that Christian doctors did not avoid touching them as upper-caste Hindus did, etc., they were impressed. Christians were known, he said, to have a *sevā bhāv* (serving nature). And though they were not identical to those of Ghasidas, *Satnamis* would have found Christian social views comparable to their guru's.

Religion as Social Vision

The evidence is substantial that material factors contributed to the growth of the Christian community in Chhattisgarh. But as the foregoing discussion suggests, there were a variety of other factors, some of which cannot be reduced to the rational calculation of economic ends and means. Max Weber accepted the argument that rational actors behaved according to the dictates of self-interest. But what distinguished him from Marx was his theory of "ideal interests" — the notion that values and ideas could also be interests, and could influence human behavior. "Not ideas, but material and ideal interests, directly govern men's conduct," Weber argued, "Yet very frequently the 'world images' that have been created by 'ideas' have, like switchmen, de-

72. Ramdas Lamb, *Rapt in the Name: The Ramnamis, Ramnam, and Untouchable Religion in Central India* (Albany: State University of New York Press, 2002), pp. 175ff.

73. The distinction between positional and structural change comes from M. N. Srinivas, *Social Change in Modern India* (Berkeley: University of California Press, 1966), p. 7.

termined the tracks along which action has been pushed by the dynamic of interest. 'From what' and 'for what' one wished to be redeemed and, let us not forget, 'could be' redeemed, depended upon one's image of the world."[74] While admitting that material interests fueled historical locomotion, he asserted that human action, directed by ideals, *wert-rational* (value-rational) behavior, could sometimes throw the switch and divert the train.

It is my contention not only that ideal interests played a significant role in the conversion of *Satnamis* to Christianity, but that certain behavior which seems at first glance to be directed by purely instrumental reasoning might upon deeper investigation prove to be more complex. For example, is the desire to survive in time of famine not at one and the same time an ideal and material interest? Is the satisfaction of basic needs such as food and shelter a value or a material interest? Can the desire for material improvement be clearly distinguished from that for dignity and respect? Can an economic pursuit be considered purely material when preceded by an offering to a god or goddess?

In village Chhattisgarhi life, where the activities and motions of everyday life are accompanied at every juncture by religious rituals and gestures, the line dividing "secular" and "religious," and thus material and ideal, cannot be easily uncovered. Hinduism may hold the ascetic renunciant up as an ideal, but for Hindu "householders" material pursuits are not considered inimical to religious goals. They are in fact not even considered distinct.[75] One's religious identity encompasses all aspects of life — *dharm*, after all, conditions not only what westerners would consider religious behavior, but also social and economic goals *(arth)*. Those who became Christian in Chhattisgarh looked to their new faith for direction in all of these arenas.

I have argued above that the affordability of Christian rituals was particularly attractive to *Satnamis* who found the expense of their religious responsibilities burdensome. Yet *Satnamis* who became Christian continued to contribute higher amounts of money to the church.[76] While these higher

---

74. From Weber's "The Social Psychology of the World Religions," in H. H. Gerth and C. Wright Mills, *From Max Weber: Essays in Sociology* (New York: Oxford University Press, 1958), p. 280. Interestingly, Weber added this passage, so often quoted by western scholars, only in later editions of the work. See Detlef Kantowsky, "Max Weber on India and Indian Interpretations of Weber," in *Recent Research on Max Weber's Studies of Hinduism,* ed. Detlef Kantowsky (London: Weltforum, 1986), p. 14.

75. See P. Y. Luke and John B. Carman, *Village Christians and Hindu Culture: A Study of a Rural Church in Andhra Pradesh, South India* (London: Lutterworth, 1968), p. 43.

76. "Poor" *Satnamis* spent an average of one rupee per year, the "middle-class" spent one to four rupees, and the "rich" four to ten rupees. Christians in the one congregation

amounts might actually amount to lower percentages of income, clearly there is more than purely economic interest at play here. What appears to be the case is that ideal interests, often unconscious or inchoate, contributed significantly to the appeal of Christianity for the *Satnamis* of Chhattisgarh. For those who joined the community, Christianity satisfied longings born of the experience of "untouchability," and perpetuated by Guru Ghasidas, the Satnampanth, and Hinduism more generally.

Many of the *Satnamis* who became Christian were not "converted," but rather "chose" to convert as part of a larger project to find an appropriate way of living and being in a changing world (though the "choice" was of course made in the context of socio-economic realities that were largely beyond their control).[77] Christianity was not "imposed" upon them by external factors, but adopted as one possible strategy — whether consciously or unconsciously — for the resolution of dissonance between the world as imagined and the world as experienced.[78]

In the context of a socially and religiously marginalized community, conversion to a "foreign" faith may be an expression of dissent, as Gauri Viswanathan and others have suggested.[79] In fact the very existence of an alternative social order — the simple possibility of "heresy" — provokes alienation from the tradition, or at least from the tradition as authoritative and given, as an objective, necessary reality.[80] As such it is most certainly a form of cultural critique. But conversion also entails *assent* to another socioreligious order, an alternative social vision.[81] Kiran Sebastian has suggested

surveyed gave an average of three rupees per year to their church. "How Much Do Satnamis Give for Religious Purposes?" ca. 1930, unsigned, AES 80-1 Sat8.

77. Cf. Karlsson, "Christian Dharma," p. 136.

78. The language of adoption versus imposition comes from J. Boel, *Christian Mission in India: A Sociological Analysis* (Amsterdam: Graduate Press, 1975), p. 9. See also J. W. Gladstone, *Protestant Christianity and People's Movements in Kerala* (Trivandrum, Kerala, India: The Seminary Publications, 1984), p. 6; and Kooiman, *Conversion and Social Equality in India*, p. 7.

79. Gauri Viswanathan, "Religious Conversion and the Politics of Dissent," in *Conversion to Modernities: The Globalization of Christianity*, ed. Peter van der Veer (New York: Routledge, 1996); and Viswanathan, *Outside the Fold*.

80. Kenelm Burridge, "Introduction: Missionary Occasions," in *Mission, Church, and Sect in Oceania*, ed. James A. Boutilier, Daniel T. Hughes, and Sharon W. Tiffany (Ann Arbor: University of Michigan Press, 1978), pp. 16-17. Berger suggests that religious *choice*, a distinctly modern possibility, inevitably undermines the givenness of tradition; see Peter Berger, *A Rumor of Angels: Modern Society and the Rediscovery of the Supernatural* (Garden City, NY: Doubleday, 1969), p. 56; and Berger, *Heretical Imperative*, chapter 1. See also Viswanathan, *Outside the Fold*, p. 76.

81. I am indebted to Dr. Richard Fox Young for the coupling of assent and dissent.

that India's *dalits* perceived in Christianity a promise, though latent and as yet unfulfilled, of being accepted as human beings and treated with respect and equality.[82] Certainly this is true in Chhattisgarh as well, but the implications of conversion as social vision are much broader than this, and involve an entire way of "being in the world."[83] Christianity offered to *Satnamis* a ready-made vision of the ideal social order and a way of living and behaving that supported it.

Satnamis who became Christian were not embracing a new cosmology or theological dogma so much as a new social ideal and a new identity.[84] Their "choice" to become Christian was motivated not only by considerations of economic profit and loss but also by values, whether or not they may have been articulated as such. It appears to be the case that *Satnamis* were joining a community they perceived to embody a value system that could accommodate and tame the shifting realities of their time while mitigating the negative impact of centuries-old social and religious prejudices.[85] That vision included "material" concerns, for what vision of well-being does not include the desire for good health, long life, and a modicum of prosperity?[86] But it

82. J. Jayakiran Sebastian, "A Strange Mission among Strangers: The Joy of Conversion," in *Vom Geheimnis des Unterschieds: Die Wahrnehmung des Fremden in Ökumene-Missions- und Religionswissenschaft*, ed. Andrea Schultze, Rudolf V. Sinner, and Wolfram Stierle (Münster: LIT, 2002), p. 202.

83. Karlsson, "Christian Dharma," pp. 152ff.

84. On conversion as the acceptance of a reconfigured social identity, see Charles F. Keyes, "Why the Thai Are Not Christians: Buddhist and Christian Conversion in Thailand," in *Conversion to Christianity: Historical and Anthropological Perspectives on a Great Transformation*, ed. Robert W. Hefner (Berkeley: University of California Press, 1993); and William L. Merrill, "Conversion and Colonialism in Northern Mexico: The Tarahumara Response to the Jesuit Mission Program, 1601-1767," in *Conversion to Christianity: Historical and Anthropological Perspectives on a Great Transformation*, ed. Robert W. Hefner (Berkeley: University of California Press, 1993).

85. For similar argument regarding converts to Christianity in Java and the Kabirpanth in India, see (respectively) Hefner, "Of Faith and Commitment," p. 119; and David N. Lorenzen, "The Kabir-Panth and Social Protest," in *The Sants: Studies in a Devotional Tradition of India*, ed. Karine Schomer and W. H. McLeod (Berkeley: Berkeley Religious Studies Series, 1987), p. 293. In a review of Virginia Postrel's *The Substance of Style*, Tom Carson argues that American consumer choices are not so much about "keeping up with the Joneses" as about *identifying* with the Joneses. Consumer choice — what kind of car to buy, for instance — has more to do with wanting to be like certain people than competing with them (and buying a Porsche associates one with a different community than buying a Prius). Here consumerism, like conversion, is about associating oneself with a community that embodies certain values and a particular social perspective. Tom Carson, "Material Girl," *Atlantic Monthly*, October 2003.

86. For a discussion of health, disease, and the "good life" among the *santals*, see

also entailed a revalorized humanity and a new way of living perceived to be more appropriate, given the circumstances. Durkheim argued that conflicts over cultural identity are not generally "between the ideal and the reality but between different ideals, between the ideal of yesterday and that of today, between the ideal that has the authority of tradition and one that is only coming into being."[87] Conversion may have made little difference in the way that others perceived and treated those who became Christian, particularly in the short term, and the vision of social equality remained an unrealized dream, even within the Christian community. But dreams, as Martin Luther King, Jr. knew, can be potent.[88]

On Not Becoming Christian

Many of the factors discussed above could turn *Satnamis* away from Christianity as well as toward it. The arrival of a famine, sickness, or the death of a child might suggest to new converts that the gods were punishing them for their betrayal, and the potential economic ostracism faced by new converts convinced many, based on material considerations, that they were better off within the Satnampanth. Similarly, marks of identity that were a matter of pride for Christians — their denial of caste differences and rejection of expensive rituals and diet restrictions — were unpalatable to many *Satnamis*.[89]

In particular, the potential disruption of death rituals, in which the role of the firstborn son was significant, continued to trouble members of the *Satnami* community. Refusal to perform the proper rituals was considered by

Sitakant Mahapatra, *Modernization and Ritual: Identity and Change in Santal Society* (Calcutta: Oxford University Press, 1986).

87. Emile Durkheim, *The Elementary Forms of Religious Life,* trans. Karen E. Fields (New York: The Free Press, 1995), p. 425.

88. This paragraph relies heavily on Mark Juergensmeyer, *Religion as Social Vision: The Movement against Untouchability in Twentieth-Century Punjab* (Berkeley: University of California Press, 1982), esp. chapter 17 and the Epilogue; and Karlsson, *Contested Belonging,* chapters 1 and 6.

89. A list of Tamil grievances against Christianity solicited by the German Lutheran missionary Ziegenbalg (1683-1719) in Tanjore in the early eighteenth century could have just as easily been gathered among *Satnamis* of Chhattisgarh. The list included the community's eating and slaughter of cows, its rejection of purificatory bathing rituals and elaborate death and marriage rites, its drinking of alcohol, and its denial of caste differences. Dennis Hudson, *Protestant Origins in India* (Grand Rapids: Eerdmans, 2000), pp. 92, 93.

Satnamis a major infraction against *dharm,* and accordingly a sense of filial piety and dread of post-mortem reprisals prevented many *Satnamis* from leaving their caste.[90] This sentiment is reflective of a larger desire among *Satnamis* to remain connected with their community and to its traditions, both in this life and the next. In the 1930s and '40s, for example, *Satnamis* in Bhathri village (near Takhatpur) gladly attended Christian meetings but, according to informants, refused to become baptized because the evangelist required them to cut their *chuṭiyās* (a lock of hair left on the back of a male's otherwise shaven head). Those who cut their *chuṭiyās* were considered outcastes, meaning that no one would perform their death rituals.

Concerns regarding marriage were also a factor in a number of conversions. *Satnamis* moved in and out of the Christian community in search of an appropriate mate for themselves or their children. Some *Satnami* families became Christian so that their child could marry an available and desirable member of the community. Other *Satnami*-Christians moved out of the community in order to obtain a brideprice for their daughters (the practice of exchanging dowry and brideprice was frowned upon by the missionaries).[91] And fear that conversion would make finding spouses for their children difficult prevented many from ever joining the community.[92]

As discussed above, *Satnamis* who became Christian were generally drawn out of their community and into the missionary realm of influence. Those who grew up in orphanages or mission stations became so thoroughly disengaged from the *Satnami* community that they were considered aliens. Christians, even *Satnami*-Christians, were seen as members of a distinct caste. To become Christian, then, was perceived to be the equivalent of abandoning one's family, friends, and community, both in this life and, perhaps, in the next.

For this reason, *Satnamis* who joined the evangelical economy were con-

90. See Evangelical missionary M. P. Davis's "Hinduism and the Christian Message," text of a 1941 address, HCS, box 1 of 4, Unsorted Correspondence and Subject Files (no folder).

91. See Gamboe, "Missionary Work of the Disciples of Christ," p. 81. The missionaries opposed the exchange of brideprice among *Satnami*-Christians, but some Christians continued the practice, undermining missionary wishes. Evangelical missionaries appear to have been somewhat more lenient. For a surprisingly nonjudgmental missionary description of brideprice negotiations involving a recent graduate of the Evangelicals' theological school in Raipur, see William Baur, "An Indian Engagement in C.P.," ca. 1928, AES 82-14 Qu2 Baur, Wm., Quarterly Reports, Articles, Newsletters, 1927-58.

92. See Donald A. McGavran to Dr. Yocum, undated letter, DCHS, UCMS Records, DOM, India, box 41, McGavran, Donald A., Mr. and Mrs. (folder: India I — McGavran, Mr. and Mrs. D. A.). See also Ethel Shreve, "A Boy Who Could Say No," *World Call,* January 1945.

sidered "caste-breakers," and "spoilers of caste." It was said of them, in Hindi, "*dharm kharāb kar dīyā*," or "*bigāṛ ho gayā*." In most instances they were immediately outcasted and considered untouchable by other *Satnamis* in the village (in many villages, however, according to informants, this enmity diminished after a period of several years). It is clear that non-Christian *Satnamis* found Christian evangelization efforts amusing and perhaps a bit tiresome — one catechist's journal is full of people poking fun at Christianity and suddenly remembering urgent business elsewhere.[93] To *Satnamis*, the traveling Christian evangelists and missionaries were entertainment, risible curiosities, freak shows. Despite this, *Satnamis* considered Christians their allies in the struggle against upper-caste hegemony, and were consistently the most interested and attentive of any community with whom Christians came in contact.

This chapter has analyzed the factors contributing to the growth of Christianity among the *Satnamis* and in Chhattisgarh more generally. But *becoming* Christian — or Muslim, or Hindu for that matter — is more than a momentary act, an event. It is a process. The following three chapters deal in a more focused way with what happened to *Satnamis* during that process, and with how the *Satnami*-Christians' old and new worldviews intertwined and mutually informed one another in the development of symbols of identity and pride.

---

93. One non-Christian listened to the catechist's criticism of Hinduism and then "heartily engaged himself to smoke opium. . . ." Diary of unnamed catechist, 4 April 1908, found in the journal of S. J. Scott, Mahasamund catechist, AES 83-5 Di54 #1. See Scott's journal also.

CHAPTER 3

The Myth of History
and the History of Myth

The fantastic is unreal only for the literal mind; the literary mind, on the other hand, allows for a certain playful re-creation of the real that is best experienced as poetry, not dogma.

Luis Gómez, *The Land of Bliss*

"Though they seem to invoke an origin in a historical past with which they continue to correspond, actually identities are about questions of using the resources of history, language and culture in the process of becoming rather than being: not 'who we are' or 'where we came from,' so much as what we might become, how we have been represented and how that bears on how we might represent ourselves."

Stuart Hall and Paul du Gay,
Questions of Cultural Identity

The question of identity — Who are we? — must always be answered, in part, with reference to the past, to tradition, to "origins," and to "who we were."[1] Nevertheless, communal identities are not static, but are in fact constantly undergoing transformations of varied consequence and celerity. The past be-

---

1. See Margaret Meibohm, "Past Selves and Present Others: The Ritual Construction of Identity at a Catholic Festival in India," in *Popular Christianity in India: Riting between the Lines,* ed. Selva Raj and Corinne Dempsey (Albany: State University of New York Press, 2002), p. 61.

comes useful as it undergirds visions of the future.[2] Therefore, as a community undergoes change, so too must its "history," or at least its interpretation of history. History is not an unalterable given, the nature of which is agreed upon by all, though it is often, within a single community, perceived to be so. Rather, history is a rich and flexible resource for justifying change (or, for that matter, defending the status quo). This is particularly so when history is embedded in oral traditions.

No community can equally recall or regard every event in its history. Communities "remember" certain episodes and "forget" others; they deem certain narratives "factual" and others "fictitious"; they emphasize certain aspects of their communal experience and turn a blind eye to others. A community's appropriation of the past is at best *selective,* and sometimes simply counterfactual. While there may be a shared heritage upon which a community's "tradition" is based, decisions about which elements of that heritage constitute its "tradition" are made in the present.[3]

Communal identities, and the histories that support them, are therefore "imagined," or "invented," a term employed by Wagner in *The Invention of Tradition,* and Hobsbawm and Ranger in *The Invention of Culture.* However, whereas Wagner understands *all* cultures to be invented (spontaneously and unconsciously), Hobsbawm and Ranger appear to suggest that the "invention" of culture is a deliberate, conscious, and politically motivated act.[4] This may be increasingly true — today's politicians do seem particularly sophisticated and cynical in their manipulation of history and public consciousness. Nevertheless, it does not appear to me that this was the case in the context of this study, and I therefore understand "invention" in the Wagnerian sense, as an organic and largely unself-conscious process. Nevertheless, the extent to which the "invention" of culture is a conscious or unconscious process cannot be confidently determined by the historian, and my preference for Wagner's understanding of the term, it must be recognized, is based largely on my own historical intuition. To suggest that identities are "invented" is therefore

2. Ainslie T. Embree, *Utopias in Conflict* (Berkeley: University of California Press, 1990), p. 13.

3. Jocelyn Linnekin, "Defining Tradition: Variations on the Hawaiian Identity," *American Ethnologist* 10, no. 2 (1983): 241.

4. See Eric Hobsbawm and Terence Ranger, eds., *The Invention of Tradition* (New York: Cambridge University Press, 1983); and Roy Wagner, *The Invention of Culture* (Englewood Cliffs, NJ: Prentice-Hall, 1975). For an insightful discussion of the differences between these two views and those who have appropriated them, see Bengt G. Karlsson, *Contested Belonging: An Indigenous People's Struggle for Forest and Identity in Sub-Himalayan Bengal* (Richmond, VA: Curzon, 2000), pp. 241ff.

not to imply that they are *inauthentic,* the conscious and wholly inaccurate manipulations of self-interested and cynical minds, but simply to assert that they are not based on fixed, unfiltered, or "objective" realities.

Oral traditions must therefore be seen as *interpretations* of events, and biased ones at that. It does not follow, however, that they have no historical value. To begin with, all history, whether oral or textual, is interpretive, and the historian should not assume that one or the other source is more "truthful." Jan Vansina suggests that rather than declare myth fictitious and history factual, historians should employ a comparative approach.[5] Taking up Vansina's challenge in her study of the interactions of indigenous Mayan peoples and the descendants of Spaniards in Latin America, Victoria Reifler Bricker has suggested that oral "legends" of the indigenous peoples were, on the whole, no less "factual" than the "histories" of those claiming Spanish descent.[6] Oral traditions are therefore potential sources of accurate information about the past if they are treated by the historian with all of the circumspection and caution applied to any kind of source. The skillful historian, Vansina argues, must sift and weigh the sources to determine which are most likely to be accurate. The job of the historian therefore becomes the "calculation of probabilities," rather than the determination of truth.[7]

Even when, by using Vansina's comparative method, one concludes with reasonable certainty that a particular oral tradition is factually inaccurate, it does not at that moment cease to be of interest to the historian. Oral traditions, even "mythic" ones, are "theories of history."[8] They are allegorical; they make a statement about something. People tell the stories of their past in a certain way because they *need it to be so.* Historical sources, oral *and* textual, can therefore provide the scholar with information about those producing them even (and perhaps especially) if it is reasonably certain that the sources are inaccurate.[9]

5. Jan Vansina, *Oral Tradition: A Study in Historical Methodology* (London: Routledge & Kegan Paul, 1965), pp. 137-38.

6. Victoria Reifler Bricker, *The Indian Christ, the Indian King* (Austin: University of Texas Press, 1981), p. 5.

7. Vansina, *Oral Tradition,* p. 185.

8. Bricker, *The Indian Christ, the Indian King,* p. 4.

9. John McRae makes a similar argument with regard to *The Platform Sutra of the Sixth Patriarch,* a text that had until recently been considered a reliable account of seventh-century Ch'an Buddhist history (but has since been proven inaccurate). He says: "Although some may despair upon discovering that [its version of history is largely legendary], the importance and validity of the *Platform Sutra* account is not compromised by its fictive nature. On the contrary, the literary and religious significance of this text . . . may be enhanced by the absence of historical veracity, [because it] is in part a creation of the col-

Accordingly, the stories that *Satnamis* and *Satnami*-Christians relate about themselves tell us more about the communities' cultural self-understandings than about their precise historical development. For just as Baba Ramchandra's *Ghāsīdāsjī kī vanśāvalī* and *Satnām sagar* had reformulated the *Satnami* past, leaders of the *Satnami*-Christian community reworked *Satnami* history in order to place Ghasidas in a spiritual lineage beginning with Christian missionaries, and thereby to portray conversion to Christianity as a return to the past, as faithfulness to the *Satnami* tradition rather than perfidy. *Satnami*-Christians reworked *Satnami* oral traditions and wove them together with elements of the Christian story, refashioning the past and contending for the right to claim the inheritance of Ghasidas.[10] This is not, however, a case of Asian mythological versus western historical thinking. In a sense, all history, as I have stated above, is "mythological." Moreover, the American missionaries themselves participated in the *Satnami*-Christian myth-making by amplifying, embellishing, perpetuating, and publishing reconfigured versions of the *Satnami* past (and thereby bestowing upon them the aura of facticity).[11]

From the beginning, missionaries in Chhattisgarh stressed the continuities between the Satnampanth and Christianity, and portrayed their faith as the culmination and fulfillment of Guru Ghasidas's message.[12] Early *Satnami*-Christians appear to have been happy to accept the missionaries' interpretation of events. But as the *Satnami*-Christian community began, in the early twentieth century, to distinguish itself more vigorously from other regional castes, including the *Satnamis,* and to improve its social standing, connections with the *Satnami* past came to be viewed as a liability. Whereas the community at first reconfigured its past to invent a "tradition" that valued the connection between Christianity and the Satnampanth, beginning early in the twentieth

lective Chinese religious imagination." John R. McRae, "The Story of Early Ch'an," in *Zen: Tradition and Transition,* ed. Kenneth Kraft (New York: Grove Press, 1988), p. 139.

10. See Saurabh Dube, *Untouchable Pasts: Religion, Identity, and Power among a Central Indian Community, 1780-1950* (Albany: State University of New York Press, 1998), p. 15.

11. The missionary participation in the mythologization of the *Satnami* past suggests that Mircea Eliade may have overstated the extent to which "modern" society had rejected "myth" in favor of "history." See Mircea Eliade, *Myth of the Eternal Return, or, Cosmos and History* (Princeton: Princeton University Press, 1954), p. xiv.

12. Christian leaders in Chhattisgarh thus placed Christianity in the same position in relation to the Satnampanth as Farquhar did in relation to all of Hinduism, that is, as its *fulfillment;* see J. N. Farquhar, *The Crown of Hinduism* (London: Oxford University Press, 1913). On Farquhar, see Eric Sharpe, *Not to Destroy but to Fulfil: The Contribution of J. N. Farquhar to Protestant Missionary Thought in India before 1914* (Uppsala, Sweden: Almqvist & Wiksells Boktryckeri AB, 1965).

century they *re*invented that tradition, minimalizing their association with the caste from which so many members of the community had come.

Tattoos and Other Embarrassing Reminders of a *Satnami* Past

Two experiences from my field research demonstrate the current Christian community's antipathy towards its historical connection to the Satnampanth. The first took place at the all-Chhattisgarh Christian *melā*, which is held each year at an island on the Seonath River at Madku Ghat. I had suspected for some time that occasionally Christians intentionally obscured their *Satnami* ancestry, because among those who claimed that they (or their parents) were famine orphans and that they therefore had no knowledge of their pre-Christian past were some whose ancestors were listed, along with their *jāti* affiliation, in the church's baptismal records. I arrived at Madku Ghat during the pre-*melā* pastors' meeting. In the course of several conversations with church leaders, I introduced myself and the nature of my work. In those public settings, no pastor admitted to having *Satnami* ancestry. But on two occasions spanning not more than a few minutes, pastors with whom I had spoken in groups tracked me down and, in private, told me that they, or their parents, had been *Satnami* converts.

The second anecdote comes from an interview in Takhatpur. I was interviewing an elderly woman with vibrant mahogany skin, who was wearing red bangles, and whose family had converted when she was quite young, but not before she had been tattooed, as were many *Satnami* children around the age of five or six. In the front room of her house on a quiet street, she spoke openly about the practice of tattooing and of her *Satnami* past, but when the interview ended and I asked to take her picture outside, hoping, to be honest, to capture the symbolic body art along with her image, she skillfully and gracefully slipped one hand over the other, covering the largest of the tattoos. Inscribed on this woman's very body, etched into the very layers of her skin, was the identity of her birth community. Though it could be obscured, it was nevertheless permanent and ineffaceable, and continued to trouble her decades after she had joined the Christian community. I didn't have the heart to ask her to expose a part of her past she clearly did not want publicly documented.

These stories illustrate the ambiguous relationship between *Satnami*-Christians and their *Satnami* past, but they also reflect the fact that the *Satnami*-Christian community has, for the most part, turned its back on its initial acceptance of the notion that membership in the Christian community was in some way continuous with involvement in the Satnampanth. That continuity had been suggested to them, on the one hand, by Indian Christian evangelists who in the early years were usually not *Satnami* and therefore had no experience of lower-caste life, and, on the other, by American missionaries who, with their western notions of achieved (versus ascribed) status, saw no shame in the *Satnami* background of Christian converts and in fact attempted to flaunt, and even manufacture, continuities with the *Satnami* past for evangelistic purposes. After embracing those continuities for several decades, the *Satnami*-Christians themselves began in the early twentieth century to distance themselves from the Satnampanth.

Inventive Converts, Mythologizing Missionaries, and the Story of Guru Ghasidas

Early in his career Oscar Lohr (the first Evangelical missionary) heard that a *Satnami* guru had prophesied the coming of a white man. The story, from an evangelistic perspective, was almost too good to be true, and in part because of it missionaries in Chhattisgarh have been obsessed with converting the *Satnamis* ever since. Lohr sent home reports predicting that Christianity would spread quickly through familial ties and that very soon the "whole tribe" would "embrace Christianity."[13] Inspired by Lohr's glowing missives, a number of energetic young Evangelical men set off for India to join the work, only to return again after a short period, disillusioned by the slow pace of conversions.[14] While individual missionaries and the missions themselves occasionally attempted to branch out to other castes, they almost always returned again to focus on the *Satnamis*.

In 1934, when Methodist missions theorist J. W. Pickett moved through the region investigating the potential for "mass movements," his commission declared that ". . . the Satnamis are the most numerous approachable caste in Chhattisgarh. It seems inevitable that a group ingathering of major proportions will occur from this caste. We are inclined to believe that when it begins, it will come as a flood."[15] The Disciples missionary Donald McGavran, who

---

13. "Third Annual Report of the Chutteesgurh Mission, 1871-72," AES 82-13a Pr91, 1870-93 (Annual Reports). See also Oscar Lohr, "Von Darchoora," *Der deutsche Missionsfreund* 4, no. 4 (1869): 1.

14. Theodore C. Seybold, *God's Guiding Hand: A History of the Central Indian Mission 1868-1967* (Philadelphia: United Church Board for World Ministries of the United Church of Christ, 1971), pp. 26-27.

15. J. W. Pickett, *Church Growth and Group Conversion* (Lucknow: Lucknow Publishing House, 1956), p. 35.

worked closely with Pickett's committee and eventually developed his own theory of "people movements," was particularly inspired by Pickett's optimism (the reverse may also have been true). For missionaries who had become dissatisfied with the deracination and dependence of converts living on or near the mission compound, the possibility of mass movements — which moved so quickly that converts remained integrated in their communities — was a source of great hope. An enthusiastic missions promoter like Lohr before him, McGavran declared Chhattisgarh a "mass movement" area — a designation misleadingly indicating the methods used, not the number or pace of conversions — and began sending sanguine reports home to the mission, convinced that the entire *Satnami* community was on the verge of becoming Christian. Like his colleague, Disciples missionary H. C. Saum had long nurtured an obsession with the *Satnamis,* and had studied everything from their history to their dietary habits, intending, throughout his career and well into retirement, to write a book on the community. (So far as I know, he never completed the project.) Saum considered it his calling to "re-interpret the essence of Satnam in the light of modern conditions and to 'revive' the Satnam of G. Das."[16]

With longer experience of disappointed expectations regarding the *Satnamis,* the Evangelical missionaries were less hopeful about the prospects of a *Satnami* mass movement. Theodore Essebaggers reported in 1937 that he did "not share Dr. McGavran's [conviction] that a mass movement is in the making. Nevertheless that [McGavran] has brought a note of hope to the entire Satnami situation cannot be gainsaid."[17] Nevertheless, even the Evangelicals admitted that they saw signs, in the 1930s and '40s, of unrest and dissatisfaction among members of the Satnampanth.[18]

Desiring to attract *Satnamis* to the Christian fold, American missionaries and Indian evangelists attempted to portray conversion as a natural and logical choice for those who believed in the message of Guru Ghasidas. The portrayal required a selective editing and rewriting of *Satnami* history, and the conscious and unconscious remythologization of Ghasidas. Christians forged this link between the Satnampanth and Christianity in two ways: First, by

16. Handwritten, informal note found in Saum's files and written in what appears to be his hand, "My Object," HCS, box 4 of 4 (folder: India-History).

17. "Baitalpur Station Annual Report, 1936-1937," AES 82-13a Pr91, Annual Reports, no. 22, 1937.

18. See, for example, Rev. and Mrs. J. C. Koenig, "Annual Reports 1935: Bisrampur and Parsabhader Stations," AES 82-13a Pr91, Annual Reports, no. 20, 1935; and Theodore Essebaggers, "Christianizing the Satnamis of Chhattisgarh, India," 1938, published article in unknown periodical, found in AES 80-1 Sat8.

emphasizing Ghasidas's alleged prophecy regarding the coming of a white-faced man and, second, by claiming that on his pilgrimage to Puri, Ghasidas came into contact with Christian missionaries.

In one of his first reports from Chhattisgarh, which was published in *Der deutsche Missionsfreund*, Lohr wrote (in German):

> Here I have to point out the reason for my favorable reception. The late guru (teacher) of the Satnamis, who was the third descendent of the founder of the sect, had at a certain occasion given the promise to his disciples, in a kind of prophetic excitement when there were ten thousand of them together, that their salvation would be brought to them by a sahib, or a white man, and that they would be guided by this person on the right way, and that they should join with him with hope and trust.[19]

Later, in an autobiography, Lohr declared, "The Chamars accepted me as the teacher whose coming their leader had predicted, who would proclaim to them the way of salvation in a better way than he himself could do."[20] It seems clear that Lohr had intentionally postured himself as this prophesied one — could he have resisted the temptation to point out that he was a white man with a message similar, in some ways, to that of Ghasidas?

Whereas Lohr's version of the account attributes the prophecy to the third *Satnami* guru, later versions of the story suggest that Ghasidas himself had uttered the prediction. For example, in an article published in *Der deutsche Missionsfreund* in 1881, Evangelical missionary Andrew Stoll claims that Ghasidas was the one who had made the prophecy. However, the phrasing of his claim — ". . . soll er . . . gesagt haben, dass bald weisse Lehrer kommen werden"[21] (. . . he is supposed to have said that a white teacher would soon come) — indicates that there was still, among missionaries, some uncertainty that the prophecy had ever occurred.[22]

Later versions of the story dispense with this uncertainty and generously fill in details. The coming leader, these versions of the story suggest, was to be a red-faced (sun-burned), *pendrā* (white), *ṭopī-vālā* (hat-wearing) man with a

---

19. Oscar Lohr, "Leiden und Freuden Unseres Missionars," *Der deutsche Missionsfreund* 4, no. 1 (1869): 5.

20. "The Autobiography of the Rev. Oscar T. Lohr, in 1900," AES 84-5 L078.

21. The use of the modal auxiliary, *"sollen,"* indicates that the writer cannot confirm the assertion. Andrew Stoll, "Chhattisgarh," *Der deutsche Missionsfreund*, June 1881, p. 45.

22. To my knowledge, the earliest unconditional assertion that Ghasidas uttered the prophecy came in 1894; see Th. Tanner, *Im Lande der Hindus oder, Kulturschilderungen aus Indien* (St. Louis: n.p., 1894), p. 35.

pothī (book) in his hand.[23] Later accounts embroidered the story yet more. For example, an unnamed writer claimed that Ghasidas told his devotees: "The red-faced one will come from a western country, wearing a hat like a *khumarī* (a local hat). He will have the *pothī* of Satnam. When he comes, accept that *pothī* of Satnam and believe in it."[24]

The following account of the prophecy, which appears to have been written by an Indian Christian (in a mixture of Hindi and Chhattisgarhi), employs western cultural peculiarities to make it unequivocally clear that Ghasidas was predicting the arrival of a European: "The foreigner that is coming will have an office [*daftar*], and will carry records [*bahī*] in his hands. He will have a fair face. He will be wearing boots [*nangariyā*] and a hat [*khumarī*]. He will not use water [to clean himself] in the toilet."[25] These accounts, particularly the later ones, appear to combine *Satnami* legends about Ghasidas's prophetic abilities with the creative embellishment of Christians and missionaries who wished to claim the prophet's mantle, along with the allegiance of his followers.

It is impossible to determine the "original" nature of the prophecy, if it existed at all. Lohr seems unlikely to have fabricated the story, since it undoubtedly raised mission board expectations (and no missionary would want to work unnecessarily under such high expectations). But if Lohr did *not* conjure up the story, then he must have heard it, or something like it, from another source. The story would best serve the purposes of *Satnami* converts, since it would in some way justify their conversion. But it seems unlikely that Lohr was simply repeating a tradition that had gained currency among *Satnami*-Christians, since Lohr's account in *Der deutsche Missionsfreund* (quoted above) appeared in the same month as the first baptisms (which means that he had written and sent it from India before there *were* any *Satnami*-Christians). Moreover, there is no evidence from *Satnami* sources that such a prophecy ever occurred. Only older *Satnamis* educated by mis-

23. See, for example, E. M. Gordon, *Indian Folk Tales: Being Side-Lights on Village Life in Bilaspore, Central Provinces* (London: Elliot Stock, 1909), p. 5; Bessie Farrar Madsen, "Come and Teach My People: A Call from India," *Missionary Tidings*, June 1914, p. 57; and H. C. Saum and Mildred Saum, "Followers of the True Name," *Mungeli News Letter*, March 1935, p. 3.

24. "*Satnāmī panth aur satnām ki pothī* (The Satnami Panth and the Book of Satnam), undated, unsigned, found in HCS, box 1 of 4 (folder: Satnami Mss.).

25. "*Satyanāmī panth ke aguve ki śikṣā tathā bhaviṣya-vāṇī* (The Leader of the Satyanami Sect's Teachings and Prophecy), undated, unsigned, found in HCS, box 3 of 4 (no folder). As this version of the prophecy indicates, there was some ambiguity in the prediction with regards to whether it applied to missionaries or British officials.

sionaries seem to have any knowledge of it. For example, one *Satnami* informant reported that Ghasidas had prophesied the arrival of white-faced people with golden hair who would come from the East (the closest area of missionary and British strength was in and around Cuttack and Puri, to the East) with books under their arms, preaching about *"satya."* When asked where he had heard the story, he said, "The *padris* [missionaries] told it like that." He later insisted that both missionaries and older *Satnamis* told the story in this way.

Though it is impossible to determine the original source of the alleged prophecy, one possible (and not unlikely) explanation of its existence is that some *Satnami* guru, whether Ghasidas or a member of his *paramparan,* uttered a saying or a prophecy which had no particular import for the *Satnami* community and was thus quickly forgotten, but which, when heard by Christians, took on an entirely new meaning and significance. As the remembered "prophecy" became passed around from Christian to Christian (and particularly as it found its way to Christian leaders, including the missionaries) it could plausibly have become more refined, precise, and detailed.

For example, one can imagine that a *Satnami* guru, privy to information from afar and hearing of the rise of the British Raj, may have uttered some prediction regarding the coming of white men who had a fondness for hats and books. One can also imagine, if the guru had heard of the nature of the British government, that he might have considered these men potential adversaries and therefore instructed his followers not to resist them openly. Remembering the prediction as Christians, members of the *Satnami*-Christian community could easily and without realizing it have interpreted the words differently, as a prophecy regarding the coming of missionaries. To my mind, this is a more plausible scenario than that offered by Dube, who suggests that the predictions of a coming "white" man may have originated in Ghasidas's encounter with the *śvet* (white, connoting purity) *Satpuruś,* which could have been assimilated to the figure of the white-skinned *(pendrā)* missionary.[26]

We are, of course, in the realm of pure speculation at this point. But I speculate not so much to invent my own history, nor even to advance a theory about what was most likely to have been the case, but merely to suggest that it is entirely possible that the Christian story of Ghasidas's prophecy had its source in some real (but transmuted) event in the history of the Satnampanth. Moreover, I desire, once again, to draw attention to the fact that the line between myth and history is very often rather blurry.

Whereas the Christian account of Ghasidas's prophecy may have been

26. Dube, *Untouchable Pasts,* p. 198.

drawn from some "real" if insignificant element of the *Satnami* tradition, Christian accounts of the Guru's pilgrimage to Puri, and what happened along the way, appear to be largely imagined, the inventions of *Satnami* converts and their Christian leaders. Nevertheless, though they may be fictions, they are *plausible* fictions, and therein lies their power. The most common traditional *Satnami* version of events suggests that Ghasidas encountered *Satpuruṣ* while on a pilgrimage to the Jagannath temple in Puri. Early British reports of Ghasidas's inspiration, such as that in Grant's 1870 *Gazetteer of the Central Provinces,* follow this account and mention no connection between Ghasidas and missionaries. This suggests that before the arrival of missionaries the *panth* itself did not believe there to be a connection between Ghasidas and Christianity.[27] Likewise, British ethnographic texts and gazetteers published well into the twentieth century follow this traditional version of the story.[28] So do contemporary *Satnami* accounts.

Christian rescensions, which assert that Ghasidas acquired his message from Christian missionaries whom he encountered on his pilgrimage to Puri, first emerged around the turn of the century. A pamphlet written by Mary Kingsbury is typical, and is among the earliest archival records of the emerging Christian version of the story:

> There is a tradition that [a *Chamar*] went on a pilgrimage to the famous shrine of Juggernaut, and while there he heard a white *Guru,* or teacher, who spoke about the sin of idolatry, saying there was only one true God, and that He alone should be worshiped. When this man, who was named Ghussee Das, returned to his country, he determined to establish this new religion among his people. In order to do this, he separated himself from them for a while, going into the jungle to live, and telling his people that God would give him a message, and he would come again and deliver it to them . . . When, after about six months, he did appear, the people received him as a prophet. . . . You will judge aright from this account, that Ghussee Das must have listened to a missionary preaching when he was at Juggernaut, and that although many things

27. Charles Grant, ed., *The Gazetteer of the Central Provinces of India* (New Delhi: Usha, 1984). See also "Notes on the Sutnamee Chumars of the Raepore District from Information Gathered Orally from the Gooroo, Agur Dass, and His Disciples, and from Chumars Generally in 1868," unsigned supplement to Temple's 1867 *Gazetteer of Central India,* HCS, box 3 of 4 (no folder).

28. See, for example, A. E. Nelson, *Central Provinces District Gazetteer: Raipur District* (Bombay: British India Press, 1909); and Robert Vane Russell, *The Tribes and Castes of the Central Provinces of India,* vol. 1 (London: Macmillan, 1916).

were confused in his mind, he had received a little of the truth which remained with him and bore some fruit.[29]

In 1909, Disciples missionary E. M. Gordon echoed Kingsbury's account, asserting that it was "more than likely that during his stay in Jagganath
[Ghasidas] heard the preaching of the early missionaries."[30]

Already by 1897, however, some Evangelical missionaries were asserting
that the encounter between Ghasidas and missionaries occurred in Cuttack
(not Jagganath).[31] In 1934, H. C. Saum wrote to a certain Rev. Lazarus, pastor
of the Baptist Church at Cuttack, asking whether Lazarus could verify the
"tradition" regarding Ghasidas's visit to the city. No record exists of a reply
from Lazarus, but Saum's letter indicates that by that time another detail had
been added to the traditional Christian version of the story — that the missionaries were Baptist (no other missionaries were active around Cuttack at
that time).[32] In a book published in 1990, but based primarily on his experiences in the 1930s and '40s, Disciples missionary Donald McGavran, an invet-
erate mythologizer, suggested that Ghasidas might have, in fact, met William
Carey himself — a possibility, of course, but a most unlikely one.[33]

Early in the twentieth century, most accounts of Ghasidas's encounter
with Baptist missionaries in Cuttack acknowledged it as "tradition" or "reputed" history, though to my knowledge only one missionary explicitly expressed skepticism about the story.[34] By the 1930s and '40s, however, most
Christians accepted the story as a "true" account. It appears to be the case that
Satnami converts "remembered" the heretofore unknown details of Ghasi-

29. Mary Kingsbury, *Bilaspur* (Indianapolis: Christian Women's Board of Missions,
n.d.), p. 5. The text, unfortunately, is undated, and Kingsbury worked nearly continuously
in Bilaspur from 1885 until her retirement in 1925. But internal evidence, including the
spelling of "Ghussee Das," suggests a publication date between 1895 and 1905.

30. Gordon, *Indian Folk Tales*, p. 4.

31. See Julius Richter, *History of Missions in India*, trans. Sydney H. Moore (New York:
Revell, 1906), p. 251. Richter here quotes an unknown Evangelical mission publication of
1897.

32. H. C. Saum to Rev. Lazarus, 20 November 1934, HCS, box 4 of 4 (folder: Satnamis).
It is unlikely that Baptist missionaries would have remembered a visit from an unknown
Satnami who had not yet been established as a powerful Guru, so even a negative response
would not necessarily have ruled out the possibility of an encounter with Ghasidas. For
one text that identifies the missionaries as Baptist (but gives no specific names), see Saum
and Saum, "Followers of the True Name," p. 3.

33. Donald A. McGavran, *The Satnami Story: A Thrilling Drama of Religious Change*
(Pasadena: William Carey Library, 1990), pp. 1, 12.

34. See McGavran, J. G. (father of Donald), to H. C. Saum, 26 April 1931, HCS, box 3 of
4 (no folder).

das's pilgrimage, which were subsequently embellished by myth-making Christian leaders, American and Indian.

The story would have appeared plausible to those who wished it to be so. Ghasidas shared with missionaries their distaste for "idolatry," their focus on worshiping a single deity, and their rejection of distinctions based on caste. All of these things are rather uncommon among "orthodox" Hindus. Moreover, Christians and missionaries noted, Ghasidas had spoken often of *satya*, which can be rendered, at least superficially, as "true" or "truth" and linked to Christian passages using analogous language.[35] It is not at all surprising, given these rather striking similarities between the message of Ghasidas and that of Christians, that *Satnami*-Christians and missionaries should "discover" a connection between the two. And it is, after all, still possible that Ghasidas *did* encounter missionaries at some time during his peregrinations.[36]

Yet to leap from commonality to inspiration is historiographically dangerous. All of the themes shared by Ghasidas and Christian missionaries were also shared by the poet-saints of the *sant* tradition. *Sants* like Kabir rejected the worship of divine images; they professed their devotion to a single God without anthropomorphized qualities; they undermined distinctions based on caste, and they spoke of *satya* — unlike the missionaries and like Ghasidas — in a way that employed its full semantic range of meanings (including not only "truth," but also "being," and "ultimate reality"). Certainly no connection to Christianity is *necessary*, and the far-greater similarities between Ghasidas, Jagjivandas, and the *sants* make any substantial influence from Christianity unlikely.

To say that the stories told by Christians about Ghasidas are at least partially fabricated is not to suggest that they are unimportant. Rather, the mythological nature of these Christian renditions of the *Satnami* story encourages a shift in focus from the stories to those telling them. Christian versions of *Satnami* history — and, to be fair, many *Satnami* versions as well — must be read not as statements of fact and chronological narrative, but as apologue, as allegory. To my mind, the stories themselves are not as important as what they say about the story*tellers*.

---

35. Christians adduced Ghasidas's emphasis on truth as evidence that he had heard passages such as "I am the way, the truth, and the life" (John 14:6 KJV), and "Ye shall know the truth, and the truth shall make you free" (John 8:32 KJV).

36. There was a Baptist mission in Cuttack beginning around 1822.

"A Voice Calling in the Wilderness"[37]

The reinterpreted, Christianized, Ghasidas provided the *Satnami*-Christian community with a link not only to its past, but also to the larger Christian story. The Guru was portrayed as both a conduit of the Christian message and as a precursor of Christian missionaries. According to the Christian version of events, conversion to Christianity became not only the logical choice for those wishing to abide by Ghasidas's quasi-Christian message, but also represented a return to the newly discovered Christian roots of his inspiration. Rather than abandoning their tradition, *Satnami* converts to Christianity were returning to the mythic past.

Consciously or unconsciously, leaders of the *Satnami*-Christian community began to fashion Ghasidas in the image of John the Baptist. Ghasidas made it easy for them; he fit the bill. Like John the Baptist he was an eccentric character, a bit wild and wooly; he preferred to spend his time in the wilderness, and his unrefined and unlettered nature contrasted dramatically with the literate purveyors of the dominant religious orthodoxy. According to a missionary author, Ghasidas said:

> . . . a day will come when the True Name will make his people pure. When my elder brother comes (or one *greater* than I) he will teach the old book from house to house and in that day there will be drinking from the same pool the lion and the cow (— meaning that they will not devour each other as does the caste system). I, the prophet, am not the true name, nor do I have the old book of the True Name. I am not able to give you the entire secret, but he who will come in the future, will reveal the true God to you. . . . A WHITE MAN WEARING A HEAD COVERING (helmet). HE WILL HAVE THE OLD BOOK IN HIS HAND, AND WILL TELL YOU THE SECRET OF THE TRUE BOOK [emphasis in the original].[38]

In this striking *mélange* of religious mythologies, the missionary puts into Ghasidas's mouth the words of John the Baptist, "There cometh one mightier than I after me" (Mark 1:7 KJV; see also Matt. 3:11 and Luke 3:16), and places him squarely within the Hebrew and Christian prophetic tradition by having

37. A phrase from Isaiah 40:3 (KJV), and applied by the authors of Matthew (3:3), Mark (1:3), Luke (3:4), and John (1:23) to John the Baptist, Jesus' predecessor.

38. "The Christian Approach to the Satnami," undated (ca. 1935), probably written by Donald A. McGavran, DCHS, UCMS Records, DOM, India, box 41, McGavran, Donald A., Mr. and Mrs. (folder: India II — McGavran, Mr. and Mrs. Donald).

him utter a localized version of Isaiah's prophecy: "The wolf also shall dwell with the lamb, and the leopard shall lie down with the kid; and the calf and the young lion and the fatling together; and a little child shall lead them" (11:6 KJV). This missionary was not alone in portraying Ghasidas as a Christian precursor and Christian missionaries as the fulfillment of his prophecies.[39] A tract written around 1920 by the Evangelical catechist and pastor Ramnath Bajpai (who added "Simon" to his name when he was baptized) says:

As Ghasidas told you that white sahib would come and would bring along with him the name of [Truth] or True name, [so you should] open your eyes and see that the white faced sahabs [*sic*] have come, and they really preach about Jesus Christ the True name. . . . Get hold of him and come out of the mud. Ghasidas told you that when those white sahebs [*sic*] come there will be the dawn of [a] True age with the effect that tigers and cows would drink water from the same drinking place or ghat [a stone stairway down to water] together. Is it not true? Yes, it is true, Brahmins and the Chamars drink water from the same pipe.[40]

After forming Ghasidas in the image of John the Baptist, leaders of the *Satnami*-Christian community went on to assert that the *Satnami* community had fallen from the standards set by its guru. The source of Ghasidas's message, after all, had been pure, and whatever slight differences there may have been between Christianity and the message preached by Ghasidas were attributed to the brevity of his exposure to Christianity, his illiteracy, or his simplicity. According to these accounts, it was Ghasidas's successors, especially Balakdas, who debased a movement that Christian leaders regarded as

39. McGavran claimed that when he and others preached to *Satnamis*, they would say, "Your own guru, Ghasi Das, foretold a hundred years ago that there would come a red-faced man with a big hat and a big book in his hand. Well, this is the red-faced man and this is the big book. Listen to what it says. It *amplifies* what Ghasi Das proclaimed." McGavran, *Satnami Story*, p. 42.

40. *Some Facts about the Satnamis* (undated; 1921?). The tract, which I discovered in the files of the Disciples missionary H. C. Saum, is a typescript English translation of an originally Hindi text. It is undated and unsigned. But in a letter from H. C. Saum to Evangelical missionary Dr. Jacob Gass (25 May 1935), Saum quotes from the tract and attributes it to "your man, Rev. Ramnath Bajpai." Seybold reports that Bajpai was ordained on 25 April 1920 and died on 16 December 1922; see Seybold, *God's Guiding Hand*, p. 71. Therefore, the text could have been written no later than 1922 and, assuming Saum was correct in designating Bajpai a "Reverend," no earlier than 1920. Both the tract and the letter were found in HCS, box 2 of 4; the tract was loose (no folder) and the letter was in a folder entitled "Bishrampur History Data."

positive overall, and who had dragged the *Satnami* community down once again into polytheism and — referring to a rarely performed fertility rite called *satlok* which involved ritualized sexual intercourse — immorality.[41] Though the scabrousness of the *Satnami's* alleged sexual profligacy provided an evocative foil on which the Christian community's relative chastity and sexual fidelity appeared all the more striking, it was the movement of *Satnamis* away from their founder's rejection of image worship that most provoked the consternation of Chhattisgarhi Christians and missionaries.

After the 1920s, while *Satnami* leaders were attempting *rapprochement* with upper-caste Hindu leaders and were sanskritizing their rituals and beliefs, Christians attempted to convince them that they were *not* Hindus,[42] and reminded them that Hindus had formerly considered them "outside the fold." As Christians presented the choice, *Satnamis* could either embrace Ghasidas's prohibitions against image-worship by becoming Christian, or reject Ghasidas's instructions in order to seek the approbation of oppressive upper-caste Hindus. By asserting that the Satnampanth had fallen away from the unspoiled message of its founder, Christians were able to portray conversion to Christianity not as a rejection of the Satnampanth, but, as one *Satnami*-Christian put it, a return "*back* to Satnam."[43] Joining the Christian community was about rediscovering and embracing the original but now vi-

---

41. See, for example, Simon Patros, *Simon Patros of India: A Miracle of God's Grace* (St. Louis: Board of International Missions, Evangelical and Reformed Church, Inc., 1954), p. 43. For more on *satlok*, see Dube, *Untouchable Pasts*, pp. 103-5.

42. One Evangelical catechist who complimented *Satnamis* on their monotheism reported, "They take great pleasure to hear that they are higher than Hindus, because they have given up idolatry and worship the one true God. . . ." Entry in diary, unnamed catechist, 22 February 1908, found in the journal of S. J. Scott, Mahasamund catechist, AES 83-5 Di54 #1.

43. Emphasis added. Hira Lal, *Satnām ke pās lauṭ āo* (Come Back to Satnam, ca. 1938), published tract (with no publication details), found in HCS, box 2 of 4 (folder: Tularam). Missionaries also sounded the theme of fallenness. See Nelle Grant Alexander, *Disciples of Christ in India* (Indianapolis: United Christian Missionary Society, 1946), p. 9; Edith Moulton Melick, *The Evangelical Synod in India* (St. Louis: Eden Publishing House, 1930), p. 25; and Emil W. Menzel, *I Will Build My Church: The Story of Our India Mission and How It Became a Church* (Philadelphia: Board of Missions, Evangelical and Reformed Church, 1943), p. 18. British officials shared with missionaries the notion that monotheism was the highest form of religion, and therefore considered polytheism a corruption. Nelson asserted, "The crude myths which are now associated with the story of Ghāsi Dās . . . furnish a good instance of the way in which a religion, originally of a high order of morality, will be rapidly degraded to their own level when adopted by a people who are incapable of living up to it." Nelson, *Central Provinces District Gazetteer*, p. 81. See also Grant, ed., *Gazetteer*, p. cxxx.

tiated message of Ghasidas, about digging through the detritus of a corrupt religion and discovering its unspoiled source. Non-Christian *Satnamis* do appear, however, to have been cognizant of the fact that the information contained in published works could also be manipulated by those who created them. As early as 1908, Chhattisgarhis had developed a modicum of skepticism towards the texts distributed by their Christian neighbors. Some villagers responded to a catechist's claim that he had books that would disprove their religion by saying, ". . . these books have been printed by you, you may insert whatever you like . . ."[44]

Inventing Tradition: M. M. Paul's *Satyanāmī Panth*

As the preceding discussion suggests, leaders of the Disciples' Christian community appear to have been far more interested in the history of Ghasidas than their Evangelical leaders. Nevertheless, in no single text is the Christian reinvention of Ghasidas and the Satnampanth more clearly, more comprehensively, or more coherently laid out than in *Satyanāmī panth: śrī gosāīn ghāsīdās giraud vāsī* (Satnam Panth: Shri Gosain Ghasidas of Girod,[45] 1937), written by M. M. Paul, an Evangelical catechist and pastor working (at the time) in Pithora.[46] After 1937, all Christian accounts of the *Satnami* story appear to draw inspiration from *Satyanāmī panth*. But it was not the first text of its kind. I have already mentioned Simon Ramnath Bajpai's earlier text, *Some Facts about Satnamis* (ca. 1921). Paul's text shares much in common with Bajpai's and at times the two are nearly exact replicas, from the fundamental arguments they make, to the account and interpretation of Ghasidas's story, to the quirky idiomatic expressions they employ (such as their admonition that *Satnamis* should "get out of the mud" and follow the true Satnam). Paul's claim to have heard his version of the story from an early *Satnami* convert notwithstanding (Bajpai does not make this claim), it is clear that he was either familiar with Bajpai's earlier tract, or that both drew upon an as-yet-undiscovered *Ur*-text, whether a written work or a fairly common oral account. Bajpai and Paul both worked for the Evangelical mission, and it is therefore entirely plausible that Bajpai's work was passed along to Paul for updating and publication.

44. Entry in unnamed catechist's journal for 26 September 1908, found in the journal of S. J. Scott, Mahasamund catechist, AES 83-5 Di54 #1.

45. The Hindi text spells it "Giraud," but "Girod" is the spelling more common today.

46. "*Śrī* is a customary mark of respect, and *gosāīn* is an honorary title, the latter usually given to holy men. All translations of the text, which was written in Hindi and Chhattisgarhi, are mine. Special thanks to Mr. Manish Tiwari for help with thorny passages.

Satyanāmī panth is by far the more rhetorically powerful of the two texts. If Bajpai's is basically a story, though an undeniably biased and pedantic one, Paul's is an impassioned, sustained polemic. Beginning with the epigraph of *Satyanāmī panth*, "Ye shall know the truth, and the truth shall make you free" (John 8:32), Paul weaves together *Satnami* and Christian myths by playing with the communities' respective emphasis on "truth" *(sat, satya)*. According to Paul's account, Ghasidas first encounters the term among followers of Jagjivandas, and is later surprised to hear the word used by Christian preachers in Cuttack. Paul refers to both Jesus and God as Satyanam or Satnam. From the title page to the closing line, Paul attempts to present Christianity as the fulfillment of Ghasidas's (and therefore the *Satnamis'*) quest for the True Name.[47]

Paul begins *Satyanāmī panth* by establishing the ground of his authority. For some time, he claims, he had been searching for someone who had known Ghasidas personally who could tell him more about the Guru. Eventually he met a man — other texts and oral accounts agree that it was Anjori (or Anjorus) Paulus, a *Satnami* among Lohr's first converts — who had associated with Ghasidas in his youth and who, seeing the degradation of the *panth* after the Guru's death, had become a Christian. Moreover, to be certain that Anjori's account was true, Paul asserts, he tested it before "large crowds of *Satnamis* in which the *panth's* great *mahants*, its lower *mahants*, its wise *bhandārīs* and its old men had been present. No one was able to deny [Anjori's account], but gave witness that now was the time that they should accept Satyanam Jesus — only by *his* grace could they arrive at a higher state."[48]

Paul then recounts the events of Ghasidas's life. In his youth, Ghasidas impressed his family with his devotion to the gods. Eventually, his family suggested he marry, which he did, and he and his wife, Saphura, had four sons. After the death of their favorite son, which neither the intervention of *baigās* nor Ghasidas's faithful worship, vows, and austerities could prevent, the anguished and disillusioned future guru began wandering. Around Lucknow, he

---

47. Though Bajpai's text also refers to Jesus as the "True Name," Paul's emphasis on *sat/satya*, and his use of the term to draw a line from Jagjivandas (unmentioned by Bajpai) to the preachers in Cuttack, is much more original. In 1935, missionary E. C. Davis wrote a tract that also linked Jesus and the Satnam. The text is repeatedly punctuated with the phrase *"jay satyanām — jay yīshu* [hail to Satyanam — hail to Jesus]." See E. C. Davis, *Satnām Panth Darśak* (Jabalpur: Mission Press, 1935).

48. M. M. Paul, *Satyanāmī Panth: Śrī Gosāīn Ghāsīdās Girod Vāsī* (Allahabad: The Mission Press, 1937), pp. 7, 21. Neither the claim that he had met Anjori Paulus nor that he tested the account before large crowds of *Satnamis* appears in Bajpai's text.

encountered members of the Satyanami Panth, founded by Jagjivandas in 1760, and noticed that they were greeting each other with "Satyanam." Inspired, Ghasidas took initiation as Jagjivandas's disciple. Jagjivandas, the text claims, had been the disciple of Ramanuja, who was a disciple of Ramanand, who was Kabir's guru. In this way, Paul connects Ghasidas, via the spiritual lineage of Ramanand, with the great *sant,* Kabir.[49]

After some time, Ghasidas left Jagjivandas and returned to his village, Girod. There the people were even more impressed than before by his evident holiness and encouraged him to take a pilgrimage to Jagannath on their behalf. Ghasidas agreed and set off for Puri with his brother:

> Along the way, when they had come close to Cuttack, they stopped under a tree, near a group of makeshift dwellings, to spend the night. In order to arrange for the evening meal, Ghasidas went to the bazaar and there, far off, saw a crowd, and going to stand near it, began to listen. He heard the word, *"satya,"* and was astonished, thinking "What is this word? *I* heard this truth from my guru, Jagjivandas, two years ago. How has this truth-speaker gotten here?" So he stood on his tip-toes and looked into the crowd and saw some preachers of truth who were relating the true message. Among these preachers was one white *sahib.* So Ghasidas stood there and listened to the preachers, who said, "There is only one True Supreme Lord [*parameśvar*] who created heaven and earth and nurtures and protects all of his creatures. And when his creation was doomed because of sin [*pāp*], this True Lord sent his Satyanam Jesus into this world in order to save it . . . This Satyanam Jesus said, 'I am the truth, the life, and the way.[50] Whoever believes in me will not perish but will receive eternal life. This Satyanam Jesus' life, work, and statements were all absolutely true. Until this very day, no one possessing true knowledge has been able in that Satyanam to find even the slightest trace of sin. Those of you who worship wood and stone, or go to Jagannath and perform prostrations of worship to an image made of *nīm* wood, the Satyanam considers this a great evil.[51]

49. It is curious that Christian authors, following the lead of *brahmans* like Babachandra, felt it necessary to bolster Ghasidas's Hindu credentials. Paul, *Satyanāmī Panth,* pp. 2-3.

50. Notice the rearrangement of the words of John 14:6 (NRSV), "I am the way, and the truth, and the life," in order to highlight "truth."

51. Paul, *Satyanāmī Panth,* pp. 5-6. The account of Ghasidas's experiences in Cuttack is quite similar to that found in Bajpai's text.

Ghasidas completed his shopping in the bazaar and then sought out the preacher and conversed with him some more. He left thinking:

> In truth images neither speak nor move. They have eyes but see nothing. Likewise they have ears, but they heard nothing when I called at the time of my son's sickness. They have mouths, but when I cried out before them none responded. . . . Therefore, I will not go to see the image [at Jagannath]. The best thing would be for me to return to my village, Girod, and there relate to my people the message of this Satyanam about which I've heard.[52]

Upon his return, a great crowd of *Chamars* gathered in expectation of receiving Jagannath *prasād* from Ghasidas. He counseled them:

> O brothers, what *prasād* have you come to me for? All of these things are useless. I met the white *sahib* and he patiently told me the story of Satyanam . . . Keep in mind, brothers, that I am not your guru. I am like a *ganda* who announces the order of the government in our villages. Just like that, I am announcing the orders of my guru. The white *sahib* will bring the one Satnam . . . He will come with the old book [*junnā dabdar*] — then the *brahmans'* books will become insignificant. . . . Listen *babus*, at that time . . . the cow and the lion will drink water from the same *ghāṭ*.[53]

Ghasidas concluded his speech with a call to action: "Now give up the killing of goats and pigs; give up taking the name of Ram; throw out your [images of] gods and goddesses and Mata, and repeat the name of the Satnam that the white *sahib* will bring along with him."[54]

After a preaching tour from 1820 to 1830, Ghasidas withdrew to the Sonakhan jungle, and became a forest-dweller (*vānaprasth*, the third of four traditional stages in life, called *āśramas*, traditionally followed only by members of the upper castes), chanting *"satyanām"* as he went along. People came to have *darśan* of the holy man, and soon temples grew up around his abode. His followers believed that he could perform miracles, and the water in which

52. Paul, *Satyanāmī Panth*, p. 7.
53. Paul, *Satyanāmī Panth*, p. 7. Bajpai's version of Ghasidas's sermon is nearly identical to this one. Dube also provides an excerpt from this page in the text, translated slightly differently, but oddly elides passages without indication; see Dube, *Untouchable Pasts*, p. 198.
54. Paul, *Satyanāmī Panth*, p. 8.

his toes had been symbolically washed, called *amṛt jal* (ambrosia water), became prized for its miraculous medicinal powers. It was thought to cure the lame, the sick, and the infertile.

Much of the persuasive power of Paul's text derives from its plausibility. Paul follows the traditional *Satnami* account of Ghasidas rather closely, diverging only when necessary to make a point. His redactions are more additive than substitutional, and the story of Ghasidas thus remains recognizable. Though not from Chhattisgarh himself, Paul frequently employs earthy, demotic Chhattisgarhi idioms, particularly when narrating the words of the Guru. That is not to say, however, that Paul never strays from the *Satnami* version of events. For example, Ghasidas's deathbed instructions to his disciples intersperse instructions regarding traditional *Satnami* dietary and religious restrictions with exhortations like "Love everyone as yourself," "Do not believe in ghosts and spirits," "Make your lifestyle pure," and "Watch for the coming of a guru."[55]

After recounting the story of Ghasidas's death, Paul traces the degeneration of the *panth* and the debasement of Ghasidas's message that took place during the time of subsequent gurus, especially Balakdas. Paul accuses Balakdas of having "mixed his father's noble teachings with dirt" (*apne pitā kī bhalī śikṣā ko miṭṭī men milā diyā*).[56] Balakdas, Paul claims, turned *ramat* and the sale of *amṛt jal* (which was perhaps initially given for free) into a business in order to support his lavish and self-indulgent lifestyle. Moreover, Balakdas institutionalized sexual profligacy by introducing practices such as *satlok*, which Paul describes in a puzzlingly circuitous and abstruse manner, arguing that Christians should not speak directly about such things.[57] According to Paul, the degeneration of the *panth* continued even after the assassination of Balakdas. During the reign of his successors, who maintained his standards of opulent living, the *Satnamis* were bilked of what little Balakdas had left them and became destitute. Even though Balakdas's successors were not nearly as corrupt as he was, the damage had been done, and *Satnamis* ceased to trust their gurus, because, as the proverb says, "the one who has been burned [drinking hot] milk, will sip buttermilk only with care" (*dūdh ka jalā huā mahī ko bhī phūk phūk kar pītā hai*).[58]

In the midst of this corruption and despair, writes Paul, a more trustworthy guru arrived: ". . . in 1868, when all of the *Satnami* and *Chamar* people

55. Paul, *Satyanāmī Panth*, pp. 9-10.

56. Paul, *Satyanāmī Panth*, p. 11.

57. A slightly more graphic description of these rituals, along with a similarly stated discomfort with discussing them, appears in Bajpai's text.

58. Paul, *Satyanāmī Panth*, p. 13. In Hindi, the proverb employs the present tense.

were oppressed by the Brahmans and Rajputs and were in an absolutely fallen state, Satyanam put it into the heart of his devotee [*bhakt*], the missionary, that he should in some way lift them up. Therefore, Padri O. T. Lohr Sahib began to proclaim the Satyanam, Jesus."[59] Missionaries and their benign colonial supporters, Paul asserts, effected a miraculous improvement among the *Satnamis:*

> Nowadays there are *Satnamis* who are seen in a good state, but not because of their *dharm* or the work of the gurus, but because of the light spread around by westerners. Schools where no distinction remains between *Satnamis* and others were established in large villages by the honorable government and the missionaries. Whatever knowledge one desires can be obtained. So many received learning, because of which the eyes of the *Satnami* are being opened and the evil practices among them . . . have come to an end or are coming to an end. . . . [*Satnamis*] should express heartfelt thanks to the honorable government and the well-wishing missionaries that today *Satnami* people move about on equal footing with Hindus and Muslims and do business with them. If there were a *Hindu* Raj, then today [the Hindus] would protect and nurture a dog with them in the house, and would wash it and clean it, and would not despise it even if it got dirty and came to them — yet oh how much they would [still] despise the *Satnamis*! If they would be in power, then, *Satnamis*, what state would you be in?[60]

The logic, claims Paul, is simple. Ghasidas foretold the coming of the white *sahib* who would bring the Satyanam, and he instructed his followers to listen to what the coming *sahib* would say. Everything the Guru predicted had come to pass with the arrival of the missionaries. Accordingly, Paul suggests that every *Satnami* should: "Seize [the Satyanam Lord Jesus Christ] and become an obedient servant of your guru, Gosain [Ghasidas]. A disciple is one who conducts himself according to the command of his guru. What is the state, today, of the boys and girls of those who obeyed their guru and took the only Satyanam into their homes [i.e., the Christians]? Today very big brahmans bow their heads before them. So, brothers, get out of the mud and come [*cikhlā mā se nikar āvo*]."[61] The one who performs *pūjā* to a Hindu deity cannot be a real *Satnami*, Paul asserts. "A Satyanami is one who acknowledges

---

59. Paul, *Satyanāmī Panth*, pp. 14-15.
60. Paul, *Satyanāmī Panth*, p. 17.
61. Paul, *Satyanāmī Panth*, pp. 19-20.

the truth, that is to say, one who acknowledges the only *paramesvar* and conducts himself according to His commandments. So if you want to be called true Satyanamis, then accept the Satyanam Jesus. . . ."[62]

Only at the very end of twenty-four pages does Paul provide a basic and hasty catechesis:

> [Satyanam Jesus] took on the outward appearance of a human in order to save sinners and neglected people. And taking on a body of kindness and excellence he lived for thirty-three years in this world. He cured the sorrows of the despairing and the diseases of the ailing. He gave life to the dead, and forgave the sins of the iniquitous. In the end he took the yoke of sin upon himself and was killed on a cross. On the third day of his entombment, very early on a Sunday morning, he courageously snatched life from death, this Satyanam Jesus Christ. Remaining alive for forty days he appeared to his disciples and others, eating and drinking with them. Finally, encouraging his disciples, he said, "Now I have told you about the great love of the True Lord, about his wishes and how to live according to them. Now I go to the place [*dhām*, a term which implies both "abode" and "splendor" or "radiance," and which Hindus associate with the supreme being and with paradise] from which I came. But remember that I am with you always. Go to all *jātis* and give them the message of the only Satyanam. And give baptism [*baptismā denā*] to anyone who comes to acknowledge the one Satyanam. . . . Saying these things, he ascended into heaven. Now in the end days he will come again just as he went to heaven. In that time he will judge everyone according to the balance of his or her works. Friends, now that you have read these things, think about it, whether you are a *Satnami* or not.[63]

In the text, Paul appeals to the *Satnamis'* presumed desire for respect and equitable treatment. Jesus, Paul maintains, came to earth for those "suffering, base persons, and paupers, who very 'wise' and wealthy people considered so worthless that they were not able to go into their temples. . . ."[64] When it became clear that Jesus would not prevent these low people from hearing his message, the highborn and "wise" abandoned him. As in this passage, Paul repeatedly contrasts the egalitarian spirit of Jesus and Christians with the

---

62. Paul, *Satyanāmī Panth*, p. 22.

63. Paul, *Satyanāmī Panth*, pp. 23-24. This almost creedal formulation does not appear in Bajpai's text.

64. Paul, *Satyanāmī Panth*, p. 20.

haughtiness of *brahmans*. The *junnā dabdar* of the missionaries would destroy the learning of the *brahmans,* he writes, and whereas the *brahmans* judge others according to archaic rules distinguishing pure from impure, Satyanam Jesus "looks inside," where the "the fruits of one's nature are on display."[65] The last line of the text makes Paul's message clear: "In the Christian religion [*dharm*] there is no untouchability, so those who desire [this] should accept the Satyanam."[66]

Conclusion

Though it is nearly impossible to ascertain how many, and what kind of people read the tract, M. M. Paul's *Satyanāmī panth* established the standard Christian version of the *Satnami* story, and most subsequent accounts of the events, on both the Disciples and Evangelical mission fields, follow the outlines of his narrative. The text drew authority from the fact that it was *written;* it was a tangible, durable, stable document. The importance of this fact, in a context of low literacy and high regard for literate specialists, cannot easily be overstated.

In fact, *Satyanāmī panth* and Bajpai's *Some Facts about Satnamis* contributed to the standardization of the previously diverse and more fluid oral tradition from which they had been drawn. During an interview with Christians from Ganeshpur, all accounts of the story of Ghasidas roughly followed the shape of Paul's version of events, but the informants were divided on whether they had heard the story from elders or read it in "some book." Similarly, during his field research, Dube encountered a Christian whose oral history of Ghasidas also closely followed Paul's account. When asked where he had heard it, the man appeared upset and said, "It is the true thing," adding that it was *likhit itihās* (written history).[67]

In *Did the Greeks Believe in Their Myths?*, Paul Veyne argues that in any culture or historical epoch, "truth" is determined by the "constitutive imagination," which is to say that the criteria for judging truth from falsity are socially and historically conditioned. For the Greeks, for example, "A program of truth existed in which it was accepted that someone, Hesiod or someone else, told the truth when he reeled off the names that passed through his mind or spouted the most unbridled Swedenborgian fantasies. For such people psy-

---

65. Paul, *Satyanāmī Panth*, p. 21.
66. Paul, *Satyanāmī Panth*, p. 24.
67. See Dube, *Untouchable Pasts*, p. 204.

chological imagination is a source of veracity."[68] Historical "truth" was, for the Greeks, information "obtained by someone else" and "authenticated by consensus over the ages."[69]

For Indians in the first half of the twentieth century, similar criteria for determining truth existed. Truth was information obtained from a reliable guide, a guru or brahman priest, or, perhaps more importantly in this context, recorded in *written texts*. Even *Satnamis*, particularly those who had contact with Christians or were educated in their schools, were influenced by Paul's written "history" of their *panth*. In the 1950s, *Satnami* leaders were still concerned about the effects of *Satyanāmī panth* on the *Satnami* community. Naindas and Anjordas, leaders of the Satnami Mahasabha, both testified about the text before the Christian Missionary Activities Enquiry. Anjordas told the committee that missionaries had been saying that Ghasidas met missionaries at Cuttack and that Ghasidas had become a Christian. Anjordas then referred to Paul's *Satyanāmī panth* as evidence of missionary wrongdoing, saying:

A book [alleging that Ghasidas had been inspired by Christian missionaries] has been published and widely circulated amongst the Satnamis. On such type of preaching many Satnamis have become Christians. . . . To my knowledge, about a thousand Satnamis became converts after the story was circulated. I do not know how many Satnamis actually read the book containing the story of Ghasidas. Many Satnamis who are in possession of the book . . . have not read it.[70]

Naindas, who was at the time a member of the state's legislative assembly, added:

Adi [the original] Guru is Ghasidas . . . [Satnamis] will be agitated, if he called himself Christian. People will be prepared to die in a fight with anybody who would say that the Adi Guru was a Christian. The Christian Missionaries go round all the villages, telling the people that as Satnamis they remained down-trodden in Hindu society, that the true

68. Paul Veyne, *Did the Greeks Believe in Their Myths? An Essay on the Constitutive Imagination* (Chicago: University of Chicago Press, 1988), p. 103.

69. Veyne, *Did the Greeks?*, pp. 27, 6.

70. Sita Ram Goel, ed., *Vindicated by Time: The Niyogi Committee Report on Christian Missionary Activities (1956)* (New Delhi: Voice of India, 1998), p. II.B.98. The Christian Missionary Activities Enquiry is discussed at length in the Conclusion.

Satnami is to be found in the Christian Scriptures, and that they should give up the Hindu society and join Christianity.[71]

Another *Satnami* witness, Bajirao Niru, who was also a member of the state legislature, argued that Paul's *Satyanāmī panth* included "offensive references to some of our Gurus."[72] Clearly Paul's text and the version of events it contained influenced far more *Satnamis* than merely those who had become Christian.

But notice, however, that Anjordas, Naindas, and Bajirao do not directly contest the factual *veracity* of Paul's account, only its effect on the *Satnami* community. There is not yet in this context a conception of historical truth that requires the marshalling and documenting of evidence from primary sources. Veyne suggests that it was historical controversy, in fact, which gave rise to modern western criteria for determining truth. He writes, ". . . before the age of controversy, before the time of Nietzsche and Max Weber, facts existed. The historian had neither to interpret (since facts existed) nor prove (because facts are not the stakes of a controversy). They had only to report the facts, either as a 'reporter' or a compiler."[73] M. M. Paul appears to have lived in a time "before the age of controversy," and the missionaries were not so different as to require the scrutinization of Paul's sources. Indeed, they were for the most part fully enough satisfied with Paul's myth — useful as it was for their own purposes — to perpetuate it whenever possible.

Ironically, the most avid peddlers of the Christianized Ghasidas chronicle were not *Satnamis*. The missionaries, of course, had no ethnic connection to the *Satnami* community. And though a native of Chhattisgarh, Bajpai was a *brahman* who converted in 1882 after becoming convinced (by a *brahman* catechist) that Ghasidas had accurately predicted the arrival of missionaries.[74] Paul was neither a *Satnami* nor a Chhattisgarhi. He was, rather, a native of Uttar Pradesh, and was born into a Tiwari *brahman* family converted by Methodist missionaries during his youth.[75] He worked first

---

71. Goel, ed., *Vindicated by Time*, p. II.B.78.

72. Goel, ed., *Vindicated by Time*, pp. II.B.78-79.

73. Veyne, *Did the Greeks?*, p. 12.

74. Seybold, *God's Guiding Hand*, p. 29.

75. Missionaries appear to have believed Paul's claims to be of *brahman* stock. Satnami-Christians, however, were unconvinced, and a rumor circulated to the effect that Paul's family had belonged to a sweeper caste. The truth of the rumor cannot be ascertained and may reflect the resentment of local Christians who felt that Paul, an outsider, sometimes treated them disrespectfully. One Christian informant reported that Paul commonly denigrated Chhattisgarhi Christians, whether they had been *Satnami* or not, by say-

as village headmaster near Bishrampur, then as a catechist. Finally he was ordained in 1921, and began working as a pastor in Pithora, Mahasamund, and other areas.

For the first decades of Christian history in Chhattisgarh, non-*Satnamis* such as the missionaries and these *brahman* authors appear to have had the authority to "represent" members of the *Satnami*-Christian community — and even members of the *panth* — to themselves. A report from a *Satnami* village by Evangelical missionary H. A. Feierabend states it artlessly: "We spent late evenings telling these ignorant people what the founder of their religion had taught, how their later leaders had [misled] them and [how] they had forsaken the original lofty teachings, and how the truth for which the founder was longing was to be found in Christ, the coming of whose disciples he had prophesied."[76]

Similarly, Disciples missionary Adelaide Frost reported an interesting encounter with an orphan girl in her care:

> Playfully and thoughtlessly I said to Jumini, "Who are you?" She was surprised at my question and could not understand why I should ask it. Seeing she took it seriously, I became serious, too, and wished her to tell me what she would reply to such a question from a stranger. She became thoughtful, and made some replies to which I raised objections. I should have forgotten this, but Jumini followed me around, silent most of the time, but addressing me every little while in a questioning tone. For fully half an hour she was by me. Finally, Phebe [another orphan girl] said: "Say, 'I'm a Christian.'" This satisfied me and Jumini, too, and she has not mentioned it again.[77]

The dialogue, in which a missionary helps an Indian orphan girl "discover" her own identity, indicates the relationship of early *Satnami*-Christian converts to foreign missionaries and their often upper-caste, non-Chhattisgarhi, and therefore similarly "foreign" evangelists, pastors, and catechists. One

---

ing things such as *tum log to sab camrā hain* (*You* people are all *camrās*). Some of Paul's ancestors report that he (not his parents) had converted, and that until his death he continued to act like a *brahman*, taking regular baths, according to informants, in a certain way as part of what he considered his cultural (not religious) heritage. It is curious, given the fact that Paul appears to have looked down upon the *Satnamis*, that he should be the one to stabilize oral accounts linking his Christian community to the low-caste *panth*.

76. "New Opportunities and Difficulties in Evangelistic Work," 1936, AES 82-14 Qu2, Feierabend, H. A., Quarterly Reports, Articles, Newsletters, 1933-1941.

77. Adelaide Gail Frost, "In the Orphanage," *Missionary Tidings*, July 1898, p. 62.

wonders, what was the nature of the self-representations that Frost rejected? Did Jumini identify herself by *jāti*? By gender? By her place of birth? By a religion other than Christianity? By a nationality?

Amplifying and embellishing *Satnami* and Christian accounts of the *Satnami* history, the early leaders of the *Satnami*-Christian community attempted to forge a retroactive link to the past for their converts from the *panth*. With no firsthand experience of the degradations of lower-caste life, missionaries and non-*Satnami* Christian leaders such as Bajpai and Paul emphasized the continuities between Ghasidas and Christianity, believing themselves to be increasing the likelihood of *Satnami* conversions. It appears that in the early years of the community's life, *Satnami*-Christians valued the connection between Ghasidas and Christianity. The myth of the Guru's encounter with missionaries in Cuttack helped *Satnami*-Christians feel connected to the larger Christian story, as if they were treading paths mapped by God long ago. Similarly, the remembered prophecy of Ghasidas regarding the coming of white men made it appear as if *Satnamis* who converted to Christianity were fulfilling their *Satnami* destiny as well.[78] The reworked versions of the *Satnami* story helped *Satnami*-Christians justify their conversion and maintain a sense of communal pride.

Nevertheless, beginning in the early decades of the twentieth century, as Christians began to successfully distinguish themselves from *Satnamis* in the eyes of other communities in the region and gain a modicum of social respect and status, they sought at the same time to obscure their primarily lower-caste origins. For many Christians, membership in the community represented an *escape* from the everyday humiliations of lower-caste life. They did not wish to view themselves, or have others view them, as *Satnami*-Christians, but as Christians — a new, and at least slightly higher caste.

Until the famines of the 1890s, *Satnamis* who became Christian appear to have maintained contacts with their unconverted kin. But the famines radi-

---

78. Prophecies regarding the coming of "white men," remembered or otherwise, are of course not unique to the *Satnamis*. Such prophetic utterings have helped smooth the transition of non-Christian communities to Christianity in many parts of the world, including Africa (the Mbaka and Gedeo), China (the Lisu), Burma (the Wa, Karen, and Kachin), and the Pacific (the "Cargo Cults"); see Don Richardson, *Eternity in Their Hearts*, rev. ed. (Ventura, CA: Regal Books, 1984). Hefner also recounts the story of a Javanese convert to Christianity in the Tengger highlands who claimed that the arrival of Christianity on the island had been foretold by Javanese mystics centuries earlier; Robert W. Hefner, "Of Faith and Commitment: Christian Conversion in Muslim Java," in *Conversion to Christianity: Historical and Anthropological Perspectives on a Great Transformation*, ed. Robert W. Hefner (Berkeley: University of California Press, 1993), p. 112.

cally altered the nature of the Christian community.[79] By the beginning of the twentieth century, a large portion of those who became Christian had grown up in orphanages and boarding schools. Christians who were nurtured in these institutions, even those who had lived in *Satnami* families before entering them, were cut off from the beliefs and practices of their *Satnami* relatives.

A Disciples missionary's description of the difficulty, in the 1930s and '40s, of getting native evangelists to work in the villages, gives some indication of the distinctions that had emerged among Christians, *Satnamis,* and other village Chhattisgarhis: "When I said to them, 'Leave this Christian community and go live in a village,' they would reply, 'You are telling us to do something very difficult. There we will be the only Christians of experience. There we'll be living in the midst of strange, low-caste people. We'll have to conform to village patterns. We will have to obey the feudal lord. We men may be able to do all this, but our wives will feel frightened. Our children will grow up with children who are not Christian and whose ways of life do not appeal to us at all.'"[80] As the passage indicates, the Christian community in Chhattisgarh had begun, at least by the beginning of the twentieth century, to function as a caste, and was reluctant to associate with "strange, low-caste people."[81]

According to Christian informants, *Satnamis* considered those who became Christian "spoilers" of the caste, and generally declared them untouchable for a period of several years, during which they refused to share wells, water, or food with them. While *Satnamis* begrudgingly admired *Satnami-Christians* for their education, their newfound dignity, and their (sometimes)

79. "Twelfth Annual Report of the Chutteesgurh Mission, 1881-82," AES 82-13a Pr91, 1870-83 (Annual Reports).

80. Though McGavran's reliability as a historian has been called into question above, there is no evidence to suggest that this firsthand account of his experience is inaccurate — indeed, the information would have been somewhat embarrassing to McGavran. He would, therefore, have had no conceivable reason to fabricate it. McGavran, *Satnami Story,* pp. 75-76.

81. From the early missions of Francis Xavier among the *Paravas,* many Christian communities in India have followed the same trajectory, becoming, functionally, a caste; see Susan B. Kaufmann, "A Christian Caste in Hindu Society: Religious Leadership and Social Conflict among the Paravas of Southern Tamilnadu," *Modern Asian Studies* 15, no. 2 (1981): 209. For a discussion of caste among Christians and Muslims in India, see "The Dominant Caste in Rampura," in M. N. Srinivas, *Collected Essays* (New York: Oxford University Press, 2002), p. 194. On a Christian community that managed to retain its ties to the caste from which it emerged, see Heike Liebau, "Country Priests, Catechists, and Schoolmasters as Cultural, Religious and Social Middlemen in the Context of the Tranquebar Mission," in *Christians and Missionaries in India: Cross-Cultural Communication since 1500,* ed. Robert Eric Frykenberg (Grand Rapids: Eerdmans, 2003), p. 83.

greater wealth, they resented them for their disloyalty to the community. In most cases, however, *Satnamis* soon began again to associate with Christians, often in secret at first, but then with increasing openness and confidence. Some *Satnami* informants admit to having secretly broken the ban on these inter-community relations. Christians — especially those who had recently converted — continued to associate with *Satnamis,* and those who wished to recant and enter the community once again could do so relatively freely.[82] But even though both Christians and *Satnamis* attest that the two communities got along well, there was no sense by the beginning of the twentieth century that one could be both *Satnami* and Christian (my use of "*Satnami-Christian*" to refer to Christians of *Satnami* ancestry notwithstanding). And Christians and *Satnamis* still get along well in the village setting, despite the anti-conversion propaganda of local Hindu nationalist parties that pits *Satnamis,* depicted as unwitting dupes, against Christians, portrayed as predatory missionaries.

Higher-caste communities generally also treated Christians as a distinct community, and with slightly more respect than the *Satnamis.* However, despite respecting them for providing educational services to villages that would not have had access to instruction otherwise, upper-caste communities still considered Christians to be members of the lower castes. For example, one group of Christian schoolteachers in a non-Christian village provoked the anger of the local higher castes when they insisted, on the advice of a missionary, on drawing water where the higher castes did.[83] Even the missionaries were considered untouchable by some. One Evangelical missionary's dress touched the water pot of a Chhattisgarh villager who exclaimed, "*Chūā ā gayā!*" (It's been touched!), giving the missionary an opportunity to tell the woman that "the caste system was inaugurated by the devil and that all the inconsistent caste rules which they observe are useless."[84]

Ironically, the shift in Christian attitudes regarding the *Satnami* past gained momentum at the very moment when missionaries, fired by Pickett's studies to pursue a mass movement among the *Satnamis,* were working hard

---

82. Theophil Twente to Paul A. Menzel, October 1923.

83. Martin P. Davis, *Sadhu Hagenstein: A White Man among the Brown* (St. Louis: The Board for Foreign Missions, Evangelical Synod of North America, 1930), p. 149.

84. Elise Kettler, "Indian Inconsistencies," undated, AES 82-14 Qu2, Kettler, Elise, Quarterly Reports, Articles, Newsletters, 1910-1933. Similarly, on an evangelical tour in Gaitara, where the dust was "an inch and a half thick," neither *Satnami* nor Hindu would give Evangelical missionary Helen Freund a cot to sit on (a basic sign of hospitality), because they considered her unclean. Untitled and undated document found in AES 82-14 Qu2, Freund, Mrs. H. G. (Helen Mueller), Quarterly Reports, Articles, Newsletters.

to emphasize the Christian community's connection with the *panth* by, among other things, publishing tracts such as Paul's. While the connection established between Christianity and the Satnampanth by the reinterpretation of Ghasidas had perhaps at one time been psychologically comforting and mythically integrative, it increasingly became an embarrassment, a liability, and the community began subtly to ignore and reject it. For example, redactors of Paul's *Satyanāmī panth* (1941) occasionally replaced "Satyanam" with "Jesus Christ," weakening the connection between the two.[85] The *bhajans* of a Chhattisgarhi Christian evangelist and songwriter, Blind Simon Patros (who will be discussed in Chapter 6), were similarly transformed.

Paul's attempt to reframe *Satnami*-Christian history may strike the modern reader as an unsavory enterprise. Yet one must keep in mind that Paul was working well within his own culture's framework for constructing truthful historical accounts. "Here is where the shoe pinches the tightest," writes Veyne. "For what conforms to the program of truth in one society will be perceived as imposture or elucubration in another. A forger is a man working in the wrong century."[86] I have argued, in this chapter, that *Satnami*-Christian identity was invented and reinvented drawing upon the flexible resource of history, upon a past selectively remembered and variously reconstructed. Such, indeed, is the case of all communal identities, including our own. For, as Veyne has argued, "It is we who fabricate our truths, and it is not 'reality' that makes us believe. For 'reality' is the child of the constitutive imagination of our tribe."[87]

85. For one instance of the change, see the second edition of M. M. Paul, *Satyanāmī Panth: Śrī Gosāīn Ghāsīdās Girod Vāsī* (Raipur: The Christian Book Depot, 1941), p. 19.

86. Veyne, *Did the Greeks?*, p. 105.

87. Veyne, *Did the Greeks?*, p. 113.

CHAPTER 4

Allopathic Medicine and the Allure of Efficacy

It is surely a cardinal principle of modern historiography that one does not treat any human group as a tabula rasa, automatically registering the imprint of external cultural influences. Rather, one treats it as the locus of thought-patterns that determine rather closely which of the influences will be accepted and which rejected.

Robin Horton, "On the Rationality of Conversion"

Eliza Kent has observed, ". . . it is striking how, in the Indian context, written representations of conversion reproduce existing class distinctions by stressing the interior dimension for elite converts and the exterior dimension for low-caste converts."[1] It is indeed striking, but not at all surprising, given that an analysis of the "interior dimensions" of conversion can only be attempted in cases where the convert has left behind a detailed and — since we are dealing here with history — *written* testimony. The most likely converts to leave behind such firsthand description are those who were well educated before they converted — figures like Nehemiah Goreh or Brahmabandhab Upadhyay.[2] There were very few highly educated converts like Goreh or Upadhyay in

1. Eliza F. Kent, *Converting Women: Gender and Protestant Christianity in Colonial South India* (New York: Oxford University Press, 2004), p. 6.
2. On Goreh, see Richard Fox Young, *Resistant Hinduism: Sanskrit Sources on Anti-Christian Apologetics in Early Nineteenth Century India* (Vienna: Indological Institute, University of Vienna, 1981); and Richard Fox Young, "Some Hindu Perspectives on Christian Missionaries in the Indic World of the Mid Nineteenth Century," in *Christians, Cultural Interactions, and India's Religious Traditions*, ed. Judith M. Brown and Robert Eric

central Chhattisgarh, however, and I have therefore chosen to concentrate on the more public, observable effects of conversion.

Before the advent of post-colonial scholarship, many investigations of the transformations wrought in colonized countries by western powers conceived of those changes as a conflict between "tradition" and "modernity." Already in the 1960s, however, scholars such as Rudolph and Rudolph began to question this easy dichotomization of societies and spoke of the potential "modernity of tradition" and of traditional "vestiges" in modern societies.[3] While there is no doubt that contact with western missionaries contributed to the "modernization," "rationalization," and — to use the term Weber borrowed from Schiller — "disenchantment"[4] of Chhattisgarhis, this chapter and the next aim to demonstrate that the process involved much more muddled complexity and circuitousness than any theory of an evolutionary "development" could take into account. The ever-present admixture of modernity and tradition was made plain to me while attending a business seminar in Raipur sponsored by Rai University. In the city's poshest hotel, surrounded by the trappings of modern luxury and technology, two visiting Dartmouth professors who were speaking on business communication skills were asked if their research had found "communication without technology or speech" to have any use in the business world. After a great deal of confusion it was determined that the questioner was asking the American professors whether their research had shown telepathy to be a useful business communication tool.

It is for this reason that I discuss religious change of *Satnamis* in Chhattisgarh under the rubric of "tradition" and "innovation," for though what American missionaries introduced in Chhattisgarh was unarguably new, the missionaries were not always themselves purely "modern" subjects.

Charles Ryerson has noted that one can speak of social change either "structurally" (i.e., according to measurable indicators of social transformations, such as the movement from ascribed to achieved status) or "culturally," that is, how it informs and is informed by a people's "cultural conscious-

---

Frykenberg (Grand Rapids: Eerdmans, 2002), pp. 55ff. On Brahmabandhab, see Julius Lipner, *Brahmabandhab Upadhyay: The Life and Thought of a Revolutionary* (Oxford: Oxford University Press, 1999).

3. Lloyd I. Rudolph and Susanne Hoeber Rudolph, *The Modernity of Tradition: Political Development in India* (Chicago: University of Chicago Press, 1967), pp. 3-5. Dube also speaks of the "silent magic of modernities." See Saurabh Dube, *Untouchable Pasts: Religion, Identity, and Power among a Central Indian Community, 1780-1950* (Albany: State University of New York Press, 1998), p. viii.

4. See Donald G. MacRae, *Weber* (London: Fontana, 1973), p. 84.

ness."[5] I am more interested in the latter, in how the comportment, sentiments, and convictions of those *Satnamis* who became Christian influenced, and were influenced by, the trajectory of their social transformation. Nevertheless, the "structural" and "cultural" aspects of religious and social change are not easily disentangled. This chapter and the next will accordingly deal with both.

Whatever the reasons *Satnamis* became Christian, they did so as part of their own experiments in the production of personal and cultural identities. Clearly missionary articulations of "true Christianity" would have influenced *Satnami*-Christian self-perceptions.[6] Yet at the same time Chhattisgarhi Christians altered missionary "representations" in accordance with their own needs and self-understandings. Chhattisgarhis embraced a "foreign" faith, but not necessarily the full and specific agenda of its promulgators.

Neither did Chhattisgarhis assess the new religion according to its own criteria. They generally did not join the Christian community because of its "self-evident" logical or revelatory superiority, which was in any case self-evident only to those who accepted its epistemological prejudices and presuppositions. Rather, they judged Christianity according to indigenous standards, which involved, above all, considerations of efficacy.[7] Those who embraced Christianity did so, generally speaking, not because it made greater sense on some intellectual plane, but largely because, given the unique cir-

---

5. Charles A. Ryerson, III, *"Meaning and Modernization" in Tamil India: Primordial Sentiments and Sanskritization* (Ann Arbor: University Microfilms International, 1979), p. 5.

6. On the ability of external "representations" to influence a community's self-representation, see James Clifford, "On Ethnographic Allegory," in *Writing Culture: The Poetics and Politics of Ethnography*, ed. James Clifford and George E. Marcus (Berkeley: University of California Press, 1986), p. 116.

7. Comaroff and Comaroff assert that the Tshidi read Methodism "through the filter of their own culture." Jean Comaroff and John Comaroff, "Christianity and Colonialism in South Africa," *American Anthropologist* 13, no. 1 (1986): 16. Similarly, Kooiman suggests that "Travancore converts embraced Christianity in accordance with their own values and without completely rejecting their own cultural past." Dick Kooiman, *Conversion and Social Equality in India* (New Delhi: South Asia Publications, 1989), p. 203. Likewise, Jordan argues that Christian ideas in China were recognized as "truth" only to the extent that they could be shown to be in congruence with the established wisdom of the Chinese tradition. David K. Jordan, "The Glyphomancy Factor: Observations on Chinese Conversion," in *Conversion to Christianity: Historical and Anthropological Perspectives on a Great Transformation*, ed. Robert W. Hefner (Berkeley: University of California Press, 1993), p. 289. See also Robert W. Hefner, "Introduction: World Building and the Rationality of Conversion," in *Conversion to Christianity: Historical and Anthropological Perspectives on a Great Transformation*, ed. Robert W. Hefner (Berkeley: University of California Press, 1993), p. 37.

cumstances of life in late nineteenth- and early twentieth-century Chhattis-garh and their own personal and cultural projects, they concluded that it "worked" (and worked better than other alternatives).[8] The development of a *Satnami*-Christian identity was therefore a *dialogic* (or perhaps *trialogic*) process involving missionaries, local Christians, and the Indian social and cultural context.[9]

In Fritz Lang's classic 1925 film *Metropolis,* the ultra-modernity of an imagined city in the year 2026 is indicated by the aerial presence of six or seven Wright brothers–era airplanes circling boxy (and relatively short) skyscrapers. The new, as with the yet-to-come, can only be imagined based on what has already been experienced or "known." This chapter discusses how it was that *Satnami*-Christians came to embrace *angrezī* (English), or allopathic medicine. In it I argue that, in many cases, Chhattisgarhis assessed the value of this heterogenetic innovation based on orthogenetic standards of utility and value. In the next chapter I then continue the discussion by analyzing attitudinal (and actual) changes among *Satnami*-Christians with regard to the proper behavior and treatment of women, and put forth the hypothesis that the *Satnami*-Christian community assimilated the Victorian values of missionaries *selectively,* based not only on considerations of "Christian" propriety, but also on indigenous Indian notions of "respectable" womanhood.

Medicine, Health, and Hygiene

For *Satnamis,* as for other village Chhattisgarhis, there were three basic lines of defense in times of sickness: home remedies, *baids* (ayurvedic practitioners), and *baigās*. As in other parts of the world, some Chhattisgarhi home

8. There were times, however occasionally, when events of great moment — such as dreams or visions — convinced Chhattisgarhis to become Christian. For example, see Leta May Brown, *Hira Lal of India: Diamond Precious* (St. Louis: Bethany Press, 1954), p. 158; and Ethel Shreve, "Christian Testimonies," *World Call,* January 1952, p. 47. See also Donald and Mary McGavran to Dr. and Mrs. Saum, 2 October 1941, HCS, box 2 of 4 (folder: Air Mail from Don). More often than not, however, those who became Christian did so after a period of observation and testing.

9. On social change as a "dialogic" process, see Eugene F. Irschick, *Dialogue and History* (Berkeley: University of California Press, 1994), p. 8. This text is also quoted and discussed in Heike Liebau, "Country Priests, Catechists, and Schoolmasters as Cultural, Religious and Social Middlemen in the Context of the Tranquebar Mission," in *Christians and Missionaries in India: Cross-Cultural Communication since 1500,* ed. Robert Eric Frykenberg (Grand Rapids: Eerdmans, 2003), p. 84.

remedies were salubrious, or at least had no negative effect. Others were downright deleterious.[10] Chhattisgarhis also consulted *baids*, local healers versed in the restorative powers of certain roots, leaves, and other materials.[11] A third option — though the three were not necessarily pursued in order — was to consult a *baigā*.[12] *Baigās* are a class of quasi-priests from various tribes and lower castes skilled in the diagnosis and healing of ailments and diseases, particularly those that derive from the activity of malignant spirits (such as *bhūts* and *churails*[13]), witches, and disgruntled local deities.[14] For Chhattisgarhis, most illnesses were of this class, making the region, as one Evangelical missionary put it in 1920, a "veritable Eldorado for the conjurer and exorcist."[15] Some *baigās* specialized in healing particular ailments, but most were general practitioners, and while some *baigās* roamed about in search of work, others made contracts with entire villages. Though *baigās* generally worked with individual clients, there were times, particularly during epidemics, droughts, or famines, when entire villages would employ a *baigā* to perform a ritual called "making the village."[16] *Baigās* were also contracted to predict the future, to chase off tigers (sometimes with disastrous results), and to predict the gender of unborn children.

Baigās were especially renowned for their skill in exorcism, and employed

10. For example, two innocuous treatments involved applying compresses of salt and paddy husks for stomach pain or of leaves and oil for headaches. Two less innocuous remedies involved treating infant stomach ailments such as colic with a hot iron applied to the stomach, and eye problems with pepper juices and powders. Disciples missionary E. M. Gordon suggested in 1909 that 90 percent of adult Indians in the Bilaspur area carried on their bodies scars from the former of these practices. E. M. Gordon, *Indian Folk Tales: Being Side-Lights on Village Life in Bilaspore, Central Provinces* (London: Elliot Stock, 1909), p. 27.

11. *Baid* is a colloquial form of the more formal Hindi word, *vaidya*, i.e., an ayurvedic specialist.

12. *Baigās* are sometimes also called *ojhās* and *guṇīyās*.

13. *Bhūts* are male ghosts, and *churails* are the ghosts of women who die while pregnant or in childbirth.

14. There is general agreement that *Gonds* make the best *baigās*. For more on this and *baigās* in general, see Lawrence A. Babb, *The Divine Hierarchy: Popular Hinduism in Central India* (New York: Columbia University Press, 1975), pp. 197ff.

15. H. H. Lohans, *Come Over and Help Us: Mission Work of Our Evangelical Church in Chhattisgarh, India* (St. Louis: Eden Publishing House, 1920), p. 21. Found in AES 81-8 Lo78.

16. Christians were very often pressured into participating in these rituals, against their will, by others who felt that their absence would threaten the efficacy of the ritual, but the *"Biśrāmpur kalīsiyā kī viṣeś ājñāyeṃ"* (Special Rules of the Bishrampur Church), 1890, forbids Christian participation in the rite. Found in AES 83-3 Bis54.

elaborate methods for the expulsion of nefarious spirits.[17] The term *"baigā"* probably derives from that of a central Indian tribe with a reputation for sorcery. Popular terms for their art, such as *jhaṛ-phūnk* (exorcism by means of charms, incantations, and blowing — *phūnkna* — in the ear), *jādū-ṭonā* (the practice of magical arts), and *tantra-mantra* (charms and incantations), give an indication of their methods.

Baigās were also called upon to expose the ill-natured *ṭonhīs* (witches) responsible for a village's misfortunes. *Baigās* recommended a variety of ordeals in order to determine the guilty party. Sometimes they would speak the name of each woman in the village over a candle (a flickering flame indicated the culpable party). At other times, *baigās* recommended that women suspected of witchcraft be tied in a bag and plunged in water. Those who floated were deemed guilty and those who sunk declared (often posthumously) innocent.[18] Another method was to make each woman in a village touch a certain pole believed to have magical properties. The hand of the guilty *ṭonhī*, it was suspected, would wither or swell after the contact. Not surprisingly, marginal female figures — widows, outsiders, or the childless — were often "discovered" to be the culprits of witchcraft.[19] Once discovered, witches were liable to be beaten, shaved, maimed, or killed, or to suffer any number of other humiliations. British records as early as 1909 declared that belief in *ṭonhīs* was beginning to fade, due to "culture-contact and the advance of education," but the practice and suspicion of witchcraft continues in rural Chhattisgarh to this day, as it does in many other areas of rural India.[20]

At the beginning of the nineteenth century, most Protestant mission societies working in India equated evangelism with preaching, the translation of

17. Informants averred that the ritual performances sometimes involved sleights of hand employed to convince the patient that the source of their pain — a needle, thorn, etc. — had been removed from their body. For a firsthand description of the "successful" exorcism of an unconscious man who had been bitten by a scorpion, see M. P. Albrecht, "Wizards in Action," undated, AES 82-14 Qu2, Albrecht, M. P., Quarterly Reports, Articles, Newsletters (2).

18. Major P. Vans Agnew, "A Report on the Subah or Province of Chhattisgarh Written in 1820 A.D.," AES 80-1 Sub1.

19. Babb, *Divine Hierarchy,* p. 205.

20. Quote from Rajendra Verma, *Raipur* (Bhopal: District Gazetteers Department, Madhya Pradesh, 1973), p. 110. See also A. E. Nelson, *Central Provinces District Gazetteer: Raipur District* (Bombay: British India Press, 1909), p. 85. For a recent instance of alleged witchcraft in Raipur, see Indo-Asian News Service, "'Witches' Keep Dussehra Crowd in Thrall," *The Times of India (Online Edition),* 23 October 2003; and Press Trust of India, "SP Gets Wife Killed for Practising Voodoo," 2003, accessed 24 December 2003; available from http://www.timesofindia.com.

scriptures, and the establishment of schools. Medical work, or "clinical Christianity" as some came to call it, was not believed to be of any use in the propagation of Christianity. That attitude began to change midway through the century, and by the end of the nineteenth century medical missions were considered an integral aspect of evangelism. One reason for the shift was theological — late nineteenth-century theologians came to embrace a much more expansive view of the gospel. Another reason was the advance of western medical theory and practice. Whereas at the beginning of the nineteenth century western medicine had enjoyed little success in combating "tropical" illnesses, by the end of the century it could boast a more robust and sophisticated understanding of medical etiology and the treatment of disease.[21]

Mission work in Chhattisgarh began during this period when medical missions were beginning to gain a foothold in Protestant missionary societies, and from the start, missionaries in Chhattisgarh explicitly and implicitly linked Christianity to allopathic medical treatment. The first missionary in Chhattisgarh, Oscar Lohr, had been, after all, trained in medicine and was the son of a surgeon, and even those who had no medical training dispensed medicines and treatment to any who came. In mission hospitals and dispensaries the linkage became more explicit. Patients were sometimes required to sit through a sermon or devotional service before receiving treatment, and missionaries often made a show of praying before diagnosing and treating a patient.[22] Catechists and Bible-women on their rounds would supplement their evangelical message with tips on disease, sanitation, and hygiene. In the 1930s and '40s, religious leaders as diverse as Gandhi and members of the liberal American "Laymen's Foreign Missions Inquiry" criticized missionaries in India and elsewhere for implying a connection between the power of allopathy and that of Christ.[23]

21. For an excellent overview of the growth and development of Protestant medical missions in India as well as a fuller discussion of the themes of this paragraph, see Rosemary Fitzgerald, "'Clinical Christianity': The Emergence of Medical Work as a Missionary Strategy in Colonial India, 1800-1914," in *Health, Medicine and Empire: Perspectives on Colonial India,* ed. Biswamoy Pati and Mark Harrison (Hyderabad, India: Orient Longman, 2001).

22. In the second decade of the twentieth century, Disciples medical doctors and their staff gave preferential treatment to those who had tickets received at the daily worship service. See Homer P. Gamboe, "The Missionary Work of the Disciples of Christ in India and Its Development" (B.Div. thesis, The College of the Bible, 1918), pp. 32, 64.

23. William Hocking, professor of philosophy at Harvard at the time, was chairman of the Inquiry. See Laymen's Foreign Missions Inquiry Commission of Appraisal, *Re-Thinking Missions: A Laymen's Inquiry after One Hundred Years* (New York: Harper & Brothers, 1932).

Missionaries in Chhattisgarh preceded their treatment with prayer not for cynical evangelical purposes but because they believed that there *was* a connection between the power of God and the efficacy of allopathic medicine. After all, they reasoned, the Christian God had enabled western (read: Christian) scientists to discover this more effective medicine. Moreover, they sincerely believed that prayer would increase the effectiveness of the treatment. For these missionaries, allopathy and faith in God, the Christian God, could simply not be disconnected. Allopathy was *Christian* science.[24] The missionaries knew they were in possession of generally superior medical knowledge, but wished the power of that medicine to be understood as flowing from the Christian God, as they themselves understood it.[25]

For this reason, missionaries were especially interested in highlighting the flaws of local medicine. They reacted to its most damaging forms with a mixture of revulsion and sarcasm. Some sense of the missionary view of local *baigās*, and, to a lesser extent, ayurvedic practitioners, can be gained from a photograph in Milton Lang's 1932 *The Healing Touch in Mission Lands* (see p. 141). The photograph captures the author, Dr. Lang, and his wife standing on the verandah of the mission hospital, dressed in radiant white gowns. In front of them stands, according to the caption, a native "doctor," the quotation marks around "doctor" making clear Lang's low estimation of the *baigā's* abilities.[26] A few missionaries seemed even to take some pleasure in dramatic demonstrations of the futility of traditional methods. All were convinced that the introduction of allopathic medicine would disrupt the "heathen superstitions" of Chhattisgarhis. Evangelical missionary Milton Lang wrote in 1932, "The might of medical missions lies . . . in the demonstration, that by attacking disease at its source and in preventative medicine, belief in evil spirits, demons, malign gods and goddesses, and witchcraft must vanish."[27] In oppos-

---

24. If "modernity" can be measured according to the extent to which "religion" (or "magic") is distinguished from "science," then we must therefore assert that these missionaries were not purely modern figures. For more on this, see Terence Ranger, "The Local and the Global in Southern African Religious History," in *Conversion to Christianity: Historical and Anthropological Perspectives on a Great Transformation*, ed. Robert W. Hefner (Berkeley: University of California Press, 1993), p. 90.

25. An entry in the diary of an unknown catechist captures this ambiguity. On evangelizing tour, Evangelical missionary Tillmanns said a prayer for a sick *Teli* and "promised to send some medicines instructing him at the same time that he should depend more upon God than medicine." Entry for 4 September 1908, found in journal of S. J. Scott, Mahasamund catechist, AES 83-5 Di54 #1.

26. Milton C. Lang, *The Healing Touch in Mission Lands* (St. Louis: Eden Publishing House, 1932), p. 59.

27. Lang, *Healing Touch*, p. 25.

Dr. and Mrs. Lang, Johann Compounder and native "doctor." The "doctor's" drugs are on the verandah to the left

ing these beliefs and practices, missionaries were playing a role well established in the imagination of western Christians of the time. One missionary admitted that before coming to India he considered himself a thespian and enjoyed being cast as the villain. One such role was that of a "village medicine man [opposed] to the egress of Christianity into his village."[28]

One catechist speaking to a Hindu merchant in Mahasamund had clearly absorbed this way of thinking: "If your science is true, contradict the English Science [*sic*] and ask any educated Hindu which one is true," he reported saying. "If your Science is false then your religion is also false."[29] Christian evangelists, Indian and American, were perhaps taking their cue from earlier colonial officials, such as the Scottish educator John Wilson, who attempted to discredit scientific views associated with Hinduism. (One Hindu responded by pointing out the Bible's scientific infelicities.)[30] Christianity, according to those who promulgated it, was intimately related to western science. Some went so far as to suggest that the achievements of western science were the result of the Christian God's pleasure with western (i.e., Christian) scientists. Building upon this presupposition, Christian missionaries and evangelists argued that any scientific error contained in Hindu scriptures must of necessity invalidate the entire religion.

Another set of pictures in Lang's *Healing Touch in Mission Lands* reflects the missionary understanding of the purpose of medical work (see p. 143).[31] The first photograph captures a scrofulous leper as he arrived at the Chandkuri Leper Asylum in Baitalpur. His beard is untrimmed. The man's hair is wild and tangled. He wears a *langoṭī* (loin cloth, a half-*dhoti*), a shawl, and a scraggly shirt exposing a good portion of his hairy chest. All pieces of clothing are dirty and dust-colored. The second captures the same man one hour later. In it his hair is cut short and oiled in place. His beard is shaven. His new, blanched-white shirt is buttoned to the collar, and he wears a proper white *dhoti*. He no longer wears the shawl. The changes are all apparently external, but the missionaries were cognizant of the fact that the modifications they effected were more than skin deep, that they were in fact deeply altering the be-

---

28. H. G. Freund, "The Indian Personal Attitude toward Illness," 1936, AES 82-14 Qu2, Freund, Dr. H. G., Quarterly Reports, Articles.

29. Entry in unnamed catechist's journal for 13 June 1908, found in journal of S. J. Scott, Mahasamund catechist, AES 83-5 Di54 #1.

30. See Richard Fox Young, "Receding from Antiquity: Hindu Responses to Science and Christianity on the Margins of Empire, 1800-1850," in *Christians and Missionaries in India: Cross-Cultural Communication since 1500,* ed. Robert Eric Frykenberg (Grand Rapids: Eerdmans, 2003), p. 194.

31. Lang, *Healing Touch,* p. 95.

Above—Part of Chandkuri's 600 Lepers
Below—A leper on entrance to the Asylum. The same man
an hour later

havioral patterns of Chhattisgarhis, both those who became Christian and those who did not.

Medical Itineration and the Allure of Efficacy

Upon becoming Christian, *Satnamis* were quickly introduced to allopathic medicine and encouraged to make use of the missions' medical facilities. Though today one might consider such a shift in behavior a religiously neutral one, in fact informants indicated it became for *Satnami*-Christians one of the most important and visible signs of their communal identity. Conversion to Christianity, it was understood by all, involved whole-hearted reliance on western medical treatment, or allopathy, and a vigorous rejection of the medico-spiritual care of *baigās*. There is evidence that in significant ways the reality matched the perception. Those who became Christian did appreciably alter their response to medical problems and emergencies.

On the other hand, the transformation was not always as abrupt and thorough as was the perception. Most elderly Christian informants' first responses to my questions were unqualified — those who became Christian went immediately to the hospital with their medical difficulties. But when pressed, those same informants frequently revealed a history of meandering medical itineration and experimentation. Particularly until the 1930s, some Christians continued to consult *baigās* first, often in secret, resorting to dispensaries and hospitals only after the prescribed treatment had failed or matters got out of hand. Christians, according to informants, were particularly likely to consult *baigās* when dealing with diseases such as cholera, smallpox, or other afflictions assumed to be the work of cantankerous spirits or irascible deities.[32] For example, some Christians believed that *baigās* and their *mantras* were more effective than allopathic treatment for the treatment of snakebites, traditionally considered the work of a snake godling, Nag Dev. Even when not directly consulting *baigās*, Christians did sometimes employ their *mantras*, which like pieces of medical advice elsewhere in the world were traded and passed around among friends. After becoming Christian, informants indicated, some *Satnamis* perceived to be in possession of efficacious

---

32. The same was apparently true of Christians in the Dornakal Diocese and among Malayali *Shanars*. See, respectively, Susan Billington Harper, "The Dornakal Church on the Cultural Frontier," in *Christians, Cultural Interactions, and India's Religious Traditions*, ed. Judith M. Brown and Robert Eric Frykenberg (Grand Rapids: Eerdmans, 2002), pp. 189ff.; and Kooiman, *Conversion and Social Equality in India*, p. 189.

mantras continued to dispense them to others for what they considered to be altruistic reasons.

As one would expect, those who lived near Christian hospitals and dispensaries were more likely to rely fully on allopathic treatment than their remote counterparts. But even those with full and easy access to hospitals were liable occasionally to consult with *baigās*. In particular, it was common for those receiving long-term treatment, such as a course of antibiotics, to become impatient with the pace of their improvement and seek out other help while still following an allopathic regimen.

In comparison with *Satnamis*, however, it becomes apparent that Christian claims to have taken on a new posture and comportment in relation to medical problems were more than empty propaganda. At first, non-Christian *Satnamis* continued to employ *mantras* and consult *baigās* even after hospitals and dispensaries opened in their area. However, after a lag of some time — informants estimated between five and ten years, less for those who lived closest to hospitals and dispensaries — *Satnami* behavior began to resemble that of Christians, who, having found the treatment efficacious, recommended it to their non-Christian relatives and friends.

The lag may be partly explained by the fact that Christians were made aware of the availability of hospitals and dispensaries, and were encouraged to use them by missionaries and catechists who also made their bullock carts available as emergency transportation. Christians may also have paid less for services at certain medical facilities. In addition, certain misconceptions prevented *Satnamis* from making more expeditious use of Christian medical facilities. For example, due to the fact that many accepted allopathic treatment only on the verge of death, a high percentage of hospital patients died while under treatment. Certain *Satnamis* and other rural Chhattisgarhis interpreted this to mean that Christian doctors were actually killing patients, or at least that the hospital was a place where one went to die.[33] Many *Satnamis* seem also to have had a fear of large, open, high-ceilinged rooms of the sort that abound in hospitals. In 1898, Disciples mission-worker, Lillian Miller, and her husband, both doctors, reported that "The number of 'in-patients' is small; partly . . . because there still exists, among the women, much prejudice against and fear of a hospital. It is hard for them to realize that so large a room is not inhabited by evil spirits."[34] These fears and prejudices did eventu-

33. Hulda D. Meyer, "The Hospital — A Place to Be Feared, or Don't Ever Go Near the Hospital," ca. 1927, AES 82-14 Qu2, Meyer, Mrs. Armin F. (Hulda D. Klein), Quarterly Reports, Articles, Newsletters.

34. Lillie B. Miller and E. C. Miller, "Medical Work, from September 1, 1897, to August 16, 1898," *Missionary Tidings*, December 1898, p. 178.

ally break down, especially during the famines, when many non-Christians were forced into contact with mission institutions.[35] But even in the 1940s, non-Christian Chhattisgarhis were still wary of the dispensaries and clinics and would only with hesitation or in dire need resort to them.[36]

The delayed *Satnami* embrace of allopathic medicine also, however, represents a divergence in attitudes. Whereas *Satnamis* who became Christian seem almost immediately to have lost their *visvās* (confidence, belief) in *baigās* and in the appeasement of Hindu deities for medical purposes — or at least declared that they had — those who did not convert retained their *visvās* until *angrezī* medicine had proven its efficacy, a process that took many years. Even after *Satnamis* had lost their *visvās* in *baigās,* however, many continued to consult them due to the strength of tradition and the threat of social ostracism for those who visited hospitals, according to informants. Visiting a Christian medical facility meant mixing with members of another community, some of whom had been members of castes *Satnamis* considered "untouchable" (such as the sweepers). Because of this, until the mid-1930s, *Satnamis* who visited Christian facilities risked being outcasted.[37] But in the 1930s and '40s, *Satnamis* came to accept Christian medical facilities as a ritually neutral sphere, and henceforth visited them with greater frequency.[38]

The shift in Christian medical behavior was more than empty gesture. It symbolized, for Christians, the rejection of "heathen superstitions" in favor of what they perceived to be life- and health-giving allopathic medicine. After asking about Christian medical practices during their childhood, I asked a number of informants about what *Satnamis* were doing when they became sick or hurt. On more than one occasion a Christian informant responded, "They were dying." During my own research, I found that there were often proportionately many fewer elderly *Satnamis* than Christians in some vil-

35. Ada McNeil, "Bilaspur Medical Work," *Missionary Tidings,* November 1901, p. 218.

36. M. A. Wobus, "Annual Reports, 1944-45, Parsabhader," 1945, AES 82-13a Pr91, Annual Reports, no. 30, 1945.

37. H. G. Freund, "The Indian Personal Attitude toward Illness," 1936, AES 82-14 Qu2, Freund, Dr. H. G., Quarterly Reports, Articles. Another reason Chhattisgarhis considered allopathy ritually polluting was the perception that liquid medicine was mixed with alcohol. See entry in diary, unnamed catechist, 10 May 1909, found in the journal of S. J. Scott, Mahasamund catechist, AES 83-5 Di54 #1.

38. Richard Young has suggested that by the 1880s in India, Copernican scientific cosmology had become a "religiously neutral, culturally relative datum of mundane knowledge." While this was probably true of astronomical science in certain more educated and cosmopolitan regions of India, medical science did not attain this neutral status among *Satnamis* in Chhattisgarh until at least half a century later. See Young, "Receding from Antiquity," p. 184.

lages, suggesting, perhaps, a certain amount of truth to the perception. Though the oral evidence seems to suggest that Christians were indeed living longer and healthier lives, the statistical evidence is ambiguous. For example, the 1911 census of the Central Provinces and Berar (which included information on Chhattisgarh) recorded infirmities by "selected castes, tribes or races."[39] Whereas, for instance, 0.3 percent of *Chamars* in the region were suffering from blindness, only 0.16 percent of Christians were unable to see (the regional average was 0.2 percent). However, a larger percentage of Christians suffered from all other infirmities listed, including insanity, deafness, and leprosy.[40] This may reflect that Christianity did not, in fact, appreciably improve the health of members of the community, but it is more likely a reflection of the number of people with disabilities, mental and physical, who found care in Christian institutions and subsequently converted. This is almost certainly true in the case of leprosy, where the discrepancy is the highest.

Oral evidence from both Christians and *Satnamis* does suggest, however, that becoming Christian gave Chhattisgarhis a better chance of avoiding or successfully dealing with potentially life-threatening diseases. The evidence is particularly strong with regard to epidemics. Rural Chhattisgarhis considered smallpox a manifestation of the strange pleasure of the goddess Shitala, or Mata. Those who showed signs of the disease were worshiped as the deity, and those who succumbed were believed to have been specially chosen by her. Similarly, cholera was considered the work of evil spirits or witches. Whereas the arrival of smallpox was considered semi-auspicious, and therefore often led to the infection of the victim's close family members, signs of cholera caused Chhattisgarhis to abandon their homes and even, sometimes, the sick and dying, thus spreading the disease to other villages.[41]

Many things contributed to the greater success of Christians in dealing with these diseases: their willingness to be inoculated, their better hygiene, their use of well water (rather than stagnant water from the *tālāb*), and the fact that they resorted earlier to medical care. It appears that from the beginning, becoming Christian offered protection from epidemics. Lohr re-

---

39. India Census Commissioner, *Census of India, 1911*, vol. 10 (Part 2, Statistics) (Calcutta: Superintendent Government Printing, 1911), p. 110.

40. Statistics for insanity: Christians .04 percent, *Chamars* .01 percent, average .02 percent; for deafness: Christians .05 percent, *Chamars* .03 percent, average .04 percent; for leprosy: Christians .84 percent, *Chamars* .04 percent, average .05 percent.

41. Charles Grant, ed., *The Gazetteer of the Central Provinces of India* (New Delhi: Usha, 1984), pp. xxv, cxxxi.

ported in 1880 that though neighboring villages had been hit with cholera for three years in a row, it affected Bishrampur only in the third, and then only minimally.[42]

Christianity also brought the dubious advantage of a higher birthrate and larger families. *Satnamis* considered mothers and children especially susceptible to the spiritual malignancy of *tonhīs, bhūts,* and *nazar* ("evil eye") around the time of childbirth. Traditional *Satnami* birthing and childcare practices, many of which were intended to protect against these spiritual threats, were not always entirely beneficial to the health of those involved. Some practices had little appreciable effect, good or bad, such as surrounding the mother and child with charms and amulets, or making children less attractive — and thus less likely to provoke the jealousy of malicious spiritual powers — by darkening their eyes with makeup and giving them uncomely names. Other practices were more injurious. After parturition, for example, *Satnami* women were secluded indoors, denied food (except for a liquid mixture of ginger, coriander, turmeric, and other spices given only after two days), and kept from bathing until a ceremony on the sixth day, called *chatthī*.[43] Moreover, *Satnami* births were generally attended by midwives, called *dāīs,* who often had very little training and were known for their poor hygiene (because of their association with the pollution of childbirth, only lower-caste Hindus would work as *dāīs*). Birth in a Christian hospital ensured better care, more hygienic surroundings, and swift emergency aid, if necessary.

Christian parents also tended to avoid practices that were detrimental to the health of newborns. Following the instructions of missionaries, Christian parents avoided giving their children opium, which *Satnamis* used to keep children from crying while they were in the fields, and which they believed increased a child's strength.[44] Christians also generally took colicky children to the hospital for treatment, rejecting the traditional home-remedy of applying a hot iron to their stomach. In addition, Christians gave water to their fe-

---

42. "Tenth Annual Report of the Chutteesgurh Mission, 1878-80," AES 82-13a Pr91, 1870-83, Annual Reports. Christians were not, however, immune from epidemics. The community was hit hard by the worldwide influenza pandemic in 1918-19, and a cholera epidemic seriously infected the Mungeli community in 1919. See H. C. Saum to Herbert (no surname), 28 May 1919, HCS, box 1 of 4 (no folder).

43. George Weston Briggs, *The Chamārs* (Calcutta: Association Press, 1920), p. 66; and Robert Vane Russell, *The Tribes and Castes of the Central Provinces of India,* vol. 2 (London: Macmillan, 1916), p. 413.

44. Simon Patros, *Simon Patros of India: A Miracle of God's Grace* (St. Louis: Board of International Missions, Evangelical and Reformed Church, Inc., 1954), p. 12.

verish children, a practice avoided by traditional *Satnamis,* who would not give children water for six months to a year after birth.[45]

Because of these behavioral changes, and because of the decline in infant mortality, Christians began to have noticeably larger families, and some evangelists and missionaries — Donald McGavran most prominent among them, according to informants — emphasized the point as an advantage in becoming Christian. Some *Satnamis* came to believe that Christian rituals and beliefs had a more powerful protective effect on children and began to seek them out. One *Satnami,* for example, came to Christians after his wife became pregnant. He had lost six children with two different women and was hoping to procure the "protection of Jesus Christ" for the seventh.[46] Christians were also prone to interpret their fertility as an advantage of their religious affiliation. One unidentified Christian woman from Bilaspur asked to have her child christened because, she said, "I always notice that a baby keeps *good health* after it is christened, and so I always have it done as soon as possible!"[47] There were others, however, who understood the greater success of Christians as a function of the fact that more of them gave birth in the hospital, and accordingly began following suit.

By the 1940s, most Chhattisgarhis with access to hospitals or dispensaries turned first to allopathic care for medical treatment. Whereas until the early part of the twentieth century *Satnamis* and *Satnami*-Christians in remote areas seem to have turned first to *baigās,* and then to allopathy only as a last recourse, the itinerary began to reverse in the 1930s and '40s, leading to a situation in which nearly all Chhattisgarhis for whom it was practicable went first to hospitals and dispensaries, and then only out of desperation or impatience to *baigās.*[48]

Despite the fact that they continued occasionally to consult *baigās* in times of infirmity, Christians clearly considered allopathic medical treatment a symbol of their religious and social transformation. But if becoming Chris-

---

45. Victor Rambo, "Call the Doctor!," *World Call,* February 1931, p. 22.

46. Donald A. McGavran, *The Satnami Story: A Thrilling Drama of Religious Change* (Pasadena: William Carey Library, 1990), pp. 102-3.

47. Edith Elsam, "English Work at Bilaspur and Other Stations on the B. N. R'y.," *Missionary Tidings,* November 1899, p. 193.

48. There were still in the 1940s, and even today, a large number of Chhattisgarhis for whom going to a hospital or clinic would require a prohibitively long walk or expensive bus or train ride. For this and other reasons, local forms of healing have not disappeared. The same is true in South Africa, where the government is now considering licensing local healers, as India's government now does; see Michael Wines, "Between Faith and Medicine, How Clear a Line?" *New York Times,* 18 August 2004.

tian meant the refusal of the *baigā's* medico-spiritual treatments, it did not mean the wholesale rejection of local forms of healing.

Some *Satnami*-Christians continued their employment of *mantras*, for example, long after becoming a Christian. In 1941, in Jora, an isolated village roughly eight miles east of Takhatpur that is only now getting its first *pakkā* road, a *Satnami* pandit named Jahani decided to become Christian after an intense and vivid dream. In the dream, which came on the night Disciples evangelists first visited the village, Pandit Jahani saw Jesus on the cross, suffering horribly and then dying in agony. Convinced that it was a sign from God, Jahani took his young son, early in the morning, and went to visit the evangelists. When he arrived, he was trembling and on the verge of tears, and the evangelists thought that he was suffering from a fever. But they accepted his story, and after some instruction he was baptized by Disciples missionary Donald McGavran.[49]

Pandit Jahani had been known as something of a part-time healer, and villagers came to him for efficacious *mantras*. Even after his conversion, he continued to employ these magical phrases for the sake of curing himself and others. His nephew, a *Satnami*, claims that Jahani thought nothing of it, believing himself to be doing good and providing a needed service to his neighbors. An exchange between the Pandit's son and me demonstrates — in addition to differences between our unconscious assumptions regarding the nature of divinity — how it was that Pandit Jahani justified his continued use of *mantras*, which contain names of Hindu gods, even after becoming a Christian:

> BAUMAN: What was the source of the *mantras'* efficacy? Why did they
> work?
> MATTHEW JAHANI: In every *mantra* is the name of God.
> BAUMAN: Which god?
> MATTHEW JAHANI: [That was] no question of his, which.[50]

Whereas most Christians avoided any suggestion of reliance on the mystical methods of the *baigās,* many continued to employ the ayurvedic com-

---

49. Matthew Jahani and Jagat Ram, interview by author, Jora, CG, 17 February 2004. Matthew Jahani is the son of Pandit Jahani, and still a Christian. Jagat Ram, a *Satnami,* is the Pandit's nephew. Interestingly Matthew, an accomplished poet obsessed with the "Christian" aspects of Ghasidas's message, interprets his father's dream psychologically as the product of a vivid imagination provoked by graphic evangelizing. McGavran's account of Jahani's conversion suggests that economic considerations may have been a motivating factor. See Donald A. McGavran, "The Growing Church in India," vol. 2 (unpublished newsletter), April 1942, found in HCS, box 4 of 4 (folder: Missionaries).

50. McGavran, "The Growing Church in India," vol. 2.

pounds of *baids* and the trial-and-error experimentation of home remedies. For some, the shift from *Satnami* to Christian was symbolized as much by a visit to the *baid* (rather than the *baigā*) as a trip to the hospital.[51] Some even accepted medicines from *baigās*, as long as they were not accompanied by *mantras* or *jhaṛ-phūnk*. Whereas converts would have previously considered the *baigā's* efficacy to be a matter of personal charisma, of spiritual power, they came to understand the efficacy of his medicines, like those of the *baid*, to be a function of the scientific properties of their ingredients.[52] *Satnami*-Christians came to distinguish local magic from local medicine and rejected only the former.

In fact, among *Satnamis* who became Christian, *baids* seem to have increased in importance, perhaps because they represented an acceptable connection with the past. Christians supplemented allopathic treatment with ayurvedic remedies — not always a good idea, medically — without the guilt and secrecy associated with consulting *baigās*. Those without access to medical facilities generally consulted *baids*. Many *Satnami*-Christians relate stories of ayurvedic methods succeeding when allopathic treatments had not.[53] *Satnami*-Christians did not hesitate to learn and practice ayurvedic medicine. For example, one *Satnami*-Christian baptized in the 1940s (and still living when I conducted my fieldwork) trained under a *baid* after becoming a Christian and has since earned a reputation for helping infertile women with his medicinal compounds. Christians may also have been drawn to the practice of ayurvedic medicine because *baids* were generally members of the higher castes, whereas *baigās* were almost always members of the lower castes or tribes. Ayurvedic medicine, therefore, had upper-caste associations. In fact, one of the reasons that non-Christian *Satnamis* tended to prefer *baigās* to *baids* was that they received better treatment at the hands of the former (because the upper-caste *baids* despised them for their lower-caste status).

Even the missionaries accepted and respected *baids* as legitimate practi-

51. Rabha converts made this same distinction; see Bengt G. Karlsson, *Contested Belonging: An Indigenous People's Struggle for Forest and Identity in Sub-Himalayan Bengal* (Richmond, VA: Curzon, 2000), p. 183.

52. According to informants, one *Satnami*-Christian pastor was on such good terms with a particular *baigā* that he hosted him in his house when the healer came through town. The pastor accepted from the *baigā* only ayurvedic medicines, though it was well known that the *baigā* employed a wider arsenal of methods in his practice.

53. Two common ayurvedic prescriptions at the time were the ingestion of a paste made from the leaves of *nīm* (*Melia Azadirachta*) trees for fevers, and of the *jīrā* (cumin) plant for stomach ailments. Subsequent investigations have found many ayurvedic treatments to have a sound scientific basis, and the government of India currently supports the research and development of ayurvedic medicines.

tioners of medicine, if perhaps limited in their abilities. Disciples missionary Dr. Mary T. McGavran described an encounter with a "tall and dignified" *baid* named Chandarsa: "Once I had a patient with a wound I could not get to heal. After I had failed for a month, [Chandarsa] persuaded her to let him try, and in three days she was practically well. When he told me why I did not cure her I felt so foolish. He very kindly said: 'Miss Sahib Ji, there are some things you know and some things I know.'"[54]

While the mind-set of *Satnami*-Christians was bending in a modern, scientific direction, ayurvedic medicine provided a link to the past. Because it had no explicit magical or religious associations, ayurvedic medicine could be *Christianized.* The efficacy of ayurvedic medicine lay not in any magical or spiritual power, but in the scientific properties of various florae — florae created, Christians asserted, by a Christian God. One *Satnami baigā* from the Takhatpur area who converted to Christianity around 1934 continued his practice, simply replacing his *mantras* with prayer and pruning his methods back to those of a *baid.* It would be unkind, he believed, to have useful knowledge and not share it. According to his adopted son, the man, Sobha Sinh, converted because he suffered from a malady he could not himself cure. Going to the mission hospital, he received treatment and, eventually, fully recovered. Sinh had also become convinced of the futility of worshiping his gods and goddesses while watching all of his young sons die of various afflictions. In the minds of converts to Christianity, therefore, ayurveda, placed in the proper context, complemented allopathy and was consonant with other Christian beliefs and practices. It was an old practice understood in a new way.

Christian Medicine as "Strong Magic"

These medical itineraries follow the outlines of what Milton Singer called the "cultural metabolism of an innovation." Orthogenetic innovations, he argued, pass through a number of stages on their way to becoming traditionalized. First, they are quarantined in enclaves (such as a foreign military fort or mission compound) and utilized only with discomfort and fear by those who enter the enclaves. Second, the quarantined space becomes "ritually neutralized" as innovations come to be more accepted and important to a wider range of people. In this stage, the mingling with other castes and foreigners necessitated by utilization of the innovations becomes acceptable, and no

54. Mary T. McGavran, "The Healing of India," *World Call*, December 1919, p. 22.

longer leads to ritual pollution. In a third stage the innovations become a "typological option" in the culture (e.g., *angrezī* medicine comes to be an option along with ayurvedic medicine). In the fourth stage, foreign innovations become a commonly accepted part of indigenous culture. In the fifth stage, during which innovations become fully traditionalized, they receive "myths of origin." (For example, neo-Hindus have argued that the Vedas presaged the production of airplanes.)[55]

In Chhattisgarh during the late nineteenth and early twentieth centuries, allopathic medicine worked its way through each of the first three stages, more quickly among Christians and more slowly among *Satnamis* and other Chhattisgarhis. However, contrary to Singer, who seems to suggest that only at the end of the process is the innovation fully traditionalized, the evidence points to the possibility that allopathic medicine was in fact understood in traditional terms from the moment it arrived. The shift among *Satnami-*Christians does not represent a straight-line transformation from "magical" or "enchanted" to "scientific" and "rational" thinking, nor does it reflect a shift from "tradition" to "modernity." Rather, *Satnamis,* Christians, and other Chhattisgarhis understood and judged the methods of *angrezī* medicine according to traditional categories from the very moment they were introduced.

There is evidence, for instance, that Chhattisgarhis understood the Christian prayers that accompanied their medical treatment as a form of *mantra,* and by consistently linking their treatment with prayers and petitions, Christian doctors, both American and Indian, implicitly perpetuated this understanding. According to informants, non-Christians even requested that Christian doctors pray with them during times of illness, believing in the efficacy of their spoken words. Chhattisgarhis also understood the mission doctors' practice of taking a patient's pulse within the context of *nārī bhed,* an ayurvedic method of diagnosing — and potentially healing — diseases by taking *(bhednā)* the pulse *(nārī).* (Those who practice *nārī bhed* are called *"nārī baids."*) It was a well-established belief in Chhattisgarh that certain people, especially *baids* and *baigās,* possessed the ability to accurately determine the cause and severity of a person's ailment simply by touching their wrist.[56]

---

55. For more, see Milton Singer, *When a Great Tradition Modernizes* (New York: Praeger Publishers, 1972), pp. 389ff. On a "myth of origin" that the Arya Samaj used to justify the appropriation of modern technology and scientific knowledge in the nineteenth century, see Kenneth W. Jones, *Arya Dharm: Hindu Consciousness in 19th-Century Punjab* (Berkeley: University of California Press, 1976), p. 164.

56. The practice is still quite common in rural Chhattisgarh today. While I was conducting research, one of my translators felt my pulse during a minor illness and declared that I would soon recover (I did).

Furthermore, it was commonly believed that certain people could cure illnesses with the same method. These beliefs came to be transferred to the mission doctors who, of course, always felt their patients' pulses. Hira Lal, a *Satnami*-Christian who had a long career in the mission hospital at Mungeli, was believed to practice the art of *nāṛī bhed* and to have the "healing touch," as was his mentor, Dr. Anna Gordon.[57] Dr. Harold Freund, an Evangelical missionary doctor, was pressed by a certain fiery old non-Christian man named Chandra Prasad to check his pulse at every possible moment, believing that it was this contact with the doctor that was keeping him alive well beyond the one month the doctor had predicted he would survive a heart illness.[58]

Habib and Raina have argued that scientific empiricism was associated with Christianity by many Indians and served at times as an inducement to conversion.[59] It is possible that this was the case among those Indians already educated in the classical sciences of Indian antiquity, but for most Chhattisgarhis the allure of allopathic medicine was not that it was based on empirical science, but that it was perceived to be more efficacious. Chhattisgarhis were accustomed to exploring a variety of medical treatments in the pursuit of better health, and all methods, "traditional" *and* "innovative," were judged according to their effectiveness.[60]

Conversion to Christianity brought information about and access to *angrezī* medicine, and converts were able to quickly see for themselves its strengths and weaknesses. Allopathic methods were accepted or rejected on this same basis only, and the allure of efficacy helps to explain why Christians continued their medical itineration even while their ostensible reliance on allopathic methods remained an integral aspect of their identity.[61] It also

57. Gordon, *Indian Folk Tales*, p. 98.

58. The man's caste is not mentioned. "The Touch of the Physician's Hand," ca. 1940; and H. G. Freund, "The Indian Personal Attitude toward Illness," 1936, both in AES 82-14 Qu2, Freund, Dr. H. G., Quarterly Reports, Articles.

59. Irfan Habib and Dhruv Raina, "The Introduction of Scientific Rationality into India: A Study of Master Ramchandra," *Annals of Science* 46 (1989): 601. Quoted in Young, "Receding from Antiquity."

60. Similarly, Arun Jones argues that the Igorot also judged the usefulness of various medical methods according to the criteria of efficacy. Arun W. Jones, *Christian Missions in the American Empire: Episcopalians in Northern Luzon, the Philippines, 1902-1946* (New York: Peter Lang, 2003), pp. 228-29.

61. B. A. Pauw asserts that the southern African Xhosa complemented allopathic medicine with visits to diviners and medicine men so that they would not be "tempting God by taking unnecessary risks." B. A. Pauw, "The Influence of Christianity," in *The Bantu-Speaking Peoples of Southern Africa*, ed. W. D. Hammond-Tooke (Boston: Routledge &

helps explain why *Satnamis*, who initially avoided the mission's medical facilities, eventually began to make use of them, though still without ever fully rejecting other methods. In this context, conversion to Christianity was not the equivalent of conversion to modernity or "scientific" ways of thinking. Rather, Christians understood and judged *angrezī* medicine according to traditional Chhattisgarhi criteria. They *traditionalized* change.

Moreover, when a method of treatment proved to be efficacious, that efficacy was perceived to be a function not of its scientific, but its *religious* properties. Especially until the 1940s and '50s, Christians in Chhattisgarh understood the greater perceived potency of allopathic medicine to be the result of its association with the Christian God, not a function of more scientific methods or better medical training.[62] They would say prayers before leaving home for treatment and arrived with *viśvās* that they would be cured. But there is a linguistic difficulty in dealing with this issue. Informants generally spoke of having (or losing) *viśvās* in allopathy, ayurveda, or the work of *baigās*. But the term's semantic range covers everything from "trust" and "confidence" to "faith" and "belief," making it difficult to determine whether a person's stated *viśvās* in certain forms of medicine (or lack thereof) was of an experiential or religious kind (and suggesting, as well, that the distinction did not exist in the minds of Chhattisgarhis).

Non-Christian *Satnamis* also perceived allopathic medicine to be imbued with a religious power, and attributed its healing abilities to the strength of the Christian god (the lowercase "g" is necessary here to indicate the inclusive attitude of *Satnamis* toward divinity), an attribution that sometimes led them to doubt the efficacy of their own deities.

Rosemary Fitzgerald asserts that, "For the most part, those [Indians] willing to place themselves under the medical care of a mission seem to have shrugged off the religious overtones in their treatment, perhaps taking the view of a Brahman patient who reportedly declared: 'The doctrine of the Christian is bad but their medicine is good.'"[63] This was certainly true, to a certain extent, in Chhattisgarh. Yet non-Christians in the region seem also, at

---

Kegan Paul, 1974), pp. 436ff. Pauw's argument is also quoted and discussed in Deryck Schreuder and Geoffrey Oddie, "What Is 'Conversion'? History, Christianity and Religious Change in Colonial Africa and South Asia," *Journal of Religious History* 15, no. 4 (1989): 499.

62. When asked what people believed to be the source of allopathic medicine's efficacy during their childhood, informants born in the 1910s and '20s tended to speak of its association with Christian faith, whereas informants born in the late 1930s and 1940s were more likely to speak of things like better hygiene, the better training of their healthcare practitioners, and better medicines.

63. Fitzgerald, "'Clinical Christianity,'" p. 129.

times, to have integrated the medical efficacy of Christianity into pre-existing modes of thought. For example, when healed at a Christian medical facility, *Satnamis* frequently presented mission doctors with gifts of money, fruit, eggs, or grain for the Christian god.[64] It was common among *Satnamis* for those who had requested and received healing from a particular deity to offer the god or goddess a thank offering. It was also commonly known that certain deities were better at healing than others.

It is therefore clear that *Satnamis* were able to comfortably incorporate the medical power of the Christian god into their own belief systems without producing an uncomfortable degree of cognitive dissonance. Corinne Dempsey claims that whereas scholarly representations of religion tend to portray it as a means of delineating belief, local Christians in India and adherents of other religions around the globe tend often to understand it more as a "conduit of miraculous power."[65] This was certainly true in Chhattisgarh, and because of this the greater perceived medical efficacy of another deity did not necessarily demand the rejection of one's own.

However, wanting in whatever way possible to please the Christian god before seeking his aid — the common terms for deity being masculine — some did begin to adhere to Christianity. In the 1940s, Samunwa, a *Satnami* from Beltukri who had visited *baids* and *baigās* in search of a cure for his rheumatism, heard Christian preachers proclaiming that "Jesus heals." Thinking Jesus would only heal him if he first got baptized, he requested Disciples missionary T. N. Hill to perform the rite. Only afterwards did he go to the hospital where he was healed. Fearing social ostracism (or worse), he sold all his possessions in Beltukri, moved to Mungeli, was given a job at the hospital, and immediately, he says, lost all his *viśvās* in *baids* and *baigās*.[66]

William Merrill asserts that the Tarahumaras in colonial Mexico were attracted to the Jesuit mission in part by the possibility of gaining access to the priests' "supernatural" ability to cure Old World diseases. Similarly, Charles Keyes has argued that by introducing medical care and curing diseases, Christian missionaries working among the Thai came to be regarded as "men of prowess."[67] Clearly Samunwa and other Chhattisgarhis, both *Satnami* and

---

64. Lang, *Healing Touch*, p. 66.

65. Corinne Dempsey, "Lessons in Miracles from Kerala, South India: Stories of Three 'Christian' Saints," in *Popular Christianity in India: Riting between the Lines*, ed. Selva Raj and Corinne Dempsey (Albany: State University of New York Press, 2002), p. 134.

66. Samunwa (informant uses only one name), interview by author, Mungeli, CG, 27 March 2004.

67. See, respectively, Charles F. Keyes, "Why the Thai Are Not Christians: Buddhist and Christian Conversion in Thailand," in *Conversion to Christianity: Historical and Anthropo-*

Christian, viewed missionary medicine not as the triumph of Baconian science but rather as strong magic that drew its power from association with the Christian god. Rather than supplant local medico-spiritual beliefs as the missionaries had hoped and expected, allopathic demonstrations of power were understood in traditional terms and simply served to increase the prestige of mission doctors and the Christian deity.[68] Missionaries tended to interpret the conversion of those who had received medical care as a response to Christian compassion, but it seems just as likely that in many cases *Satnamis* and other Chhattisgarhis were responding to a demonstration of medical power.

While asserting that "magic" had been "the greatest enemy to human progress,"[69] missionaries continued to believe that prayer and faith contributed to the efficacy of their medical treatments, and so did little in word or deed that would have contradicted those who saw in allopathic medicine the power of a Christian god. Some missionaries even explicitly encouraged the perception by involving themselves in the same medico-spiritual battles *baigās* would have joined. For example, during one of his village visits, Disciples missionary Donald McGavran awoke to the sounds of wailing. His host, a Hindu, believed himself to be possessed of an evil spirit that attacked in the night, and was overcome with what he considered a mortal illness. McGavran took his Bible and, moving around to each corner of the stricken man's bed, ordered Satan to depart. Within an hour the man was entirely healed.[70]

---

logical Perspectives on a Great Transformation, ed. Robert W. Hefner (Berkeley: University of California Press, 1993); and William L. Merrill, "Conversion and Colonialism in Northern Mexico: The Tarahumara Response to the Jesuit Mission Program, 1601-1767," in *Conversion to Christianity: Historical and Anthropological Perspectives on a Great Transformation,* ed. Robert W. Hefner (Berkeley: University of California Press, 1993).

68. One missionary who had helped a woman recover from a fever-induced coma was known far and wide to have the power of raising people from the dead, a symbol of spiritual power. See Brown, *Hira Lal,* p. 136. Another story having nothing to do with medicine illustrates the point. In the early part of the twentieth century Disciples missionary John McGavran, father of Donald, swam out into a village *tālāb* to retrieve some ducks he had shot, in order to prove to villagers that there was no evil deity that would pull him under (thick reeds had caused the drowning of several villagers). When he safely returned to shore, villagers did not declare that there was no evil deity but rather that McGavran must have been a more powerful god. See McGavran, *Satnami Story,* p. 28.

69. A quote from an unidentified book in M. P. Davis, "Indian Touring Notes, Parsabhader," ca. 1930, AES 82-14 Qu2, Davis, M. P., Quarterly Reports, Articles, Newsletters, 1916-1935.

70. Vernon James Middleton, "The Development of a Missiologist: The Life and Thought of Donald Anderson McGavran" (Ph.D. diss., Fuller Theological Seminary, 1989). This dissertation, though (or perhaps *because*) based on interviews with McGavran, is largely hagiographical.

Christian missionaries did not generally deny the workings of evil spirits but instead relativized them by asserting that Christ held them in thrall.[71] Catechists also perpetuated the notion that allopathic medicine derived its power from a Christian god by the preaching of Jesus Christ as a healer. One catechist visited Meghanath Satnami in Labra and reported, "I preached to him and others about Christ's healing powers; while he lived on earth he cured by the word of his mouth many incurable diseases, and he is able to cure now and can do all in his power if a man looks up to him in true faith. Still it is necessary that we may use those means which God has provided for cure and pray for His blessing."[72]

Due to peer pressure and a desire to imitate other Christians and missionaries, the behavior of *Satnamis* who became Christian changed abruptly and intensely. But their ways of thinking, their fears, instincts, and prejudices, were not so quickly abandoned. For example, after being bitten by a *karait* (a very poisonous black snake) in the early 1920s, a Christian named Phagua sought help at the mission hospital in Mungeli, but begged the mission doctor to spare the serpent. Killing it, he believed, would anger Nag Dev and ensure his own death. To make a point, the missionaries had the snake killed. Phagua suffered horribly for some time but recovered fully, declaring that his recent baptism had been the cause of his recuperation.[73] It must be stressed that Phagua did not reject the idea that supernatural forces could affect one's medical state, but rather simply altered his interpretation of the event — baptism, rather than Nag Dev, became the more potent causal factor.

Interpreting the Signs

Contact with Christians did not immediately turn *Satnamis* into armchair scientists. It did, however, have an immediate effect on their interpretation of medical events, particularly momentous ones. In Chhattisgarh, medical events were not just events, but signs pregnant with meaning and requiring careful interpretation. For example, in May of 1938, a prominent *Satnami* man from Fosterpur was baptized before a large crowd of *Satnamis* who vowed to observe the effects of his baptism closely to see whether they would

---

71. Buddhist missionaries did the same in Thailand, subsuming local spirits to the laws of *karma*. See Keyes, "Why the Thai Are Not Christians," p. 266.

72. Entry in diary, unnamed catechist, February (no date), 1909, found in the journal of S. J. Scott, Mahasamund catechist, AES 83-5 Di54 #1.

73. George E. Miller, "The Serpent That Failed," *World Call*, July 1922.

be good or ill. He died the next month, and the *Satnami* community understood his death as a warning from the gods.[74]

Those who became Christian came to interpret events somewhat differently than their non-Christian counterparts. In the 1870s, an older *Satnami* woman joined the Evangelicals despite the objections of her husband. A few days after her baptism, her husband fell seriously ill. He interpreted his illness as punishment for his refusal to become Christian, was baptized on his sickbed, and recovered fully.[75] The events could easily have been understood differently. Given the traditional belief that a wife's piety is responsible for her husband's life, health, and good fortune, the husband's sickness could have been seen as punishment for the wife's decision to abandon the religion of her ancestors. Surely contact with the Christian community — the couple's grown child had become Christian — must have influenced the rejection of this convincing and culturally appropriate interpretation in favor of one that was less so.

There were limits, however, to the hermeneutical flexibility of Christian converts, as some signs were incapable of being interpreted in a Christian direction. Ramu, a Christian from Chandrapur, a town where Evangelical missionaries worked, withstood the wagging tongues of his caste-mates after his baby became ill and suddenly died. But when his wife fell sick with a fever, Ramu took the advice of his neighbors and offered some *ghī* (clarified butter) and spices to his family's former *iṣṭ-devtā* (favored, or chosen deity). His wife recovered, and he began again wearing the *kaṇṭhī* he had discarded at baptism, though he professed to a missionary that he still believed Christ was more powerful than the god to whom he made his sacrifice.[76] Here again, it seems that Ramu understood Christ not as *the* one God, but as one god among many (albeit one he was willing to believe was the most powerful). This would be consonant with the common Hindu view that devotion to a chosen deity (in this case, Jesus) does not obviate the propitiation and worship of other gods and goddesses, especially those gods and goddesses most responsible for the health of one's body, family, or village.[77]

74. McGavran, *Satnami Story*, pp. 47ff.

75. "Sixth Annual Report of the Chutteesgurh Mission, 1874-75," AES 82-13a Pr91, 1870-83, Annual Reports.

76. Ramu was probably *Satnami*, but may also have been a Kabirpanthi (since both wear the *kaṇṭhī*). The missionary believed that the wife's health had declined in response to the fear-mongering of her friends and neighbors and then improved when their words turned hopeful and encouraging once Ramu had made his offering. M. P. Albrecht, "Annual Report, 1937-38," AES 82-13a Pr91, Annual Reports, no. 23, 1938.

77. On this, see John B. Carman, "When Hindus Become Christian: Religious Conver-

In the *Elementary Forms of Religious Life* (1912), Emile Durkheim asserted, "That which science refuses to grant to religion is not its right to exist, but its right to dogmatize upon the nature of things and the special competence which it claims for itself for knowing man and the world."[78] While such may have been the case in Durkheim's Europe, in Chhattisgarh — and, we might add, large parts of the rest of the world at the time — religion was still refusing to grant science the right to dogmatize about something so fundamental as the cause of disease. A Chhattisgarhi would have admitted, when it was the case, that smallpox killed his or her child. But the important question was *why*, and the answer was more likely to involve reference to a volatile goddess — or, in the case of Christians, the mysterious will of a benevolent God — than to the airborne poxvirus pathogen.

Along with the use of allopathic medicine, greater hygiene was one of the most frequently mobilized markers of the boundary between Christians and other communities of Chhattisgarh.[79] According to informants, Christians were proud of their hygienic cooking habits, their unsoiled clothing, and their tidy, more open, better-ventilated, whitewashed *pakkā* houses. The missionaries had made no secret of preaching "soap" along with "salvation," and those who became Christian in Chhattisgarh embraced the former message as enthusiastically as the latter (if not more so). Christian village evangelists reinforced the message by inspecting Christians' houses and hassling the unfastidious.

Satnamis had a reputation for filth and slovenly behavior and were blocked from appropriating traditional markers of ritual purity. It is perhaps not surprising, then, that for the *Satnami*-Christian community, better hygiene would become such a prominent symbol of communal difference. It appears that the hygienic concern of some Christians may have been a reflection of traditional notions regarding purity and impurity. But more importantly, cleanliness brought to *Satnami*-Christians a measure of self-respect based more on basic notions of what constituted polite behavior and social refinement.[80]

---

sion and Spiritual Ambiguity," in *The Stranger's Religion: Fascination and Fear*, ed. Anna Lännström (Notre Dame: University of Notre Dame Press, 2004), pp. 148-49.

78. Emile Durkheim, *The Elementary Forms of Religious Life*, trans. Karen E. Fields (New York: The Free Press, 1995), p. 432.

79. The same was true in other regions of India. See Sundararaj Manickam, *The Social Setting of Christian Conversion in South India: The Impact of the Wesleyan Methodist Missionaries on the Trichy-Tanjore Diocese with Special Reference to the Harijan Communities of the Mass Movement Area, 1820-1947* (Wiesbaden: Steiner, 1977), p. 83.

80. While Christian villagers remained like their neighbors in much of their outlook and behavior, they took pride, according to one informant, in being "refined villagers."

Members of all strata of society — from upper-caste *malguzars* to *Telis*
and *Satnamis* — recognized a significant change in the hygiene of those
who became Christian, but not all agreed on an explanation for the transformation. Whereas Christians tended to view their cleanliness as a result of
their social "improvement" — it was the *dharm* of Christians to be clean —
Satnamis and other communities suspected that there were financial factors
involved — Christians, these latter informants argued, had cleaner bodies,
children, and homes because of their greater wealth and professionalization,
which allowed Christian wives to spend time at home (rather than in the
fields) attending to such things. All, however, agreed that education was a
factor.

For reasons of health, missionaries also urged certain diet alterations on
Chhattisgarhi Christians that occasionally brought them into conflict with
Hindu sensitivities.[81] Some of the changes were benign enough — for example, Christians, informants indicated, tended to reject the traditional
Chhattisgarhi breakfast of *bāsī* (literally, leftover food, but in this case, a mixture of water and the previous day's rice) in favor of *cāy* (tea) and *capātī* (a
thin, unleavened bread). But many Christians also ate meat without scruple,
offending the vegetarian sensibilities of *Satnamis* as well as Kabirpanthis and
upper-caste Hindus. For members of all these communities, vegetarianism
would have been the ideal, though it was not always possible for poorer
Chhattisgarhis to remain vegetarian (because meat was cheaper than many
vegetables).[82] Meat-eating was not an important element of Christian communal identity, except as an indication of their freedom from what they perceived to be vacuous restrictions. There was some at least limited support for
vegetarianism within the community. The "Special Rules of the Bishrampur
Church," drawn up in 1890, even appear to encourage vegetarianism (or at
least to prohibit the eating of carrion): "We will abstain from eating things
forbidden by the gospel, things which damage the eater, and things which the

81. Lohr reported in 1869 that all *Satnami* converts were eating meat as he had recommended; see Oscar Lohr, "Von Bisrampoor (1)," *Der deutsche Missionsfreund* 4, no. 5
(1869): 1.

82. Vegetarianism and *ahimsa* (nonviolence) towards animals was not always a part of
Indic religion; the Vedas, for example, include instructions on horse sacrifices. But from
the time of Manu's Laws (written sometime during or just before the first century BCE,
and perhaps in response to the *ahimsa* of *śraman* sects such as the Jains and Buddhists,
vegetarianism came to be incorporated into popular Hindu notions of purity and impurity. See Louis Dumont, *Homo Hierarchicus* (Chicago: University of Chicago Press, 1980),
p. 148. There is a hierarchy of meats, so to speak, beef being the most polluting, then pork,
chicken, and mutton. See M. N. Srinivas, "The Social System of a Mysore Village," in *Village India*, ed. McKim Marriott (Chicago: University of Chicago Press, 1955).

Hindus and *Satnamis* find abhorrent."[83] Nevertheless, next to the perception of Christians as caste-breakers, no other aspect of Christian practice appeared so saliently to non-Christians as a marker of Christian identity as the fact that they ate meat. The perception was so strong, in fact, that in 1907 a landowner in Mahasamund would not sell land to Evangelical missionaries because he assumed that they intended to open up a slaughterhouse.[84]

Christians were constantly harassed about their lack of vegetarianism, and Christian evangelists discovered that objections regarding this aspect of the Christian diet ended many conversations with non-Christians. In 1911, at the home of Budh Ram Mugaddam and other *Satnamis* in Pitia Jhar, an Evangelical catechist began to preach, but was interrupted by his host, who, the catechist reported, ". . . liked to hear now and then about Christianity but there is one thing he did not like [and] that is the killing of animals which is a very cruel act of Christians and others. [He said, 'Those] who do so are not worthy to be called man but brutes because it is the business of wild animals to kill one another and eat. You Christians better give up killing animals and then we can appreciate your teachings and religion; otherwise it has no effect on us.[']"[85] On the other hand, Christians viewed *Satnamis* as brutes for their perceived maltreatment of work animals.

Two disparate understandings of compassion were at play. To Christians, compassion for humans was far more important than compassion for animals, which they felt involved only alleviating the suffering of beasts (and not unnecessarily adding to it). They considered Hindus brutish not only for overworking their farm animals but for what they perceived to be a lack of compassion for other humans.[86] Hindus, on the other hand, viewed the prohibition against harming animals as an absolute — even if the purpose was to

83. "Biśrāmpur kalīsiyā kī viśeṣ ājñāyeṃ," AES 83-3 Bis54.

84. Theodore C. Seybold, *God's Guiding Hand: A History of the Central Indian Mission 1868-1967* (Philadelphia: United Church Board for World Ministries of the United Church of Christ, 1971), p. 62.

85. Entry in diary, unnamed catechist, 5 August 1911, found in the journal of S. J. Scott, Mahasamund catechist, AES 83-5 Di54 #1. See also entries for 6 November 1908, 15 January 1909, 21 May 1909, and 11 October 1909.

86. Christian missionaries and evangelists, for example, found the money spent on cow protection, which they believed should been spent for the care of humans, particularly wasteful. See Lang, *Healing Touch*, p. 58. Not all Christians agreed with the missionary rejection of *ahimsa*. For example, Evangelical missionary M. P. Davis reported in 1941 that certain Christians felt revulsion at the idea of taking animal life, and that Christian pastors sometimes avoided details of biblical stories, such as that a fatted calf was killed upon the return of the Prodigal Son, in order to avoid offending sensibilities; "Hinduism and the Christian Message," text of a 1941 address, HCS, box 1 of 4 (no folder).

alleviate their suffering — and could therefore countenance neither the mercy-killings nor meat-eating of Christians.[87]

If the local community disdained Christians for their consumption of meat, the fact that many *Satnamis* who became Christian were able to procure more respectable employment and so gave up their work in skins and bones tended to bolster their social status. Yet, despite the fact that no Christians in the Central Provinces returned leather-related occupations as their primary occupation in the Census of 1901, there were always poorer members of the community who continued to work with bones, hides, and carrion.[88] A 1925 report from Bishrampur, written by the Evangelical missionary F. A. Goetsch, illuminates the complexity of the issue for the Christian community:

> The Congregation at times becomes greatly exercised over the fact that occasionally certain members of the Church eat carrion, or occasionally kill a cow or bullock for food. Both of these acts bring the Christian Church in disrepute with the surrounding Hindu people. The greater part of our Christian community came from the Chamar caste, in which such things are done. This section of our Christian community is not entirely opposed to Christians doing the same. A section of our Church however came from castes in which this is considered an abomination, and therefore strenuously opposes these things. The teachers and catechists, who are compelled to live in Hindu communities and who are greatly looked down upon by their neighbours when it becomes known that some Christians do these things, are, even though they themselves were of low castes, very much opposed to this being done by any member of the Church. It is the problem of the Apostolic Church over again. Some of the stricter members would like to make the Indian Christian conform to the Hindu ideas of respectability and to defer to their prejudices. It is the attempt to acquire some standing

---

87. There is some evidence that Hindus later began appropriating something of the Christian understanding of compassion for humans. A 1955 article written by a Hindu bemoans the fact that Christians provided better care for orphans than Hindus did. Article from the Nagpur Hindi weekly, *Naya Khoon* (i.e., *Nayā khūn*, the next generation), 21 January 1955 (pages not given). Translated by Samuel Maqbul-Masih as "The Gulf between Religion and Humanity," found in DCHS, UCMS Records, DOM, India, box 59 (folder: Masih, Dr. and Mrs. Samuel, 1948, 1953, 1954-63).

88. In the same year, 11.8 percent of *Chamars* in the Central Provinces returned a trade in hides, leather, or shoemaking as their primary occupation. There are no separate statistics for *Satnamis*. India Census Commissioner, *Census of India, 1901*, vol. 8 (Part 2, Statistics) (Bombay: Government Central Press, 1902-3).

among the other communities. . . . Instead of working and praying for such regenerated lives, a section of our community is seeking to gain respectability by conforming Christian habits in non-essentials to the life of the people round about. I am going with them in so far that I am seeking to stop the eating of carrion and the killing of cows . . . for food with all the means at my disposal in our own Christian villages, but realize that the only recognition worthwhile must come through the regenerated lives of our Churchmembers [*sic*].[89]

Until the 1930s, leaders of the Immanuel Church in Bishrampur excommunicated members of the community who continued to work in skins and bones, with the support of missionaries like Goetsch, on the grounds that the trade was a "stumbling block" to non-Christians.[90] In 1933, the "Immanuel Mandli [Congregation]," a group of Bishrampur Christians that briefly broke away from the mission over its defense of a pastor, Boas Purti, that members of the rebel congregation believed to be an adulterer, resolved that "those who are turned out from the mandli [church, or congregation] due to the occupation of bones and skin will be accepted [back] in the mandli, but if they take again this occupation and will eat the flesh of [dead animals], they will be punished heavily . . ."[91]

Eventually, however, the missionaries began to support the trade in bones as a necessary source of income for indigent members of the community. Oral accounts disagree over which missionary first directed the Bishrampur Christian community to allow its members to work with carrion. Some say that missionary M. P. Davis ended the ban. Others suggest that William Baur personally went out and picked up bones, daring the congregation to excommunicate him. Residents of Ganeshpur remember that missionary Whitcomb at first attempted to convince the local *pañcāyat* to forbid trade in skins and bones, desiring to increase the social standing of the Bishrampur Christian community, and only when the *pañcāyat* refused to ban the trade, began supporting it financially, even going so far as to construct a bone-processing plant. Even today, some Christian Bishrampur-*vālās* (residents of Bishrampur) resent this missionary decision, feeling it led to their degradation. Many Hindus in the area consider Bishrampuri Christians lower than *Satnamis*, who have by and large ended their association with carrion. In

89. "Annual Report for 1925," AES 82-13a Pr91, Annual Reports, no. 10, 1925.

90. Edith Moulton Melick, *The Evangelical Synod in India* (St. Louis: Eden Publishing House, 1930), p. 83.

91. Prem Prakash (Secretary) and Prem Dass Jacob (President), "Minutes of the Special Meeting of Immanuel Mandli," 1933, AES 83-3 Bis54.

summary, on the one hand, Christians were generally able to avoid work with leather, carrion, and bones, thereby increasing their social status. On the other, they did still allow such work for those who needed it, and were perceived far and wide to be vascular carnivores. In general, however, this latter fact appears to have had the greater influence on non-Christian impressions regarding Christianity.

Satnami-Christian dietary alterations were the result, in large part, of the community's desire to emulate other Christian catechists, pastors, and missionaries. However, the Chhattisgarhi appropriation of *angrezī* medical methods, health practices, hygienic predilections, and dietary habits did not simply replace native methods and ways of thinking. Rather, missionary norms were received and embraced (or not), in many instances, according to native criteria. Chhattisgarhis viewed the new medicine through old eyes, and appropriated it (or did not) accordingly.

CHAPTER 5

"Christian" Womanhood

Put another way, the mobilization of markers of group difference may it-self be part of a contestation of values about difference, as distinct from the consequences of difference for wealth, security, or power.

Arjun Appadurai, *Modernity at Large*

Beginning in the first quarter of the nineteenth century, western Christian women came to be much more involved with mission work in India than they had been before, though their involvement was at first quite informal. Until midway through the nineteenth century, most Protestant mission societies working in India believed that those seeking appointment as missionaries should be ordained. This preference for ordained missionaries greatly limited the number of *official* female mission workers.[1] There were many women, of course, who accompanied their husbands to the field, but because they had not been *officially* appointed, these women often had to raise independent funds to support their work. By the turn of the twentieth century, however, females on the mission field outnumbered their male counterparts, provoking an increased evangelical interest in "women's issues."[2] Women were in-

---

1. Rosemary Fitzgerald, "'Clinical Christianity': The Emergence of Medical Work as a Missionary Strategy in Colonial India, 1800-1914," in *Health, Medicine and Empire: Perspectives on Colonial India*, ed. Biswamoy Pati and Mark Harrison (Hyderabad, India: Orient Longman, 2001), p. 92.

2. Jane Haggis, "'Good Wives and Mothers' or 'Dedicated Workers'? Contradictions of Domesticity in the Mission of Sisterhood, Travancore, South India," in *Maternities and*

volved in both the Disciples and Evangelical missions from the start. The Disciples mission to India was, after all, co-sponsored by the CWBM, and India was chosen over other countries in part because of the "needs of India's women."[3]

Patricia Hill has argued that most women involved in the late nineteenth-century foreign missionary movement did not support the goals of the contemporaneous women's rights movement, and the evidence suggests that this holds true for the American missionaries in Chhattisgarh as well.[4] These missionaries, and, to a large extent, their husbands, were inspired by Victorian notions of femininity and domesticity which considered women "guardians" of the home and subordinated them to their husbands as "help-meets." At the same time, these notions emphasized the importance of companionate marriage, emotional intimacy, and mutual respect between a husband and wife.

Few aspects of Indian culture scandalized missionaries so much as the perceived maltreatment of Indian women, which not only invigorated mission societies but also, to some extent, came to be used as a justification for the imperial project itself.[5] Missionary reports abound with censorious accounts of child marriages, polygyny, temple prostitution, widow abuse, and the occasional (but infamous) *satī* ceremonies in which a widow immolated herself, or was immolated, on her husband's funeral pyre. Disciples and Evangelical missionaries considered it their duty to overturn these and other of Hinduism's "age-old" gender injustices and improve the treatment of women.[6]

A sense of what missionaries believed they were doing in India can be gained from a set of photos in a 1932 advertisement for the United Christian Missionary Society (UCMS) with the headline, "Paganism or Christianity: Which?" (see p. 169). In the first picture stands a young, naked, *brahman* girl

---

Modernities: Colonial and Postcolonial Experiences in Asia and the Pacific, ed. Kalpana Ram and Margaret Jolly (New York: Cambridge University Press, 1998), pp. 88ff.

3. Nelle Grant Alexander, *Disciples of Christ in India* (Indianapolis: United Christian Missionary Society, 1946), p. 4.

4. Patricia R. Hill, *The World Their Household: The American Woman's Foreign Mission Movement and Cultural Transformation, 1870-1920* (Ann Arbor: University of Michigan Press, 1985), pp. 35ff.

5. Eliza F. Kent, *Converting Women: Gender and Protestant Christianity in Colonial South India* (New York: Oxford University Press, 2004), p. 10.

6. In 1932, one missionary wrote, "Coupled with woman's own desire for social uplift the day will soon come when the Laws of Manu in regard to women will be relics of the Dark Ages in India. Let us do all we can to speed the coming of that day." Milton C. Lang, *The Healing Touch in Mission Lands* (St. Louis: Eden Publishing House, 1932), p. 88.

PAGANISM or CHRISTIANITY

A Christian child dedicated to a life of love, happiness and service for Christ.

WHICH?

Answer Children's Day

Through an Offering for Foreign Missions

on

JUNE 5

Supplies Ready April 5

Order from

Department of Religious Education

UNITED CHRISTIAN MISSIONARY SOCIETY

Missions Building   Indianapolis, Indiana

A Brahman child ready for dedication to the Temple.

Thanks to Don Haymes for help obtaining a usable scan of this image and permission to reprint it from the collection of *World Call* issues available at the Heritage Room of Christian Theological Seminary Library (Indianapolis, IN).

with tussled, matted hair, looking sullenly downward, who was, as the caption states, "ready for dedication to the Temple."[7] The other photo depicts a young, smiling, *sari*-wearing girl with her head covered, who, the caption indicates, is a "Christian child dedicated to a life of love, happiness and service for Christ."[8]

For many missionaries, the desire to improve the lot of India's women took the form of visiting those who were secluded under the system of *purdah*.[9] The practice of visiting women in their homes, called *zenana* missions after the Persian word for secluded women's apartments in some Indian homes, was well established when the Disciples and Evangelical missionaries began their work in Chhattisgarh. *Zenana* missionary workers visited women who, because of restrictions on appearing in public and interacting with men, would not have been able to hear the missionary message or participate in the mission's educational programs. The historical origins of the *purdah* system are uncertain and debated, though it is clear that the practice was most common among Muslims, upper-caste Hindus, and those seeking to emulate these two groups. *Zenana* missions declined toward the end of the century, primarily because the idea of female education began to take root among India's elites, but also because many mission agencies began at around this time to focus more on rural and lower-caste India, where the seclusion of women was a much less common practice.[10]

Disciples and Evangelical missionaries worked primarily among *Satnamis*, who rarely secluded their women;[11] nevertheless, they continued to

---

7. An allusion, presumably, to the Hindu practice, rare today but relatively common in this period, of "marrying" young girls to temple deities. The girls, called *devadāsīs* ("servants of God") were involved in worshiping their divine "husbands" as singers and dancers. Though in theory having nothing to do with sexuality, the potential for such an arrangement to be abused by males associated with the temples (and rumors that it was so abused) led reformers, British and Indian, to declare the practice "temple prostitution" and to work for its abolition.

8. United Christian Missionary Society, "Paganism or Christianity: Which?" *World Call*, April 1932. The UCMS, formed in 1920, was a merger of the Disciples FCMS, the CWBM, and the American Christian Missionary Society.

9. *Purdah* literally means "curtain," a reference to the drapery in certain homes that divided the domain of women from that of men. By extension, the term came to be used to refer to the system of seclusion itself.

10. Kent, *Converting Women*, pp. 141, 157.

11. For example, in 1895 Disciples missionary Ada Boyd regularly visited 24 homes in Bilaspur (26 in 1896) of which roughly a quarter were Muslim and the rest lower-caste "Hindu." See Ada Boyd, "India, Bilaspur (Annual Report)," *Missionary Tidings*, December 1895; and Ada Boyd, "India, Bilaspur (Annual Report)," *Missionary Tidings*, December 1896. The quote comes from Ada Boyd, "Bilaspur Zenana Report," *Missionary Tidings*, No-

view the "plight" of Indian women, as did most missionaries in India, through the lens of their experience with secluded women. When comparing *Satnami*-Christian attitudes and behaviors towards women with those of Indians in general, missionaries often took the practice of *purdah* to be representative of the average Indian woman's experience. Based on this asymmetrical assessment, they believed that they had achieved great gains for their *Satnami*-Christian women, who did not suffer under the "refined vices" of the upper castes.[12] *Satnami* women who became Christian did, in fact, enjoy certain benefits, but just as often, as will be discussed below, conversion to Christianity curtailed the already narrow range of behaviors and vocations considered suitable for women.

"Women's uplift," informed by Victorian notions of femininity and gentility, remained, throughout the entire period under investigation, an integral aspect of missions in Chhattisgarh. The missionary goal of "civilizing" Indian attitudes and behaviors regarding women coexisted with the *Satnami*-Christian community's desire to improve their social status according to traditional criteria, resulting in a fluid, synthetic amalgam of values and practices that Eliza Kent has called, in the context of her work on the *Nadars* of South India, a "discourse of respectability." *Satnami*-Christians did not merely accept the missionaries' notions of femininity and domesticity, but assimilated them selectively, and in a way informed by upper-caste Hindu notions of "respectable" womanhood. These dual ideals were in many ways compatible. Kent argues, for example, that Victorian and elite Indian sensibilities both "privileged women's enclosure over mobility, self-restraint over spontaneity, and self-denial over self-indulgence. . . ."[13] There was thus a pronounced affinity between Victorian and upper-caste Indian notions of female propriety and respectability. While *Satnami*-Christians clearly assimilated many of the values and practices introduced by missionaries, they appear to have much more quickly embraced those attitudes and behaviors that reflected both heterogenetic and orthogenetic notions of social refinement and respectability. By appropriating the signs of Victorian domesticity and femininity, *Satnami*-Christians were at the same time appropriating the symbols of upper-caste Hindus, and thereby establishing, asserting, and manifesting their improved social status vis-à-vis the *Satnami* community.

---

vember 1902. By 1932 Evangelical missionaries and Bible women were visiting 4,638 homes roughly two times a year. See Lydia Kies, "Annual Report," 1933, AES 82-13a Pr91, Annual Reports, no. 18, 1933.

12. For an example of this asymmetrical assessment, see Helen A. McGavran, "Christian and Non-Christian Homes in India," *Missionary Tidings*, December 1918, p. 313.

13. Kent, *Converting Women*, p. 4.

In Chhattisgarh, as in other regions of India structured by feudal landowning arrangements, a family's status was in many ways related to its ability to protect its women from difficult physical labor and from potentially dangerous contact with unrelated men. Families wishing to indicate or assert their higher social status would therefore veil and/or seclude their women. Among less wealthy families, however, financial considerations required women to work outside the home. Women of the mostly agricultural *Satnami* community, for example, generally worked along with men in the fields. In fact, women in Chhattisgarh were more likely than women in almost any other region of North India to work outside the home, partly because of the prevalence of rice harvesting — an especially labor-intensive enterprise — and also because of the large number of *dalit* communities in the region.[14] While this afforded these women a certain limited physical mobility denied to secluded women, it also symbolized their low social status. In addition, it exposed them to unstructured interaction with unrelated men, which had its hazards. Lower-caste women were particularly vulnerable to sexual violence at the hands of higher-caste men because their community's subordination made the social price of redressing such crimes unacceptably high.[15] There is still in India today, among even the most westernized Indians, a sense of danger associated with women, especially solitary women, who do or must interact with unrelated men. One Indian Christian who had seen the movie "Home Alone" was shocked by the film — not by the fact that a child could be left behind by a family, but by the fact that the child's mother, in an effort to get back to her son, rode in the back of a truck with an all-male Polka band without getting sexually abused.

As the economic situation of *Satnami*-Christians improved, making unnecessary the extra-domicilic labor of women, Christian women began more frequently to confine their labors to the home. This pleased the missionaries,

14. On the relatively greater mobility of tribal and lower-caste women, see Peter B. Anderson and Susanne Foss, "Christian Missionaries and Orientalist Discourse: Illustrated by Materials on the Santals after 1855," in *Christians and Missionaries in India: Cross-Cultural Communication since 1500*, ed. Robert Eric Frykenberg (Grand Rapids: Eerdmans, 2003), p. 305; Joyce Burkhalter Flueckiger, *Gender and Genre in the Folklore of Middle India* (Ithaca: Cornell University Press, 1996), pp. 9-11; and Ramdas Lamb, *Rapt in the Name: The Ramnamis, Ramnam, and Untouchable Religion in Central India* (Albany: State University of New York Press, 2002), p. 165; and R. S. Mann and K. Mann, *Tribal Cultures and Change* (New Delhi: Mittal Publications, 1989), p. 201.

15. For a discussion of *Satnami* women's experiences of sexual abuse at the hands of upper-caste Chhattisgarhis, see Saurabh Dube, *Untouchable Pasts: Religion, Identity, and Power among a Central Indian Community, 1780-1950* (Albany: State University of New York Press, 1998), p. 107.

whose goal was not simply to convert Indian women to Christianity, but to "convert" them as well to the Christian ideal of loving, competent, and dedicated homemaking.[16] But it also satisfied certain traditional criteria of upper-caste Indian status by indicating that Christian men were now capable of protecting (and controlling) their wives.

Satnami-Christian Conjugality: Weddings, Widows, and Divorce

To suggest that *Satnami*-Christians may have been responding not only to missionary, but also to upper-caste Indian ideals of "respectable" womanhood is not to suggest that those who became Christian in Chhattisgarh remained unchanged. On the contrary, the behaviors and attitudes of *Satnamis* who became Christian were transformed in a variety of significant ways. The most appreciable of these transformations pertain to the community's conventions of conjugality.[17]

Satnami weddings generally followed the patterns of those of other Hindu communities, except that *Satnami* functionaries took the place of *brahman* priests and astrologers. *Satnamis* usually got married between the ages of four and thirty and pairings were arranged by the families of those to be wed, following the customs of village exogamy and sub-caste endogamy. On the first day of *Satnami* wedding ceremonies, called *cūl-māṭī* (hearth-earth), the families involved reconstructed their hearths and rubbed *halḍī* (turmeric) on the bride and bridegroom (in their respective homes). The application was repeated on the second day, and then the marriage itself took place on the third.

On the day of the wedding, the bridegroom's family traveled to the wedding grounds, carrying with them gifts (usually *saris*) to present to the bride and her family members. Once they arrived, the tails of the bride and bridegroom's clothing were tied together, and they circumnavigated a tall pole seven times. The couple was treated as if divine for the day, effecting a temporary reversal whereby the parents became as devotees to their children. After the ceremony, the bride traveled to the bridegroom's house for several days

---

16. On similar goals of missionary women in Hawaii and China (respectively), see P. Grimshaw, *Paths of Duty: American Missionary Wives in Nineteenth Century Hawaii* (Honolulu: University of Hawaii Press, 1989); and J. Hunter, *The Gospel of Gentility: American Women Missionaries in Turn-of-the-Century China* (New Haven: Yale University Press, 1984).

17. It bears mentioning that the following analysis rests on the *perceptions* of missionaries, *Satnami*-Christians, and other Chhattisgarhis. The extent to which these perceptions reflect the actual experience of those involved cannot, of course, be determined.

and then, if not yet pubescent, returned to her family's home until she came of age. After attaining puberty, she would return to her husband's home and complete the wedding with a small ceremony.[18] It appears that among *Satnamis* pubescent marriage was the norm; few *Satnami* girls remained single after the age of fifteen, though they were generally not married at as young an age as upper-caste girls. Families wishing to improve their social position did, however, generally promise their daughters at a very young age (as child marriage was a sign of traditional status).

Following missionary ideals of propriety and restraint, *Satnami*-Christian weddings tended to be much simpler, involving only a short western-style ceremony in the church, during which rings were sometimes exchanged. There was no application of *haldī*, no tying of the couple's garments, and only a rare exchange of dowry or brideprice. The "Special Rules of the Bishrampur Congregation," for example, declare, "We will not sell our daughters for money, nor will we accept a sum [*mol*] for them," but allow that, "If a girl desires some clothing, then no more than 10 rupees worth of clothing should be given or taken."[19] Child marriages in the Christian community continued to occur, but they were remarkably infrequent, and generally led to the excommunication of those who arranged them.[20] Many Christian girls continued, however, to be married just after the onset of puberty. Especially in the earlier years (but even still in the 1930s and '40s), *Satnami*-Christian families felt and responded to pressure from their friends and relatives to marry their children, especially female children, at the more traditional earlier age.[21] Nevertheless, by the 1940s and '50s there was a perceptible difference between the two communities, at least according to Christians, who attest that they married, on average, around the age of eighteen to twenty, whereas *Satnamis* were

18. This paragraph relies heavily on "Notes on the Sutnamee Chumars of the Raepore District from Information Gathered Orally from the Gooroo, Agur Dass, and His Disciples, and from Chumars Generally in 1868," unsigned typescript supplement to Temple's 1867 Gazetteer of Central India, found in HCS, box 3 of 4 (no folder).

19. "Biśrāmpur kalīsiyā kī viśeś ājñāyeṃ," 1890, found in AES 83-3 Bis54.

20. On similar changes among Christian women in Portuguese Goa, see Pratima P. Kamat, "From Conversion to the Civil Code: Gender and the Colonial State in Goa, 1510-1961," *Indian Historical Review* 27, no. 2 (2003): 68.

21. Missionaries tended to cling to female boarding school students and orphans until a later age in the knowledge that returning them to their families or letting them leave would mean their early marriage. See Donald A. McGavran, "The Growing Church in India," vol. 2 (unpublished newsletter), April 1942, found in HCS, box 4 of 4 (folder: Missionaries). On the difficulty of keeping older orphans in the orphanages, see Martin P. Davis, *Sadhu Hagenstein: A White Man among the Brown* (St. Louis: The Board for Foreign Missions, Evangelical Synod of North America, 1930), p. 114.

married at around the age of twelve to fifteen. (The Indian Christian Marriage Act of 1864 stipulated that Christian grooms must be at least sixteen years old, and that brides be over the age of thirteen.)[22] Officially there was no polygamy among *Satnami*-Christians, though occasionally Christians surreptitiously arranged polygamous unions.

In this context, Kent's "discourse of respectability" can be clearly discerned. On the one hand, *Satnami*-Christians accepted a marriage ceremony designed according to missionary values of restraint and propriety in public services. Similarly, some *Satnami*-Christians altered their conjugal practices by getting married later (or having their children married later). On the other hand, however, the upper-caste Hindu ideal of an early marriage continued to influence the community, and for those seeking (or having achieved social advancement), this influence was stronger than that of the missionaries, or of Indian Christian marriage laws, for that matter.

Upper-caste widows in Chhattisgarh, as in other parts of India, were generally forbidden to remarry. Considered the conduits of community purity, upper-caste women (far more than upper-caste men) were expected to lead a life of monogamy and extramarital chastity that extended even beyond the death of a husband. Conversely, *Satnami* widows, like those of other *dalit* communities, commonly remarried in an attenuated wedding ceremony during which their new husbands presented them with the fashion accessories forsworn by widows (such as bangles or other pieces of jewelry).[23] Widows whose husbands had died before their cohabitation generally fetched a higher brideprice (among *Satnamis* brideprice, rather than dowry, was the norm). Levirate marriage was common if the deceased husband had available brothers. In part because of the possibility of remarriage for widows, *sati* was extremely rare.

One might be tempted to interpret the exchange of brideprice (rather than dowry) as an indication that *Satnami* women were valued for their fi-

---

22. The age of consent for Christians in India is now twenty-one years for men and eighteen years for women. The Indian Christian Marriage Act of 1872 (a revised version of the Indian Christian Marriage Act of 1864), was as this book went to print available online (with all its subsequent amendments) at www.indialawinfo.com/bareacts/indchris.html#_Toc502305912.

23. After the funeral ceremony of their husbands, widows broke their bangles as a sign of their bereavement. Widows were sometimes also tonsured, and they were expected to forswear the wearing of colorful *saris*. See Walter G. Menzies, "A Contrast in Cries," *Missionary Tidings*, September 1911. Widows who did remarry were forced to relinquish control of their possessions, and sometimes lost their children to their previous husbands' families.

nancial contribution to the family, and there is some evidence that this is the case.[24] However, Prem Chowdhry has shown that in many communities, the exchange of brideprice and dowry coexist.[25] The economic contribution of women is a factor in determining whether brideprice or dowry will be exchanged, but so, too, is the relative social status of the families involved.[26] In such communities, families with a relatively low social status must pay a brideprice when seeking wives for their sons, whereas families with a relatively high social status can demand a dowry for the marriage of their male heirs. Similarly, while the possibility of remarriage for widows appears at first glance a great advantage,[27] in actuality this was not necessarily the case. In a patrilocal society such as Chhattisgarh's, the marital possibilities of widows were generally determined by the deceased husbands' families. Levirate marriage — which allowed for any accumulation of wealth or children to remain within the family — was very often the only option allowed to widows, and was not necessarily an appealing one. Furthermore, according to Hindu conjugal laws, which were consolidated by the British, widows who remarried lost any right they had to their husbands' property. The only way for them to retain their property (and sometimes even their children) was to accept a levirate remarriage or to remain unmarried.[28]

Christian inheritance laws allowed widows to retain possession of their goods and children upon the death of a husband.[29] Like *Satnamis*, Christian widows were allowed to remarry, and frequently, according to informants, those with no children did. Here, at least, it appears as if the *Satnami-*

24. For examples of this argument, see Flueckiger, *Gender and Genre*, p. 11; Indira Rajaram, "Economics of Bride-Price and Dowry," *Economic and Political Weekly* 18, no. 8 (1983); and John C. B. Webster, *A History of the Dalit Christians in India* (San Francisco: Mellen Research University Press, 1992), p. 29. The existence of brideprice (rather than dowry) can be seen either as an indication that women are considered property, chattel to be bought and sold, or that they are valued for their ability to contribute to a family's economic situation. The two interpretations are not, of course, mutually exclusive. On this topic, see Dube, *Untouchable Pasts*, p. 109.

25. Prem Chowdhry, *The Veiled Women: Shifting Gender Equations in Rural Haryana, 1880-1990* (Delhi, India: Oxford University Press, 1994), pp. 70-72.

26. On the exchange of brideprice and dowry in North India, see David G. Mandelbaum, *Women's Seclusion and Men's Honor: Sex Roles in North India, Bangladesh, and Pakistan* (Tucson: University of Arizona Press, 1988), pp. 66ff. Like the greater seclusion of women, the ability to demand dowry for one's sons is a sign of higher status and is often adopted by those undergoing the process of sanskritization.

27. For an example of this argument, see Webster, *History of Dalit Christians*, p. 65.

28. Chowdhry, *The Veiled Women*, pp. 82-87.

29. Martin P. Davis, *India Today and the Church Tomorrow* (Philadelphia: The Board of International Missions, Evangelical and Reformed Church, 1947), p. 62.

Christian community was following the norms of its own pre-Christian tradition, which were in many ways consonant with the prejudices of the missionaries. There is no evidence that the *Satnami*-Christian community began, for example, to restrict the remarriage of widows, as a community attempting to improve its social status according to indigenous criteria would do. Rather, the evidence suggests that *Satnami*-Christian widows frequently remarried, and there is some indication that their ability to determine their own marital fate actually increased.

Divorce was common among *Satnamis,* though the term implies a more formal marital arrangement than was actually the case. The community had a reputation for adulterous liaisons, and many men and women simply abandoned their spouses and took up residence with another. Frequently, women who had thus strayed were welcomed back by their husbands, who were alleged to have said flippantly, "If my cow wanders and comes home again, shall I not let her into her stall?"[30] A man wishing to make a more formal arrangement and wanting to marry an already married woman would, upon the consent of the woman's husband, simply repay the first husband for expenses incurred in his wedding. The woman and her new husband were then joined in a new, simplified ceremony, called *curī pahanānā* (to put bangles on [one's new wife]).

The *Satnami*-Christian community, on the other hand, strenuously opposed divorce among its members. As a result, the divorce rate among *Satnami*-Christians plummeted relative to that of the *Satnami* community, according to both *Satnami* and Christian informants. The increased stability of Christian marriage may reflect the health of Christian relationships, but it also reflects the strong social pressure against divorce that was brought to bear on members of the Christian community. According to upper-caste Hindu norms of conjugality, only men could seek divorce. According to Indian Christian conventions and law, neither men nor women could seek the dissolution of a marriage, except in extreme circumstances. The rarity of divorce among Chhattisgarh's *Satnami*-Christians, therefore, could be interpreted in several ways. It could, for example, indicate that Christians had assimilated the conjugal prejudices of their missionary interlocutors. Conversely, it could be taken as an indication that the *Satnami*-Christian community was using conversion as a pretense for appropriating certain of the symbols and practices of upper-caste Hindu status, as cover for their claims to higher social status. My own sense is that the apparent enthusiasm with which the *Satnami*-Christian community embraced the missionary

---

30. Robert Vane Russell, *The Tribes and Castes of the Central Provinces of India,* vol. 2 (London: Macmillan, 1916), p. 412.

ideal of monogamous and lasting marriage demonstrates the fact that *Satnami*-Christians remained at all times attuned to *both* the prescriptions of their missionary leaders and — especially as their economic and social situation improved relative to that of the *Satnamis* — the traditional insignia of upper-caste status.

It is worth noting here that in this case conversion to Christianity actually led to the *restriction* of conjugal options for women. The ease with which *Satnami* women could leave their husbands — and the evidence suggests that *Satnami* women abandoned their husbands more frequently than their husbands abandoned them — conferred upon *Satnami* women the social leverage necessary to manipulate or rearrange their relationships with men.[31] Save for the possibility of recanting (or being excommunicated), *Satnami*-Christian women lost the leverage bestowed upon their *Satnami* sisters by the possibility of second *(curī)* marriages.[32]

Satnami-Christian women found their behavior restricted in another way as well. The *Satnami*-Christian community attempted, with apparent if not complete success, to eradicate the use of foul and abusive language for which *Satnamis* — especially *Satnami* women — were well known. One Muslim informant said, "*Satnamis* spoke in a hot, angry way. Every word was *gālī* (abuse). But when they became Christian, this way of speaking changed. They came to speak in a respectful way." *Satnamis* had a reputation for skill in the raunchy and vulgar arts, and for encouraging such asperity among their children. In particular, *Satnami* women were renowned *gālīdene-vālīs* (givers of abuse, users of foul language).[33] The most vicious verbal assaults surfaced in the pribbles and prabbles of *Satnami* women, but *Satnami* women conversed contumeliously with their husbands and even their gods (because relationships with the deities were also considered coercive, based on exchange and reciprocity).[34] Though the utilization of abusive language is perhaps a more

31. Flueckiger, *Gender and Genre*, p. 11.

32. Perhaps in an effort to please their higher-caste political allies, *Satnami* conferences in the 1920s frequently resolved to punish those who ran away with other people's spouses. See untitled, unsigned, and undated account of conferences from 1925 to 1927 in HCS, box 2 of 4 (folder: Dr. Don Sat. Mss.).

33. Some examples of popular Chhattisgarh abuses, which I have translated as insipidly as possible (the reader can imagine more colorful renderings), are *bhāsarī ke* ([you are] from a vagina) and *buramārī ke* ([you are] from a penetrated vagina). *Satnami* women also might call their husbands *bharā* (pimp) or *berrā* (bastard).

34. For an account of one rather nasty argument between two women involving *gālīdenā* (the giving of abuse), see H. A. Feierabend, "The Way Our Young Men's Society Settles Quarrels," 1936, AES 82-14 Qu2, Feierabend, H. A., Quarterly Reports, Articles, Newsletters, 1933-1941.

symbolic than real freedom, it could be argued that it fulfilled an important subversive function as an example of what James Scott calls the "weapons of the weak."[35] As one coping mechanism in the repertoire of women dealing with their own subordination, abusive language allowed for the voicing of dissent and the expression of frustration. Through such language women could mock authority and ridicule those who could not be confronted directly.[36]

Though unarguably *Satnami* women who became Christian gained a great deal of conjugal security relative to their unconverted counterparts, the gains appear to have come with a diminished ability to express their disagreement with men, whether directly or indirectly. Several Christian informants suggested that one of the biggest differences between *Satnami* and Christian women was that whereas *Satnami* women said whatever they wanted to their husbands, Christian women did not say anything against theirs.[37] Christianity does appear to have bred a greater willingness, among women, to act in submission to the will of their husbands, in part because of the availability of biblical passages urging such submission. Here again, Victorian ideals regarding the restrained speech of "respectable" women resonated with traditional Indian notions of upper-caste conjugal decorum, which entailed, among other things, that wives be submissive, restrained, and self-controlled.[38]

The affinity of Victorian and upper-caste ideals, however, should not be overstated. Clearly there are similarities between the two, especially with regard to the relationship of husbands and wives. Nevertheless, further investigation would be necessary to determine whether and to what extent Victorian and upper-caste norms converge on a range of related matters, such as the relationship of widowed mothers with their sons, and single women with their fathers.

35. James C. Scott, *Weapons of the Weak: Everyday Forms of Peasant Resistance* (New Haven: Yale University Press, 1989).

36. Cf. Chowdhry, *The Veiled Women*, pp. 18-19.

37. The Christians probably overstated the extent of *Satnami* women's freedom in this regard, as other informants suggested that *Satnami* women who verbally abused their husbands were likely to provoke a physically abusive response.

38. The singing of bawdy, irreverent, and sometimes sexually suggestive songs was common to *dalit* women's communities in all of rural North India, and in its reforms the Arya Samaj frequently attempted to "purify" these communities of their "indecent" songs. Kenneth W. Jones, *Arya Dharm: Hindu Consciousness in 19th-Century Punjab* (Berkeley: University of California Press, 1976), p. 95. Likewise, Sahajanand, leader of the nineteenth-century Swaminarayan movement in what is now Gujarat, prohibited the singing of "bawdy songs." See Raymond Brady Williams, *An Introduction to Swaminarayan Hinduism* (Cambridge: Cambridge University Press, 2001), p. 25.

Women's Education and Professionalization

At the time of the missionaries' arrival, rural Chhattisgarhis did not consider it important to educate their daughters; indeed, they were at that time rarely educating their sons. Around 1900, Disciples missionary Bertha Lohr reported the reaction of a group of rural Chhattisgarhis to the idea of her starting a girls' school in their village:

> At first they seemed rather startled, and began to make all sorts of excuses. "There are very few girls here," they said, and when I told them that I saw quite enough right there for a small girls' school, they made other excuses. "They will have to go to their father-in-law's house soon [i.e. get married]," or, "What will be the use for girls to learn? They cannot earn their living by it." Some of them said, "We can not spare them from the housework. . . ."[39]

Despite these prejudices, the value of educating girls and women seems to have caught on rather quickly among *Satnami*-Christians, though for some time the duration and topics of their education differed from those of boys. At least by the 1930s, however, Christian women near Evangelical and Disciples mission stations were receiving, according to informants, roughly the same education as men, though in smaller numbers. In the popular imagination, in fact, Christianity seems to have been defined, in part, by the education of women. When asked by a Disciples missionary what the difference was between her life as a *Satnami* and as a Christian, Mungia Bai replied:

> In those days, when the gurus or other important men came to our house, my husband would say, "Don't show your face around here. This is a men's meeting." Now when you come, they say, "The women must come to learn. You women are God's daughters . . ."[40]

When given the opportunity to gain an education, lower-caste women appear to have responded with enthusiasm. Higher-caste communities in India had traditionally perpetuated the notion that women were incapable of

---

39. Bertha F. Lohr, "Bits of Talk from India, Bilaspur," *Missionary Tidings*, June 1900.
40. The idiom suggests some redaction by the missionary, but there is no particular reason to doubt the accuracy of the sentiments expressed. Donald A. McGavran, *The Satnami Story: A Thrilling Drama of Religious Change* (Pasadena: William Carey Library, 1990), p. 66.

learning, or that a woman's education might threaten her husband's health.[41] Fewer such preconceptions existed among lower-caste women.

If *Satnami*-Christian girls received much the same education as their brothers, however, it was not with the same goal in mind. In Europe, the Industrial Revolution had driven a wedge between the locus of "production" and that of "reproduction," and had given rise to the notion of "separate spheres," the idea that men worked primarily *outside* the home, whereas women were responsible for what went on *inside* the domestic abode. Informed by this Victorian sensibility, missionaries sought to train Indian men for purposeful and gainful employment, and Indian women for efficient, informed, and pious homemaking.[42] The system was self-perpetuating in a way, for greater professionalization of Christian men allowed for the greater domestication of Christian women.[43] No longer needed in the fields, those who did not pursue professional training themselves — and even many who did — entered the home, leading to an abundance of relatively highly educated Christian housewives. These educated housewives took great pride in their intelligent homemaking. Speaking of the current period but in an idiom Christian housewives at mid-century would have understood, one Christian

---

41. A. S. Altekar argues that in the Vedic period upper-caste Hindu women were educated in much the same way as men, and that it was not until child marriage became more popular — a development he traces to the first three centuries BCE — that the education of Hindu women declined. Both Altekar and I. J. Leslie suggest that until the first or second century of the Common Era, higher-caste Hindu women even underwent the *upanayana* ceremony which qualified them for study in the Vedas. See Anant Sadashiv Altekar, *The Position of Women in Hindu Civilisation, from Prehistoric Times to the Present Day* (Benares: The Culture Publication House, Benares Hindu University, 1938), pp. 11ff.; and I. Julia Leslie, *The Perfect Wife: The Orthodox Hindu Woman According to the Strīdharmapaddhati of Tryambakayajvan* (Delhi: Oxford University Press, 1989), p. 37. For a more critical view of upper-caste Hindu educational practices in the late nineteenth and early twentieth centuries (especially as they relate to women), see Pandita Ramabai, *The High-Caste Hindu Woman* (Philadelphia: Press of the J. B. Rogers Printing, 1888), p. 131.

42. Barbara Ramusack argues that British women in nineteenth-century India might properly be called "maternal imperialists" because of their desire to socialize "immature" Indian daughters according to what they considered to be more advanced Victorian ideals of womanhood. Barbara N. Ramusack, "Cultural Missionaries, Maternal Imperialists, Feminist Allies: British Women Activists in India, 1865-1945," in *Western Women and Imperialism,* ed. Nupur Chaudhuri and Margaret Strobel (Bloomington: Indiana University Press, 1992), pp. 120, 133.

43. The same was true among Tshidi Christians in South Africa. See Jean Comaroff and John Comaroff, "Christianity and Colonialism in South Africa," *American Anthropologist* 13, no. 1 (1986): 13.

woman of *Satnami* ancestry said, "We are also housewives, but the difference is we are educated and [*Satnami* women] are illiterate."

Unlike previous *Satnami*-Christian transformations discussed in this chapter, the education of women appears to have had little precedent in the practice of upper-caste Hindus. Central Provinces Census figures for 1921 and 1931, for example, indicate that Christians were educating their women at a far higher rate than local higher-caste communities such as the Rajputs and Banias (see Figures 9 and 10 in the Appendix).

Though the main goal of female education, as noted above, was competent homemaking, a small but significant number of Chhattisgarhi Christian women were trained for employment as teachers, nurses, and Bible women. In many ways, the professionalization of these women undermined both Victorian and upper-caste Hindu ideals, which agreed that the home was the most appropriate sphere of female activity. Bible women thus embodied a certain ambiguity in the Chhattisgarhi Christian community's views regarding the proper behavior of women.[44] The education of Bible women, for example, mingled topics like "the Bible," "Christian faith," and "Hygiene" with sessions on the "Art of Teaching" and "Social Problems."[45] While being trained by missionary women to propagate the evangelical ideal of "civilized" domesticity, Bible women themselves represented a different model. They were *professional* purveyors of *domestic* propriety. There was also a generational element to the community's ambivalence about the education of women — Bible women taught religious knowledge and domestic arts (e.g., sewing and knitting) to women in their homes while those same women's young girls were in school learning reading, writing, and arithmetic.

Jane Haggis argues that the missionary "goal of 'emancipating' Indian women into 'Christian womanhood' [was] overlaid with the Bible women's intention to 'emancipate' themselves from the restrictions of their low-caste

---

44. Cf. Haggis, "Good Wives and Mothers"; and Mrinalini Sebastian, "Reading Archives from a Postcolonial Perspective," *Journal of Feminist Studies in Religion* 19, no. 1 (2003).

45. On the curriculum of Bible women on the Evangelical mission field, see Helen Süger, "Report of the Committee on Biblewomen's School Curriculum and on the Revision of the Old Course of the Biblewomen," 1925, AES 82-14 Qu2, Süger, Mrs. Helen Enslin, Quarterly Reports, Articles. The evangelical mission employed between five and eight Bible women per year in the first three decades of the twentieth century. Many of these first Bible women were born outside the mission, but the proportion of Chhattisgarhi Bible women increased as the years passed by; see Helen E. Süger, "Report of 1915," AES 82-13a Pr91, Annual Reports, no. 4, 1914-15; "1922 Report," ibid., no. 7, 1922; and Elise Kettler, "Zenana Work Survey," 1924, AES 82-14 Qu2, Kettler, Elise, Quarterly Reports, Articles, Newsletters, 1910-1933.

status."[46] While she may be overlooking the extent to which missionaries shared with Bible women the goal of their "emancipation," it is clear that the professionalization of Christian women in Chhattisgarh offered them the increased social capital that came with economic improvement and a modicum of financial independence — probably as important a factor as faith in their decision to pursue work as Bible women.

In the 1940s, a study on the Evangelical mission found that while the male children of Christians with *Satnami* ancestry were working in professions in much higher numbers than women, fifteen women of *Satnami* ancestry were working as Bible women, eleven as nurses, twelve as *ayahs,* and fourteen as teachers.[47] These occupations required women to move about extensively and conduct social intercourse with a wider range of people. Given the traditional association of such behaviors with lower-caste status, and even sexual impropriety and prostitution, one might expect that the itinerations of Christian Bible women were met with suspicion by members of other communities. In fact, the evidence suggests that Christian Bible women were respected and admired wherever they went, despite the fact that their unsupervised perambulations challenged traditional notions of female propriety.

Eliza Kent has suggested that Bible women working in South India "went to great lengths to de-emphasize all traces of their sexual desirability or availability: They removed their jewels and wore white saris, drawing on widely recognized markers of virtuous widowhood in its ascetic and asexual mode. . . ."[48] The evidence suggests that, like their counterparts in South India, Chhattisgarh's Bible women (and other *Satnami*-Christian women, such as nurses) also drew upon widely understood signifiers of pious and chaste widowhood and projected an image of chastity and asexuality. Like their South Indian sisters, they eschewed jewelry and frequently wore entirely white outfits. By doing so, these and other Christian women were able to announce that they were "off limits." Their peregrinations and social engagements did not, therefore, arouse suspicion.[49]

If *Satnami* women who became Christian came more frequently to work inside the home, however, the *Satnami*-Christian community did not, it appears, embrace indigenous notions associating the seclusion of women with

---

46. Haggis, "Good Wives and Mothers," p. 95.

47. "Satnami Tragedy Continues," 1943, unsigned, AES 80-1, Sat8.

48. Kent, *Converting Women,* p. 155.

49. This does not mean, however, that *Satnami*-Christian women were invulnerable. For example, in the 1930s, the Evangelical mission still considered it unsafe to place a single female teacher in an isolated village. M. P. Davis, "Annual Report, Parsabhader, 1932/33," 1933, AES 82-13a Pr91, Annual Reports, no. 18, 1933.

higher social status. Perhaps in part due to their education, Christian women related to both men and other women with greater confidence than their *Satnami* counterparts, a shift in behavior noted by informants from a variety of communities.[50] One Muslim former *malguzar*, who had witnessed the conversion of some *Satnamis* to Christianity in his village in the late 1930s and '40s, said that whereas the "jurisdiction" of *Satnami* women ranged no farther than the walls of their home, Christian women moved about with confidence and interacted with everyone, as he put it, "courageously."

The greater "courage" of Christian women may have been related to the fact that the Christian community had succeeded in changing other communities' perceptions about their women. Though the topic has not been systematically studied, there is evidence that in the late nineteenth and early twentieth centuries, upper-caste Chhattisgarhi men, particularly those whose families wielded economic power in addition to their social status, frequently took advantage of lower-caste women's sexual vulnerability.[51] As discussed above, a community's ability to protect the chastity of its women was generally considered a mark of high social status. Given their low social (and often economic) position, *Satnami* (and other *dalit*) families in Chhattisgarh could do little about the exploitation of their women; this, in turn, perpetuated their low social standing.

The *Satnami*-Christian community, on the other hand, appears to have succeeded in indicating, in a variety of ways, that its women were sexually unavailable. Their success in this regard may have had something to do with their association with socially and politically connected missionaries, a fact that assured *Satnami*-Christian women the social and even legal support necessary to redress incidences of sexual violence. It may also have had something to do with Christian sartorial choices, which both American missionaries and Indians would have considered more modest and thus indicative of chastity.

But the evidence suggests that the *Satnami*-Christian community defended its women from the perceived threats of "outsiders" (even Christian

---

50. There were limits, of course, to the freedom of Christian women, and one Christian resident of Parsabhader was asked by his congregation to keep his daughters from roaming about after sunset. M. P. Davis, "A Fallen Pillar," ca. 1934, AES 82-14 Qu2, Davis, M. P., Quarterly Reports, Articles, Newsletters, 1916-1935. Chhattisgarh is to this day a place where the interaction of men and women is very restricted and controlled. For example, so-called *"majnūn"* (the Indian equivalent of Romeo) squads allegedly monitor the interaction of unmarried males and females in Raipur's parks, restaurants, and hotels for any sign of illicit relations.

51. Dube, *Untouchable Pasts*, pp. 106ff.

outsiders) in more active ways as well. In the early 1930s, rumors circulated among members of the Bishrampur congregation that Boas Purti, who had been given responsibility by the missionary *malguzar* for the everyday supervision of village affairs, had seduced and impregnated an unmarried Bishrampur native named Rebekka. In what missionaries considered a "poorly conducted trial," the Immanuel church council (which was dominated by Indians at the time) considered the matter, declared Purti guilty, and removed him from church membership.[52] Missionaries disagreed with the church council's ruling, and Purti appealed the matter to the India Mission District (IMD). The IMD, still firmly under control of the missionaries, ruled that the church council's declaration of guilt had been rash and was not adequately supported by evidence. Accordingly, the IMD retained Purti as its representative in Bishrampur and declared that he was not to be put "out of caste," as the Immanuel church council had hoped he would be.[53]

Leaders of the Immanuel congregation responded by breaking with the missionaries and forming a schismatic body. They held their first meetings in the nearby Ganeshpur church, elected a president and secretary, and proceeded to agitate for recognition of their independent status.[54] They threatened lawsuits and sent letters to the home board of the Evangelical mission (one with 163 signatures). They drew up their own laws and regulations. Missionaries responded by locking them out of the Ganeshpur church building and forcing them to find other facilities. Leaders of the schismatic group were removed from mission employ and prevented from accessing the church's assets. Though rancorous, the dispute was resolved two years later, in 1935, when the two sides agreed, with the help of a mediator, to reunite.

No individual issue can be singled out as the cause of this controversy. One element in the story was the paternalist attitude of missionaries towards the Indian Christians, and their willingness, through the IMD, to overturn a decision arrived at legally by the Immanuel church council. The *Satnami*-Christian community's desire for autonomy had been growing for some time, a reflection of calls for independence on the nationalist stage. A year or two before the Purti scandal erupted, for example, missionaries had found a notice posted by Christians on an *imli* (*tamarindus indicus*) tree near the Bishrampur bungalow demanding *"balvā"* and *"svatantratā"* (revolution and independence).

52. M. P. Davis, "A Report of the Bisrampur Church Trouble," 1934, AES 83-3 Bis54.
53. For a fuller discussion of this controversy and its many layers of potential interpretation, see Saurabh Dube, *Stitches on Time: Colonial Textures and Postcolonial Tangles* (Durham, NC: Duke University Press, 2004), pp. 60-73.
54. M. P. Davis, "A Report of the Bisrampur Church Trouble," 1934, AES 83-3 Bis54.

In addition to calling for greater autonomy, the notice requested the removal of all non-Chhattisgarhi mission employees. Bishrampur's Christians had been frustrated for some time that the mission frequently imported Christians from other parts of the country for leadership positions in the mission. Boas Purti was one of those imported for work in the mission, and many of the schismatic leaders had been ousted from positions they once held in the mission.[55]

Nevertheless, the evidence also suggests that another important element in the story was the Bishrampur community's desire to protect its women from perceived "outsiders" and "aliens." The Purti scandal arrived on the heels of a previous one in which another man imported from outside Bishrampur, Kenswar, had been found guilty of adultery with Naomi, a native of Bishrampur, and had been put out of the church.[56] The Bishrampur community, it appears, understood itself as a community with boundaries worth defending.

One way of defending these boundaries was to encourage and enforce the practice of endogamy, as did other communities in the region. For example, the "Special Rules of the Bishrampur Congregation," written by church leaders with the help of missionary Lohr, prohibit marriage with members of other communities. The rules state: "We will not give our boys and girls in marriage to outsiders [*anyadeśiyoṃ*, literally, people from another land, foreigners or aliens]."[57] The rules do, however, allow for marriage to "outsiders" if they first become Christian.

During the Purti controversy, members of the rebel congregation wrote to P. A. Menzel, who was at the time secretary of the mission, asserting that, "In American Mission Station Bisrampur there are servants as doctors, masters and clerks who have been called from other parts of India (outside mission) by your missionaries. Many of these have spoiled the character of our young Christian ladies."[58] Here the Bishrampur community's concern about the scarcity of jobs coalesced with their desire to defend the chastity of the community's women.

More importantly, however, the statement reflects the influence of both missionary and upper-caste Indian attitudes and ideals. Knowing (and presumably having to some extent assimilated) the missionary abhorrence of adulterous liaisons, the schismatic community attempted to draw sympathy

55. Davis, "A Report of the Bisrampur Church Trouble," 1934, AES 83-3 Bis54.
56. Davis, "A Report of the Bisrampur Church Trouble," 1934, AES 83-3 Bis54.
57. "Biśrāmpur kalīsiyā kī viṣeś ājñāyeṃ," 1890, AES 83-3 Bis54.
58. Quoted in Dube, *Stitches on Time*, p. 64.

from the mission secretary by raising the specter of spoiled virginity. At the same time, given that in India the purity of a caste was believed to be related to the chastity of its women, the Bishrampur community's fiercely vindictive attitude towards Kenswar and Purti suggests that it was concerned not merely with the chastity of its members, but also with the maintenance of its communal borders. Such maintenance required, among other things, the protection of women from the predations of alien men. By protecting its women from outsiders such as Kenswar and Purti, the Bishrampur community was therefore staking a claim to higher communal purity, and thereby higher ritual and social status according to indigenous criteria.

Christianization as Sanskritization?

Christians in Chhattisgarh considered their treatment of women far more admirable than that of their neighbors, and their behavior in this regard became one of the most significant signs of the group's identity and difference. Not surprisingly, in interviews and testimonials found in missionary sources, *Satnami*-Christians attribute their "improved" behavior with regard to women to their spiritual "regeneration," to strong teaching on the "Christian" treatment of women, to vigilant monitoring by village evangelists and missionaries, to education, and to the prohibition against polygyny. Without a doubt, *Satnami*-Christian women enjoyed certain social and sexual protections unavailable to their *Satnami* sisters, and one is therefore tempted to say that the differences between *Satnamis* and *Satnami*-Christians on matters of conjugality and female education indicate the assimilation of Victorian notions of femininity, gentility, and domesticity.

There is good reason, however, to conclude that the transformation of Christian attitudes and deportment with regard to women represents not a simple rejection of old and retrogressive values and behaviors in favor of new and progressive ones, but also the appropriation and reconfiguration of pre-existing upper-caste Hindu mores and mien. Could it be a mere coincidence that the most significant of innovations embraced by the *Satnami*-Christian community were consonant not only with missionary conceptions of female "respectability," but also with those of upper-caste Hinduism?

The transmutation of *Satnami*-Christian values must be understood, therefore, not merely as a process of denaturation and acculturation, but also as the magnification of pre-existing cultural tendencies, and in particular the tendency, among both lower- and higher-caste Hindus, to consider self-restraint, domestic semi-confinement, and submissiveness as marks of female "respectability." The evidence suggests that while couching their appropriation of the marks and signs of respectable womanhood introduced by missionaries in terms of religious conversion and spiritual regeneration, the *Satnami*-Christian community never lost sight of indigenous notions of female decorum. The reforms most eagerly embraced by those *Satnamis* who became Christian were those that were consonant with both indigenous and "foreign" ideals.

Both of these ideals valued restraint, self-control, and sexual chastity among women, and both agreed that the most appropriate sphere of female activity was in the home. Therefore, while there were certain advantages for *Satnami* women in becoming Christian, some of the changes initiated by conversion to Christianity entailed the greater restriction of women's behavior and a contraction of their sphere of influence. Christian marriage laws and social mores discouraged divorce, and thus stripped Christian women of the social leverage enjoyed by *Satnami* women due to their ability to abandon unsatisfactory relationships. Similarly, Christian prejudices against foul and abusive speech removed one *Satnami* mechanism for the expression, by women, of dissent and frustration.

For the most part, the process of sanskritization, as a mechanism of social mobility, was unavailable to *dalit* communities.[59] Though, as discussed in Chapter 1, certain concessions were made to the *Satnamis* by upper-caste political figures in the early decades of the twentieth century, the community had no real hope of rising above their lower-caste status by sanskritizing their myths and rituals. Christianity, however, represented a quasi-neutral space where the signs and behaviors of upper-caste Hinduism could be appropriated without provoking the ire of these cultural elites. While *Satnami*-Christians appropriated neither Sanskritic gods and goddesses nor symbols such as cow-protection, they did, in the process of assimilating certain missionary values and ideals, also bring their social structures and practices more (though never fully) in line with traditional ideals of upper-caste social propriety. Over time, their social position vis-à-vis the *Satnami* community improved as a result.

Conclusion

I have attempted in this and the previous chapter to sketch the emergence of a *Satnami*-Christian identity in relation to the issues of *angrezī* medicine and Indian Christian womanhood, and to show that the development of that

---

59. Louis Dumont, *Homo Hierarchicus* (Chicago: University of Chicago Press, 1980), p. 56.

identity involved the reciprocating interaction of "tradition" and "innovation." What occurred in Chhattisgarh in the late nineteenth and early twentieth centuries in relation to these issues did not involve a process of deculturation and reculturation. Rather, it involved the complex intermingling and amalgamation of a variety of cultural attitudes and behaviors — western, *dalit,* and upper-caste Hindu. It involved the renovation of tradition, and the traditionalization of change.

Missionaries attempted to "indigenize" Christianity in Chhattisgarh by making certain "concessions" to Indian religious forms. For example, they encouraged Christians to remove their shoes before entering Christian churches, to sit on the floor rather than on pews, and to retain segregation by gender in worship. These alterations, while no doubt appreciated by Chhattisgarhi Christians, were nevertheless superficial, and, I would argue, not nearly as consequential as the organic indigenizations discussed in this and the previous chapter, by which I mean those that originated in the unconscious apprehension of novelty from a conventional perspective and of convention from a novel perspective.

Significant behavioral and attitudinal changes accompanied the conversion of *Satnamis* and other Chhattisgarhis to Christianity. But these are not as significant, to my mind, as the *perception* of change. The perception, both at the time and in the community's current collective memory, is that those who became Christian underwent a swift and thoroughgoing transformation of their conduct and dispositions. Such would be utterly implausible except for the fact that Chhattisgarhis, like other Indians, understood Christianity as a religious community with unique moods, manners, and temperaments — as a *dharm* and not just as a system of beliefs.[60]

Joining the community meant more than accepting beliefs, but also entailed the embrace of the community's ethos, including its ways of acting, dressing, eating, marrying, remarrying, and relating. Indeed, the evidence suggests that many *Satnamis* knew very little about Christianity when they joined the community, but they understood and, for the most part, embraced its peculiar traditions. Their behavior, to use Weber's typology once more, was *traditional,* though in this case they were assimilating a "new" tradition. Interestingly, though Christian missionaries frequently castigated *Satnamis* for holding tenaciously to traditions they did not fully understand, it appears

---

60. On Christianity as *dharm,* see Bengt G. Karlsson, "Entering into the Christian Dharma: Contemporary 'Tribal' Conversions in India," in *Christians, Cultural Interactions, and India's Religious Traditions,* ed. Judith M. Brown and Robert Eric Frykenberg (Grand Rapids: Eerdmans, 2002), p. 53.

that in many cases converts to Christianity embraced a range of Christian peculiarities simply because they were part of what was perceived to be the Christian *dharm.*

Nevertheless, the historical record indicates that the reality was much more complicated than the perception.[61] The Christian community frequently excommunicated its members for a variety of infractions.[62] For example, from 1909 to 1947, the Evangelical mission at Bishrampur excommunicated, on average, 12.3 members per year (in the same period the congregation's membership ranged from 1,007 to 1,541). On the Mahasamund and Pithora stations, the Evangelical mission excommunicated roughly 6.7 people per year between 1919 and 1947 (during which period the station's membership fluctuated between 120 and 544).[63] Sexual and marital improprieties — adultery, divorce, child marriage, polygamous unions, etc. — were the most common causes of removal from the community, but the consumption of alcohol, spousal abuse, "idol"-worship, quarreling, and criminal behaviors were also common provocations. What these statistics suggest is that over time the reality came to resemble the perception more closely. Bishrampur, which was well established by 1909, excommunicated only about 1 percent of its members per year, whereas the community at Mahasamund, a relatively new station in 1919, was excommunicating roughly 5 percent of its membership *per annum.*

Ultimately, however, lapses such as these — cracks in the façade of public self-perception — do not inordinately disrupt the coherence of communal identities, because those identities are essentially *imagined;* they are constructed, whether consciously or unconsciously, of histories and social circumstances viewed with punctilious and fussy selectivity (and sometimes in utter denial of the "facts," as discussed in Chapter 3). From the communal identities discussed in this and the previous chapter, we now turn to six individuals who negotiated their own personal identities in unique and diverse ways.

61. On similar discrepancies between perception and reality in, respectively, the Dornakal diocese and Travancore, see Susan Billington Harper, "The Dornakal Church on the Cultural Frontier," in *Christians, Cultural Interactions, and India's Religious Traditions,* ed. Judith M. Brown and Robert Eric Frykenberg (Grand Rapids: Eerdmans, 2002), p. 199; and Dick Kooiman, *Conversion and Social Equality in India* (New Delhi: South Asia Publications, 1989), p. 169.

62. The discipline of Chhattisgarhi Christians itself would prove an interesting study of continuity and discontinuity in view of the fact that church discipline very often resembled that of caste *pañcāyats.* Both churches and castes employed ostracism and fines to punish erring members and sometimes obliged the excommunicated to feed their caste fellows before reinstatement.

63. These numbers are somewhat inflated due to the fact that the entire family of the offender was excommunicated along with him or her.

CHAPTER 6

Satnami *and Christian Stories:*
"Human Recapitulations of a Social Transformation"

In his short but seminal monograph, *Islam Observed* (from which the phrase in the chapter title above is taken), Clifford Geertz describes the modern social and religious transformations of Muslims in Indonesia and Morocco by analyzing the lives of certain prominent individuals whom he considers human "metaphors."[1] If these men "did not wholly make the history of their times," he writes, "they surely embodied it . . . they sum up much more than they ever were."[2] While he recognizes the dangers of seeing history through the lens of individual personages, especially dramatic personages, he nevertheless succeeds in portraying the variety of responses to social and religious change with more subtlety than might have otherwise been possible.[3]

In this chapter I attempt to do the same. None of the characters, described here in roughly chronological order,[4] affected the history of India, or even Chhattisgarh, in any substantial way. But each was a leader in his commu-

---

1. Geertz, *Islam Observed: Religious Development in Morocco and Indonesia* (New Haven: Yale University Press, 1968), p. 25.

2. Geertz, *Islam Observed*, p. 74.

3. Similarly, Bellah analyzes the life of Ienaga Saburo as a window into the social transformations affecting modern Japan. See Robert Bellah, "Ienaga Saburo and the Search for Meaning in Modern Japan," in *Changing Japanese Attitudes toward Modernization*, ed. Marius B. Jansen (Princeton: Princeton University Press, 1965). Both Geertz and Bellah are quoted in Charles A. Ryerson, III, *"Meaning and Modernization" in Tamil India: Primordial Sentiments and Sanskritization* (Ann Arbor: University Microfilms International, 1979), pp. 20-21.

4. Though all five of the characters considered in this chapter were born between 1868 and 1947, the parameters of my study, they all survived beyond that period. Despite this, I have chosen to follow their stories until their respective deaths.

nity.[5] Moreover, each demonstrates a different aspect, or different aspects, of the encounter between *Satnamis* and Christianity in the late nineteenth and early twentieth centuries. One was born to *Satnami*-Christian parents, two converted from the Satnampanth to Christianity, one remained a *Satnami* his whole life, and another converted to Christianity only to rejoin the Satnampanth later in life. Like Geertz's metaphors, they sum up much more than they ever were.

Today, these figures' stories are undergoing a process of mythification. Of this process, Mircea Eliade asserted that ". . . popular memory finds difficulty in retaining individual events and real figures. The structures by means of which it functions are different: categories instead of events, archetypes instead of historical personages. The historical personage is assimilated to his mythical model (hero, etc.), while the event is identified with the category of mythical actions (fight with a monster, enemy brothers, etc.)."[6] In the collective memory of *Satnamis* and *Satnami*-Christians, the stories of the following five individuals have already begun to undergo a process of mythical accretion. The historical characters are becoming archetypes and merging slowly with narrative categories. They are symbolic placeholders, dramatic individuals whose stories can embody different meanings, reinforce different values, and teach different lessons, depending on who tells them. Yet it is still possible, in the case of each figure, to ascertain something of their "history." Their stories reflect the values and beliefs of those who tell them, but they also demonstrate something of the infinite variety of individual experience.

"Doctor" Hira Lal[7]

In 1875, Hira Lal was born in Ramgarh, a village divided from Mungeli by the river Agar, the diminutive nature of which embarrasses the town's current

---

5. Despite my consistent and aggressive attempts, I could find no female character that figured prominently in the oral or textual histories of these communities. This is indeed regrettable, but reflects the greater prominence of male characters (over and against female) in the memories of the *Satnami*-Christian community.

6. Mircea Eliade, *Myth of the Eternal Return, or, Cosmos and History* (Princeton: Princeton University Press, 1954), p. 43.

7. The two most comprehensive sources of information on Hira Lal's life are Leta May Brown, *Hira Lal of India: Diamond Precious* (St. Louis: Bethany Press, 1954); and Tihari Masihdas, *Jīvan Caritr Tathā Sevā Kārya: Śrīman Ḍākṭar, Kaisar I. Hind, Hīrālāl Sāhib* (Bilaspur: n.p., 1953). This latter text can be found at HCS, box 3 of 4 (no folder). Brown was a Disciples missionary, and her work was written in English and based on interviews,

residents. Hira Lal's grandfather, Rama Satnami, had wor
Tiwari *brahman* family in Mungeli. A son in the *brahmu*
leaving a widowed daughter-in-law, Sahudra Bai. Rumors e
was an inappropriate relationship between Rama and the
They denied it, but a plan was hatched to spirit the two away w
be together (suggesting, to my mind, that they did indeed have
beyond the everyday).[8] Sahudra's family threatened to kill Rama,
intervened on his behalf.[9] The couple left the area for two years, w
Sahudra's family's anger had subsided, and then returned to Ramg.
Satnamis quietly accepted them back into the community.[10] Becau
upper-caste origins, Sahudra's defense of Rama, and her faithfulness
later in life, she became a legend among the *Satnamis* of Ramgarh.

Sahudra and Rama soon had several children. Like a good *brah*
Sahudra wanted to have their oldest son, Shiv Lal, betrothed at the age of s,
Narbadiya, the daughter of the *malguzar* of Karidongri. Their second s
Ganeshlal, was also married young, to a *Satnami* named Bisaihin. Sudden
Shiv Lal died, and Rama decided that Ganesh should take Narbadiya as a sec
ond wife. Ganeshlal and Narbadiya gave birth to Hira Lal, on 9 November 1875.

Hira Lal's father, Ganesh, and his grandfather, Rama, were both ardent
Satnamis, and passed their piety on to Hira Lal. Bisaihin Bai, Ganeshlal's first
wife, moved away from the family, and Narbadiya died when Hira Lal was
only seven. So Hira Lal's *brahman* grandmother, Sahudra Bai, acted as mother
to him and to his siblings. Sahudra made arrangements for Hira Lal's wedding when he was only seven years old, marrying him off to Sonarin Bai (who
was only three at the time).

Sahudra was said to love Hira Lal very much, and prophesied that *īśvar*

---

correspondence, and Hira Lal's autobiography. Masihdas was a Disciples catechist, and his
text is written in Hindi.

8. Tihari Masihdas's biography of Lal does not include this suggestion of scandal. Instead, he reports that at first Sahudra would always curse at Rama because of his lower-
caste status, particularly when meeting him after having performed her morning ablu-
tions. But seeing his religious devotion, she started believing that he must have been the
reincarnation of some pious soul. Meanwhile, Rama always prayed to God to give him a
good higher-caste girl as a wife, and thought himself blessed that he was lucky enough to
see this "*brahman* goddess [*devi*]" each morning after his bath. While this may indeed have
been the nature of their early relationship, it seems likely that Masihdas creatively embellished the story for rhetorical purposes (e.g., to suggest that such a liaison was not in and
of itself immoral). Masihdas, *Jivan Caritr*, pp. 3-5.

9. Leta May Brown to H. C. Saum, 14 January 1953, HCS, box 1 of 4 (no folder).

10. Masihdas compares Rama and Sahudra's flight from persecution to that of Mary
and Joseph, the parents of Jesus. Masihdas, *Jivan Caritr*, p. 7.

he Lord, God) would do some special work through him.[11] But she balked
hen Hira Lal began to work as a coolie for the Wesleyan missionary, George
ackson, who arrived in 1887 (Jackson was associated with the Disciples mis-
ion, and was later replaced by Disciples missionaries). Sahudra attempted to
counteract the missionaries' influence over her grandson by performing acts
of devotion and going on religious pilgrimages. Her fears that the "caste-
breaking" missionaries would convert her grandson were well founded, but
Hira Lal did not immediately become a Christian.

During his youth, Hira Lal associated with a mischievous group of boys
who found pleasure in disrupting Jackson's evangelical meetings. Jackson
gave the boys responsibilities at the meetings in order to win them over, and
soon they were not only paying attention, but showing up early to help set up.
The group of boys, which included a number of *Satnamis* and one *brahman*,
occasionally discussed what they had heard. They were interested, but wished
that they could continue in their own religion while believing in Jesus, because they were fearful of offending their gods. One of Jackson's evangelists,
an Indian named Padri De, told them that the Christian God of love could
cast out fear, and that no harm would come to them even if they abandoned
their families' deities.[12]

Inspired by De's words and the missionary's assurance that Christians,
even *Satnami*-Christians, could become anything they wanted to be, one boy
in the group proclaimed with a vow that he intended to become a Christian.
More thoughtful by nature, Hira Lal held back, and some time later retreated
into a mango grove to contemplate the matter. While he was absorbed in his
own thoughts, something landed on his back, knocking him to the ground and
giving him a rather good fright. It was only afterwards, when he heard a fren-
zied whooping, that he realized he had literally had a monkey on his back. Hira
Lal retold the story to his friends, to the amusement of all. But "solemn, sober
Ghasiya" said, "*Bhaiya* [older brother, a term of respect], should you laugh
thus? Perhaps it was the monkey god, Hanuman, who sent one of his own offspring to warn you to have nothing to do with these Christians."[13] Ghasiya's
interpretation of events was plausible, and was perhaps the most logical infer-
ence for a *Satnami* to make. One boy in the group agreed with him and began
to tremble with fear. But after some reflection, Hira Lal declared that he did
not think Hanuman had sent the monkey. "I have a feeling in my heart," he
said, "that it was the Jesus God saying to me, 'Stop your hiding. Cease fearing.

---

11. Masihdas, *Jīvan Caritr,* p. 8.
12. Brown, *Hira Lal,* pp. 76-80.
13. Brown, *Hira Lal,* pp. 76-80.

Quit trembling.'" Hiralal vowed to become Christian, and was joined by five of his *Satnami* friends.[14] The fact that Hira Lal interpreted the event in this way, rejecting the more culturally plausible interpretation provided by Ghasiya, suggests that he had already been inclined to become Christian. As with those who interpreted medical events as a sign that they should become Christian (see Chapter 4), Hira Lal's decision was determined not so much by his experience, but by his *interpretation* of that experience.

Meanwhile, Sonarin Bai, Hira Lal's "wife" (they were not yet cohabiting), who had been working for Mrs. Jackson, indicated her desire to become a Christian. Once Mr. Jackson ascertained that she was serious and knowledgeable about the Christian faith, he agreed to baptize her. Hira Lal also questioned Jackson about baptism, and decided to join the Christian community, but wished to do so in secret. Jackson convinced him to speak to his grandmother first, and set a date for Hira Lal and Sonarin Bai to be baptized. When Hira Lal made an appeal to Sahudra, she called his uncle and brother-in-law, who came and tied him up to prevent the boy from attending the ceremony.[15] Only Sonarin appeared at the arranged time, and therefore she became the first Christian to be baptized in the area.[16]

Hira Lal was living under what amounted to house arrest, but after some time managed to surmount the wall of his family's courtyard. As he emerged from the thorn bushes lining the wall, he saw Sonarin's brother, Pran, who was going to the annual Ganesh *pūjā* at Ratanpur. Hira Lal was known to be a good dancer, and had participated in the festival before.[17] Rather than turn Hira Lal in, Pran convinced Sahudra to allow her grandson to travel to the holy city. At first, Hira Lal saw the *pūjā* as an escape from his difficult situation, and appears to have sincerely intended to dance at the event. But along

---

14. Brown, *Hira Lal,* p. 104. Like Masihdas, Brown employed a good deal of creative re-creation in her account of Hira Lal's life. But there is no reason to doubt that the event itself occurred, and it appears in a number of other texts in roughly the same form. Ghasiya did eventually become a Christian, and fathered three generations of Christian evangelists and schoolteachers.

15. Brown, *Hira Lal,* p. 109. For a slightly different account of the events, see H. C. Saum, "Hira Lal, of Mungeli, India," *World Call,* August 1923, p. 45.

16. Masihdas claims that Sonarin Bai abandoned Lal when he chose to become a Christian, and that Lal was therefore the first baptized. Masihdas's rendering of the story employs a common trope in the biography of Indian Christian men (the initially reticent but later obedient wife), a fact that does not necessarily invalidate it. Masihdas, *Jīvan Caritr,* p. 15. But Brown and other sources suggest a reading closer to the one presented here.

17. Dancing at the Ganesh *pūjā* involved dressing up like women and imitating them in song.

the way he had second thoughts, abandoned his future brother-in-law, and went to meet the Disciples missionaries at Bilaspur. The missionaries assigned Hira Lal to work with a new Indian evangelist heading for the Mungeli area, Joseph Jadhav.

The Jacksons had left Mungeli, and so Hira Lal came to work for their replacements, Disciples missionaries Dr. Anna and Mr. E. M. Gordon. In 1891, Mr. Gordon baptized Hira Lal. A crowd gathered and attempted to prevent Hira Lal from reaching Majhgaon Ghat (where the rite was to be performed), but to no avail. When Hira Lal emerged from the water a baptized Christian, Govardhan, the Mungeli *malguzar,* sprayed him with abuses. Hira Lal then crossed the river and headed for his home in Ramgarh in order to inform his grandmother of his baptism. Hearing the news, Sahudra and other members of her family beat their breasts, wept, and abused their now outcaste son. Bisaihin Bai, who had returned to the family, said that if she had known he would convert when she bathed him as a baby, she would have taken the stone on which he now sat and pressed him to death.[18]

A few months later, Hira Lal and Sonarin were remarried according to Christian customs. The missionaries began to teach Hira Lal Hindi and lessons from the Bible. Soon he reported that he had read through the book of Samuel and was planning to read through the New Testament.[19] Hira Lal was fifteen, and began working closely with Dr. Anna Gordon. Later, Hira Lal, who had been impressed with the healing abilities of missionary doctors, asked Dr. Gordon whether he might work for her as a medical assistant. She believed that Hira Lal was well equipped for the job and mentioned it to Mr. Gordon, who decided instead for unknown reasons to send Hira Lal for Bible training.

Eventually, however, Hira Lal came to work as a compounder for Dr. Gordon. Hira Lal learned quickly. He occasionally took training courses in medicine, and was trusted by the missionaries to perform minor surgeries. Sources disagree on whether Hira Lal ever did *officially* become a doctor, but he was known to *Satnamis* far and wide as "Doctor" Hira Lal, and was eventually awarded the prestigious Kaiser-I-Hind award by the British government.

Brown writes, "His fame as a physician grew steadily. He was thought to

---

18. Brown, *Hira Lal,* p. 121.

19. It is not surprising that Hira Lal might have enjoyed the book of Samuel, given the fact that its accounts of great rulers and their escapades resemble those in the Hindu Epics. It is clear that Chhattisgarhi converts enjoyed the epic-style stories of the Hebrew scriptures more than the American missionaries. A diary of an unnamed Evangelical catechist, for example, is full of references to biblical stories about Saul, David, Jonathan, etc., but contains few references to the New Testament. The diary is found in the journal of S. J. Scott, Mahasamund catechist, AES 83-5 Di54 #1.

have a healing touch. People wanted him to touch them, as there seemed to be virtue in his kindly hands. Often he was requested to see hopeless cases just for his prayers and comforting words and fellowship."[20] Brown, like other missionaries, interpreted Hira Lal's popularity as a physician to be a function of his kindness and good character, and, to be sure, this was part of his appeal. But it also appears that Chhattisgarhis, both Christian and non-Christian, understood Hira Lal's talent as a healer within traditional modes of thought. They perceived him, informants indicated, to be a skilled *nāṛī baid.* Whether Hira Lal perpetuated the perception or not is difficult to determine. After all, allopathic doctors do almost always check a person's pulse. Moreover, many doctors in Chhattisgarh who had no belief in *nāṛī bhed* still made certain to touch their patients on the wrist, because patients would not trust their diagnoses otherwise.

Hira Lal's medical prowess and wise but humble, affable character contributed to his reputation among *Satnamis* in the region. *Satnami* leaders would go out of their way to visit Dr. Lal, and he enjoyed entertaining them at his home. He toured frequently, as both an evangelist and a physician, and his arrival in faraway villages would draw great crowds.[21] *Satnamis* heeded his religious and medical advice. *Satnami*-Christians accepted his corrections and rebukes (more so than they did those of the missionaries).[22]

It was largely due to the work of Hira Lal, and the great esteem in which *Satnami* leaders held him, that in February of 1917, around thirty Chungia *Satnami* leaders, many of them *malguzars,* organized a meeting in Set Ganga, near Fosterpur, to discuss the possibility of becoming Christian. They invited Hira Lal to come and make the case for Christianity.[23] Some of the leaders had already made the provocative decision to eat with Hira Lal, and appeared unworried about the social consequences of doing so (a sign that they were thinking very seriously about conversion). Disciples missionary H. C. Saum arranged for funds to clear the debt of any *malguzars* who converted, expecting that after conversion they would have their debts called in by offended moneylenders.

Heavy rains prevented the arrival of all but twelve of the main leaders. But between the time these leaders had planned the event and the day of the actual meeting, they had all made up their minds to remain *Satnami.* The turning point appears to have been a meeting of the leaders at Sarangpur the

20. Brown, *Hira Lal,* pp. 207-8.

21. Homer P. Gamboe, "We're in Mungeli," *World Call,* September 1931, p. 34.

22. Homer P. Gamboe, "The Missionary Work of the Disciples of Christ in India and Its Development" (B.Div. thesis, The College of the Bible, 1918), p. 47.

23. Lal himself had been a Chungia *Satnami.*

night before the planned meeting at Set Ganga. The *malguzar* of Gorakhpur, whose caste affiliation is unknown, feared that the leaders would become Christian, and requested the Sub-Inspector of Police at Kunda to speak to them. The Sub-Inspector gave the *malguzars* a "thorough scolding" and, terrified, the *malguzars* gave up their promise to become Christian.[24]

The next day, Hira Lal and an entourage of Disciples missionaries and evangelists arrived at Set Ganga. Hira Lal told the crowd that Ghasidas had "learnt all the good teachings from [Christian] Padris while he was on his way to a shrine. When he came back he told his followers . . . ['a fair man will come with a hat like an umbrella and a Holy Book in his hand. When he comes you should accept his teachings.[']"[25] Despite Hira Lal's appeal, the *malguzars* stated that they would become Christian, but only after four years. Few, if any, were true to their word. Hira Lal took it as punishment from God that the Sub-Inspector became ill and quickly died, that the *malguzar* in whose house the Sarangpur meeting was held broke his leg, and that "all these malguzars who were Satnamis, were seized by some disease or other and died . . ."[26]

Though Hira Lal's primary work was in the mission hospital at Mungeli, he worked as an evangelist as well. Missionaries credited him and his reputation for a large portion of the conversions in the area. One claimed that half of the Christians in Mungeli were relatives of Hira Lal.[27] Intelligent but reputedly not eloquent, Hira Lal related best with *Satnamis* in informal contexts, and in the Chhattisgarhi dialect. Nevertheless, there is a Hindi tract attributed to his name entitled *Satnām ke pās laut āo* (Come Back to Satnam).[28]

24. From the autobiography of Hira Lal, dictated in Hindi and translated into English by Robert Mohan, a missionary who worked briefly with the Disciples. Both the Hindi and English versions are lost, but a two-page excerpt of the English text is included in a letter from Leta May Brown to H. C. Saum, 16 May 1952. See also H. C. Saum, "Mass Movement Which Failed and Why," ca. 1936. Both found in HCS, box 1 of 4 (no folder).

25. From Mohan's translation of Hira Lal's autobiography, ibid.

26. From Mohan's translation of Hira Lal's autobiography, ibid.

27. Bert Wilson, "With the Men and Women of All Lands Who Have Answered Our Call," *World Call*, October 1920, p. 16.

28. Hira Lal, *Satnām Ke Pās Laut Āo* (n.p.: n.d.). Found in HCS, box 2 of 4 (folder: Tularam). While reading the refined Hindi of this text, some informants expressed surprise that Hira Lal, who learned Hindi only later in life, had been the author. At least one *Satnami*-Christian who worked with Donald McGavran believes that the Disciples missionary may have penned the tract himself. It is possible that McGavran, believing the ends to justify the means, would have written a tract for Hira Lal and had the "doctor" add his signature. I find it more plausible, however, given that the tract appears to me more Chhattisgarhi than American in *content*, that after Hira Lal dictated or wrote the text him-

The text, addressed to "my dear Satnami brothers,"[29] provides an interesting glimpse into the methods and thought patterns of those attempting to convert members of the Satnampanth. Unlike the Hindu deities, Hira Lal asserts, the *"pakkā prabhu* [Lord, God]" had only a single, blameless *avatār* — Jesus, Satyanam, the "way, the truth, and the life."[30] Moreover, the Bible is the book of Satnam prophesied by Ghasidas. Like the evangelists discussed in Chapter 3, Hira Lal suggested that the *Satnamis* had fallen away from the undefiled message of their original Guru. With minute detail, he described the pervasive worship of images among Satnamis, and urged them to come *back* to Satnam, to become "real *Satnamis*" *(aslī satnāmī ban jāo).*[31]

Sahudra Mata and Bisaihin Bai had for some time after Hira Lal's conversion considered him a traitor, and Sonarin Bai's parents had moved to Bilaspur after her conversion, in part due to the embarrassment it caused them. Later in life, however, Hira Lal and Sonarin were able to reestablish relations with their estranged parents. In 1892, Sonarin Bai became pregnant. Anxious about her first experience of giving birth, she went into labor and remained so for six days. Suddenly, Sahudra appeared, took charge, cleared the room, and calmed Sonarin, who soon gave birth to her child. Sahudra named the child, and remained in contact with her grandson's family thereafter. But she still seethed with anger whenever she saw Mr. Gordon, and "with great venom would spit out the words, 'Caste destroyers!'"[32] Two years later she died, still a *Satnami.*

Later, Hira Lal happened to come upon Bisaihin Bai in Ramgarh and received an unusually pleasant greeting. She pointed to her emaciated youngest son, who succumbed periodically to fits of coughing. Hira Lal told his stepmother to send the child to the hospital, and she accepted his instruction. The child recovered and Bisaihin came to live on the mission compound, near her stepson's house.[33]

On another day, Sonarin's mother and father appeared at the door of Hira Lal and Sonarin's home. It was a bittersweet reunion, because it was occasioned by death. The couple had lost two of their children in the previ-

---

self (probably in Chhattisgarhi), sounding some of the common evangelical themes of the missionaries and full-time evangelists, the text was significantly reworked and refined for publication by a missionary like McGavran. I will therefore speak of the text as if its author was Hira Lal, though the reader should keep the authorial uncertainty in mind.

29. Lal, *Satnām Ke Pās*, p. 1.
30. Lal, *Satnām Ke Pās*, pp. 1, 3.
31. Lal, *Satnām Ke Pās*, p. 3.
32. Brown, *Hira Lal,* pp. 133-34.
33. Brown, *Hira Lal,* p. 162.

ous eight days, and they had with them only an infant who was suffering from an unknown malady. They told Hira Lal, "We greatly fear that an old woman in our neighborhood there in Bilaspur whom we unintentionally offended has set a spell over our house. She has worked her charms against our two elder sons and they are gone. Now she has bewitched this little one."[34] Interestingly, Sonarin's parents believed themselves to have fallen under the evil eye of a witch, and yet came to Christians for help. Dr. Gordon administered medicine for dysentery and the child recovered. Attempting to convince his parents-in-law of the *medical* nature of their child's illness, Hira Lal told them, "You people believe in witchcraft, but this child has a disease."[35] Soon thereafter, Sonarin's father, Mahesh, had a dream in which someone spoke to him and said he would find full repose in Christianity. He asked Hira Lal to interpret his dream, which of course Hira Lal was happy to do. Mahesh and his wife were taught the basics of Christianity and baptized a few months later.

Hira Lal continued to work for the mission until his retirement. In 1955, soon after his eightieth birthday, he suffered a heart attack from which he never recovered. Christians, Hindus, and *Satnamis* filed passed his hospital bed to receive *darśan*.[36] One morning he said to his family, "Now you go and take your food and rest. I'm all right. I'll be here with you till 3 or 4 o'clock today."[37] He died that afternoon, on 16 December, at 3:30. For Hindus, *Satnamis,* and Christians who already considered him a saint, his accurate prediction of impending death, the mark of a true holy man, confirmed his sanctity.

Śimon Draṣṭahīn (Simon the Sightless)

In 1903, a *Satnami*-Christian woman from Bishrampur traveled the twenty-four miles to Hira Lal's hospital at Mungeli in order to seek the famous doctor's opinion regarding her three-month-old son's blindness. The child had begun crying uncontrollably three days after its birth, and the woman and her husband knew something was awry. They tried local cures for about a month, but without success. After these failed to cure the boy's blindness, they sought

---

34. Brown, *Hira Lal,* p. 157.

35. Brown, *Hira Lal,* p. 158.

36. Unsigned, untitled account of Hira Lal's last days, ca. 1956, DCHS, UCMS Records, DOM, India, box 19 (folder: Christian Hospital, Mungeli).

37. Leta May Brown, "Forever with the Lord," 1956, DCHS, UCMS Records, DOM, India, box 59 (folder: Lal, Dr. Hira).

help from the Evangelical missionaries at Bishrampur.[38] The boy's blindness had progressed to the point that the missionaries could do nothing. After another two months had passed the boy's mother, out of desperation, set off for Mungeli with her child, hoping to see the famous Dr. Lal. Dr. Lal told her, with regret, that there was no hope.[39] The blind child was Simon Patros,[40] who would become a famous regional musician loved by Hindus and Christians alike.

Before Simon's birth, his mother, Kari, abandoned her *Satnami* husband and moved to Bishrampur to live with her parents, who had become Christian after her marriage. Simon's father, Vishnath, was an orphan who had run away from his grandparents, with whom he lived, and had gone to live with the missionaries, whom friends told him would give him shelter. In Bishrampur the two began living together. After some religious instruction and a period during which the missionary made them live apart to satisfy his religious scruples, the couple was baptized, married, and given a small plot of land in the adjoining village of Ganeshpur. Kari became Rachel; Vishnath became Patros (Peter).

When it became clear that Simon would not recover his eyesight, the newly converted couple's happiness at the birth of a son turned to sorrow, and they began to wonder, as some of their *Satnami* neighbors were suggesting, whether Simon's infirmity was not the result of his (or their) sins from a previous birth.[41] Simon sensed from a very young age, a relative of Simon indicated, that his parents did not love him as they did their other children. Once during his infancy, he "fell" from an uncle's lap into an earthenware pot full of smoldering ashes. The severity of the wounds suffered in the incident led some to conjecture that the fall was not entirely accidental.[42]

---

38. Oral accounts of Simon's youth attribute his blindness to *cecak* (smallpox), or *choṭī mātā* (chickenpox), but his autobiography gives no such details.

39. Simon Patros, *Simon Patros of India: A Miracle of God's Grace* (St. Louis: Board of International Missions, Evangelical and Reformed Church, Inc., 1954), p. 9. Simon himself believed that the Evangelical missionaries could have healed him if they had been consulted in a timely fashion. In a different version of the story, Simon's parents both travel to the hospital, and upon hearing the bad news, throw themselves at Dr. Lal's feet, believing that he wanted money before treating the child. See M. P. Albrecht, "Blind Simon," undated, AES 84-9b Simo5.

40. Simon sometimes signed his name as *Śimon Draṣṭahīn* (Simon the Sightless). See "*Jūbilī kā gīt.*" (Jubilee Song, ca. 1927), AES 82-14 Qu2, Twente, Th. H., Quarterly Reports, Articles, Newsletters. Today, however, he is more commonly known as Simon (pronounced "Shee-MONE") Patros.

41. Patros, *Simon Patros of India*, p. 10.

42. M. P. Albrecht, "Blind Simon," undated, AES 84-9b Simo5.

As a result of not going to school, Simon came to associate with a rather unruly group of children, and oral Christian accounts of Simon's youth describe his juvenile mischievousness as fondly and lovingly as Hindus speak of Krishna the Butterthief's youthful impishness. He was, nevertheless, one of the most attentive students in Sunday school, and could easily remember and repeat the stories teachers told in class. Later in life, his ability to correct people's reading of scriptures based on his memory of the verses became legendary.

He also possessed a rather fantastical imagination, probably a side effect of his blindness. He experienced the Easter passion narratives so profoundly, for example, that he was fourteen before he realized that Jesus was not *actually* crucified somewhere every Good Friday. In a passage that not only offers a glimpse into Simon's young mind, but also indicates disparate cultural understandings of "myth," one Evangelical missionary reported:

> All stories to him were fairy stories; those that he heard in the village as well as those that he heard in Sunday School and church. When attending a childrens [sic] meeting one day, the missionary said that she was going to tell them a true story that day. The meeting over with, Simon could hardly wait until he got to the missionary. "What," [he said,] "Are there true and false stories? Is not the story of the mouse and the cat just as true as the story of Daniel?" Hearing that this was not the case caused him several sleepless nights.[43]

Certainly Simon's mythic imagination contributed to his success as a musician and songwriter later in life.

Simon's musical skills increased along with his knowledge of Christianity. His father owned a small shop, and one older woman who came to make purchases often sang Chhattisgarhi folk tunes, which Simon appears to have picked up rather easily. According to informants, he loved singing village tunes such as *Candainī, Alha,* and *Paṇḍvānī.* Missionaries and church leaders noticed his musical abilities, and the catechist, Yishu Prakash, gave him a drum. Simon's father, who also loved to sing, became proud of his son's musical abilities. He made his son a simple one-stringed instrument, taught him to play it, and began to speak more kindly to him.[44] Despite the fact that he lacked the requisite educational background, the mission sent Simon to its seminary in Raipur in 1920.

43. Albrecht, "Blind Simon," undated, AES 84-9b Simo5.
44. Albrecht, "Blind Simon," undated, AES 84-9b Simo5.

Simon's parents lived in the Christian colony of Ganeshpur, but they had not fully abandoned their pre-Christian religious practices. They continued, in secret, to worship Hindu deities (especially Nishana), honoring them on auspicious occasions and appealing to them for help in mundane affairs. They had even worshiped Simon as a vessel of Mata when he contracted smallpox as a child. They ritually washed his feet in milk, and then drank it as a sign of their adoration of the *devī*. But whenever missionaries visited, they quickly and quietly removed the evidence of such practices.[45]

In Sunday school, Simon and his brother had heard the story of the Hebrew prophet, Gideon, who tore down his father's altar to Baal (Judges 6:25ff.), and had vowed to destroy their parents' image of Nishana someday. Their father, Vishnath, considered the image sacrosanct, and believed that his own father and younger brother had died as a result of having discarded theirs. For some time, fear of divine reprisal prevented the boys from fulfilling their vow. One summer, while on break from his theological training, however, Simon was rooting around in the family house and happened upon the basket with which the family covered the altar of Nishana (a mound with a stake driven in the middle).[46] Simon resolved to get rid of the altar and waited until his family was out of the house on a market day. He describes the pivotal experience in his autobiography:

> At four o-clock of that day in the month of May, I prayed [to] God for strength and courage like that of Gideon to destroy the idol. I removed the basket which covered it and began to pull the staff out of the ground. As I did so, I felt a strong impulse directing me not to pull it out, and I was frightened; but another and stronger impulse drove me to do so and throw it away. The words of my father came to mind, "This idol has killed your grandfather and uncle." My mind filled with conflicting ideas and I began to lose courage. In this extremity I turned to God and asked for help. I tried again to pull out the staff but could not. In desperation I turned to God and said, "Lord Jesus, give me the strength to gain the victory over this devil." As I touched the idol again, the devil made his final attempt to thwart me and I felt I would surely die. I was shaking, tears rolling down my cheeks; I thought I would stop

45. Patros, *Simon Patros of India*, p. 15. For more on the worship of those infected by smallpox, see E. M. Gordon, *Indian Folk Tales: Being Side-Lights on Village Life in Bilaspore, Central Provinces* (London: Elliot Stock, 1909), pp. 33-35.

46. Albrecht places the incident much earlier, when Simon was around ten years old, but probably conflates the initial vow with the actual act. My account follows that found in Simon's autobiography. M. P. Albrecht, "Blind Simon," undated, AES 84-9b Simo5.

breathing. I sat down to regain composure; I felt I was defeated and would not be able to remove the idol from our home.

Finally I summoned my courage again and prayed, "Lord Jesus, now I am going to pull that devil out. If I can do it this time I will know that thou art almighty and victorious. If I cannot do it I will believe that the god of my forefathers is true. Having prayed thus, I made my final attempt. All conflict had ceased, and with peace and strength in my heart and a smile upon my face, I grabbed hold of the Nishana and pulled it out of the ground. I put all the collected things of the god into an earthen pot, and covering myself with a towel, I went out of the village toward the brook [where I discarded the idol].[47]

Simon's father feared for his son's life, but decided to see what would happen before making any decisions. Simon remained healthy throughout the summer and even improved in health, significantly affecting the strength of the family's confidence in the Christian God.

Simon completed his degree at the top of his class in 1923, and was assigned a *caprāsī* (a peon, or orderly) named Ruben — his "eyes," as local Christians called him. Simon married a schoolteacher's daughter named Shanti (Peace), who, informants indicated, fully embodied her name. Then he moved to Baitalpur to work among lepers in the asylum there. At one point he contracted leprosy, but was quickly healed. Some in the Christian community, perhaps revealing the influence of the Hindu view of infirmity as karmic retribution, questioned his fitness for the job with the language of the Hebrew scriptures: "For whatsoever man he be that hath a blemish, he shall not approach; a blind man or a lame . . ." (Lev. 21:18 KJV). Missionaries defended him with another passage: "Jesus answered, 'Neither hath this man sinned, nor his parents: but that the works of God should be made manifest in him'" (John 9:3 KJV).[48]

In Baitalpur, Simon began to develop his musical skills more formally, teaching himself to play several instruments, including the *tabla, dafālī* (a small tambourine) and *cikārā* (a stringed, bowed instrument in the *sarangi* family). Later in life, Simon also learned to play the harmonium, but the instrument for which he was best known was the *tambūrā*, a long-necked instrument made from a gourd, with four strings that are plucked, usually in accompaniment of a singer. Just after Simon arrived in Baitalpur, Evangelical

---

47. Patros, *Simon Patros of India*, pp. 44-45.

48. Notice, again, that the Hebrew scriptures seem more consonant with the pre-Christian worldview of Chhattisgarh's Christians than the New Testament. Patros, *Simon Patros of India*, p. 33.

missionary Theophil H. Twente reported that the blind evangelist's musical innovations had touched off an "awakening" in the congregation.[49]

Simon gave his first formal concert at the annual Chhattisgarhi Christian *melā* at Madku Ghat. First, he put the story of the Prodigal Son to the tune of *Alha*, a well-known Bundelkhandi folk song traditionally sung with lyrics describing the heroic deeds of two brothers, Alha and Udal. Later, he sang a *kīrtan* on the conversion of Paul.[50] (*Kīrtans* are traditional devotional songs composed of a chorus [*pallavi*] and several verses [*caraṇam*], and usually expounding a theme or telling a story. They are especially associated with devotion to Krishna.) The crowd was electrified and collected funds to support his musical development. One even suggested that Simon should be designated a *bhaṇḍārī*, which Simon translates as "head singer," but which also has strong *Satnami* associations (the literal meaning of *"bhaṇḍārī"* is "supervisor" or "steward"). In any case, it is clear that Simon's use of indigenous musical forms appealed to most Indians far more than the Hindi translations of western hymns to which they were accustomed.[51]

After this episode, Simon began to perform *kīrtans* more regularly. Along with *bhajans*, *kīrtans* are the most common form of devotional song among Hindus in village India, and are often sung in the spring and summer months when farmers are seeking divine protection and favor for the hot and rainy months to come.[52] The songs are sung in a group setting, though they are usually led by someone considered particularly skilled. *Kīrtan* performances generally involve not just one song, but a series of songs punctuated by poetic explication and elucidation. Like those of his Hindu counterparts, Simon's *kīrtans* took place outside, in a village *maidān* (open field, park), over the

---

49. Twente to Paul A. Menzel, October 1923, AES 82-13a Pr91, Annual Reports, no. 8, 1923.

50. Patros, *Simon Patros of India*, p. 39.

51. On two far more widely known South Indian Christians who employed Tamil musical, poetic, and theological forms in the production of Christian songs, see Dennis Hudson, "Hindu and Christian Parallels in the Conversion of H. A. Krishna Pillai 1857-1859," *Journal of the American Academy of Religion* 40, no. 2 (1972); and Indira Viswanathan Peterson, "*Bethlehem Kuṟavañci* of Vedanayaka Sastri of Tanjore: The Cultural Discourses of an Early-Nineteenth-Century Tamil Christian Poem," in *Christians, Cultural Interactions, and India's Religious Traditions*, ed. Judith M. Brown and Robert Eric Frykenberg (Grand Rapids: Eerdmans, 2002). The Hudson text is discussed in John B. Carman, "When Hindus Become Christian: Religious Conversion and Spiritual Ambiguity," in *The Stranger's Religion: Fascination and Fear*, ed. Anna Lännström (Notre Dame: University of Notre Dame Press, 2004), p. 143.

52. For more on rural devotional songs, see Susan S. Wadley, "Texts in Context: Oral Tradition and the Study of Religion in Karimpur," in *American Studies in the Anthropology of India*, ed. Sylvia Vatuk (New Delhi: Manohar Publications, 1978), pp. 326ff.

course of a few days or a week. He would play for several hours at a time and late into the evenings. Usually, he was accompanied by *tabla, majīrā* (miniature cymbals), and (later) harmonium players. He often performed seated on a dais — the same dais, in non-Christian villages, where Hindus played their *kīrtans* and held *Rāmāyaṇa* recitations. But occasionally he performed in the *Paṇḍvānī* style, in which musicians would jump and dance while playing. In these more animated settings, the crowd often joined the performers in laughter and dance.

Simon's *kīrtans* drew large crowds, sometimes of hundreds of people, from all castes and religious communities. *Satnamis* and Hindus in the region speak highly of his performances even to this day. Though non-Christians enjoyed Simon's *kīrtans* primarily for their entertainment value, some indicated that they respected Simon as a religious teacher. They were impressed by his religious passion, by his devotion *(bhakti)* to Jesus.

Virtually all Hindu scriptures are written in a poetic form and thus lend themselves easily to musical interpretation. Such is not the case for most Christian scriptures, and so Simon was forced to create his own lyrics. He is remembered for his evocative skill, for his ability to bring the drama and emotions of biblical narratives to life. Informants remember him singing the stories of Samson and Delilah, Queen Esther, Ananias and Saphira, and Jesus' birth, among others. His crowds were not infrequently brought to tears during his musical descriptions of poignant scenes such as Jesus' crucifixion, or the dissipation and destitution of the Prodigal Son. To those raised on recitations of the *Rāmāyaṇa* and *Mahābhārata*, many of these stories, particularly those from the Hebrew scriptures, must have seemed of a rather familiar type.

The biblical Parable of the Prodigal Son, for example, reflects a social situation similar to that of the Chhattisgarhis. They would have understood the agonies of famines such as the one described in the parable, and shared the biblical audience's revulsion towards the swine among which the son was forced to live and eat. But Simon added touches of local nuance to his renditions of the stories, localizing them in order to draw in his audience. For example, in his Prodigal Son *kīrtan,* the father is portrayed as a great *malguzar,* and the son a torpid vagrant who indolently plays marbles rather than going to school.[53] Neither of these details appears in the biblical account (Luke

---

53. Perhaps because of his early lack of education, Simon's evangelical message frequently involved exhortations regarding education. Evangelical missionary Theophil H. Twente drew together and published a collection of "Chhattisgarhi" folktales, and stated that Simon's help in the project was invaluable. Interestingly, there are some striking additions to the stories. For instance, to the end of Twente's version of the well-known Indian parable of the "tenth man," in which ten men who have just crossed a river panic as each of

15:32). Simon also added an emotive description of the father's sorrow at the son's premature request, and suggests that the son threatened to strike the father with an axe if he would not soon give him his inheritance. In another detail not found in the biblical version, the Prodigal Son's friends make suggestions as to how he should spend his newfound wealth. One encourages him to buy a village and become a great *zamindar,* but the son eventually decides to throw something like a long-drawn-out bachelor party. Simon drew life out of every sentence of scripture, and could transform a short biblical passage into an artistic event lasting an entire evening.[54]

Simon also composed around 250 *bhajans* for use in the congregational setting. (*Bhajans* are songs of a diverse, loosely organized genre of relatively simple devotional music used in communal worship settings.) He recorded the songs in two large registers that he kept with him at all times.[55] Though he created music for some of his *bhajans,* in most cases Simon put his own Christian lyrics to the tune of well-known Chhattisgarhi folk songs, such as the *Bihāv Gīt* (Wedding Song) and *Suā Nāc* (Parrot Dance), or common *rāgs,* such as the *Bhajan, Tambhūrā,*[56] *Gazal,* and *Dādrā.*[57] These folk songs are popular at Hindu festivals and weddings in Chhattisgarh, and many of them are still in use today. Simon considered the tunes themselves religiously neutral, writing in his autobiography, "[Some tunes] carry a filthy association. A tune is not bad in itself. It is like a blank piece of paper on which messages good or bad can be written. It is like a vessel in which palatable or bitter food can be served. Nothing is bad in itself. It becomes bad when we make improper use of it. So I learned these village tunes."[58]

---

them counts only nine men, forgetting to count himself, is added the moral, "Such are the fruits of illiteracy. Therefore we should become educated lest we show ourselves fools . . ." (p. 56). The addition may have been Twente's, but he seems to be under the impression that his collection is of *original* folktales. Thus it is quite likely that the addition was actually Simon's. Theophil H. Twente, ed., *Chhattisgarh India Folk Tales* (North Tonawanda, NY: Bodoni Press, 1938).

54. Much of the information in this paragraph comes from Theodore Twente, "The Gospel in Chhattisgarhi Garb," undated, AES 82-14 Qu2, Twente, Th. H., Quarterly Reports, Articles, Newsletters.

55. Hedwig Schaeffer, "The Minstrel of Chhattisgarh," undated, AES 84-9b Simo5.

56. "*Tambhūrā*" is a local variant of "*tambūrā.*"

57. For more on these Chhattisgarhi musical forms, and collections of the lyrics traditionally sung to them, see Sharif Mohammad, *Madhyapradesh Kā Lok Sangīt* (Bhopal: Madhyapradesh Hindi Granth Akādmī, n.d.); Hanumant Naidu, *Chattisgarhī Lok-Gīton Kā Loktātvik Tathā Manovaijānik Anuśīlan* (Nagpur, Madhya Pradesh, India: Viśvabhāratī Prakāśan, 1987); and Dayashankar Shukla, *Chattisgarhī Loksāhityă Kā Adhyayan* (Raipur: Jyoti Prakāshan, n.d.).

58. Patros, *Simon Patros of India,* p. 26.

Some of Simon's *bhajans* are catechetical, and articulate basic themes of Christian doctrine, like sin and soteriology, or the story of Jesus' birth, teachings, death, and resurrection. The words of a song sung before each of Simon's *kīrtans* and modeled after a form of Hindi poetic meter called *savaiyā*, for example, offers a creed-like statement in four verses and covers creation, God's forgiveness, and Jesus' incarnation and resurrection.[59] Other *bhajans* fall within the *bhakti* tradition, and express the composer's love and devotion for Jesus the Guru. In one song, set to the *Goran bihāv rāg* (a tune used in *Gond* weddings), Simon writes, "I have seen so many gods and goddesses / They died like humans / But Yishu Masih [Jesus the Messiah], you are righteous, / Thus I have made you my Guru."[60] The anti-idolatry theme adumbrated in this passage is a common one for Simon. A line from a song based on the *Tambhūrā rāg* asserts, "Iron idols rust, and wooden idols spoil / Those who choose a Guru without thinking suffer much."[61] Like those of this *bhajan*, some of Simon's lyrics appear to be aimed directly at the *Satnamis*. Another song, also set to the *Tambhūrā rāg*, emphasizes that earthly gurus are "without conscience" and "bear false witness against each other."[62] Yet another refers to Jesus as the "Sat Guru."[63]

Healing is another regular theme in Simon's *bhajans*, perhaps not surprisingly, given his own blindness and the fact that he worked for many years at the Baitalpur leprosarium. Those afflicted by leprosy in Simon's audiences would have understood lyrics such as those in one song, set to the *Gazal rāg*, in which God is portrayed in the aspect of a doctor, washing wounds and applying ointment. In the same song, the interminable and impossibly loud sound of the insects that bore through the rafters of rural Indian homes becomes a metaphor for sin. "The worms of sin are in my heart / Gnawing, gnawing, gnawing, the worms bore on. Because of this I weep." (In the phrase translated here as "gnawing, gnawing, gnawing," Simon repeats the onomatopoeic Chhattisgarhi word, *kuṭ*, that approximates the sound of the wood-

59. Simon Patros, *Chhattisgarhi Christian Bhajans* (Raipur: Evangelical Book Depot, 1940), #2. Special thanks to Samsheer Samuel and Matthew Jahani for help with translating the Chhattisgarhi lyrics of these songs. I also benefited from an unpublished text by Evangelical missionary J. C. Koenig, who translated one verse from each *bhajan*; "Transliteration and Translation of First Verses of *Chhattisgarhi Christian Bhajans*," undated, AES 83-16 Mu88.

60. Patros, *Chhattisgarhi Christian Bhajans*, #7.

61. Patros, *Chhattisgarhi Christian Bhajans*, #20.

62. This is not so much a reference to Ghasidas as to his successors, his sons and grandsons who did not live up to his reputed probity. Patros, *Chhattisgarhi Christian Bhajans*, #16.

63. Patros, *Chhattisgarhi Christian Bhajans*, #23.

boring insects.)[64] For Simon, who understood his blindness not as karmic punishment but as an opportunity for his God to be glorified, physical and spiritual disabilities were analogous. In one *bhajan,* he writes, "I haven't yet seen You, of what use are these eyes? / Appear now before me. This I am asking of You. / Those who don't hear your voice are deaf / Come and speak to my ears, / This I am praying."[65] Another song, written for the jubilee celebration of the Evangelical mission, contains the stanza, "Truly we were blind; we had not seen Jesus. / Mission mother came and opened our spiritual [*ātmik*] eyes."[66]

The lyrics of some of Simon's *bhajans* bear no resemblance to those traditionally associated with the *rāgs* on which they are based. For example, Simon set a description of Jesus' birth that closely follows the biblical account to the tune of the popular *Suā nāc,* a harvest song of playful lyrics addressed, metaphorically, to a parrot (*suānā*).[67] But in other lyrics, Simon builds upon the ideas, images, and emotions related to the *rāgs,* transforming these evocative associations by situating them in a new context. For instance, in the chorus of a *bhajan* set to the *Kevaṭ kahānī rāg,* a tune usually accompanied by lyrics containing *kahānīs* (stories) about *Kevaṭs* (members of the fisher and ferrier *jāti*), Simon portrays Jesus as a ferryman: "Savior of life, captain of the boat, O beloved Jesus / Ferry me across the river, ferry me across the river." The first verse continues the metaphor, "The river is too deep and my boat is so old / Jesus, my beloved ferryman (*Kevat*), ferry me across the river."[68]

In a *bhajan* based on the *Bihāv Gīt,* Simon exploits the grammar and style of the song's traditional lyrics for evangelical purposes. The *Bihāv Gīt* is actually a series of songs used at different stages during traditional Hindu weddings, and is still in use today (though not by Christians). The tune employed by Simon is from the section of the tune called "*telcaghī,*" which is sung while the bride is being anointed with oil (*tel*). Though Simon's lyrics involve the birth of Christ, their style clearly borrows from that of the *Bihāv Gīt.* Simon transforms the aesthetic coupling of the traditional lyrics into an effective catechetical tool. Compare:

64. Patros, *Chhattisgarhi Christian Bhajans,* #12.

65. Patros, *Chhattisgarhi Christian Bhajans,* #35.

66. "*Jūbilī kā gīt*"(Jubilee Song), ca. 1927, AES 82-14 Qu2, Twente, Th. H., Quarterly Reports, Articles, Newsletters.

67. Patros, *Chhattisgarhi Christian Bhajans,* #4. For more on the *Suā nāc,* see Joyce Burkhalter Flueckiger, *Gender and Genre in the Folklore of Middle India* (Ithaca: Cornell University Press, 1996), pp. 77ff.

68. Patros, *Chhattisgarhi Christian Bhajans,* #15.

Bihāv Gīt

Where, O Ginger, where, O Ginger,
were you born?
Where have you taken birth [avatār]?
In the Marar [vegetable grower's jāti]
pārā, Marar pārā, sister, I have taken
birth.
I have taken birth in the world [pirthī].
Where, O karsā [earthen pot], where, O
karsā, were you born?
Where have you taken birth?
In a black anthill [possibly a metaphor
for a kiln], a black anthill, sister I have
taken birth.
I have taken birth in the Kumharā
[potter caste's] pārā.
Where, O māur [a feathered,
ceremonial crown], where, O māur,
were you born?
Where have you taken birth?
In the jungle and bushes, in the jungle
and bushes, sister, I have taken birth.
In the Marar pārā I have taken birth.
Where, O parrā [a woven bamboo
plate], where, O parrā, were you born?
Where have you taken birth?
In the mountains and hills, in the
mountains and hills, sister, I have taken
birth.
In the Kanrarā [the caste that makes
parrās] pārā I have taken birth.
Our bride, our bride, so beautiful.
Teli [member of the oil-pressing jāti],
press oil and give it to us.[69]

Simon's Bhajan

From which country, from which
country [have you come]?
In which country have you taken birth
[avatār]?
From the land of heaven, the land of
heaven [I have come].
I have taken birth in the world
[duniyā].
Jesus tell me, Jesus tell me, from whose
womb did you take birth?
In Bethlehem, in Bethlehem, I took
birth from Mary's womb.
What was your covering, what was your
covering?
Where did you find your bed and
bedding?
I covered myself in rags. I covered
myself in rags.
Straw was my bedding, and I slept in a
sheep's manger.
Why have you done this, why have you
done this?
What is the great work for which you
came?
I have come for sinners. I have come
for sinners.
I have come to save sinners.
How did you save the sinners? How did
you save the sinners?
How have you rescued them from sin?
For the sake of sinners, for the sake of
sinners,
I have shed my blood.
You have shed your blood. You have
shed your blood.
Tell me the secret of how you saved
sinners.
I have shed my tears. I have shed my
tears.
I died, was raised, and purchased the
life of sinners.

69. This is a translation of the Chhattisgarhi *Bihāv Gīt* found in Naidu, *Chattisgaṛhī Lok-Gīton Kā Loktātvik Tathā Manovaijānik Anuśīlan*. The original is in Khairagarhi Chhattisgarhi, slightly different than the Ratanpuri Chhattisgarhi employed in the area of my research. The difference does not, however, appreciably affect the meaning of the lyrics.

It is not surprising, given Simon's loving, masterful use of Chhattisgarhi and his skillful utilization of local lyrical and musical forms, that his *bhajans* were exceedingly popular. Simon's songbook, *Chhattisgarhi Christian Bhajans,* which contained around sixty of his songs (some editions had fewer), was first published in 1937, and was reprinted nearly every year until the end of the 1940s. It was among the mission's best-sellers each year, and sometimes topped the list. By the end of its run it had sold over fifty thousand copies. This number is particularly striking when one keeps in mind that in the 1930s there were fewer than fifteen thousand Christians in *all* of Chhattisgarh, and that less than 10 percent of the general population could read.[70] Clearly Simon's popularity was such that large numbers of non-Christians and illiterate Chhattisgarhis were purchasing his *bhajan* books.

Despite his popularity among non-Christians, and his thorough knowledge of Hindu and *Satnami* mythology, Simon remained committed to the view that Christianity was a superior religion. He never directly attacked Hinduism or the Satnampanth, though he sometimes criticized practices such as child marriage. Yet he did not dilute his message in order to gain popularity. He asked his audience to be quiet for prayers and spoke to them about repentance, salvation, and the afterlife. Even today, non-Christians in the region who I interviewed remember snippets of his Christian message. He did not appear to use his musical skills for the express purpose of evangelism, though his passion and devotion often had evangelical repercussions; many *Satnami* converts attributed their initial interest in Christianity to Simon's *kīrtans.*

Blind Simon Patros translated the myths and beliefs of Christianity into an indigenous musical idiom, and appealed, above all, to the *Satnami* community from which his parents had come. In the lyrics of a song set to the *Bhajan rāg,* placed prominently for effect at the very beginning of his *bhajan* book, Simon refers four times to Jesus as "Satnam." Clearly Simon was attempting, like M. M. Paul and Ramnath Bajpai, to forge a connection between the Satnampanth and Christianity. But just as the Christian community later rejected the implication of these authors' works, so too did it reject the implications of Simon's.

Near the end of my time at the 2004 Madku Ghat *melā,* after four days of revelry, sleeping in tents, and bathing in rivers, I was interviewing a young woman who knew some of Simon's songs. I showed her a copy of Simon's songbook, which I had discovered in an American archive and taken along to India. Pointing at the first *bhajan,* the one in which Simon refers so frequently

---

70. M. P. Davis, "The Mission Pen," 1941, AES 82-13b St2 7a, Literature Committee (Publications).

to Jesus as "Satnam," I asked her whether she knew the traditional Chhattis-garhi words of the song. Taking a look at the songbook, and noticing the word "Satnam," she declared Simon's lyrics to be the pre-Christian, traditional Chhattisgarhi words to the tune. In the version of Simon's song that she knew, the words had been changed; the references to "Satnam" had been removed. Later redactors of the song, apparently uncomfortable with the emphasis Si-mon laid on the continuities between the *Satnami* and Christian faith (with the encouragement of missionaries), had expurgated his use of the *Satnami* di-vine name. Musicians, poets, and older Chhattisgarhi Christians, especially those who were born in the 1910s and '20s, bear a certain nostalgia for Simon's songs and for his ability to draw continuities between Christianity and the Satnampanth. But members of more recent generations that I interviewed have, generally speaking, rejected those reminders of the *Satnami* past.

Tularam Paul

Tularam was born in Lata, a small, predominantly *Satnami* village just south of Takhatpur, around 1910. His parents were wealthy farmers, and owned ap-proximately thirty-five acres of land on which they paid forty rupees of *lagān* (tax).[71] They were *pakkā Satnamis,* members of the Jahari sub-sect who wore all white and rigorously adhered to the religious and dietary prescriptions of Ghasidas. They despised both members of the *panth* who did not so strin-gently obey the Guru and the few *Satnamis* from the village who, during Tularam's childhood, had converted to Christianity.

In his teens, Tularam ran away from his village in order to get educated at the Disciples' mission school (his father would not allow him to attend the village school). Because of his education, Tularam became the *Satnami mukhiyā* (headman) for Lata and around a dozen surrounding villages. He was considered wise, helpful, sociable, and generous.[72] He arbitrated disputes and acted as judge in conflicts involving *Satnamis.* Even after his conversion, *Satnamis* (and occasionally members of other castes) employed him as a me-diator. His responsibilities were more secular than religious, though he was, according to informants, in charge of organizing religious activities such as

71. Tularam Paul, *Main Ne Satnām Kaise Pāyā* (n.p., n.d.). The title's translation is "How I Found the True Name." Found in HCS, box 1 of 4 (folder: Tularam). Just as Hira Lal's tract appears to have been significantly edited or perhaps even penned by missionary collaborators, the authorship of this "autobiography" remains uncertain.

72. "The Story of Tularam, Indian Convert," ca. 1945, probably written by H. C. Saum and found in HCS, box 1 of 4 (no folder).

nāch-gammat (a celebration involving dancing, *nāchnā,* and other forms of amusement, *gammat*) and *rās līlā* (a popular Hindu drama celebrating Krishna's divine dalliance with the cowherding girls of Vrindavan). Because of his prominence in the community, Tularam's eventual conversion to Christianity drew much attention and provoked strong emotions. There are two common versions of how it was that Tularam came to be a Christian, and though they are not necessarily mutually exclusive, they do highlight different aspects of the story.

In the most frequently rehearsed version of the story, Tularam is portrayed as a pious young man who was constantly in search of truth, and increasingly disillusioned with the state of the Satnampanth. Tularam's *Main ne satnām kaise pāyā* suggests that as a young man he came to believe that few *Satnamis* obeyed the precepts of Guru Ghasidas, and as a result, he began to question the validity of the *panth's* rules and regulations. He says he "made it his job" to seek out the truth in conversation with the community's pandits, *mahants,* and gurus.[73] Still he found no peace. Eventually, Tularam invited Agamdas, the *Satnami* Guru, and a number of *mahants* to his home for a three-day meeting. He posed a series of questions to his interlocutors: When was the Satnam born? What did the Satnam command *Satnamis* to do? Are we, the *Satnamis,* obeying his command?[74]

The intent of the first question is uncertain. Does it suggest that Tularam was disturbed by the lack of historical information regarding the Satnam? Was it his exposure to the "historical" Jesus that led him to wish for such information, or a fundamental misunderstanding of what "Satnam" referred to? The second two questions are more direct, and reflect Tularam's discomfort with what he perceived to be a disparity between the teachings of Satnam, as mediated through Guru Ghasidas, and the actual behavior of *Satnamis,* especially *Satnami* leaders.

Those present told Tularam his search was legitimate, but could provide no answers to his questions. One suggested to him that he might find knowledge about Satnam by studying the *Rāmāyaṇa,* or by performing *pūjā.* But Tularam knew that the *Rāmāyaṇa* did not mention Satnam and believed that Ghasidas had expressly forbidden the worship of images. Having rejected these solutions, Tularam encountered a Christian preacher, whose words captured his attention *(mere man ko bāndh liyā).*[75] The preacher told him,

73. Paul, *Main Ne Satnām Kaise Pāyā,* p. 2.

74. Paul, *Main Ne Satnām Kaise Pāyā,* p. 2.

75. Paul, *Main Ne Satnām Kaise Pāyā,* p. 3. Seeing the religious unrest of Tularam and his friends, and hoping to convince them to become Christian, Disciples missionaries de-

"Blessed [*dhanya*] are those who are hungry and thirsty for righteousness [*dharm*], for they will be filled."[76] Tularam began to read the Bible and noticed that it forbade idol worship and bore no trace of untouchability. He concluded that this book, rather than the *Rāmāyaṇa*, or, for that matter, any other Hindu book, was the book of Satnam. One *Satnami* informant even suggested that Tularam's discontent with the Satnampanth largely resulted from the sect's lack of a holy book, and that in the meeting with *Satnami* leaders Tularam had said he would become a Christian unless the leaders could produce a book containing information on Satnam.[77] In any case, Tularam decided to become a Christian in 1937, took baptism before a large crowd, and added "Paul" to his name.[78]

Around 1954, while testifying before the government of Madhya Pradesh's Christian Missionary Activities Enquiry, Tularam reiterated the main points of this version of his conversion story:

> I used to be addressed contemptuously as belonging to the Chamar community. That was being done by [my] Hindu teacher. In my childhood I used to hear from the elders of my community that Satnamis belonged to a [distinct] community from Hindus and that instead of uttering the name of Ram they should utter Satnam. But in actual practice I found that all customs and manners exhibit the same as those of Hindus. . . . I, therefore, started enquiries about other religions. . . . Once I had gone to Takhatpur market where copies of [the] Hindi Bible were being sold. I purchased one book and studied it for one year. One im-

---

cided in January of 1937 to do "intensive evangelistic work" in their villages. Tularam became a Christian soon thereafter. See "The Story of Tularam, Indian Convert," ca. 1945, probably written by H. C. Saum and found in HCS, box 1 of 4 (no folder).

76. Paul, *Main Ne Satnām Kaise Pāyā*, p. 3. The quotation is from Matthew 5:6.

77. Govind Das Patre, interview by author, Takhatpur, CG, 23 February 2004. The reason the existence of a book was so important for Tularam, Patre maintained, was that he wished to have an objective source of rules and regulations. He found the decrees of *Satnami* leaders rather arbitrary and all too human, and scriptures such as the *Rāmāyaṇa* biased in favor of the upper castes.

78. J. R. Paul, stepson of Tularam Paul, confirmed this version of events, though his account differs in minor details; interview by author, Takhatpur, CG, 27 March 2004. A similar account appears in Disciples missionary Mildred M. Saum's "Tularam of Latta — Outstanding Convert from the Depressed Classes," undated, HCS, box 2 of 4 (folder: Tularam). Saum suggests that one of the reasons Tularam was disillusioned with the *Satnami* leadership was that a *bhandārī* to whom Tularam had entrusted the protection of his house, his mother, and his sister during his absence, had taken advantage of the situation and claimed Tularam's sister as his wife, with the complicity of the sect's head guru.

portant feature influenced my mind, namely, that it preached social equality amongst all men.[79]

Tularam also described his invitation to *Satnami* leaders in the area: "When I had further gone towards this religion I sent round verbal intimation to my community members saying that I propose to embrace Christianity at a subsequent day and if they could point out a better way of life . . . they should attend and convince me accordingly. . . . No foreign or Indian Missionary ever gave me any allurement or promise or temptation of material gain to induce me to embrace Christianity."[80]

Another version of the story that exists only in oral accounts is nevertheless worth recounting because it is told by one of Tularam's sons.[81] Just before his death, the story goes, Tularam's father told Tularam that he believed he would have success in the afterlife only if Tularam would arrange for the *Gītā pāṭh* to be read by a *brahman* after his death. When his father died, Tularam visited a number of pandits, but they refused to perform the ceremony for a *Satnami*. Accordingly, calling together a number of his fellow *mukhiyās*, he announced that he was going to join the Christian community, in which he could find converted *brahmans* to fulfill his father's request. After conversion, he traveled to South India upon the recommendation of missionaries, and there found some *brahman*-Christians to perform the ritual.

It is difficult to determine which of these versions of the story is more accurate, and as I have asserted earlier, they are not necessarily mutually exclusive. It could be that Tularam's inability to fulfill his father's request, and the low social status of the *Satnami* community it highlighted, was one of the sources of his disillusionment. Clearly the first version of events follows a more recognizable and stereotypical evangelical Christian trajectory involving a spiritual malaise leading to a dramatic experience of crisis and then conversion. Not surprisingly, this is the story that Christian leaders — including, apparently, Tularam himself — told and published, causing it, perhaps, to supplant others as the "true" story. One wonders, however, whether the second version of events is not in some way also reflective of Tularam's actual experience. The first, more evangelical version of Tularam's conversion reads

79. Sita Ram Goel, ed., *Vindicated by Time: The Niyogi Committee Report on Christian Missionary Activities (1956)* (New Delhi: Voice of India, 1998), pp. II.B.105-6.

80. Goel, ed., *Vindicated by Time*, p. II.B.106.

81. Oddly, the account of the son, I. D. Paul, conflicts with published accounts and even with that of his half-brother, J. R. Paul. Nevertheless, for various reasons I consider I. D. Paul a trustworthy source, and his version of events as plausible as others. Interview by author, Takhatpur, CG, 19 February 2004.

like a gloss, like a testimony honed in its repeated rehearsal. Could it be that Tularam really did convert in order to secure his father's desired death rituals, but that, after having done so, he came, through contact with missionaries and other Christians, to consider his testimony inadequately evangelical and, with the help of others, adjusted it accordingly?

Whatever the actual nature of the events leading to Tularam's decision to become a Christian, there remained one problem with which he had to deal before joining the community: his polygamous marriage. Tularam was already married when his older brother, Uday Ram Paul, died. Following the traditions of levirate marriage, Tularam took Uday Ram's wife, Tijya, and eventually her two children, as his own. Having decided to become a Christian, Tularam asked his first wife, Sona Bai, who was childless, whether she would join him. Sona Bai, who had been born into a very strict, pious, *Satnami* family, refused to join him, and went to live with her parents. Tularam sought her out there and gave her one last chance, but she told him he could spoil his caste if he wished, but she would not.[82] Tularam and the missionaries were somewhat relieved by her pertinacity, for it meant that Tularam could divorce her and become a Christian with only one wife. Though tradition did not require him to do so, Tularam gave Sona Bai goods worth a substantial amount of money.[83] Tijya Bai, Tularam's second wife by levirate marriage, willingly became Christian along with him and several others in 1937.

Soon after converting, Tularam became an evangelist and pastor of the church at Lata. Informants indicate that in conversations with non-Christians, Tularam spoke of Christianity as a source of peace, as a solution to life's suffering, and an answer to life's questions.[84] Once, when Tularam was in the mission hospital at Mungeli, he was asked by a fellow *Satnami* religious leader, a patient in the hospital, why he was becoming Christian. Tularam replied that it was because of his *dukh* (suffering, sorrow, distress). Thinking he had financial problems, the patient implied that he could help him out of debt. Tularam clarified, saying that his *dukh* was the result of his loss of *viśvās* in the possibility of finding salvation in the *Satnami dharm*.[85]

82. Mildred M. Saum, "Tularam of Latta — Outstanding Convert from the Depressed Classes," undated, HCS, box 2 of 4 (folder: Tularam).

83. See "Experiences of India Missionaries," undated, probably written by H. C. Saum, HCS, box 2 of 4 (folder: Customs of Chamars); and "The Story of Tularam, Indian Convert," ca. 1945, also probably written by H. C. Saum, ibid., box 1 of 4 (no folder).

84. See also, Paul, *Main Ne Satnām Kaise Pāyā*, p. 1.

85. The encounter was reported secondhand by a missionary, probably H. C. Saum, and is likely to reflect the missionary's idiom (this is particularly true for Tularam's alleged use of "salvation"). But the fact that the missionary employed the Hindi word *dukh*, sug-

To *Satnami* audiences, Tularam portrayed Ghasidas much as his Evangelical counterparts, M. M. Paul and Ramnath Bajpai, had before him: as a prophet and precursor of Christian missionaries. Like them he also emphasized the "decline" of the Satnampanth.[86] But unlike these two authors, who were *brahmans*, Tularam highlighted his own *Satnami* birth, and asserted his continued membership in the *panth*, saying, "Satnami brothers, don't think that by becoming Christian I have abandoned the Satnamis. I have not abandoned you. I am showing you a new path. I am still your brother and a member of your caste [*āpkā bhāī aur jātvālā*]."[87] As an evangelist, Tularam challenged *Satnamis* to debates, but respected their practices. Around 1947, a group of *Satnamis* in Dand criticized the carnivorousness of Christians. Tularam, a natural leader, told them, according to informants, that if they would become Christian, he and his associates would leave off eating meat.

Nevertheless, Tularam would eventually serve time for a murder perpetrated in his village. *Satnamis* were in the majority in Lata, but the village was owned by *brahman malguzars*. These *malguzars* had always seen Tularam as a threat, as he was the *Satnami* leader and as wealthy as they were. Furthermore, after his conversion to Christianity Tularam appears to have challenged their hegemony more directly than before. As a result, the *brahmans* of the village began to harass him. They allowed their animals to graze in his fields, and then, around 1942, they dragged him before the courts, claiming that he had urinated on the image of their god. It appears that the complaint was an attempt, by the *brahmans*, to derail a plan to build a Christian church on some of Tularam's property, which bordered that of the village temple. After several years, according to Tularam's son, the case was settled out of court and the Christians built their church.[88]

Then, around 1967, three *Satnami* boys, at least one of whom had recently converted to Christianity, fought with a *Marar* boy over access to irrigation for their fields. The encounter created bitterness on both sides (the *Marars* supported the *brahman*-led faction in the village), and later a larger fight broke out between a group led by the three *Satnamis* and another led by the *Marar*, who was supported by a number of *brahmans*. During the ensuing scuffle, the *Marar* was killed. The *brahmans* told government investigators that Tularam and the village's other *Satnami patel*[89] (village head), Joshish

<hr />

gests that Tularam indeed spoke of his difficulty in this way; see "The Story of Tularam, Indian Convert," ca. 1945, HCS, box 1 of 4 (no folder).

86. Paul, *Main Ne Satnām Kaise Pāyā*, pp. 1-2.
87. Paul, *Main Ne Satnām Kaise Pāyā*, p. 4.
88. J. R. Paul, interview by author, Takhatpur, CG, 27 March 2004.
89. After Independence, *mukhiyās* came to be known as *patels*.

Ram, had personally beaten the boy to death. The investigators originally recommended only the three *Satnami* boys for prosecution, but perhaps under pressure from higher-caste powers, the prosecutors eventually pressed charges against a much larger group of *Satnamis* and Christians, including Tularam and Joshish Ram. Though everyone else was eventually exonerated, Tularam and Joshish Ram were convicted, and sentenced by the Bilaspur District Sessions Court to twenty years in prison. Tularam appealed his sentence to the High Court at Jabalpur. He was again convicted, but this time the sentence was reduced. Again he appealed the ruling to the Delhi Supreme Court, but because of a backlog the court was not at the time hearing appeals on cases involving shorter sentences. After seven years of incarceration, Tularam was released from the Raipur jail. He died of natural causes midway through the 1980s.

Ratiram

In 1944, a letter from Disciples missionary H. C. Saum indicates that Tularam was being harassed by Ratiram, the *malguzar* of Kevta Devri, a village just south of Takhatpur and near Lata.[90] The *malguzar*, a prominent *Satnami* leader born around 1875, had always had a reputation for being a bully and a ruffian. In the 1930s, as discussed in Chapter 2, around twelve families left his village over what they perceived to be his exploitative, violent, and despotic ways. When they left, Ratiram vowed to take their fields and thereby increase his wealth. Only an intervention by Donald McGavran and other Christians on the Disciples mission field, after some of the families who had left the village converted and asked for help, prevented the *malguzar* from carrying out his threat. If he was not at the time fiercely opposed to Christianity, he became so, and in the 1940s reports of his harassment of the Christian community became increasingly common.

In addition to the threatening presence, in Kevta Devri, of Christians with access to the power and influence of their missionary patrons, Ratiram's steadfast opposition to Christianity may have also been the result of his involvement (at one time as president) in the Satnami Mahasabha. An unsigned missionary description of a Mahasabha meeting that probably occurred in the late 1920s gives an indication of the *malguzar*'s political program and activities:

90. H. C. Saum to "Jennie V. and Veda B.," 24 April 1944, HCS, box 2 of 4 (folder: Pendridih Village).

The Satnamis held a Sabha once in Bematara. One of the Satnami leaders from near Mungeli [Ratiram] was present to distribute the Janau [*janeū*]. Some Government officers and lawyers were also present. The Satnami leader cleverly prepared their minds to accept the Janau. He told them that their Guru Gassidas [*sic*] and Guru Ramanand were disciples of the same Guru. He also told them that he had advised the Commissioner that he purposed to distribute to the Satnamies this new lever of social uplift and urged every one to wear this. Some 700 Janaus were given out there, as reported. In the Sabha a lawyer asked this same leader why the Chamars [were] becoming [C]hristians? His false reply was that only those are becoming [C]hristians who, having transgressed some religious duties, are excommunicants. It is of interest and significance also at this juncture to know that the Satnami leader who is a well-to-do malguzar, and who is most honoured today by the Government has now, and has for some time had, in his house, an Arya pundit.[91] A part of the pundit's duties seem to be to facilitate the popularity of the wearing of the Janau by the Satnamies; also to help to hinder persons from becoming [C]hristians, and to take a hand in hastening the return of persons to their former castes, who have become [C]hristians. . . . This malguzar Satnami leader is Mr. Ratiram who is the newly appointed member of the [Central Provinces] Legislative Council in Nagpur.[92]

Ratiram was close to the levers of *Satnami* power in other ways; his daughter was given as the second or third wife of Agamdas, a *Satnami* guru and fellow leader of the Mahasabha.[93] At the time, however, Ratiram's more overt harassment of Christians had not yet begun. The missionary author of the text above concludes by saying, "[Ratiram] has been much concerned for the uplift of his caste people and is working hard to accomplish this end. He has the confidence and good will of the Government. He is a worthy man. It surely

---

91. Though not as active in this area as in other parts of India, the Arya Samaj did attempt not only to bring Hindus who had converted to Christianity back to the fold, but also to "purify" (i.e., sanskritize) the rituals of more sectarian Hindu religious communities such as the *Satnamis*.

92. "Miscellaneous Items of Interest as Reported from Various Places," undated, unsigned, found in HCS, box 2 of 4 (folder: Census). Ratiram was appointed as the depressed-classes representative to the C. P. Assembly; see Saurabh Dube, *Untouchable Pasts: Religion, Identity, and Power among a Central Indian Community, 1780-1950* (Albany: State University of New York Press, 1998), p. 153.

93. H. C. Saum to "Dear Davis Friends," 20 February 1953, AES 80-1 Sat8.

behooves us to work with, and not [against] such men as he is. He has been friendly and approachable, and has a fair knowledge of Christ."[94]

Beginning at the end of the 1930s, however, after a *Satnami*-Christian community had been established in Kevta Devri, Ratiram's opposition to Christianity became more direct.[95] Disciples missionary Donald McGavran reported that:

> [The people in Kevta Devri] who have become Christians are the [farmers] who still have some land left and who suspect that Ratiram is intending to filch from them by hook or crook what land they have left — they are the anti-Ratiram party. As a result it looks to [Ratiram] as if we are strengthening the hand of his opposing party. Really of course our being there will promote harmony in the long run, though it will tend to prevent [Ratiram] from getting further land from his peasants by hook and crook. He beat up one Christian. I asked the DSP for an inquiry. Got it. [Ratiram] was very much put out, but has behaved since then. . . . The situation is tense, and the tenants, especially the Christians, are afraid that they are going to be beaten up or otherwise destroyed.[96]

A year later one *Satnami*-Christian was rather soundly bastinadoed by the *malguzar:* "Ratiram . . . deliberately beat a Christian man there for being a Christian, and all the Christians stood by listening to the screams for five minutes. My heart is still sick about that — there was nothing we could do. I tried a dozen avenues in [Bilaspur]. No proof!! No proof with ten good Christians standing and listening. . . . Yet that group gathered in my daftar and said to me, 'Sir we go back to be beaten again.'"[97] Other *Satnami*-Christian residents of Kevta Devri also ended up in the Takhatpur hospital as a result of their encounters with Ratiram and his thug-associates.[98]

At the end of his life, Ratiram's attitude toward the Christian community

---

94. H. C. Saum to "Dear Davis Friends," 20 February 1953, AES 80-1 Sat8. Ratiram also gave the Christian Leper Asylum at Jerhagaon a substantial gift of one hundred rupees around 1926; see Deputy Commissioner of Bilaspur to Superintendent of Leper Asylum, 3 May 1926, HCS, box 4 of 4 (folder: Satnamis).

95. Incidentally, the Kevta Devri church was founded by Ratiram's nephew, Rangia. Donald A. McGavran to "Jennie V.," H. C. and Mildred Saum, 31 July 1941, HCS, box 2 of 4 (folder: Don McGavran).

96. Donald A. McGavran to H. C. and Mildred Saum, 21 May 1942, ibid.

97. Donald A. McGavran to unknown recipient, 31 July 1943, ibid.

98. "The Christian Approach to the Satnami," undated, probably written by Donald A. McGavran, DCHS, UCMS Records, DOM, India, box 41, McGavran, Donald A., Mr. and Mrs. (folder: India II — McGavran, Mr. and Mrs. Donald).

softened. His change of heart appears to have been the result of medical aid he and his son, Beni Madhav, received from the mission, and of the gifts sent to them by Disciples missionary Donald McGavran, who was attempting to win over the father and son. Ratiram may also have taken on a more accommodating air out of necessity, given that more than half of his village's residents had become Christian. Nevertheless, Disciples evangelist Tihari Masihdas reported that in 1952, after another battle of wills between McGavran and Ratiram, the *malguzar* had told him that he felt McGavran should be "ground to dust and burnt to ashes."[99] Masihdas reminded him that McGavran and the Christians had "the stick of law [*chaṛī kānūn*]" on their side and suggested that he give up his harassment.[100] He did, but only because death compelled him. After being treated for some time by Hira Lal at the Mungeli hospital, Ratiram died in 1952.[101]

Beni Madhav

Ratiram died a *Satnami*, but within a few months of his death, his son, Beni Madhav, was baptized along with his wife, Jagmotibai, and several others. Given the prominence of his father in the *Satnami* community and in regional politics, Madhav's conversion created quite a stir.[102] Like his father, Madhav, who was born around 1920, had a reputation for lascivious, vicious, and tyrannical behavior. To this day, the mere memory of his behavior is capable of provoking an emotional response in those who experienced it.[103] Women tried to avoid his lechery and men stayed out of his way.

At some point, however, Madhav's attitude towards Christianity, like that of his father, began to soften. Already in 1937, Disciples missionary H. C. Saum

99. Masihdas, *Jīvan Caritr,* p. 46.

100. Masihdas, *Jīvan Caritr,* p. 47.

101. One husband and wife who were married in Mungeli while Ratiram was undergoing treatment at the hospital reported that Ratiram ate meat for the first time at their wedding in 1953. It is uncertain whether this is an indication of his changing attitudes towards Christians or simply the result of the fact that the wedding presented him with an opportunity to indulge his curiosity (he was, after all, powerful enough not to fear social ostracism).

102. The mere fact that Madhav had been convinced to become a Christian was repeatedly raised as a grievance against the Christian community during the Christian Missionary Activities Enquiry conducted in Chhattisgarh and other regions of Madhya Pradesh in 1954 and 1955. See Goel, ed., *Vindicated by Time,* pp. II.A.67, 71, 74.

103. One informant broke into tears when describing how Madhav had abused him and forced him to go call a woman to entertain him.

reported that Madhav was considering becoming Christian.[104] As locals tell it, one factor in his transformation appears to have been a promise, from Disciples missionary Donald McGavran, that if he converted he would be sent to America for education (the promise was never fulfilled).[105] There is a distinct paucity of details, and only circumstantial evidence, but it is possible that another reason Madhav may have been attracted to Christianity was that the missionaries helped him (and Jagmotibai) overcome their infertility. According to informants, in 1945, hoping to help secure the birth of a son for Beni Madhav, Ratiram had gathered together a great heap of rice to distribute to villagers in a ritual called *parvat dhān* (hill of rice). Madhav and Jagmotibai, his second wife,[106] did eventually have several children, including a son, after the birth of which the couple decided to become Christian. Whether this conversion had anything to do with the birth of the son or not cannot be determined.

Madhav himself described his conversion experience for the Christian Missionary Activities Enquiry (see Conclusion) around 1954. In his testimony, he responded to some of the rumors circulating about his motivations for becoming Christian: "I became a Christian in November 1952. I read the Bible and voluntarily became a Christian. No inducement was offered to me to become a Christian nor was any allurement held out to me for going to America. I cannot desire of going to America as I do not know English. . . . Before I became a Christian, I had on several occasions heard [the] preaching of pracharaks [preachers]."[107]

Responding to a cross-examination, Madhav continued, "Even during the life-time of my father, I had been thinking of becoming a Christian, but due to respect for [the] old man, I had to obey his instructions not to become Christian. I was first drawn towards Christianity on hearing the preaching of a blind preacher [Simon Patros?] who used to visit our place about five years ago. . . . I had purchased a Hindu Bible for Rs. three, I have studied up to 4th Hindi class."[108] Curiously, Madhav's testimony ends with what would seem a

---

104. H. C. Saum to Paul Parker, 28 June 1937, HCS, box 4 of 4 (folder: Prayer, Jesus P.).

105. This allegation, repeated by other informants as well, would be unlikely except for its Christian source. One can't imagine why Christian informants would fabricate a story such as this, which proves the point of their critics, i.e., that *Satnamis* who became Christian were induced to convert by promises of education, money, or travel. For a Hindu who makes similar claims, see Goel, ed., *Vindicated by Time*, p. II.A.77.

106. Some sources indicate that this was his third wife. The disagreement may be rooted in the informality of *Satnami* "marriage."

107. Christian Missionary Activities Enquiry Committee, *Vindicated by Time*, vol. 2, part B, p. 101.

108. Goel, ed., *Vindicated by Time*, p. II.B.101.

damning admission, "I do not know how many chapters the Bible contains and from what story it begins. I do not know with what story the Bible ends. I cannot recite any verse from the Bible. I do not know [the] Lord's Prayer."[109]

At the encouragement of missionaries, Madhav wrote a tract before his baptism indicating when and where he would be baptized and inviting *Satnamis* and *Satnami*-Christians to attend. Many did.[110] The tract was entitled "I Am Not Leaving Satnam, I Am Finding Him," and indicated Madhav's desire, according to missionaries, to remain *Satnami* after conversion, to be a "Satnami Christian."[111] After his conversion, Madhav enthusiastically joined the Christian community. Freed from *Satnami* restrictions regarding respect for animal life, he bought a gun, according to his son, and began hunting.[112]

But Madhav's fortunes soon took a turn for the worse. Despite having inherited all his father's property, he began squandering away his wealth. Some say his pecuniary deterioration was the result of a newfound love of drinking wine and eating meat (habits that informants say he picked up *after* becoming Christian). Then the Christian neophyte contracted tuberculosis. Within a matter of years he had returned to the *Satnami* fold.

Accounts of his reconversion vary. Some assert that he was pressured into leaving the Christian community by his sister, Karnu Mata, the wife of Guru Agamdas, and in any case it is clear that Karnu and her family cut their ties with Madhav after his conversion to Christianity. Others assert that he reconverted because McGavran did not follow through with his promise to send him to America. Still others suggest that Madhav was disillusioned by the fatalistic attitude towards his disease displayed by doctors in the mission's hospital and tuberculosis sanatorium. He overheard one doctor telling another that his case was hopeless and it would be best to do nothing, a course of action Madhav interpreted as tantamount to murder. The exact reasons for his reconversion are impossible to determine, but it seems likely that a combination of difficulties such as these, along with pressure from his sister's and father's families, caused him, around 1957, to return again to the Satnam-panth, where he remained until his death around 1990.

---

109. Goel, ed., *Vindicated by Time*, p. II.B.101.

110. H. C. Saum to "Dear Davis Friends," 20 February 1953, AES 80-1 Sat8.

111. As was the case with tracts written in the name of Hira Lal and Tularam, it is uncertain to what extent the tract, or even its title, reflects the thinking of Madhav. On the tract, see "The Christian Approach to the Satnami," undated, DCHS, UCMS Records, DOM, India, box 41, McGavran, Donald A., Mr. and Mrs. (folder: India II — McGavran, Mr. and Mrs. Donald).

112. Baldev (informant, the son of Madhav, uses only one name), interview by author, Kevta Devri, CG, 19 February 2004.

Conclusion

These five figures demonstrate a range (but not *the* range) of *Satnami* responses to the encounter with Christianity in the late nineteenth and early twentieth centuries. They are individual representations of a social and religious transformation. Several themes run through the narratives of these figures. By way of conclusion, I will highlight three.

One of the most prominent of themes is *marginality*. Hira Lal and Tularam's interest in Christianity was born out of a sense of social inferiority that awakened in them a desire for social improvement and respect. Sensing that they could not adequately address that desire within the Satnampanth, both eventually converted. Ratiram, the *Satnami* leader, was also keenly aware of his community's social marginality, but attempted to address it through the dual processes of politicization and sanskritization. In addition to his *Satnami* ancestry, Blind Simon knew the brokenness of physical disability. Just as conversion allowed Hira Lal and Tularam to address their sense of social dislocation, Simon found in Christianity a forum in which to address his (and others') physical infirmity.

A second theme evident in the stories of the *Christians* presented here is their desire to draw connections between Guru Ghasidas, the Satnampanth, and Christianity. Like the authors discussed in Chapter 3 (Ramnath Bajpai and M. M. Paul), Hira Lal, Tularam, Simon, and Madhav each attempted, in one way or another, to convince themselves and others that Christianity represented the fulfillment — rather than the rejection — of Guru Ghasidas's message and the social and religious longings of the Satnampanth. This conviction is evident in Simon's utilization of *Satnami* religious vocabulary in his Christian compositions, as it was in the preaching and post-conversion tract-writing (influenced as it may have been by missionaries) of Hira Lal, Tularam, and Madhav.

While each of these figures spoke openly about what they perceived to be the Satnampanth's degraded beliefs and practices, their stories demonstrate, in various ways, that conversion to Christianity, in this context, did not require the wholesale rejection of Indian culture. For example, Simon the musician reveled in the use of local musical, devotional, and performance styles, and Hira Lal the allopathic "doctor" continued to use (or at least to give the appearance of using) local medical methods.

A third prominent theme in these narratives is the social disruptiveness of Christian conversion. Hira Lal, Tularam, and Madhav each strained relationships with close relatives — mothers, grandmothers, wives, fathers, and sisters. Each of their conversions also produced resistance and a backlash within the *Satnami* community. They were therefore *doubly marginalized,* as it were (at least temporarily). For Ratiram, the conversion of farmers in Kevta Devri represented an undesirable social disruption. The landlord's newly Christian tenants found in Christianity novel resources for social assertion, physical resistance, and legal advocacy in the face of oppression, and thereby altered arrangements of power and authority within the village. Likewise, Tularam's conversion to Christianity (combined with his wealth) threatened upper-caste village leaders in Lata and led, ultimately, to his imprisonment. But if conversion to Christianity occasionally *caused* social disruption, it also, as the story of Blind Simon indicates, sometimes provided an alternative for those who found themselves in unhappy social situations. Blind Simon would not have been born a Christian, after all, if his formerly *Satnami* mother and father had not sought out the mission's shelter.

These men *are* metaphors, not only representing the variety of responses to Christianity in nineteenth- and twentieth-century Chhattisgarh, but also providing a conduit through which contemporary Christians — indigenous and foreign — can read new meanings back into their "historical" past. The meanings of the stories, of course, depend on who is telling them. As such, they are myths — no longer "just" stories, but stories imbued with a surplus of symbolic significance capable of being repeatedly reconfigured and reimagined.

Conclusion

The fundamental assumption of this study is that culture is a living thing, an evolving, always-emergent entity. Drawing on the work of Benedict Anderson, Stuart Hall, Paul du Gay, Peter Berger, Bengt Karlsson, and James Clifford, I have argued that cultural identities are "social facts," and are largely "imagined," or "invented." This is often true for the "traditions" and "histories" that nourish cultural identities as well.

Religion is one aspect of culture, and both conditions and is conditioned by it. Moreover, keeping in mind that social structures of power, dominance, and subjugation influence the articulation and experience of religion, I have suggested, with Geertz, that religion is a system of rituals and symbols that serves to fuse the world as lived and experienced with the world as imagined. There are a variety of potential catalysts of religious change, one of the most significant of which is fundamental social disruption of the kind that irreparably alters the world as lived. The encounter of *Satnamis*, a sectarian *dalit* Hindu community, with evangelical Christianity between 1868 and 1947, came on the heels of a series of such social, economic, and environmental disruptions.

The encounter between *Satnamis* and evangelical Christians in the late colonial period did not simply entail the "imposition" of western attitudes and behaviors on "hapless natives." Rather, it involved a cultural *transaction*. This book has focused on the *Satnami* side of that transaction, on the ways in which *Satnamis* who became Christian were transformed, as well as on the ways in which they altered, metabolized, and indigenized the religion and culture introduced by American missionaries in the process of appropriating them for their own use.

227

The arrival of missionaries in Chhattisgarh did not *provoke* the social and religious ferment among *Satnamis,* but rather gave direction and shape to how *some* members of the community responded to it. The missionaries carried with them a whole range of cultural assumptions, implicit and explicit, which were made attractive by, among other things, their putative association with structures of colonial power. Though in many ways an unintentional consequence of their work, the evangelical activities of missionaries in Chhattisgarh affected far more than the religious orientation of those with whom they came into contact. *Satnamis* who became Christian (as well as many who didn't) assimilated a variety of attitudes, beliefs, and behaviors, and appropriated a range of potent symbols from their western (and westernized Indian) interlocutors.

The *Satnami*-Christian identity that developed in Chhattisgarh between 1868 and 1947 drew upon the values and insignia of western Christianity in order to demarcate communal distinction and difference. Allopathic medicine, education, literacy, chastity, and refined domesticity all became potent symbols of pride and belonging. Nevertheless, in this context, conversion did not entail the simple deracination of those who became Christian. Though *Satnami*-Christians appropriated many of the signs and markers of evangelical religion, they did so *selectively.* Religions are not only imposed, but also adopted (and *adapted*), and the trajectory of the *Satnami*-Christian community's transformation was therefore significantly guided by the community's pre-Christian consciousness, by more general Indian notions of social rank and respectability, and by the attitudes and values of Chhattisgarhi culture.

For example, though allopathic medicine, western-style education, and literacy programs were heterogenetic innovations, they were not, according to missionaries, central aspects of Christianity. Missionaries considered the soteriological effects of their faith to be its primary benefit, and complained endlessly, particularly after 1900, that converts and even non-Christians "mistook" these "secondary" benefits for the essence of Christianity. The enthusiasm with which the *Satnami*-Christian community embraced these new practices and behaviors, therefore, indicates that the community did not simply accept Christianity as it was presented to them, but rather, consciously or unconsciously, extracted from the encounter with western Christians those things that best helped them respond to the physical, spiritual, and social exigencies of their time and place.

Moreover, though it appears at first glance as if the emerging *Satnami*-Christian identity drew heavily from a western symbolic repertoire, the community altered the significance and meaning of western symbols by mobilizing them in an entirely new cultural context. In Chapter 4, for example, I asserted that *Satnamis* and *Satnamis* who became Christian judged allopathic medicine according to indigenous criteria. When and to the extent that they assimilated western attitudes toward and responses to sickness, health, and healing, they did so, in general, not because they had accepted the scientific basis of western medicine and rejected the medico-spiritual methods of the *baigās*. Rather, they embraced allopathic medicine because it proved better according to indigenous criteria, criteria that are frankly little different from our own, and involved, above all, considerations of *efficacy.*

Likewise, though *Satnami*-Christians frequently mobilized their "respectable" gender roles and relations as a marker of communal identity, they were not by doing so simply indicating their full espousal of missionary notions regarding the proper roles and treatment of women. In late nineteenth- and early twentieth-century Chhattisgarh, the social status of a family or community was in many ways a function of its ability to protect its women from the outside, and most importantly from the gaze or sexual advances of unrelated men. Whenever possible, therefore, higher-caste women were kept secluded within the strictly controlled confines of the family compound, or even a specific section of it. A community's social status was also associated with the perceived chastity of its women. Upper-caste Chhattisgarhi women were therefore not allowed to divorce their husbands, nor (generally) to remarry if they became widowed. Therefore, the *Satnami*-Christian community's appropriation of Victorian values of feminine domesticity, modesty, monogamy, self-restraint, and chastity — an appropriation that pleased the missionaries — also enabled them to contest their social inferiority as *dalits* and establish an implicit claim to higher status in the local caste hierarchy. In this way at least, the process of Christianization was compatible with the process of sanskritization.

Though it must be acknowledged that *Satnami* women who became Christian gained a certain degree of social security and stability, the *Satnami*-Christian assimilation of these values of feminine respectability in many ways entailed the restriction of female converts' mobility and a contraction of their spheres of influence. As in many other *dalit* communities, *Satnami* women had frequently, out of necessity, worked outside the home. This public exposure reinforced the community's low status and ritual impurity, but it also allowed women an enlarged range of physical mobility and social intercourse and ensured that they would be valued for their contribution to the family economy. *Dalit* women possessed a modicum of social leverage, therefore, which their higher-caste counterparts lacked. This leverage was compounded by the fact that among *dalit* communities such as that of the *Satnamis,* marriages could be dissolved rather easily (by either party).

Women could trade on their economic value by leaving (or threatening to leave) husbands who treated them poorly. It was this social leverage that *Satnami*-Christian women lost as their community adopted western Christian (and upper-caste) conventions of female domesticity, femininity, and marriage (which, of course, included the discouragement of divorce).

As argued in the Introduction and in Chapters 4 and 5, the nature of the *Satnami*-Christian community's transformation was thus significantly conditioned by pre-existing *Satnami* structures of thought, belief, and behavior, by the community's social organization, methods of determining "truth" and utility, and by its psycho-social hopes, fears, and dreams. The foregoing discussion has demonstrated the ways in which these fundamental realities altered elements of western Christianity as they were incorporated into the *Satnami*-Christian consciousness. In the process of constructing a distinct communal identity, *Satnami*-Christians borrowed much from the American missionaries and Indian evangelists with whom they conversed, but altered everything they took.

There were even occasions, as discussed in Chapter 3, when the community rejected symbols of identity that were suggested to them by these same conversation partners. The most striking example of such a rejection involved the *Satnami* past. Christian leaders, both American and Indian, consciously or unconsciously reconfigured the *Satnami* past in order to portray conversion to Christianity as the culmination of a process begun by Guru Ghasidas himself. The roots of Ghasidas's message were to be found, they maintained, in an encounter with missionaries in Cuttack, Orissa. This innovation situated Ghasidas, and thus the entire *Satnami* community, within the larger Christian story, and suggested that conversion did not represent the abandonment of the Guru's ideals, but rather their recovery. Similarly, Christian leaders, working perhaps with information "remembered" by converts themselves, suggested that Ghasidas had predicted the arrival of a "white-faced man with a book under his arm." Ghasidas was thus reimagined as a forerunner of Christianity, a latter-day John the Baptist. Again, the implication, for *Satnamis*, was that becoming Christian was an act of obedience and faithfulness, fulfillment of the tradition rather than perfidy.

Though in the early years of its history in Chhattisgarh, the *Satnami*-Christian community appears to have embraced this version of the *Satnami* history as its own, and even, perhaps, participated in its construction, it later came to regard all reminders of the *Satnami* past, expressed or implied, as a liability. As the *Satnami*-Christian community gained ground in wealth, education, and social status, it sought, in a variety of ways, to distance itself from its low-caste roots. Texts such as those written by the *brahman* evangelists M. M. Paul and Ramnath Bajpai (Chapter 3), and the songs of Blind Simon Patros (Chapter 6), which stressed continuity with the *Satnami* story, were redacted, rejected, or forgotten. (Identity formation, it must be stressed, involves not only selective remembering, but also selective forgetting.) These symbolic indicators of a truly *Satnami*-Christian identity, which to early members of the community were a matter of pride and a justification of their conversion, came, as the community advanced socially and economically, to feel imposed, unnecessary, and illegitimate. Though they had once "imagined" themselves as the inheritors of Ghasidas's lineage, in the 1930s and '40s *Satnami*-Christians reimagined themselves as Christians with a different past, a past unmarred by association with the degradations of lower-caste life.

Where does this leave us with regard to the questions posed in the Introduction? Does Christianization, as alleged by the forces of *Hindutva*, entail denationalization? And can it be legitimately claimed, as many Hindu nationalists allege, that most conversions to Christianity come about as a result of force, fraud, inducement, or allurement? I will return to these questions in the last pages of the book. But first, we must look briefly at the experience of the Chhattisgarhi Christian community in the post-Independence era.

Chhattisgarhi Christianity in the Post-Independence Era

When, at Partition in 1947, British India was divided into two nations, India and Pakistan, a large number of Indian Muslims moved to Pakistan, where they would be in the majority. Their migration, and the parallel migration of Hindus from what became Pakistan to India, touched off untold violence and resulted, perhaps, in the death of a million. The migration of Muslims to Pakistan also further decreased the numerical strength of the Muslim community in India. As relations between India and Pakistan soured in the post-Independence period, therefore, this community became increasingly suspect in the eyes of the Hindu majority. Likewise, Sikhs in the Punjab came into conflict with other Indians for a variety of reasons, not least among them the fact that many of their leaders called repeatedly for an independent Sikh territory. Tensions between Hindus, on the one hand, and Muslims and Sikhs, on the other, have provoked violent conflicts, usually in the form of riots but sometimes also in the form of military action, several times since 1947. For the most part, however, such violence has not affected the Christian community. (An extraordinary recent exception to this trend is the brutal killing of an Australian missionary, Graham Stuart Staines, and his two sons in the state of Orissa on 23 January 1999.)[1] Nevertheless, communal tensions between Christians and non-Christians have been a regular feature of independent India. Chhattisgarh's Christians have had a role in the history of these tensions disproportionate to the size of the community.

The Christian Missionary Activities Enquiry

The first news of all-Indian interest to involve the Chhattisgarhi Christian community was the Christian Missions Activities Enquiry sponsored by the government of Madhya Pradesh and led by Bhawani Shankar Niyogi, a retired High Court Chief Justice in the state.[2] In 1952, the Government of India turned down an unprecedented number of visa applications for new missionaries, and in 1953, India's Home Minister, Dr. Kailash Nath Katju, commented in the Lok Sabha that foreign missionaries who "were engaged in social welfare work, medical work and education" were welcome, but that missionary attempts at proselytization were "undesirable."[3] Dr. Katju also noted that he had received several complaints from officials in Madhya Pradesh alleging that missionaries in the Surguja and Bilaspur districts of Chhattisgarh (which was, at the time, a part of Madhya Pradesh) had "offended the feelings of the non-Christian local population" by luring Chhattisgarhis to Christianity with "monetary temptation" and sometimes threats. Katju further intimated that an enquiry was under way.[4]

In the same period, there was in Chhattisgarh a distinct increase in the anti-conversion activities of organizations such as the Arya Samaj.[5] Even be-

---

1. See "Australia-Born Missionary, Children, Burnt Alive in Orissa," 1999, accessed 23 January 1999; available from http://www.rediff.com; and Michael Fischer, "The Fiery Rise of Hindu Fundamentalism," *Christianity Today* (Online Edition), 1 March 1999.

2. The six-man commission included only one Christian, and Chhattisgarhi Christians considered him too marginally Christian to share their concerns and sentiments.

3. See Sebastian C. H. Kim, *In Search of Identity: Debates on Religious Conversion in India* (Oxford: Oxford University Press, 2003), p. 61.

4. Sita Ram Goel, ed., *Vindicated by Time: The Niyogi Committee Report on Christian Missionary Activities (1956)* (New Delhi: Voice of India, 1998), p. B.III.39.

5. The Arya Samaj, established by Dayananda Sarasvati in Bombay (1875) and Lahore (1877), resisted the growth of Christianity by adopting many of its methods of proselytization. Especially after establishing the *Arya Upadeshak Mandalī* (Arya Instruction/Missionary Society) in 1882, the Samaj attempted to undermine Christian evangelists by deploying Arya preachers to debate Christians on the streets of cities and villages. See Kenneth W. Jones, *Arya Dharm: Hindu Consciousness in 19th-Century Punjab* (Berkeley: University of California Press, 1976), pp. 47, 139ff. Some of Dayananda's programs of re-

fore Independence, missionaries reported that Christian workers were frequently heckled by Arya Samajists when they were working in the cities,[6] and around 1914, the organization was actively involved in attempts to disrupt the mission's Sunday school work among non-Christians.[7] H. A. Feierabend, reporting to the mission board in 1940, stated, "The Hindu sect of Arya Samajists, though numerically small, is quite influential and very active trying to counteract missionary influence. They had a meeting here recently in which their leader, who sometimes privately professes to be a secret Christian, ridiculed the idea that Christ should die for our sins."[8] Arya Samaj and RSS activities appear to have increased after Independence. In 1955 an Evangelical Indian pastor in Raipur reported: "Prior to one year, the relations between Christians and non-Christians were cordial but due to the activities of Rashtriya Swayamsevak Sangh and Arya Samajists, they have been disturbed, and strained. Arya Samajist preachers go in the rural areas of Raipur and indulge in abusing Christians and their religion by such [slogans] that they are beef-eaters, horse-eaters, eating the flesh of their Guru, Jesus, etc. [presumably a reference to the Eucharist], and that Jesus was born of adultery."[9]

The Arya Samajists did convince some Christians to reconvert to Hinduism, but on the whole the *Satnami* and *Satnami*-Christian communities appear to have held them at arm's length. For example, when in 1936 the Arya Samaj published and distributed a pamphlet entitled *Pādrī sāhib se bacho* (Stay Away from the Padri Sahib!), a Mennonite missionary whose territory bordered that of the Disciples and Evangelicals reported that she had encountered a *Satnami* who had changed the title to *Pādrī sāhib ham ko bachāo* (Padri Sahib, Rescue Us!).[10] The evidence suggests that for the most part

---

form were rather progressive, for the time, and were consonant with those of missionaries. For example, he advocated lifelong marriage and education for all (including, to some extent, women) while denouncing caste-based inter-dining taboos. See J. T. F. Jordens, *Dayānanda Sarasvatī: His Life and Ideas* (Delhi: Oxford University Press, 1978), p. 285.

6. See Emil W. Menzel, *I Will Build My Church: The Story of Our India Mission and How It Became a Church* (Philadelphia: Board of Missions, Evangelical and Reformed Church, 1943), p. 101.

7. Walter G. Menzies, "India," *Missionary Tidings*, November 1914, p. 286.

8. H. A. Feierabend to The Foreign Mission Board of the Evangelical Synod of North America, 19 August 1940, in AES 82-14 Qu2, Feierabend, H.A., Quarterly Reports, Articles, Newsletters, 1933-1941.

9. Goel, ed., *Vindicated by Time*, p. II.B.87.

10. Aldine C. Brunk, "Things I Have Seen and Heard in Indian Villages," in the Archives of the Mennonite Church USA (Goshen, Indiana), Hist. Mss. 1-445, Aldine C. Brunk Collection, Diaries. The Arya Samaj appears to have been much more active on the "Old" Mennonite Mission field lying to the southwest of the Evangelical and Disciples mission

Christians in Chhattisgarh viewed these more radical nationalist and reform organizations as adversaries and antagonists rather than as allies.

Due, however, to the social unrest caused by tensions between Hindus and Christians, the state launched a preliminary inquiry into conversion to Christianity. Christians denied claims of wrongdoing, and countered with the assertion that the Christian community was being persecuted in direct and indirect ways by the Hindu majority. Provoked by these events (and seeking political gain vis-à-vis their political rivals, members of the more secular Congress Party), the Jana Sangh in Madhya Pradesh launched an "Anti-Foreign Missionary Week."[11]

To investigate these matters, the government of Madhya Pradesh announced, on 14 April 1954, that it would constitute a committee charged with making a thorough inquiry into the matter.[12] Because it was led by Dr. Bhawani Shankar Niyogi, the committee came to be known as the Niyogi Committee, and the report it produced in 1956 came to be known as the *Niyogi Report*. The official publication name, however, *Report of the Christian Missionaries Activity Inquiry Committee,* indicates somewhat more clearly the focus of the investigation.

Over the next two years, the Committee toured the state extensively, making contact with over eleven thousand people, interviewing several hundred, and accepting written testimonies from several hundred more.[13] One of the areas from which they gathered information was Chhattisgarh. The Commission held meetings in Raipur, Mahasamund, Bilaspur, Takhatpur, Mungeli, and Jerhagaon. The Committee also widely distributed a detailed questionnaire. Nearly four hundred responses were returned, roughly 90 percent of them from Hindus.

The Committee's findings are summarized in the following paragraph from the report:

---

fields. On the Arya tract, also see Martin P. Davis, *India Today and the Church Tomorrow* (Philadelphia: The Board of International Missions, Evangelical and Reformed Church, 1947), p. 28.

11. The protest was called off when the government announced its enquiry. Christopher Jaffrelot, *The Hindu Nationalist Movement in India* (New York: Columbia University Press, 1996), p. 164.

12. A copy of the original resolution appears in the *Report* at I.167. For more on the context of the enquiry, see Kim, *In Search of Identity,* pp. 60ff. For a discussion of the *Report* in the context of an article on the impact of (western) missionary money on the Indian Christian community, see Frampton F. Fox, "Foreign Money for India: Anti-dependency and Anticonversion Perspectives," *International Bulletin of Missionary Research* 30, no. 3 (2006).

13. Goel, ed., *Vindicated by Time,* p. I.2.

There was no disparagement of Christianity or of Jesus Christ, and no objection to the preaching of Christianity and even to conversions to Christianity. The objection was to the illegitimate methods alleged to be adopted by the Missionaries for this purpose, such as offering allurements of free education and other facilities to children attending their schools, adding some Christian names to their original Indian names, marriages with Christian girls, money-lending, distributing Christian literature in hospitals and offering prayers in the wards of in-door patients. Reference was also made to the practice of the Roman Catholic priests or preachers visiting new-born babies to give 'ashish' (blessings) in the name of Jesus, taking sides in litigation or domestic quarrels, kidnapping of minor children and abduction[14] of women and recruitment of labour for plantations in Assam or Andaman as a means of propagating the Christian faith among the ignorant and illiterate people. . . . The concentration of Missionary enterprise on the hill tribes in remote and inaccessible parts of the forest areas and their mass conversion with the aid of foreign money were interpreted as intended to prepare the ground for a separate independent State on the lines of Pakistan.[15]

Among the most common allegations were that Christians were given preferential treatment at mission schools and hospitals, that they abused Hindu gods and goddesses in their preaching, that they slaughtered and ate cattle, and that they induced illiterate and ignorant Hindus to convert with promises of land, money, education, or respectable (and available) wives.[16] Another common allegation was that conversion to Christianity promoted allegiance to America and "denationalized" Indians.[17] In short, the problem with missionaries was, to use the words of a group of non-Christians from Mahasamund (in present-day Chhattisgarh): "Inducements shown. Hinduism abused and talk of anti-national things."[18]

It is clear that the Committee was not entirely unbiased. There was only one Christian on the Committee, and he proved to be rather uninterested in

14. The regularity of claims of kidnapping and abduction is particularly astounding.
15. Goel, ed., *Vindicated by Time*, p. I.3.
16. Goel, ed., *Vindicated by Time*, pp. II.A.52-77.
17. Several witnesses expressed fears that if the Christian community increased in size, it would begin to demand a separate homeland. Some pointed, as evidence, to the Jharkhand movement that at the time was quite strong just to the northeast of Chhattisgarh. Goel, ed., *Vindicated by Time*, pp. II.A.52, 57, 70, and 72.
18. Goel, ed., *Vindicated by Time*, p. II.A.55.

(or incapable of) being an advocate for Christians in the area.[19] And whereas most of the Christian claims of harassment were dismissed outright as spurious and baseless, the Hindu testimonies were accepted, it seems, at face value. Moreover, the questionnaire distributed by the Committee was a travesty of impartial inquiry, and repeatedly asked leading, even baiting questions. One question, for example, was: "Are any of the following methods used [for conversion]?" Several possible answers were offered: loans, help in litigation, employment, marriage, threats of hellfire and damnation, etc.[20]

One eloquent Catholic writer responded to the questionnaire, accusing it, with some justification, of "perfidious suggestion," and "barefaced impertinence,"[21] adding, "Surely, the members of the Committee are fully aware that such a series of veiled charges — for often these are not questions, but scarcely veiled accusations — is a potent means to exacerbate sectarian feeling, and to incite religious fanatics to lay charges against those whom they dislike, yes, false charges without number."[22] Catholics in the region were so thoroughly incensed, in fact, by the inquiry that they petitioned the government of Madhya Pradesh to end it. The appeal fell on deaf ears, and the archbishop of Nagpur therefore directed his flock to cease cooperating with the committee's work.[23]

Nevertheless, while the questionnaire was clearly not up to contemporary sociological standards, and while a good number of the testimonies recorded by the committee were biased and others probably fabricated, what is most surprising about the *Report* is the quality and fairness of sections that cover Christian history, Christian ecumenism, Christian missions, and missionary strategy. Committee members had done their homework. They had read dozens of missionary reports from local and international organizations, such as the International Missionary Council (IMC). The *Report* refers to writings by J. W. Pickett, Roland Allen, William Hocking, M. M. Thomas, and Arnold Toynbee, as well as to the published proceedings from IMC meetings at Whitby and Tambaram. Admittedly, many of the authors named above were critical of missionary practices common at the time and the *Report* did not, perhaps, adequately acknowledge the fact that these authors — with the exception of Hocking — still believed in the Great Commission. Despite this, however, the *Report* was often quite generous in its recognition of Christian

19. Goel, ed., *Vindicated by Time*, pp. I.170-71.
20. Goel, ed., *Vindicated by Time*, p. II.A.182.
21. Goel, ed., *Vindicated by Time*, respectively, pp. II.A.200, 203.
22. Goel, ed., *Vindicated by Time*, p. II.A.198.
23. Copies of Catholic correspondence with the Madhya Pradesh government and the Niyogi Committee are included in the *Report*. Goel, *Vindicated by Time*, pp. II.B.1-49.

contributions to Indian society, and at one point even waxed utopian about a "real welding of Indian spirituality and Hebrew ethics."[24]

Upon the conclusion of their Enquiry, Niyogi's Committee made several recommendations. It suggested, for instance, that missionaries "whose primary object [was] proselytization should be asked to withdraw," that the Indian churches should "establish a United Independent Christian Church in India" without being dependent on foreign support, and that the "use of medical or other [professional] services as a direct means of making conversions should be prohibited by law."[25] The *Report* also suggested that the right of religious propagation, enshrined in the Constitution, be amended to stipulate that the right extended *only to citizens of India*.[26] Some of the Committee's suggestions were implemented in Madhya Pradesh's 1968 "Freedom of Religion" bill, which in many ways restrained the Christian community's evangelistic activities.[27] Many Hindus welcomed the report, some declaring that it had "exposed," or "disrobed" *(naṅga kar diyā hai),* and thereby disgraced the missionaries and the missionary enterprise in general.[28] The Enquiry also became a rallying point for various anti-conversion organizations, such as the Arya Samaj, the Jan Sangh, and the RSS, and their local manifestations.[29]

The Destruction of Gass Memorial Centre

It is difficult to gauge the exact effect of the *Report* in Chhattisgarh. As indicated in previous chapters, the testimony of prominent Chhattisgarhi Christians (e.g., Tularam Paul) and opponents of Christianity (e.g., Mahants, Naindas, and Anjordas) appears in the *Report*. And witnesses critical of Christian missionaries repeatedly pointed to Beni Madhav's conversion (see Chapter 6), which was of course made all the more sensational and infuriating, in their view, because of his father's famous opposition to Christianity, as

24. Goel, ed., *Vindicated by Time,* p. I.159.

25. Goel, ed., *Vindicated by Time,* p. I.163.

26. Goel, ed., *Vindicated by Time,* p. I.164.

27. In the 1930s and '40s, the princely states of Surguja and Raigarh had passed laws prohibiting or regulating conversion. These laws were revoked, however, when at independence the states were incorporated into Madhya Pradesh. Copies of the laws can be found in AES 80-1 Hin58 (1).

28. Goel, ed., *Vindicated by Time,* p. vii.

29. Unsigned "Youth Deputation of India Disciples of Christ Churches," 1956, in DCHS, UCMS, DOM Files, India, box 14 (folder: Bilaspur 1956 Visit Memorandum). The tone of the report, however, suggests that the activities of these organizations were not a local or imminent threat.

proof that missionaries were luring people to the faith with promises of various kinds. In any case, the Enquiry brought greater attention to the work of missionaries in the Chhattisgarh region, and led to a number of articles and opinion pieces in local and regional newspapers. The debate continued throughout 1956 and 1957. Then, on 26 August 1957, Chhattisgarh again made national headlines when the Gass Memorial Centre, a reading room and center of Christian social and beneficent activities in Raipur founded by the Evangelical mission (the rebuilt version of which was my residence for several months), was ransacked and destroyed by a mob of around 9,000 people. Missionary reports suggested that the attack took on a general anti-Christian character and was encouraged by organizations such as the RSS and the Hindu Mahasabha that considered Hinduism an integral aspect of India's national identity (and were thus opposed to Christian proselytization).[30]

The immediate cause of the riot, however, was an incident that had taken place ten days earlier. On 16 August, a patriotic play was to be presented in the Centre's auditorium as part of Independence Day celebrations. During preparations for the performance, the Centre's director, Reverend Gurbachan Singh, who had accompanied the Niyogi Committee during its investigative tour and was thereby seen by many as a representative of the Chhattisgarh Christian community, noticed that the performers had brought with them an image of a Hindu god.[31] He asked that it not be used in the service because of the Centre's Christian affiliation. Singh and other Christians maintain that Singh did not attend the performance, and learned only later that the image had been used, contrary to his request.[32]

A local newspaper, however, ran a story accusing Singh of having forcibly removed the idol, and suggested that he had also stamped enthusiastically

30. Theodore C. Seybold, *God's Guiding Hand: A History of the Central Indian Mission 1868-1967* (Philadelphia: United Church Board for World Ministries of the United Church of Christ, 1971), pp. 133ff. During the Niyogi investigation, the Working Committee of the Hindu Mahasabha met in Raipur and discussed a plan, as a local paper put it, "to combat the growing menace of the Foreign Missionaries' activities. . . ." Ruth May Harnar to Don West, 15 August 1954, HCS, box 1 of 4 (no folder).

31. Singh was also seen as an employee of foreign missionaries, rather than of a church run by Indian nationals. This was in part the result of the former President of the COCC's suggestion, in his testimony to the Niyogi Commission, that whereas he (the President) was paid very little because he worked for an institution run and financed by Indians, Singh was making a much larger sum as an employee of the Evangelical mission. Just after the President's testimony, a Hindu testified that Singh was "a pro-American person." Goel, ed., *Vindicated by Time*, p. 65. In 1965, Singh would be elected as moderator of the United Church of North India.

32. Seybold, *God's Guiding Hand*, pp. 133ff.

upon it. Moreover, the story suggested that the Centre had flown its flag at half-mast on Independence Day. Singh's response and denial, sent to the paper, were never printed. Students began to organize protests and send letters to the editor. On 26 August, the protesters moved on the Centre, and after pelting it with stones, forced their way inside and began destroying furnishings and office equipment. Books and Bibles from the library, the best Christian library in the region at the time, were torn to pieces, removed from the Centre, or otherwise destroyed. Protesters wrote anti-Christian slogans on the walls. Finally, some protesters poured gasoline around the Centre and set it aflame. The throng of protesters prevented fire engines from reaching the scene and the building was destroyed. Police officers, greatly outnumbered, opened fire on the rioters, killing one student.[33]

The crowd's anger was directed especially at Singh, who was hiding in the building. While the crowd searched for him, he managed to escape with the help of an aggressive police van driver who forced his way through the mob and then spirited the director to safety. Many local Christians, including missionaries, left Raipur for the villages, though they were able, after some days, to return. Some violence spilled over into other areas — effigies of Singh were burned as far away as Saraipali (just east of Mahasamund) and Jabalpur — but for the most part it remained confined to Raipur.[34] The event did, however, make national headlines.

The violent nature of this particular clash was exceptional. One local Sikh I interviewed attributed the destruction to a gang mentality, exclaiming at one point in our interview, "Mob violence — what can you do?" (Being Sikh, he knew something about the potentially devastating effects of mob violence, and vividly described standing behind his family home's locked doors with all of his weapons loaded and ready during India's 1984 anti-Sikh riots.) In any case, never since 1957 has the Chhattisgarh Christian community experienced anything similar.

Nevertheless, as indicated in the Introduction, Hindu nationalist organizations such as the RSS and the VHP continue to stoke popular anxiety regarding the conversion of Indians to Christianity for political gain. And occasionally that anxiety manifests itself in violence towards Chhattisgarh's roughly 400,000 Christians. For example, in February of 2007, news sources reported that a mob led by the Dharm Sena ("Army of Dharm") attacked a

---

33. Seybold, *God's Guiding Hand*, pp. 133ff.

34. Ruth Unrau, *A Time to Bind and a Time to Loose: A History of the General Conference Mennonite Church Mission Involvement from 1900-1995* (Newton, KS: Commission on Overseas Mission, General Conference Mennonite Church, 1996), pp. 114ff.

pastors' conference in Raipur, injuring ten. Nevertheless, political rhetoric and isolated incidences of violence aside, relations between Christians and Hindus in Chhattisgarh today appear, for the most part, relatively cordial.

Conclusion

Having given some sense of the Chhattisgarhi Christian experience in the post-Independence era, I return now, finally, to those broader questions that have been constantly lurking in the margins of this study (and that I have promised, at various points, to address). Is the Christian community in Chhattisgarh the result of conversion by means of "force, fraud, and inducement"? And does Christianization entail denationalization? As an answer, which must of course remain partial and tentative, I offer the following conclusions based on the findings of this study.

First, there is no such thing as a "disinterested" conversion. As I argued in Chapter 2, the decision to convert, or — in the case of many women and children in the colonial period — to follow one's husband, father, or brother into a new religion, has its source, at all times, in self-interest. People simply do not convert to religions that they do not find in some way attractive. Attractiveness, however, comes in many colors. Some converts find the moral and ethical prescriptions of the new religion more appealing than those associated with their former worldview. Others are attracted to a new religion by the clear and convincing answers it provides to life's (and death's) puzzles, by the possibility of knowing — with certainty — one's place in this world and ultimate fate, and thereby being able to live and act with confidence. Some are attracted by a worldview that makes rational sense, or at least more rational sense than their previous worldview, and therefore gives them both intellectual and psychological peace. Others are attracted by the promise of a nurturing community they could not find in their former religion. Some are attracted by the educational, vocational, and economic possibilities made available by association with the new community. Others — and many of Chhattisgarh's *dalits* must be among them — are attracted by a social vision that promises to treat them with greater dignity and respect. Other forms of attraction include aesthetic beauty, social potential, and political power.

The existence today of many western converts to Hinduism demonstrates the rather obvious fact that Christianity is not the only "attractive" religion. The point to be emphasized here is therefore that all converts, whether to Hinduism, Christianity, or another religion, *get something out of their conversion*. They follow their own self-interests, whether those interests be material, ideal, or — as I suspect is generally the case — a mixture of both. Moreover, and this is an important point, people get something out of *not* converting as well, for surely self-interest, material and ideal, has prevented as many conversions as it has prodded.

Most people would, we can be relatively certain, object to conversions by "force" or "fraud." Additionally, most reasonable people would object to "allurements" of the most crass and cynical kind: *quid pro quo* offers of money, land, jobs, or a spouse. These are relatively simple matters. But what of more subtle forms of allurement and attraction? For example, does the theoretical and real promise of education for one's children constitute allurement? Does competent, effective, and considerate medical care — even when delivered without expectations about or even the encouragement of conversion — constitute allurement? Education and medical service seem benign enough, and many Hindus would not object to Christians being involved in providing them. Nevertheless, to the extent that the ability to provide educational and medical services suggests that Christians have special access to "western" knowledge, scientific ability, and, as is very often the case, money, it is not unreasonable to suggest that the ability of Christians to provide education and effective healthcare in parts of India where the government itself cannot do so constitutes a kind of allurement. Power, as manifest in these and other ways, is aphrodisiacal, and given Christianity's association with the west and western power in the popular imagination (and very often in reality), all converts to Christianity must therefore remain vulnerable to the allegation of having converted for less than "purely spiritual" reasons. Indian Christians themselves are aware of this ambiguity. With candor and some dismay, one well-educated Christian told me several days after my arrival in Chhattisgarh that if the government proclaimed all Christians should be killed, 70 percent of them would convert to Hinduism.

My argument, however, is that such allegations and their denial ultimately miss the point (which, I wish to stress, is not the same as declaring them wrong). If all conversions are self-interested, as I have argued, as well as all non-conversions, then the salient point is not which converts have been inappropriately induced to convert and which have not (since all have, arguably, been induced), but rather which kinds of religious allurement, if any, should be considered acceptable in a civil society. But the same standard, according to this logic, must be applied not only to conversion, but also to non-conversion and reconversion.

The second general point I wish to make is that *all identities, including of course national ones, are forged, not discovered*. Therefore, the notion that Christianization entails denationalization rests on the false assumption that the nation is an immutable essence, a stable entity. It is not. Clearly Christianization in Chhattisgarh did lead many converts to have divided loyalties, both because they were attracted to the beliefs and practices associated with a worldview that was at odds, to some degree, with that which dominated Indian society, and also because Christian theology contains a prophetic element that prevents it, ideally, from becoming too comfortable in any temporal kingdom. (If Christian loyalties in a place like the United States do not seem as divided to observers as they do in India, it is only because the Christian prophetic voice in the United States has become muted. Those most likely to give it voice have instead, in the last several decades, busied themselves waving the patriotic flag of what they consider to be, in more or less pure form, a "Christian" nation.)

Converts to Christianity in India are denationalized only according to a definition of the nation that declares it essentially timeless, and essentially Hindu. This is, of course, the definition given to the Indian nation by those associated with the *Hindutva* movement in contemporary Indian politics. Given that communal identities are socially constructed and socially negotiated, and that history and tradition are malleable resources in this project, it should come as no surprise that *Hindutva* ideologues should draw so selectively from the past in their reconstruction of a national identity for India's future. That is not the issue; to condemn such a selective reconstruction of identity would be to condemn all identities. The issue, rather, is whether that is the only national identity possible, and whether there might be another way of inventing a tradition and an identity for the Indian nation that would more effectively allow it, and the communities, both majority and minority, that constitute it, to achieve their goals. That is the question India now debates, and how the question is answered will have significant and long-term effects in India and beyond.

The final point that emerges from this study is that no religion is purely indigenous. The *Hindutva* construction of an India essentially Hindu rests on the assertion, rejected by some contemporary scholars, that the Aryans originated within the boundaries of the Indian nation. It rests, moreover, on the assertion that the Aryan scriptures, the Vedas, are the basis of true Hinduism, despite the fact that many clear differences exist between the religious worldview of the Vedas and that of the majority of contemporary Hindus. It is not my intention to evaluate the veracity of these assertions. I only wish to point out that those wishing to argue that India is *essentially* Hindu, or at least those wishing to argue that Hinduism is *essentially* Indian, would also have to prove that throughout its millennia of history Indian Hinduism was impervious to outside influences, hermetically sealed off from the broader world of ideas, whether religious or philosophical. This much, I suspect we can agree, cannot be proven.

Nor is any religion purely foreign. No religion can simply move from one cultural context to another without being affected by the culture of the new context. Transplantation is therefore an inadequate metaphor for what happens in such a case, unless one keeps in mind that a transplanted organism will be considerably altered by the constitution of the soil and the climate into which it is transplanted.

This is particularly clear in the case of the *Satnami*-Christians. The development of a *Satnami*-Christian identity in the late nineteenth and early twentieth centuries was a two-headed process, involving not only the assimilation of heterogenetic beliefs, values, and practices, but also their concomitant indigenization and orthogenetic alteration. Through it, the *Satnami*-Christians attempted to adapt to the social givens of their time by selectively assimilating the values and behaviors of both colonial and indigenous powers, which were oftentimes at odds with one another.

Satnami-Christians exploited this unsettled nature of authority in Chhattisgarh to their advantage. By converting to Christianity, *Satnamis* were able to call their degradation as *dalits* into question. They embraced "Christian" notions of equality, inchoate as they may have been at the time, and a reward system based on achievement rather than ascription. Denied the symbols of traditional status, they seized upon western marks of worth, such as education, literacy, and professionalization. Conversion did represent, in this sense, dissent from the traditional social system, an effort to circumvent it by appealing to an alternate source of social authority.

But conversion was not merely, as it is sometimes portrayed, an attempt to opt out of the system. Christians retained their regard for the symbols of traditional status, and appropriated them when possible. For example, the *Satnami*-Christian community utilized the protective cover of Christianity to appropriate insignia of upper-caste status, such as the domestication and protection of women, as discussed in Chapter 5. Additionally, one wonders whether the almost obsessive cleanliness of the *Satnami*-Christian community, frequently mobilized as a symbol of communal pride, did not also reflect a certain respect for traditional notions of purity and impurity. Moreover, throughout the period under study, the *Satnami*-Christian community never fully settled the question of whether Christians should be employed in trades involving carrion, bones, and leather. As discussed in Chapter 2, members of the community whose impecunious circumstances required them to carry out such work called upon the western disregard for ritual notions of impurity to justify their activity, often with missionary support. But when rising economic and educational standards allowed sections of the community to rise above such demeaning work, they encouraged other members of their community to abandon it (as had wealthier members of the Satnampanth). Clearly members of the *Satnami*-Christian community retained a certain regard for the traditional markers of individual and communal status. *Satnamis* who became Christian, therefore, were not simply expressing dissent, but were rather seeking to engage their social context as effectively as possible by selectively appropriating the symbols of both traditional and western status. To the extent that they opted out of the system, they did so, in a leapfrog maneuver, in order to reenter it later *on their own terms and at a higher level.* Their faith was therefore not entirely foreign.

No cultural consciousness is constructed of entirely autochthonous elements, of purely indigenous symbols, ideas, and practices. Because of this, cultural distinctiveness resides not in its ("indigenous" and "essential") accidents, but rather in the way disparate and eclectic elements are woven into a comprehensive (and comprehensible) whole. During her fieldwork in Chhattisgarh, Joyce Burkhalter Flueckiger encountered a village headman who described his own hybrid but integrated culture as *khicṛī*, literally a cooked mixture of rice and lentils.[35] It is culture in this comprehensive sense — however eclectic in its ingredients — which provides continuity in times of change, and which dictates the nature and extent of that change. Chhattisgarhi *Satnamis* in the late nineteenth and early twentieth centuries were undergoing a period of social tumult and disruption. There were many responses, of which conversion to Christianity was but one. Those who became Christian drew upon the symbols of both colonizer and colonized, and refashioned them into a coherent, meaningful, and effective collective identity that enabled them to change the world, or at least their experience of it.

---

35. Joyce Burkhalter Flueckiger, *Gender and Genre in the Folklore of Middle India* (Ithaca: Cornell University Press, 1996), p. 13.

Appendix: Charts and Statistics

Figure 1

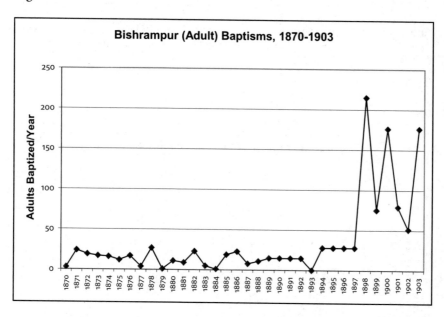

Source: Bishrampur Baptismal Registry, EA 83-1a Bap22. After 1889, the older children of converted families were occasionally included in the figures.

Figure 2

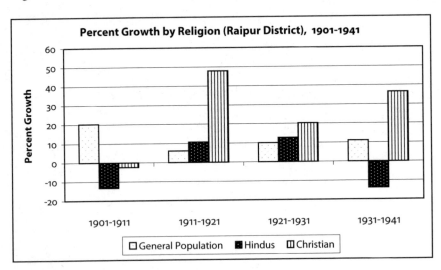

Source: Census figures, 1911-1941. Hindu growth figures in Figures 2 and 3 are skewed by changing definitions of Hinduism, especially with regard to whether "animism" or "tribal" religion is included.

Figure 3

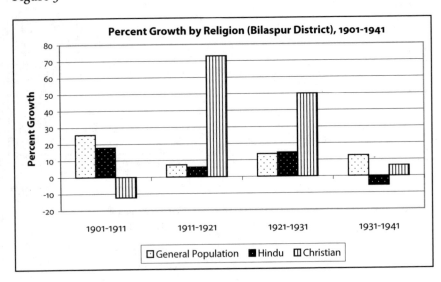

Source: Census figures, 1911-1941.

Figure 4

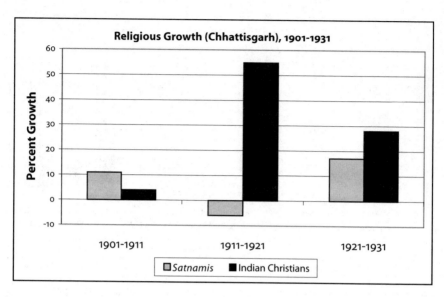

Source: Census figures, 1911-1931.

Figure 5

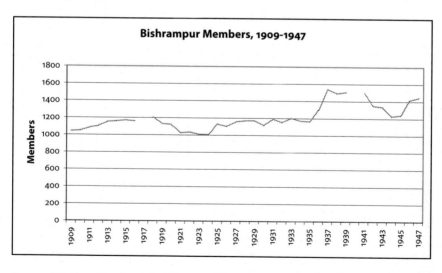

Source: EA 82-15 St2, Statistical Reports. Figures are missing for 1917 and 1940.

Figure 6

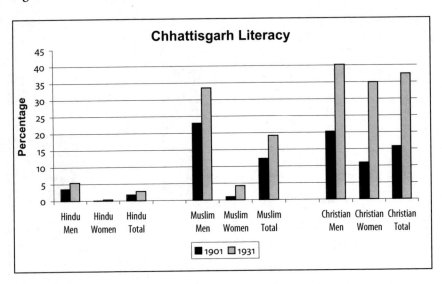

Source: Census figures, 1901, 1931. Figures refer to literacy in the vernacular.

Figure 7

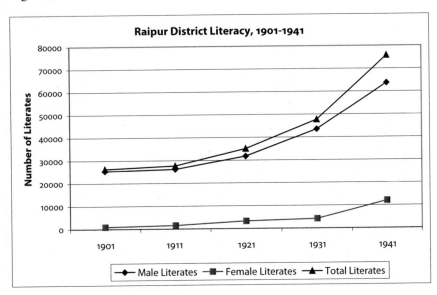

Source: Census figures, 1901-1941. Figures refer to literacy in the vernacular.

Figure 8

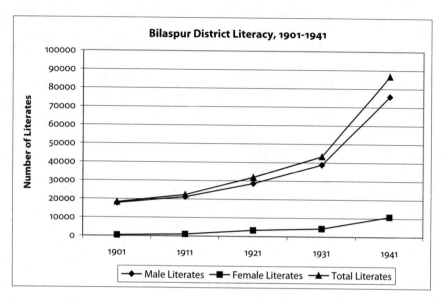

Source: Census figures, 1901-1941. Figures refer to literacy in the vernacular.

Figure 9

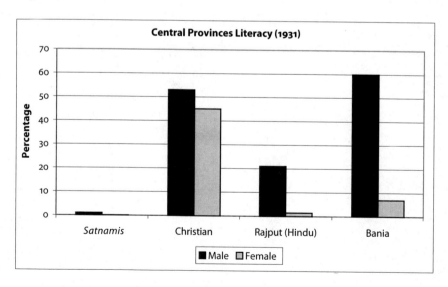

Source: Census figures, 1931. Figures refer to literacy in the vernacular.

Figure 10

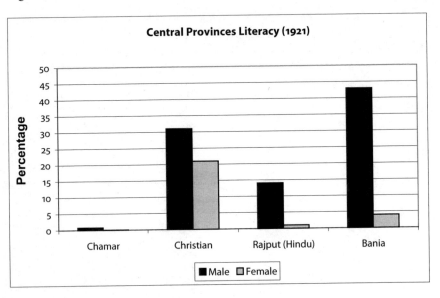

Source: Census figures, 1921. Figures in 1921 did not yet distinguish *Satnamis* from *Chamars* and refer to literacy in the vernacular.

Glossary

ādivāsī   lit. original inhabitant, a member of an indigenous tribe

amṛt jal   lit. nectar water, water in which a *Satnami* guru's foot has been ceremonially washed

angrezī   English

avatār   a descent, incarnation

baid   an ayurvedic practitioner

baigā   a local spiritual-medical healer

begar   forced labor

bhajan   a devotional hymn

bhakti   devotion, devotional religious movements

bhaṇḍārī   *Satnami* village priests

bhūt   a ghost

camṛā   hide or skin

camrā   a serious insult

caraṇāmṛit   "nectar of the feet," water in which the guru's feet have been washed

Chungia   endogamous sect within the Satnampanth that allowed the use of tobacco

curī   bangles, or, a marriage ceremony symbolized by the exchange of bangles

chuṭiyā   lock of hair left on the back of a male's otherwise shaven head

daftar   an office

dāī   a midwife

darśan   a vision, or sight (usually of a respected person or deity)

devī   a/the goddess

dharm   tradition, custom, law, duty

dvīj   twice-born

gaddī   the *Satnami* guru-seat

gālī   a curse, abuse, invective

gālī denā   to give abuse, to curse

gauṇṭiyā   village heads under the Maratha land-revenue system

ghāṭ   steps down to water

Gītā pāṭh   recitation of passages from the *Gītā*

gosāīn   an honorary title often applied to holy men

haldī   turmeric

īśvar   Lord, Master, God

janeū   the sacred thread

jāti/jāt   an endogamous group, a caste or sub-caste

jhaṛ-phūnk   exorcism by means of charms, incantations, and blowing in the ear

junnā dabdar   the old book

khalsā   land revenue system instituted by British in 1854

khumarī   a local Chhattisgarhi hat

kīrtan   a long devotional song, usually expounding a theme or telling a story

kaṇṭhī   necklace made of beads from the *tulsi* (basil) plant

langoṭī   a loincloth, a half-*dhoti*

līlā   divine "play" or "sport"

mahant   a regional *Satnami* leader

melā   religious fair

mukhiyā   village or area headman

munshi   lay preacher

nām   a name

nāṛī   a pulse

nāṛī baid   one who practices *nāṛī bhed* (see below)

nāṛī bhed   the traditional diagnosis (and sometimes alleviation) of disease by feeling the pulse

nīm   a tree, *Melia Azadirachta*

nirguṇ   without qualities

pakkā   fitting, proper, well-built, ripe, full-fledged, cooked, etc.

pañcāyat   local caste or village governing and arbitrating body

panth   a community of followers, a spiritual lineage

pārā   quarter, neighborhood

parameśvar   a term used frequently by Hindus for the supreme being or a particular god

pāramparan   guru lineage

parganā   a district under the Maratha land-revenue system

paṭel   district supervisor under the Maratha land-revenue system

pendrā   white

prabhu   master, lord, ruler, God

prasād   food offered to the gods

pothī   a book

purohit   a family or village priest, generally *brahman*

pūjā   worship or homage, generally involving symbolic offerings

qaum   a large religious community

rāg   a musical mode or melody

ramat   the *Satnami* guru's tours of solicitation and discipline

śākhā   branch (as of an institution or association)

saguṇ   with qualities

sanskār   a life-cycle ritual

sant   poet-saint

sat/satya   true, truth

satlok   *Satnami* fertility rite involving ritualized intercourse

Satpuruṣ   the true supreme person, or source of the universe

śrī   an honorary title for men

Suā Nāc   the Parrot Dance

sūbāhdār   a local governor under Maratha rule

tālāb   a village tank, reservoir

thekedār   village administrators on *zamindari* estates

tonhī   a witch

topī-vālā   one wearing a hat

varṇa   one of four primary communities delineated in the Vedas

viśvās   confidence, belief

zamindar   landlord

Works Cited

Alexander, Nelle Grant. *Disciples of Christ in India.* Indianapolis: United Christian Missionary Society, 1946.

Altekar, Anant Sadashiv. *The Position of Women in Hindu Civilisation, from Prehistoric Times to the Present Day.* Benares: The Culture Publication House, Benares Hindu University, 1938.

Anant, Arpita. "Anti-Conversion Laws," *The Hindu (Online Edition),* 17 December 2002.

Anderson, Peter B., and Susanne Foss. "Christian Missionaries and Orientalist Discourse: Illustrated by Materials on the Santals after 1855." In *Christians and Missionaries in India: Cross-Cultural Communication since 1500,* edited by Robert Eric Frykenberg, pp. 295-314. Grand Rapids: Eerdmans, 2003.

Asad, Talal. "Comments on Conversion." In *Conversion to Modernities: The Globalization of Christianity,* edited by Peter van der Veer, pp. 263-73. New York: Routledge, 1996.

"Australia-Born Missionary, Children, Burnt Alive in Orissa." 1999. Accessed 23 January 1999. Available from http://www.rediff.com.

Babb, Lawrence A. "The Satnamis — Political Involvement of a Religious Movement." In *The Untouchables in Contemporary India,* edited by Michael J. Mahar, pp. 143-51. Tucson: University of Arizona Press, 1972.

———. *The Divine Hierarchy: Popular Hinduism in Central India.* New York: Columbia University Press, 1975.

Badrinath, Chaturvedi. "Max Weber's Wrong Understanding of Indian Civilization." In *Recent Research on Max Weber's Studies of Hinduism,* edited by Detlef Kantowsky, pp. 45-58. London: Weltforum, 1986.

Bellah, Robert. "Ienaga Saburo and the Search for Meaning in Modern Japan." In *Changing Japanese Attitudes toward Modernization,* edited by Marius B. Jansen. Princeton: Princeton University Press, 1965.

Berger, Peter. *The Social Construction of Reality: A Treatise in the Sociology of Knowledge.* Garden City, NY: Doubleday, 1966.

———. *The Sacred Canopy: Elements of a Sociological Theory of Religion.* Garden City, NY: Doubleday, 1967.

———. *A Rumor of Angels: Modern Society and the Rediscovery of the Supernatural.* Garden City, NY: Doubleday, 1969.

———. *The Heretical Imperative: Contemporary Possibilities of Religious Affirmation.* Garden City, NY: Anchor Press/Doubleday, 1980.

The Bhagavad-Gīta. Translated by R. C. Zaehner. New York: Oxford University Press, 1973.

Boal, Barbara. *The Konds: Human Sacrifice and Religious Change.* Warminster, Wilts, England: Aris & Phillips, 1982.

Boel, J. *Christian Mission in India: A Sociological Analysis.* Amsterdam: Graduate Press, 1975.

Boyd, Ada. "India, Bilaspur (Annual Report)," *Missionary Tidings,* December 1895, pp. 157-58.

———. "India, Bilaspur (Annual Report)," *Missionary Tidings,* December 1896, pp. 167-68.

———. "Bilaspur Zenana Report," *Missionary Tidings,* November 1902, pp. 218-19.

Bricker, Victoria Reifler. *The Indian Christ, the Indian King.* Austin: University of Texas Press, 1981.

Briggs, George Weston. *The Chamārs.* Calcutta: Association Press, 1920.

Brown, Leta May. *Hira Lal of India: Diamond Precious.* St. Louis: Bethany Press, 1954.

Burridge, Kenelm. "Introduction: Missionary Occasions." In *Mission, Church, and Sect in Oceania,* edited by James A. Boutilier, Daniel T. Hughes, and Sharon W. Tiffany, pp. 1-34. Ann Arbor: University of Michigan Press, 1978.

Buswell, Robert E. *The Zen Monastic Experience.* Princeton: Princeton University Press, 1992.

Carman, John B. "When Hindus Become Christian: Religious Conversion and Spiritual Ambiguity." In *The Stranger's Religion: Fascination and Fear,* edited by Anna Lännström, pp. 133-53. Notre Dame: University of Notre Dame Press, 2004.

Carson, Tom. "Material Girl," *Atlantic Monthly,* October 2003, pp. 115-18.

Carstairs, G. M. *The Twice-Born: A Study of a Community of High-Caste Hindus.* London: Hogarth Press, 1957.

Charsley, Simon. "Sanskritization: The Career of an Anthropological Theory," *Contributions to Indian Sociology* 32, no. 2 (1998): 527-49.

Chatterjee, Partha. "Agrarian Relations and Communalism in Bengal, 1926-1935." In *Subaltern Studies I: Writings on South Asian History and Society,* edited by Ranajit Guha, pp. 9-38. Delhi: Oxford University Press, 1982.

———. "Caste and Subaltern Consciousness." In *Subaltern Studies VI,* edited by Ranajit Guha, pp. 169-209. Delhi: Oxford University Press, 1989.

Chowdhry, Prem. *The Veiled Women: Shifting Gender Equations in Rural Haryana, 1880-1990.* Delhi, India: Oxford University Press, 1994.

Clifford, James. "Introduction: Partial Truths." In *Writing Culture: The Poetics and Politics of Ethnography,* edited by James Clifford and George E. Marcus. Berkeley: University of California Press, 1986.

———. "On Ethnographic Allegory." In *Writing Culture: The Poetics and Politics of Ethnography,* edited by James Clifford and George E. Marcus. Berkeley: University of California Press, 1986.

Cohn, Bernard. "The Changing Status of a Depressed Caste." In *An Anthropologist among the Historians and Other Essays,* edited by Bernard Cohn, pp. 255-83. Delhi: Oxford University Press, 1987.

Comaroff, Jean, and John Comaroff. "Christianity and Colonialism in South Africa," *American Anthropologist* 13, no. 1 (1986): 1-22.

———. *Of Revelation and Revolution: Christianity, Colonialism, and Consciousness in South Africa.* Chicago: University of Chicago Press, 1991.

Council for World Mission. "VHP Rails against Christians in Chhattisgarh." 17 December 2003. Accessed 17 December 2003. Available from http://www.cwmission.org.

Davis, E. C. *Satnām Panth Darśak.* Jabalpur: Mission Press, 1935.

Davis, Martin P. *Sadhu Hagenstein: A White Man among the Brown.* St. Louis: The Board for Foreign Missions, Evangelical Synod of North America, 1930.

———. "The Satnami Tragedy," *Evangelical Herald,* 1 June 1933, p. 429.

———. *India Today and the Church Tomorrow.* Philadelphia: The Board of International Missions, Evangelical and Reformed Church, 1947.

Dempsey, Corinne. "Lessons in Miracles from Kerala, South India: Stories of Three 'Christian' Saints." In *Popular Christianity in India: Riting between the Lines,* edited by Selva Raj and Corinne Dempsey, pp. 115-40. Albany: State University of New York Press, 2002.

Dirks, Nicholas B. "The Original Caste: Power, History and Hierarchy in South Asia," *Contributions to Indian Sociology* 23 (1989): 59-77.

———. *Castes of Mind: Colonialism and the Making of Modern India.* Princeton: Princeton University Press, 2001.

Douglas, Mary. *Purity and Danger: An Analysis of Concepts of Pollution and Taboo.* London: Routledge & Kegan Paul, 1966.

Dube, Saurabh. *Untouchable Pasts: Religion, Identity, and Power among a Central Indian Community, 1780-1950.* Albany: State University of New York Press, 1998.

———. "Conversion to Translation: Colonial Registers of a Vernacular Christianity," *South Atlantic Quarterly* 101, no. 4 (2002): 807-37.

———. *Stitches on Time: Colonial Textures and Postcolonial Tangles.* Durham, NC: Duke University Press, 2004.

Dumont, Louis. *Religion/Politics and History in India: Collected Papers in Indian Sociology.* Paris: Mouton, 1971.

———. *Homo Hierarchicus.* Chicago: University of Chicago Press, 1980.

Dumont, Louis, and David Pocock. "Pure and Impure," *Contributions to Indian Sociology* 3 (1959): 9-39.

Durkheim, Emile. *The Elementary Forms of Religious Life*. Translated by Karen E. Fields. New York: The Free Press, 1995.

Eliade, Mircea. *The Myth of the Eternal Return, or, Cosmos and History*. Princeton: Princeton University Press, 1954.

Elsam, Edith. "English Work at Bilaspur and Other Stations on the B. N. R'y," *Missionary Tidings*, November 1899, pp. 192-93.

Embree, Ainslie T. *Utopias in Conflict*. Berkeley: University of California Press, 1990.

Farquhar, J. N. *The Crown of Hinduism*. London: Oxford University Press, 1913.

Feierabend, Herman Hans. *Life of a Jungle Missionary: Herman August Feierabend*. U.S.A.: n.p., 1999.

Fernandes, Walter. *Caste and Conversion Movements in India: Religion and Human Rights*. New Delhi: Indian Social Institute, 1981.

Fischer, Michael. "The Fiery Rise of Hindu Fundamentalism," *Christianity Today*, 1 March 1999, p. 46.

Fitzgerald, Rosemary. "'Clinical Christianity': The Emergence of Medical Work as a Missionary Strategy in Colonial India, 1800-1914." In *Health, Medicine and Empire: Perspectives on Colonial India*, edited by Biswamoy Pati and Mark Harrison. Hyderabad, India: Orient Longman, 2001.

Flueckiger, Joyce Burkhalter. *Gender and Genre in the Folklore of Middle India*. Ithaca: Cornell University Press, 1996.

Forrester, Duncan B. "The Depressed Classes and Conversion to Christianity, 1860-1960." In *Religion in South Asia: Religious Conversion and Revival Movements in South Asia in Medieval and Modern Times*, edited by G. A. Oddie, pp. 35-66. New Delhi: Manohar Publications, 1977.

Fox, Frampton F. "Foreign Money for India: Antidependency and Anticonversion Perspectives," *International Bulletin of Missionary Research* 30, no. 3 (2006): 137-42.

Frost, Adelaide Gail. "In the Orphanage," *Missionary Tidings*, July 1898, p. 62.

Frykenberg, Robert Eric. "On the Study of Conversion Movements: A Review Article and a Theoretical Note," *Indian Economic and Social History Review* 17, no. 1 (1980): 121-38.

———. "Emergence of Modern 'Hinduism' as a Concept and as an Institution." In *Hinduism Reconsidered*, edited by Günther-Dietz Sontheimer and Hermann Kulke, pp. 29-50. New Delhi: Manohar Publications, 1991.

———. "Introduction: Dealing with Contested Definitions and Controversial Perspectives." In *Christians and Missionaries in India: Cross-Cultural Communication since 1500*, edited by Robert Eric Frykenberg, pp. 1-32. Grand Rapids: Eerdmans, 2003.

Fuchs, Stephen. *Rebellious Prophets: A Study of Messianic Movements in Indian Religions*. New York: Asia Publishing House, 1965.

Gamboe, Homer P. "The Missionary Work of the Disciples of Christ in India and Its Development." B.Div. thesis, The College of the Bible, 1918.

———. "We're in Mungeli," *World Call,* September 1931, p. 34.

———. "The Story of a Well," *World Call,* December 1942, pp. 27-28.

Geertz, Clifford. *Islam Observed: Religious Development in Morocco and Indonesia.* New Haven: Yale University Press, 1968.

———. *The Interpretation of Cultures.* New York: Basic Books, 1973.

Gerth, H. H., and C. Wright Mills. *From Max Weber: Essays in Sociology.* New York: Oxford University Press, 1958.

Gladstone, J. W. *Protestant Christianity and People's Movements in Kerala.* Trivandrum, Kerala, India: The Seminary Publications, 1984.

Goel, Sita Ram, ed. *Vindicated by Time: The Niyogi Committee Report on Christian Missionary Activities.* New Delhi: Voice of India, 1998.

Gordon, E. M. *Indian Folk Tales: Being Side-Lights on Village Life in Bilaspore, Central Provinces.* London: Elliot Stock, 1909.

Government of Chhattisgarh. "Official Website, Govt. of Chhattisgarh." 2004. Accessed 28 June 2004. Available from http://www.chhattisgarh.nic.in/profile/corigin.htm#seed.

Grant, Charles, ed. *The Gazetteer of the Central Provinces of India.* New Delhi: Usha, 1984.

Grimshaw, P. *Paths of Duty: American Missionary Wives in Nineteenth Century Hawaii.* Honolulu: University of Hawaii Press, 1989.

Guha, Ranajit. "The Prose of Counter-Insurgency." In *Selected Subaltern Studies,* edited by Ranajit Guha and Gayatri Spivak. Delhi: Oxford University Press, 1988.

Habib, Irfan, and Dhruv Raina. "The Introduction of Scientific Rationality into India: A Study of Master Ramchandra," *Annals of Science* 46 (1989): 597-610.

Haggis, Jane. "'Good Wives and Mothers' or 'Dedicated Workers'? Contradictions of Domesticity in the Mission of Sisterhood, Travancore, South India." In *Maternities and Modernities: Colonial and Postcolonial Experiences in Asia and the Pacific,* edited by Kalpana Ram and Margaret Jolly, pp. 81-113. New York: Cambridge University Press, 1998.

Halbfass, Wilhelm. *India and Europe: An Essay in Understanding.* Albany: State University of New York Press, 1988.

Hall, Stuart, and Paul du Gay, eds. *Questions of Cultural Identity.* London: Sage, 1996.

Harper, Susan Billington. "The Dornakal Church on the Cultural Frontier." In *Christians, Cultural Interactions, and India's Religious Traditions,* edited by Judith M. Brown and Robert Eric Frykenberg, pp. 183-211. Grand Rapids: Eerdmans, 2002.

Hefner, Robert W. "Introduction: World Building and the Rationality of Conversion." In *Conversion to Christianity: Historical and Anthropological Perspectives on a Great Transformation,* edited by Robert W. Hefner, pp. 3-44. Berkeley: University of California Press, 1993.

———. "Of Faith and Commitment: Christian Conversion in Muslim Java." In *Conversion to Christianity: Historical and Anthropological Perspectives on a Great*

Transformation, edited by Robert W. Hefner, pp. 99-125. Berkeley: University of California Press, 1993.

Hill, Patricia R. *The World Their Household: The American Woman's Foreign Mission Movement and Cultural Transformation, 1870-1920.* Ann Arbor: University of Michigan Press, 1985.

Hobsbawm, Eric, and Terence Ranger, eds. *The Invention of Tradition.* New York: Cambridge University Press, 1983.

Horton, Robin. "On the Rationality of Conversion," *Africa* 45, no. 3 (1975): 219-35.

―――. *Patterns of Thought in Africa and the West: Essays on Magic, Religion, and Science.* New York: Cambridge University Press, 1993.

Hudson, Dennis. "Hindu and Christian Parallels in the Conversion of H. A. Krishna Pillai 1857-1859," *Journal of the American Academy of Religion* 40, no. 2 (1972): 191-206.

―――. *Protestant Origins in India.* Grand Rapids: Eerdmans, 2000.

Hunter, J. *The Gospel of Gentility: American Women Missionaries in Turn-of-the-Century China.* New Haven: Yale University Press, 1984.

Hunter, William Wilson, Sir, James Sutherland Cotton, Sir Richard Burn, and Sir William Stevenson Meyer, eds. *Imperial Gazetteer of India,* vol. 8. Oxford: Clarendon Press, 1908.

Inden, Ronald. *Imagining India.* Oxford: Blackwell, 1990.

India Census Commissioner. *Census of India, 1901,* vol. 8 (Part 2, Statistics). Bombay: Government Central Press, 1902-3.

―――. *Census of India, 1911,* vol. 10 (Part 2, Statistics). Calcutta: Superintendent of Government Printing, 1911.

―――. *Census of India, 1921,* vol. 11 (Part 2, Statistics). Nagpur: Government Press, 1923.

Indo-Asian News Service. "'Witches' Keep Dussehra Crowd in Thrall," *The Times of India (Online Edition),* 23 October 2004.

Irschick, Eugene F. *Dialogue and History.* Berkeley: University of California Press, 1994.

Jaffrelot, Christopher. *The Hindu Nationalist Movement in India.* New York: Columbia University Press, 1996.

―――. *Dr. Ambedkar and Untouchability: Fighting the Indian Caste System.* New York: Columbia University Press, 2004.

James, William. *The Varieties of Religious Experience.* New York: Mentor Books, 1958.

Jha, Makhan. "Ratanpur: Some Aspects of a Sacred City in Chhattisgarh." In *Chhattisgarh: An Area Study,* edited by Ajit Kumar Danda, pp. 34-45. Calcutta: Anthropological Survey of India, Govt. of India, 1977.

Jones, Arun W. *Christian Missions in the American Empire: Episcopalians in Northern Luzon, the Philippines, 1902-1946.* New York: Peter Lang, 2003.

Jones, Kenneth W. *Arya Dharm: Hindu Consciousness in 19th-Century Punjab.* Berkeley: University of California Press, 1976.

Jordan, David K. "The Glyphomancy Factor: Observations on Chinese Conversion."

In *Conversion to Christianity: Historical and Anthropological Perspectives on a Great Transformation,* edited by Robert W. Hefner, pp. 285-304. Berkeley: University of California Press, 1993.

Jordens, J. T. F. *Dayānanda Sarasvatī: His Life and Ideas.* Delhi: Oxford University Press, 1978.

Juergensmeyer, Mark. *Religion as Social Vision: The Movement against Untouchability in Twentieth-Century Punjab.* Berkeley: University of California Press, 1982.

Kamat, Pratima P. "From Conversion to the Civil Code: Gender and the Colonial State in Goa, 1510-1961," *Indian Historical Review* 27, no. 2 (2003): 61-86.

Kammerer, C. A. "Custom and Christian Conversion among Akha Highlanders of Burma and Thailand," *American Ethnologist* 17, no. 2 (1990): 277-91.

Kananaikil, Jose. *Christians of Scheduled Caste Origin.* New Delhi: Indian Social Institute, 1986.

Kantowsky, Detlef. "Max Weber on India and Indian Interpretations of Weber." In *Recent Research on Max Weber's Studies of Hinduism,* edited by Detlef Kantowsky, pp. 9-43. London: Weltforum, 1986.

Karlsson, Bengt G. *Contested Belonging: An Indigenous People's Struggle for Forest and Identity in Sub-Himalayan Bengal.* Richmond, VA: Curzon, 2000.

————. "Entering into the Christian Dharma: Contemporary 'Tribal' Conversions in India." In *Christians, Cultural Interactions, and India's Religious Traditions,* edited by Judith M. Brown and Robert Eric Frykenberg, pp. 133-53. Grand Rapids: Eerdmans, 2002.

Kaufmann, Susan B. "A Christian Caste in Hindu Society: Religious Leadership and Social Conflict among the Paravas of Southern Tamilnadu," *Modern Asian Studies* 15, no. 2 (1981): 203-34.

Keay, F. E. *Kabir and His Followers.* Calcutta: Association Press, 1931.

Kent, Eliza F. *Converting Women: Gender and Protestant Christianity in Colonial South India.* New York: Oxford University Press, 2004.

Keyes, Charles F. "Why the Thai Are Not Christians: Buddhist and Christian Conversion in Thailand." In *Conversion to Christianity: Historical and Anthropological Perspectives on a Great Transformation,* edited by Robert W. Hefner, pp. 259-84. Berkeley: University of California Press, 1993.

Khan, Mehboob. "Mother India." Edited by Wajahat Mirza and S. Ali Raza. Bombay, 1957.

Kim, Sebastian C. H. *In Search of Identity: Debates on Religious Conversion in India.* Oxford: Oxford University Press, 2003.

Kingsbury, Mary. "Orphanage Work in India," *Missionary Tidings,* December 1896, pp. 190-91.

————. *Bilaspur.* Indianapolis: Christian Women's Board of Missions, n.d.

Kooiman, Dick. "Untouchability in India through the Missionary's Eye," *Itinerario* 7, no. 1 (1983): 115-25.

————. "Mission, Education and Employment in Travancore (19th Century)." In *Conversion, Competition and Conflict,* edited by Dick Kooiman, Otto van den

Muijzenberg, and Peter van der Veer, pp. 185-215. Amsterdam: Free University Press, 1984.

———. *Conversion and Social Equality in India.* New Delhi: South Asia Publications, 1989.

Kooiman, Dick, Otto van den Muijzenberg, and Peter van der Veer, eds. *Conversion, Competition and Conflict.* Amsterdam: Free University Press, 1984.

Lal, Hira. *Satnām Ke Pās Laut Āo.* n.p., n.d.

Lamb, Ramdas. *Rapt in the Name: The Ramnamis, Ramnam, and Untouchable Religion in Central India.* Albany: State University of New York Press, 2002.

Lang, Milton C. *The Healing Touch in Mission Lands.* St. Louis: Eden Publishing House, 1932.

Laymen's Foreign Missions Inquiry Commission of Appraisal. *Re-Thinking Missions: A Laymen's Inquiry after One Hundred Years.* New York: Harper & Brothers, 1932.

Leslie, I. Julia. *The Perfect Wife: The Orthodox Hindu Woman According to the Strīdharmapaddhati of Tryambakayajvan.* Delhi: Oxford University Press, 1989.

Liebau, Heike. "Country Priests, Catechists, and Schoolmasters as Cultural, Religious and Social Middlemen in the Context of the Tranquebar Mission." In *Christians and Missionaries in India: Cross-Cultural Communication since 1500,* edited by Robert Eric Frykenberg, pp. 70-92. Grand Rapids: Eerdmans, 2003.

Linnekin, Jocelyn. "Defining Tradition: Variations on the Hawaiian Identity," *American Ethnologist* 10, no. 2 (1983): 241-52.

Lipner, Julius. *Hindus: Their Religious Beliefs and Practices.* New York: Routledge, 1998.

———. *Brahmabandhab Upadhyay: The Life and Thought of a Revolutionary.* Oxford: Oxford University Press, 1999.

Lohans, H. H. *Come Over and Help Us: Mission Work of Our Evangelical Church in Chhattisgarh, India.* St. Louis: Eden Publishing House, 1920.

Lohr, Bertha F. "Bits of Talk from India, Bilaspur," *Missionary Tidings,* June 1900, p. 57.

Lohr, Oscar. "Leiden und Freuden unseres Missionars," *Der deutsche Missionsfreund* 4, no. 1 (1869): 5-6.

———. "Von Bisrampoor (1)," *Der deutsche Missionsfreund* 4, no. 5 (1869): 1.

———. "Von Bisrampoor (2)," *Der deutsche Missionsfreund* 4, no. 6 (1869): 1.

———. "Von Darchoora," *Der deutsche Missionsfreund* 4, no. 4 (1869): 1-2.

Lorenzen, David N. "The Kabir-Panth and Social Protest." In *The Sants: Studies in a Devotional Tradition of India,* edited by Karine Schomer and W. H McLeod, pp. 281-303. Berkeley: Berkeley Religious Studies Series, 1987.

———. *Kabir Legends and Ananta-Das's Kabir Parachai.* Albany: State University of New York Press, 1991.

Luke, P. Y., and John B. Carman. *Village Christians and Hindu Culture: A Study of a Rural Church in Andhra Pradesh, South India.* London: Lutterworth, 1968.

MacRae, Donald G. *Weber.* London: Fontana, 1973.

Madappattu, Jose. *Evangelization in a Marginalizing World: With Special Reference to the Marginalized Satnamis in the Diocese of Raipur.* Nettetal: Steyler, 1997.

Madsen, Bessie Farrar. "Come and Teach My People: A Call from India," *Missionary Tidings,* June 1914, pp. 57-58.

Mahapatra, Sitakant. *Modernization and Ritual: Identity and Change in Santal Society.* Calcutta: Oxford University Press, 1986.

Mandelbaum, David G. "Transcendental and Pragmatic Aspects of Religion," *American Anthropologist* 68 (1966): 1174-91.

————. *Society in India.* Berkeley: University of California Press, 1970.

————. *Women's Seclusion and Men's Honor: Sex Roles in North India, Bangladesh, and Pakistan.* Tucson: The University of Arizona Press, 1988.

Manickam, Sundararaj. *The Social Setting of Christian Conversion in South India: The Impact of the Wesleyan Methodist Missionaries on the Trichy-Tanjore Diocese with Special Reference to the Harijan Communities of the Mass Movement Area, 1820-1947.* Wiesbaden: Steiner, 1977.

Mann, R. S., and K. Mann. *Tribal Cultures and Change.* New Delhi: Mittal Publications, 1989.

Marriott, McKim. "Little Communities in an Indigenous Civilization." In *Village India: Studies in the Little Community,* edited by McKim Marriott, pp. 171-222. Chicago: University of Chicago Press, 1955.

Masihdas, Tihari. *Jīvan Caritr Tathā Sevā Kārya: Śrīmān Ḍākṭar, Kaisar I. Hind, Hīrālāl Sāhib.* Bilaspur: n.p., 1953.

McGavran, Donald A. "So He Went and Told His Brethren," *World Call,* March 1939, pp. 12-13, 27.

————. "Evangelism in Central India," *World Call,* February 1942, p. 11.

————. "Training Leaders for a New Christian Movement," *World Call,* February 1942, p. 42.

————. *The Bridges of God.* New York: Friendship Press, 1955.

————. *How Churches Grow.* New York: Friendship Press, 1959.

————. *The Satnami Story: A Thrilling Drama of Religious Change.* Pasadena: William Carey Library, 1990.

McGavran, Helen A. "Christian and Non-Christian Homes in India," *Missionary Tidings,* December 1918, pp. 313-14.

McGavran, Mary T. "The Healing of India," *World Call,* December 1919, pp. 20-22.

McNeil, Ada. "Bilaspur Medical Work," *Missionary Tidings,* November 1901, 218.

McRae, John R. "The Story of Early Ch'an." In *Zen: Tradition and Transition,* edited by Kenneth Kraft, pp. 125-39. New York: Grove Press, 1988.

Meibohm, Margaret. "Past Selves and Present Others: The Ritual Construction of Identity at a Catholic Festival in India." In *Popular Christianity in India: Riting between the Lines,* edited by Selva Raj and Corinne Dempsey, pp. 61-84. Albany: State University of New York Press, 2002.

Melick, Edith Moulton. *The Evangelical Synod in India.* St. Louis: Eden Publishing House, 1930.

Menzel, Emil W. *I Will Build My Church: The Story of Our India Mission and How It Became a Church.* Philadelphia: Board of Missions, Evangelical and Reformed Church, 1943.

Menzies, Walter G. "A Contrast in Cries," *Missionary Tidings,* September 1911, pp. 155-56.

————. "India," *Missionary Tidings,* November 1914, pp. 285-89.

Merrill, William L. "Conversion and Colonialism in Northern Mexico: The Tarahumara Response to the Jesuit Mission Program, 1601-1767." In *Conversion to Christianity: Historical and Anthropological Perspectives on a Great Transformation,* edited by Robert W. Hefner, pp. 129-64. Berkeley: University of California Press, 1993.

Meyer, Birgit. "Modernity and Enchantment: The Image of the Devil in Popular African Christianity." In *Conversion to Modernities: The Globalization of Christianity,* edited by Peter van der Veer, pp. 199-230. New York: Routledge, 1996.

Middleton, Vernon James. "The Development of a Missiologist: The Life and Thought of Donald Anderson McGavran." Ph.D. diss., Fuller Theological Seminary, 1989.

Miller, George E. "The Serpent That Failed," *World Call,* July 1922, pp. 28-30.

Miller, Lillie B., and E. C. L. Miller. "Medical Work, from September 1, 1897, to August 16, 1898," *Missionary Tidings,* December 1898, 178.

Mohammad, Sharif. *Madhyapradesh Kā Lok Sangīt.* Bhopal: Madhyapradesh Hindi Granth Akādmī, n.d.

Mullin, Ann. "Among the Depressed Classes," *World Call,* February 1937, 29.

Naidu, Hanumant. *Chattisgarhī Lok-Gīton Kā Loktātvik Tathā Manovaijānik Anusīlan.* Nagpur, Madhya Pradesh, India: Visvabhāratī Prakāsan, 1987.

Nelson, A. E. *Central Provinces District Gazetteer: Raipur District.* Bombay: British India Press, 1909.

Novetzke, Christian. "The Subaltern Numen: Making History in the Name of God," *History of Religions* 46, no. 2 (2006): 99-126.

Oddie, G. A. "Old Wine in New Bottles? Kartabhaja (Vaishnava) Converts to Evangelical Christianity in Bengal, 1835-1845." In *Religious Change, Conversion and Culture,* edited by Lynette Olson. Sydney: Sydney Association for Studies in Society and Culture, 1996.

Office of the Registrar General. "Census of India, 2001." 2001. Accessed 23 June 2004. Available from http://www.censusindia.net/results/.

"Official Census of India (Reprinted from the Missionary Herald)," *World Call,* July 1924, p. 37.

Ortner, Sherry. "Theory in Anthropology since the Sixties," *Comparative Studies in Society and History* 26, no. 1 (1984): 126-66.

Pathak, Suman Lata. "Religious Conversion and Social Change." In *Reform, Protest and Social Transformation,* edited by Satish K. Sharma, pp. 213-25. New Delhi: Ashish Publishing House, 1987.

Patros, Simon. *Chhattisgarhi Christian Bhajans.* Raipur: Evangelical Book Depot, 1940.

———. *Simon Patros of India: A Miracle of God's Grace.* St. Louis: Board of International Missions, Evangelical and Reformed Church, Inc., 1954.

Paul, M. M. *Satyanāmī Panth: Śrī Gosāīn Ghāsīdās Girod Vāsī.* Allahabad: The Mission Press, 1937.

———. *Satyanāmī Panth: Śrī Gosāīn Ghāsīdās Girod Vāsī.* Raipur: The Christian Book Depot, 1941.

Paul, Tularam. *Main Ne Satnām Kaise Pāyā.* N.p., n.d.

Pauw, B. A. "The Influence of Christianity." In *The Bantu-Speaking Peoples of Southern Africa,* edited by W. D. Hammond-Tooke, pp. 415-40. Boston: Routledge & Kegan Paul, 1974.

Pennington, Brian. *Was Hinduism Invented? Britons, Indians, and the Colonial Construction of Religion.* New York: Oxford University Press, 2005.

Peterson, Indira Viswanathan. "*Bethlehem Kuṟavañci* of Vedanayaka Sastri of Tanjore: The Cultural Discourses of an Early-Nineteenth-Century Tamil Christian Poem." In *Christians, Cultural Interactions, and India's Religious Traditions,* edited by Judith M. Brown and Robert Eric Frykenberg, pp. 9-36. Grand Rapids: Eerdmans, 2002.

Pickett, J. W. *Christian Mass Movements in India.* New York: Abingdon Press, 1933.

———. *Mass Movement Survey Report for Mid-India.* Jubbulpore, Central Provinces, India: Mission Press, 1937.

———. *Church Growth and Group Conversion.* Lucknow: Lucknow Publishing House, 1956.

Prentiss, Karen Pechilis. *The Embodiment of Bhakti.* New York: Oxford University Press, 1999.

Press Trust of India. "SP Gets Wife Killed for Practising Voodoo." 2003. Accessed 24 December 2003. Available from http://www.timesofindia.com.

Queen, Christopher S. "Dr. Ambedkar and the Hermeneutics of Buddhist Liberation." In *Engaged Buddhism: Buddhist Liberation Movements in Asia,* edited by Christopher S. Queen and Sallie B. King, pp. 45-72. Albany: State University of New York Press, 1996.

Rajaram, Indira. "Economics of Bride-Price and Dowry," *Economic and Political Weekly* 18, no. 8 (1983): 275-79.

Ramabai, Pandita. *The High-Caste Hindu Woman.* Philadelphia: Press of the J. B. Rogers Printing, 1888.

Ramanujan, A. K. *Hymns for the Drowning.* Princeton: Princeton University Press, 1981.

Rambo, Victor. "Call the Doctor!" *World Call,* February 1931, pp. 21-23.

Ramusack, Barbara N. "Cultural Missionaries, Maternal Imperialists, Feminist Allies: British Women Activists in India, 1865-1945." In *Western Women and Imperialism,* edited by Nupur Chaudhuri and Margaret Strobel, pp. 119-36. Bloomington: Indiana University Press, 1992.

Ranger, Terence. "The Local and the Global in Southern African Religious History." In *Conversion to Christianity: Historical and Anthropological Perspectives on a Great Transformation,* edited by Robert W. Hefner, pp. 65-98. Berkeley: University of California Press, 1993.

Rao, M. S. A. "Religion, Sect and Social Transformation: Some Reflections on Max Weber's Contributions to Hinduism and Buddhism." In *Recent Researches on Max Weber's Studies of Hinduism,* edited by Detlef Kantowsky, pp. 193-98. London: Weltforum, 1986.

Redfield, Robert, and Milton Singer. "The Cultural Role of Cities," *Economic Development and Cultural Change* 3, no. 1 (1954): 53-73.

Richardson, Don. *Eternity in Their Hearts,* rev. ed. Ventura, CA: Regal Books, 1984.

Richter, Julius. *History of Missions in India.* Translated by Sydney H. Moore. New York: Revell, 1906.

Risley, H. H. *The People of India.* Delhi: Oriental Books Reprint Corporation, 1969.

Roy, Arundhati. "Do Turkeys Enjoy Thanksgiving?" *Hindu,* 18 January 2004, 1.

Rudolph, Lloyd I., and Susanne Hoeber Rudolph. *The Modernity of Tradition: Political Development in India.* Chicago: University of Chicago Press, 1967.

Russell, Robert Vane. *The Tribes and Castes of the Central Provinces of India,* vol. 1. London: Macmillan, 1916.

———. *The Tribes and Castes of the Central Provinces of India,* vol. 2. London: Macmillan, 1916.

Ryerson, Charles A., III. *"Meaning and Modernization" in Tamil India: Primordial Sentiments and Sanskritization.* Ann Arbor: University Microfilms International, 1979.

Sail, Rajendra K. *Conversion in Chhattisgarh: Facts and Myths.* Raipur: Indian Social Action Forum, 2003.

Sands, Kathleen M. "Tracking Religion: Religion through the Lens of Critical and Cultural Studies," *CSSR Bulletin* 31, no. 3 (2002): 68-74.

Saum, H. C. "Hira Lal, of Mungeli, India," *World Call,* August 1923, p. 45.

———, and Mildred Saum. "Followers of the True Name," *Mungeli News Letter,* March 1935, p. 3.

Saxena, Abha, and Mitashree Mitra. "Christian Missionaries in Chhattisgarh." In *Reform, Protest and Social Transformation,* edited by Satish K. Sharma, pp. 227-37. New Delhi: Ashish Publishing House, 1987.

Schreuder, Deryck, and Geoffrey Oddie. "What Is 'Conversion'? History, Christianity and Religious Change in Colonial Africa and South Asia," *Journal of Religious History* 15, no. 4 (1989): 496-518.

Scott, James C. *Weapons of the Weak: Everyday Forms of Peasant Resistance.* New Haven: Yale University Press, 1989.

Sebastian, J. Jayakiran. "A Strange Mission among Strangers: The Joy of Conversion." In *Vom Geheimnis des Unterschieds: Die Wahrnehmung des Fremden in Ökumene-Missions und Religionswissenschaft,* edited by Andrea Schultze, Rudolf V. Sinner, and Wolfram Stierle, pp. 200-10. Münster: LIT, 2002.

Sebastian, Mrinalini. "Reading Archives from a Postcolonial Perspective," *Journal of Feminist Studies in Religion* 19, no. 1 (2003): 5-26.

Seybold, Theodore C. *God's Guiding Hand: A History of the Central Indian Mission 1868-1967*. Philadelphia: United Church Board for World Ministries of the United Church of Christ, 1971.

Sharpe, Eric. *Not to Destroy but to Fulfil: The Contribution of J. N. Farquhar to Protestant Missionary Thought in India before 1914*. Uppsala, Sweden: Almqvist & Wiksells Boktryckeri AB, 1965.

Shashikumar, V. K. "Preparing for the Harvest," *Tehelka (Online Edition)*, 7 February 2004.

Shoobert, W. H. *Census of India, 1931*, vol. 12: Central Provinces and Berar (Part 2-Tables). Nagpur: Government Printing, C.P., 1933.

Shreve, Ethel. "A Boy Who Could Say No," *World Call*, January 1945, p. 37.

———. "Christian Testimonies," *World Call*, January 1952, p. 47.

Shukla, Dayashankar. *Chattisgaṛhī Loksāhityă Kā Adhyayan*. Raipur, CG, India: Jyoti Prakāshan, n.d.

Shukla, Hira Lal. *Chattisgaṛh Rediscovered: Vedāntic Approaches to Folklore*. New Delhi: Aryan Books International, 1995.

Singer, Milton. "The Social Organization of Indian Civilization," *Diogenes* 45 (1964): 84-119.

———. *When a Great Tradition Modernizes*. New York: Praeger Publishers, 1972.

Singh, K. S. *The Scheduled Castes*, rev. ed. Calcutta: Oxford University Press, 1999.

Smith, Jonathan Z. *Imagining Religion: From Babylon to Jonestown*. Chicago: University of Chicago Press, 1982.

———. "Religion, Religions, Religious." In *Critical Terms for Religious Studies*, edited by Mark C. Taylor. Chicago: University of Chicago Press, 1998.

Smith, Wilfred Cantwell. *The Meaning and End of Religion: A New Approach to the Religious Traditions of Mankind*. New York: Macmillan, 1963.

Snow, David A., and Richard Machalek. "The Sociology of Conversion," *Annual Review of Sociology* 10 (1983): 167-90.

Srinivas, M. N. "The Social System of a Mysore Village." In *Village India*, edited by McKim Marriott. Chicago: University of Chicago Press, 1955.

———. "A Note on Sanskritization and Westernization," *Far Eastern Quarterly* 15, no. 4 (1956): 481-96.

———. *Religion and Society among the Coorgs of South India*. New York: Asia Publishing House, 1965.

———. *Social Change in Modern India*. Berkeley: University of California Press, 1966.

———. "The Cohesive Role of Sanskritization." In *India and Ceylon: Unity and Diversity*, edited by Philip Mason. London: Oxford University Press, 1967.

———. "Mobility in the Caste System." In *Structure and Change in Indian Society*, edited by Milton Singer and Bernard Cohn. Chicago: University of Chicago Press, 1968.

———. *The Dominant Caste and Other Essays*. Delhi: Oxford University Press, 1987.

———. *Collected Essays*. New York: Oxford University Press, 2002.

Stoll, Andrew. "Chhattisgarh," *Der deutsche Missionsfreund*, June 1881, pp. 45-46.

Tanner, Th. *Im Lande der Hindus oder, Kulturschilderungen aus Indien*. St. Louis: n.p., 1894.

Taylor, B. "Recollection and Membership: Converts' Talk and the Ratiocination of Commonality," *Sociology* 12 (1978): 316-24.

Thomas, George. *Christian Indians and Indian Nationalism 1885-1959*. Frankfurt: Peter Lang, 1979.

Times News Network. "Chhattisgarh: Past Imperfect." 2003. Accessed 29 September 2003. Available from http://www.timesofindia.com.

Twente, Theophil H., ed. *Folk Tales of Chhattisgarh India*. North Tonawanda, NY: Bodoni Press, 1938.

United Christian Missionary Society. "Paganism or Christianity: Which?" *World Call*, April 1932, p. 474.

Unrau, Ruth. *A Time to Bind and a Time to Loose: A History of the General Conference Mennonite Church Mission Involvement from 1900-1995*. Newton, KS: Commission on Overseas Mission, General Conference Mennonite Church, 1996.

Vansina, Jan. *Oral Tradition: A Study in Historical Methodology*. London: Routledge & Kegan Paul, 1965.

Verma, Rajendra. *Raipur*. Bhopal: District Gazetteers Department, Madhya Pradesh, 1973.

Veyne, Paul. *Did the Greeks Believe in Their Myths? An Essay on the Constitutive Imagination*. Chicago: University of Chicago Press, 1988.

Viswanathan, Gauri. "Religious Conversion and the Politics of Dissent." In *Conversion to Modernities: The Globalization of Christianity*, edited by Peter van der Veer, pp. 89-114. New York: Routledge, 1996.

———. *Outside the Fold: Conversion, Modernity, and Belief*. Princeton: Princeton University Press, 1998.

Wadley, Susan S. "Texts in Context: Oral Tradition and the Study of Religion in Karimpur." In *American Studies in the Anthropology of India*, edited by Sylvia Vatuk, pp. 309-41. New Delhi: Manohar Publications, 1978.

Wagner, Roy. *The Invention of Culture*. Englewood Cliffs, NJ: Prentice-Hall, 1975.

Weber, Max. *Economy and Society*, edited by Guenther Roth and Claus Wittich. Berkeley: University of California Press, 1978.

Webster, John C. B. *A History of the Dalit Christians in India*. San Francisco: Mellen Research University Press, 1992.

———. "Dalits and Christianity in Colonial Punjab: Cultural Interactions." In *Christians, Cultural Interactions, and India's Religious Traditions*, edited by Judith M. Brown and Robert Eric Frykenberg, pp. 92-118. Grand Rapids: Eerdmans, 2002.

———. "Missionary Strategy and the Development of the Christian Community: Delhi, 1859-1884." In *Popular Christianity in India: Riting between the Lines*, edited by Selva Raj and Corinne Dempsey, pp. 211-32. Albany: State University of New York Press, 2002.

Works Cited

Westcott, G. H. *Kabir and the Kabir Panth*. Calcutta: Susil Gupta, 1953.

Williams, Raymond Brady. *An Introduction to Swaminarayan Hinduism*. Cambridge: Cambridge University Press, 2001.

Wilson, Bert. "With the Men and Women of All Lands Who Have Answered Our Call," *World Call*, October 1920, pp. 16-17.

Wines, Michael. "Between Faith and Medicine, How Clear a Line?" *New York Times*, 18 August 2004, A4.

Wolpert, Stanley. *A New History of India*, 5th ed. New York: Oxford University Press, 1997.

Young, Richard Fox. *Resistant Hinduism: Sanskrit Sources on Anti-Christian Apologetics in Early Nineteenth Century India*. Vienna: Indological Institute, University of Vienna, 1981.

————. "Some Hindu Perspectives on Christian Missionaries in the Indic World of the Mid Nineteenth Century." In *Christians, Cultural Interactions, and India's Religious Traditions*, edited by Judith M. Brown and Robert Eric Frykenberg, pp. 37-60. Grand Rapids: Eerdmans, 2002.

————. "Receding from Antiquity: Hindu Responses to Science and Christianity on the Margins of Empire, 1800-1850." In *Christians and Missionaries in India: Cross-Cultural Communication since 1500*, edited by Robert Eric Frykenberg, pp. 183-222. Grand Rapids: Eerdmans, 2003.

Index

Index